INFAMOUS MURDERS AND MYSTERIES:
Cold Case Files and Who-Done-Its

INFAMOUS MURDERS AND MYSTERIES:
Cold Case Files and Who-Done-Its

"Sleuths and Spies" ©2009 (silhouettes of the author)
Artwork by **J. Higginbotham**

Dr. Robert J. Girod, Sr.

iUniverse, Inc.
New York   Bloomington

Infamous Murders and Mysteries
Cold Case Files and Who-Done-Its

Copyright © 2009 by Robert J Girod

All rights reserved. No part of this book may be used or reproduced by any means, graphic, electronic, or mechanical, including photocopying, recording, taping or by any information storage retrieval system without the written permission of the publisher except in the case of brief quotations embodied in critical articles and reviews.

iUniverse books may be ordered through booksellers or by contacting:

iUniverse
1663 Liberty Drive
Bloomington, IN 47403
www.iuniverse.com
1-800-Authors (1-800-288-4677)

Because of the dynamic nature of the Internet, any Web addresses or links contained in this book may have changed since publication and may no longer be valid. The views expressed in this work are solely those of the author and do not necessarily refl ect the views of the publisher, and the publisher hereby disclaims any responsibility for them.

ISBN: 978-0-595-50399-5 (pbk)
ISBN: 978-0-595-63183-4 (cloth)
ISBN: 978-0-595-61491-2 (ebk)

Printed in the United States of America

iUniverse rev. date: 12/16/2008

He is in my judgment, the fourth smartest man in London, and for daring I am not sure that he has not a claim to be third.

~ Sherlock Holmes ~
Sir Arthur Conan Doyle

*Come, Watson, come!
The game is afoot.
Not a word!
Into your clothes and come!*

~ Sherlock Holmes ~
Sir Arthur Conan Doyle

Table of Contents

Dedication and Acknowledgements	1
Preface	5
Introduction	7
PART I - Who-Done-It: Mysteries In Paradise	9
Chapter 1 - Murder on Mackinack Island (1960)	11
Chapter 2 - Triple Murder at Starved Rock State Park (1960)	56
PART II - Ghosts, Curses, and Spies Who Kill	113
Chapter 3 - The Ghosts of Mansfield Prison: Murder Behind Bars	115
Chapter 4 - The Curse of the Hope Diamond	143
Chapter 5 - The Cambeidge Five: Cloak and Dagger Murder	164
Chapter 6 - The Kennedy Assassination: Declassified (Part I)	193
Chapter 7 - The Kennedy Assassination: Declassified (Part II)	252
Part III - The Life and Crimes of the Rich and Famous	301
Chapter 8 - Mass Murder at Taliesin: The Frank Lloyd Wright Tragedy	303
Chapter 9 - The "Murder" and Ghost of Agatha Christie	318
Chapter 10 - Sherlock Holmes and Houdini: Ghost Busters	334
Chapter 11 - Murder, Hemingway, and the Florida Keys	374
Part IV - They've Killed The Marshal: 1907	405
Chapter 12 - The Murder of Marshal Columbus L. Croy	407
Chapter 13 - Marshal Croy Murder: The Prosecution and Trial	434
Chapter 14 - The Croy Murder: Defense and the Verdict	465
References	491
About the Author	501

Dedication and Acknowledgements

In memory of my late wife, Marian Elizabeth (Mimi) Girod; departed June 22, 2002.

This book is also dedicated to my two "partners in crime," Laurie and my son, Bobby, for the many hours of patience, assistance, and long days of traveling "on-location" at most of the "scenes of the crimes." Without them, this collection of writings would not have been possible and would have no purpose.

I would like to acknowledge and thank the following individuals and organizations for their assistance in compiling the facts and artifacts necessary to tell these stories. They provided essential research, reports, photographs, news archives, court records, personal accounts, and a great deal of camaraderie and hospitality during the course of these investigations.

Alice Barva, Allen County Public Library, Fort Wayne, Indiana

Carla Bauman-Franks, Allen County Public Library, Fort Wayne, Indiana

Fritz Miller, Woodburn City Council and the Woodburn Historical Society

Loretta McCann, The Woodburn Historical Society

Gaylen Stetler, The Woodburn Historical Society

The Allen County-Fort Wayne Historical Society and the History Center

Bob Nern, Allen County-Fort Wayne Historical Society and the History Center

Anee L. St. Onge, Mackinac Island Public Library, Mackinac Island, Michigan

Wesley H. Maurer, Jr., St. Ignace News / Town Crier, St. Ignace, Michigan

Dr. Robert J. Girod, Sr.

Trooper Donna Haw, Michigan State Police, St. Ignace Post #83, St. Ignace, Michigan

Detective Sergeant Robin D. Sexton, Michigan State Police, Field Detective Division, St. Ignace, Michigan

Sheriff Lawrence H. Leveille, Mackinac County Sheriff's Department, St. Ignace, Michigan

Mackinac Island Police Department, Mackinac Island, Michigan

Sheriff Thomas J. Templeton, LaSalle County Sheriff's Department, Ottowa, Illinois

The Illinois State Appellate Defender's Office, Ottowa, Illinois

Dan Churney, Staff Writer, Republican Times News, Ottowa, Illinois

Steve Stout, Utica, Illinois.

Detective Raymond M. Pierce, New York Police Department (Retired), New York, New York

Sheriff Richard Roth, Monroe County Sheriff's Office, Key West, Florida.

The John F. Kennedy Presidential Library

Stephanie Waters, JFK Presidential Library, Audiovisual Archives

The Portsmouth Public Library, Conan Doyle Collection, Arts and Cultural Development Service, Portsmouth, England

The Sherlock Holmes Museum, London, England

The Sir Arthur Conan Doyle Foundation, UK

The Harry Houdini Museum, Appleton, Wisconsin

The National Magicians' Museum and Library

The American Museum of Magic, Marshal, Michigan

The Frank Lloyd Wright Center

The Frank Lloyd Wright Foundation

The Taliesin Preservation Society

The Wisconsin Historical Society

Special thanks to Dawn M. Wooten, Copy Editor, for her assistance with the final draft.

Preface

Readers of any current daily newspapers find front-page headlines of local killings and murders. In these times and in the recent past, most of the violence surrounding these murders is related to drug trafficking.

But murder can occur in any number of contexts and author Dr. Robert Girod has provided us with many: cold cases, prison violence, curses, spies and betrayal, presidential assassination, mass murder, and more.

Dr. Girod's review of cold cases reads as you would expect of an author professionally and academically trained in police investigation. But even outside of cold cases, his professional training is inherent in his writing. He continually notes dates, times and the meetings of individuals implicated in murderous plots or escapes from misdeeds. Girod is able to do so by a careful study of police investigative reports, newspaper articles, personal interviews with detectives involved in investigating the cases, and a visit to the scenes of a number of these crimes.

The book provides numerous photocopies of reports, articles and photos which gives the reader a real life view or feel of the crime from an investigative viewpoint.

The book is not just enlightened by Girod's education and professional training; it is also entertaining in that he provides us with biographical sketches of many of the famous names found throughout his book.

These biographical sketches, however, are kept brief with just enough to fit the sketch within the context of the crime or mystery. Readers may especially enjoy the paths crossed, for example, between Sir Arthur Conan Doyle, Agatha Christie, Harry Houdini and Teddy Roosevelt.

The profound tragedy of murder is also handled with sensitivity in the case of the famous architect, Frank Lloyd Wright, and the mass murder at Taliesin.

Dr. Robert J. Girod, Sr.

    This book, mainly from its review of newspaper accounts, shows a public outraged by murder. Entire communities would get caught up in the case. The pressure for justice was keen and palpable.

    Today, with violent murders nearly commonplace and predictable, especially in our nation's metropolitan areas, society has become decidedly less sensitive and emotional about violent deaths. We should learn to care anew.

Judge Daniel G. Heath
Fort Wayne, Indiana
June, 2008

INTRODUCTION

This book is a collection of true murder and mystery tales. It may be appropriate for a case study in a course on criminology or criminal investigation, but it is also a thrilling experience for anyone who likes to read real life "who-done-its." For those of you who like to curl up with a good mystery and listen for things that "go bump in the night," I think you will find this as interesting as I do.

In fact, this collection of murders and mysteries are about cases that interest me. I am a career detective and law enforcement officer and a professor of . . . well, just about anything that (again) interests me. That is, I have worked in law enforcement at the city, county, state, federal and military levels for most of my life. I have also been an adjunct professor or associate faculty at seven universities, in six disciplines, through the doctoral level. (But that is all listed in the "About the Author" section, for those of you who like to read about the author who wrote what you are reading at the time, like I do). So that is my perspectives on these cases.

Some of these cases are solved and some are not. All involve famous (or infamous) persons and/or places. Again, they are tales that have fascinated me and I hope you find them equally interesting.

OK, enough of that; let's get right to some mysteries and adventures of the macabre. The game is afoot!

PART I

WHO-DONE-IT: MYSTERIES IN PARADISE

*I listen to their story,
they listen to my comments,
and then I pocket my fee.*
~ Sherlock Holmes
Sir Arthur Conan Doyle

CHAPTER ONE

MURDER ON MACKINAC ISLAND (1960)

They say that genius is an infinite capacity for taking pains. It's a very bad definition, but it does apply to detective work.

~ Sherlock Holmes ~
Sir Arthur Conan Doyle

The Game Is Afoot

I have visited Mackinac Island dozens of times since 1980 and it has come to be a special place to my family and me. On most of my visits I make a stop at the Mackinac Island police station and court house. On one of my earliest visits I stopped to visit with fellow officers and talk shop for a few moments. In passing, one of the seasonal officers (the island hires additional police during the tourist season) mentioned that he believed that there had been only one murder on the island that had ever been recorded. I filed this in the back of my mind for a couple of decades until one day when I told students in one of my criminology classes that I would give extra credit for a report on this case study. The report was brief, but sparked my interest in researching this further and resulted in the beginning of this book.

The murder of Frances Lacey is a Great Lakes murder mystery. The scene was Mackinac Island, Michigan, located in Lake Huron, near the Mackinac

Bridge that spans the Straits of Mackinac leading to Lake Michigan. Finding information on this case was difficult at first. But once I had identified the date and the victim, I received a great deal of help from the Michigan State Police, the Saint Ignace News and Mackinac Island Town Crier, the Mackinac Island Public Library, the Mackinac County Sheriff's Department, and others. (See acknowledgements)

Once I started investigating this case study I found that it was not the first murder on the island. On July 30, 1960, *The Detroit News* reported, "The last murder on Mackinac Island was in 1910, when a woman employee of the Grand Hotel was found in the underbrush behind it. That death was never solved." (*The Detroit News*, p. 1A, July 30, 1960) The Grand Hotel, cinema enthusiasts may remember was not only the setting for the film *Somewhere In Time* (starring Christopher Reeve and Jane Seymour), but the film classic *This Time for Keeps* (starring Ester Williams). Ironically *Somewhere in Time* was set in 1912, just two years after the first murder.

Murder Trial at Mackinac Island

Even before the 1910 mystery another murder trial was held at the Mackinac Island Court House. Though not related to the 1910 case or this 1960 case study, this is an interesting side bar worth recounting and a good way to set the historic and cultural scene for this mystery.

In the 1850s Lake Michigan was the scene of profitable fishing settlements along the lake shores. Around that time Augustus Pond set up a small fishing operation at Seul Choix Point, a small harbor about sixty miles west of the Straits of Mackinac where Lake Michigan and Lake Huron meet. Pond, his wife, Mary, and their three children had a one-room shanty-house and a smaller net house where two hired hands, Daniel Whiney and Dennis Cull, lived. (*Pond v. People*, p. 152) But all was not well in this water-winter wonderland. Another group of fishermen were "after" Pond and harassed him endlessly. David Plant, Joseph Robbilliard, and Isaac Blanchard, Jr. were Augustus Pond's rivals and enemies. The exact reason for this tumult is not clear, but some have speculated that Isaac Blanchard, Jr. had his cap set for Mary Pond and hoped to drive Augustus off through intimidation. (Stonehouse, p. 16)

On June 16, 1859, Pond's daughter told her mother, Mary, that she had heard David Plant tell another fisherman that he was going to beat up her father, Augustus. Mary, of course, told her husband about the threat and at about 8:00 p.m. that night Plant and a group of men surrounded Pond. Augustus refused to be goaded into a fight and the confrontation eventually disbanded. But Plant went to Pond's home later that same night with Joseph Robbilliard and Isaac Blanchard, Jr. A crowd of twenty or more men were with the trio as they demanded to see Pond. Augustus' wife said that he was not there and the crowd eventually left. When Augustus did come, Mary told him what had happened and Augustus stayed that night at the home of a neighbor. (Stonehouse, pp. 16-17)

The next morning, on June 17, Plant again approached Pond and threatened him with a rock. Once again Pond refused to be provoked. At about 1:00 a.m. on Saturday morning, June 18, Plant, Robbilliard, and Blanchard went to Pond's net house and started to tear it down. When Pond did not respond, they went to his house and demanded to enter. When Mary again told them that Augustus was not home, Plant demanded to enter to search for him. Mary refused and kept the door locked, so the three would-be intruders went to a neighbor's house to get him to join them. (Stonehouse, pp. 16-17) When the neighbor refused, the trio again returned to Pond's net house, approximately thirty-six feet from the Pond home. (*Pond v. People*, p. 153)

As the three men returned to tearing down Pond's net house, they dragged the sleeping Dennis Cull outside. (*Pond v. People*, p. 161) When Augustus heard the noise he came to his door and called out, "Who is tearing down my net house?" The men continued their destruction without answering and Augustus again called out, "Leave or I will shoot!" Hearing choking sounds from one of the hands, Augustus fired one barrel of his shotgun. He assumed that he had missed as the men ran away. (Stonehouse, pp. 16-17)

When morning came, Isaac Blanchard, Jr. was found on the ground in view of several of the other village homes. He was alive but bleeding from a shotgun wound. Minutes after he was found, the six-foot seven-inch, 240-pound Blanchard expired. Plant and Robbilliard, who had abandoned their associate, were nowhere to be found. (Stonehouse, p. 17)

Augustus Pond knew that he was in serious trouble. Not only had he killed Isaac Blanchard, Jr., but he knew that the Justice of the Peace for Mackinac County was Isaac Blanchard, Sr. Seul Choix was a part of Delta County, but attached to Mackinac County for judicial purposes, so Pond did not expect to receive a fair trial. He went to his brother, Louis Pond, who was the constable of Seul Choix and asked to be taken to Beaver Island to turn himself in there. While August and his two hands, Whitney and Cull, headed there in a rowboat, Constable Wilson Newton, Plant, Robbilliard, and two other men pursued them in another boat. About seven miles from Beaver Island the posse overhauled them and arrested Augustus Pond for murder. He was taken to the Mackinac County jail to await trial. (Stonehouse, p. 18) (*Pond v. People*, pp. 162-163)

The trial started on August 30, 1859, at the court house on Mackinac Island, which is not at the county seat of Saint Ignace, but on the island which is a part of Mackinac County. August's lawyers made a historic argument for self-defense that "a man's home is his castle," but in the end he was found guilty and sentenced to ten years of hard labor in a state prison. Upon appeal the Michigan Supreme Court overturned the verdict and directed a new trial. August was never retried and no other murder trial has ever been recorded as being held at the Mackinac Island court house. (Stonehouse, p. 18)

However, his case study is not about the Augustus Pond case of 1859 or the Grand Hotel case of 1910, but the 1960 murder of Frances Lacey.

Vacation Tragedy Becomes a Mystery

Bunting covered the old ferry dock to welcome the gleaming teak yachts harbored in the Mackinac Island harbor. Cooling breezes were coming from the Straits. One of the weekend visitors was Mrs. Frances Lacey from 805 Lafayette South, Dearborn, Michigan. The 49-year-old widow, Kay Sutter (her daughter), Wesley Sutter (her son-in-law), and Merry Lou Sutter (Sutter's sister) left Detroit at about 10:30 p.m. (2230 hours) on Friday night, July 22, 1960. Driving Mrs. Lacey's 1958 Mercury, they arrived in Mackinac City on the south mainland (Lower Peninsula) at about 6:45 a.m. (0645 hours) on Saturday, July 23. They had breakfast at the Post House before boarding the Arnold Ferry to arrive at Mackinac Island at about 9:30 a.m. (Michigan State Police Complaint Report 83-862-60, p. 13)

Mrs. Lacey, Mr. and Mrs. Wesley Sutter, and Miss Sutter came to vacation at Mackinac Island. Mrs. Lacey's daughter and her son, William E. Lacey, had urged her to make the trip to the island for her first vacation since her husband, Ford Lacey, died more two years earlier, in January, 1957. They said they felt she needed to get out. (*Mackinac Island Town Crier*, July 31, 1960, p. 1) (*The Detroit News*, August 22, 1969)

After checking in at the Murray Hotel, Mrs. Lacey took a carriage across the island to join the Sutters who were staying in a cottage of Wesley's mother, Mrs. Leona Schermerhorn, at British Landing. (*The Detroit News*, August 22, 1969) At 5:00 p.m. Kay and Wesley called a cab and brought Mrs. Lacey back into town – approximately four miles. They shopped for some candy and went to Mrs. Lacey's room to visit. (Three pounds of Mackinac fudge from Mays Candy Shop were found later in Mrs. Lacey's suitcase). It was agreed that Mrs. Lacey would come back to the Schermerhorn cabin the next day at 11:00 a.m., either by cab or walking. Kay and Wesley returned to British Landing at about 7:00 p.m. (Michigan State Police Complaint Report 83-862-60, p. 13 and 15) Mrs. Lacey returned to her hotel at or about the same time and spent Saturday night in room 26 of the Murray Hotel, according to the statements of the hotel chamber-maids.

Dr. Robert J. Girod, Sr.

Mrs. Frances Lacey
(Courtesy of the Michigan State Police)

The following morning Mrs. Lacey awoke early and dressed herself in a white blouse, an aquamarine skirt, and gray canvas walking shoes. She packed a pair of blue dress shoes that she planned to wear when she arrived at her destination in a plastic bag. She packed her other belongings in her brown suitcase before going to the lobby. She had paid $5.20 in advance for her room the night before, so it is believed that she placed the room key on the registration counter and her suitcase near the hotel's baggage pickup area. It is speculated that she started her trek from the Murray to British Landing at around 9:00 a.m. (Michigan State Police Complaint Report 83-862-60, p. 13) (Barfknecht, p. 113)

The Chicago-to-Mackinac yacht races were ending and there was a large crowd on the island. While a number of people were still checking into hotels, only a few were checking out. Mrs. Lacey left her room in the Murray Hotel on Sunday, July 24, 1960. Again, she had paid her bill the night before, so the busy desk clerk, a college student, found the key to her room on the counter at around 10:00 a.m. Her suitcase was in front of the counter. (*The Detroit News*, p. 1A, July 30, 1960 and August 22, 1969)

In the corner of the lobby by the stairway is a place where guests leave luggage if they have checked out but are away before leaving the island. This is intended for those who plan to return or call for their things. Detectives later speculated why her bag was positioned in front of the checkout counter, rather than stairway luggage corner. While researching this case I visited the beautiful, historic Murray Hotel. The hotel has been remodeled since 1960 and room 26 no longer exits as such. The area for storing luggage in the lobby is still there.

The Murray Hotel in 1960

(Courtesy of Wesley Maurer, the Saint Ignace News and Mackinac Island Town Crier)

While press accounts reported that the police theorized that Mrs. Lacey had breakfast at the Murray Hotel, waitresses at the Murray said that she did not have breakfast in the dining room. There were few customers that morning and the waitresses said that they would have remembered. In fact, the hotel kitchen had trouble with the gas stoves that Sunday and was unable to serve breakfast until 8:45 a.m. (0845 hours). The police, reportedly, believed that this would put her on the murder scene between 10:00 and 10:15 a.m. (1000-1015). (*The Detroit News*, p. 2A, July 30, 1960) (*Mackinac Island Town Crier*, August 7, 1960, p. 1) The conclusion made by the police may have been quite accurate as a later post-mortem (autopsy) revealed that Mrs. Lacey had cantaloupe not more than two hours before her death. (Michigan State Police Complaint Report 83-862-60, August 2, 1960)

Carriage drivers (the only taxis available on Mackinac Island) reported that they rarely had passengers going along the lake front road or as far as British Landing where Mrs. Lacey planned to go to the cottage of relatives. None of them recalled seeing her. On previous visits Mrs. Lacey was known to walk to British Landing by a path cutting through the center of the island.

This time she planned something different. (*The Detroit News*, p. 2A, July 30, 1960)

Mrs. Lacey's exact route can only be speculated. No doubt she passed the Victorian facades of gift stores, fudge shops, restaurants, hotels and other attractions that characterize the downtown of the island. It is opined that she turned west at Windemere Point where the deteriorating boardwalk led along Lake Shore Road, the eight-mile blacktop of M-185 that follows the Lake Huron shoreline of the island. After passing the Grand Hotel (the scene of the 1910 murder) atop a high bluff to her right, she is thought to have stopped to rest near the fieldstone gate entrance to the Stonecliff Estate. At the time a trail led nearly half a mile through the woods to the then sixty-year-old English-style mansion. In 1960 this was the summer retreat for the Moral Re-Armament society (MRA), a world-wide "fundamentalist" Christian organization. (Barfknecht, p. 114) Today, Stonecliff is more than 100 years old and is a beautiful resort.

What happened next is not entirely clear, but can be speculated upon by what the artifacts of the crime scene would later reveal. The serenity of Mrs. Lacey's rest was interrupted by the sound of snapping branches behind her. As she stood and turned someone hit her in the face, almost knocking her unconscious and sending her partial dental plate from her mouth to the road. She dropped her purse but, still clutching the bag that contained her shoes, she was dragged for several yards up the steep, evergreen-covered incline toward Stonecliff. There her assailant sexually assaulted her and strangled her to death with her panties. (Barfknecht, p. 114)

Conjecture suggests that the murderer removed a wallet from Mrs. Lacey's purse in the roadway, but left the purse on the shoulder of the road. He picked up her canvas oxford walking shoes and threw them into Lake Huron and carried Lacey's body further into the woods. The killer then attempted to conceal the body beneath a fallen balsam tree about two-hundred feet from the stone gate and covered her with branches. Then he secreted her bagged dress shoes under a rotting rowboat before effecting his get-away along a wooded path called Tranquil Lane. (Barfknecht, pp. 114-115)

Dr. Robert J. Girod, Sr.

When Mrs. Lacey did not show up at the Sutter-Schermerhorn cottage by noon, her family expressed concern. Sixteen-year-old Marvin Fineman was bicycling to town to get some milk and offered to take the shore road to look for Mrs. Lacey along the way. When he did not locate her and discovered that she had left her key at the hotel at 10:00 a.m., the police were notified. (*The Detroit News*, August 22, 1969) Kay Sutter later told investigators that she and her husband, Wesley, became concerned and walked to town along the Lakeshore route. They checked the Murray Hotel at 1:00 p.m. and when they did not find Mrs. Frances Lacey there, they notified the State Police. (Michigan State Police Complaint Report 83-862-60, p. 13)

The initial report taken by Trooper Herbert J. Grosse of the Michigan State Police stated that Trooper Grosse contacted the complainant, Mrs. Wesley Sutter, of 24739 Andover Street, Dearborn, Michigan. Mrs. Sutter reported that her mother "was suppose to come out to their cabin at 11:00 a.m. this date but failed to show up." His investigation reports, "A check was made at the Murray Hotel and it was learned that MRS LACEY had checked out at 10:30 a.m. this date but the desk clerk did not know where she was headed for." (Michigan State Police Complaint Report 83-862-60. p. 1) At 7:00 p.m. Kay called her brother, William, from the police station in the presence of Mackinac Island Police Chief Junior Bloomfield (the acting chief). (Michigan State Police Complaint Report 83-862-60, p. 13)

Infamous Murders and Mysteries

Michigan State Police Complaint Report 83-862-60, July 24, 1960, page 1
(Courtesy of the Michigan State Police)

"Mother and I had talked about the shore road," reported Mrs. Wesley Sutter, Lacey's daughter, as she sat on the stone steps of the Michigan State Police office. While detectives questioned people inside the post, Sutter, who was also from Dearborn, shared, "She told me she had decided to walk it even if it was longer. She asked me not to tell the others in the family for fear they would try to dissuade her. It is about four miles that way, but she was strong and was sure she could do it." No one saw Mrs. Lacey on that route for sure, but someone reported to the State Police that they had seen a lone woman by the "boat house," a landmark along that way. (*The Detroit News*, p. 2A, July 30, 1960).

The Mackinac City Police Department was requested to check the Arnold Dock at Mackinac City on the south mainland (Lower Peninsula). There they found Mrs. Lacey's Bronze 1958 Mercury, Michigan license plate KL-6077, still parked where she and her companions had left it. Trooper Grosse reported, "Car 837 and the island ambulance were used to search on the roads on the island but with nil results." He then contacted Sergeant Burnett of Station 83 (Saint Ignace Post) who told him that "he would send over a few men in the morning to assist in a foot search of the wooded areas leading to British Landing..." Assistance was "also requested from the Sheriff Dep't, the local fire department, Coast Guard and a Boy Scout group staying on the island..." (Michigan State Police Complaint Report 83-862-60, p.1)

The Search Unfolds as the Mystery Develops

West of the village on Mackinac, Lake Shore Road circles below the beautiful and historic Grand Hotel and golf courses. The shoreline road or M-185, as it is designated by the state highway system, is the only state highway that has never had a motor vehicle accident. M-185 has no intersection with another highway (other than secondary roads) and, with few exceptions, motor vehicles are not permitted on the island, which utilizes bicycle and horse-drawn transportation. Carriages and bicyclists pass and often stop at Devil's Kitchen, one of many points of interest along the road that circles the island for eight miles. Most of the way to British Landing is characterized by steep wooded slopes and the limestone shoreline. In the distance the Mackinac Bridge connects the two peninsulas of the mainland and ferries often pass from either Mackinac City on the lower (south) or Saint Ignace on the upper (north).

At 11:00 a.m. (1100 hours) on July 26, 1960, Detective Sergeant Spratto and Trooper Kenneth Yuill were sent to Mackinac Island to "make a character and financial background check on missing woman, FRANCIS LACEY and her two children, MRS. KAY SUTTER (Complainant) and WILLIAM LACEY, in an attempt to establish a possible motive for either a suicide or bodily harm by someone." Their report says that "KAY SUTTER, W/F, 22 yrs., of 24739 Andover, Dearborn, Michigan..." was "interrogated for considerable time at the U.S. Coast Guard station..." Kay Sutter told the investigators that her mother was in a "very good financial situation at present." She stated that Mrs. Lacey, "has many stocks and bonds, owns 2 – 8 family apartment buildings, 1 located at 2139 W. Grand Blvd., Detroit and the other located at 109 Leicester, Detroit, Michigan, and owns her home at 805 S. Lafayette, Dearborn, Michigan." (Michigan State Police Complaint Report 83-862-60, p. 12)

Mrs. Sutter went on to add that her mother had "personal checking, business checking and savings accounts at the Manufacturer's National Bank in Detroit and an account at the Federal Savings & Loan Association in Dearborn. The report says, "KAY thinks that her mother is worth about $125,000.00 at present" (a considerable amount in 1960). Her father, Ford V. Lacey, passed away of Leukemia on January 3, 1957. His final will left $9,000 to Kay and $9,000 to her brother, William. While the rest went to Mrs. Lacey, when Kay and William reached the age of 25 half of the profit from the two apartment buildings would go to them. (Michigan State Police Complaint Report 83-862-60, p. 12)

Kay, who was married to Wesley Sutter, was already 25. She was employed by British Overseas Airway Corporation as a ticket agent in the Book Building in Detroit, making $450 a month. She also worked a second job for a heating and air conditioning firm in Detroit. While Kay and Wesley had about $800 in a checking account at the National Bank of Detroit and some stocks and bonds totaling about $3,000, they rented their home and owned two older model cars. (Michigan State Police Complaint Report 83-862-60, p. 12)

Kay told the police that her brother, William, also aged 25, was also married and was buying a home on South Thiesen Street in Dearborn.

Until one month earlier William was employed as a salesman at Thermofax Corporation in Detroit, but was at the time unemployed and taking care of his sick uncle, Claude T. Lacey, of 1625 Murlbut, Detroit, Michigan. Kay reported, however, that her brother was "also secure financially." She told the police that about a month earlier Mrs. Lacey gave her a gold pen and "stated at the time that she didn't want WILLIAM to get it." Kay said that her mother also told her that "if anything happens to her the dishes goes to KAY." Mrs. Lacey also reportedly told a neighbor, in front of Kay, that if anything happened to her that "her washing and ironing were already done." Michigan State Police Complaint Report 83-862-60, pp. 12-13)

Mrs. Lacey's son, William E. (Bill) Lacey (one account called him Phil), age 25, was from 7758 Thiesen, Dearborn, Michigan. He and his wife arrived early on Monday, July 25, at 8:00 a.m. to help search for his mother. He described his mother as a stable person "who could take care of herself; she wasn't inclined to take off on a lark" (past tense quote). "She was a very capable person," he added. "For three years she tended to my father who had become an invalid, which requires considerable strength. She was in excellent physical condition." Mr. Lacey went on to tell reporters, "She never travels out of town by herself, but she does go around by herself in the city." (*Mackinac Island Town Crier*, July 31, 1960, p. 1, and August 14, 1960, p. 1)

A search was organized and included more than sixty lawmen and residents of the island. Divers searched the waters off the island shores. Ed Langin, of Norway in the Upper Peninsula (U.P.) of Michigan was an old hand at searches in the north woods and a dog handler for the Michigan-Wisconsin Rescue Unit. He arrived at the island late on Monday with his two prize bloodhounds, Big Red and Little Red. After being given the scent from clothing from Mrs. Lacey's suitcase they started a track along Lake Shore Road. By 2:00 a.m. (0200 hours) on Tuesday, July 26, the trackers had reached the area of the boat house. (*The Detroit News*, August 22, 1969)

During the search for Mrs. Lacey, Sheriff Charles Garries reported that tracking dogs seemed to have "picked up a scent" of Mrs. Lacey on a boardwalk parallel to the shore road at a point near the Grand Hotel. At that time the boardwalk was dilapidated and signs had been posted warning the public not to use it. "The dogs followed the scent to the end of the boardwalk," Sheriff Garries said. "Then they seemed to lose it completely," he said. "When they couldn't pick it up again after a couple hundred yards," Sheriff Garries reported to *The Detroit News*, "we took them in a car to British Landing" (where Mrs. Lacey was heading to visit relatives). (*The Detroit News*, p. 1B, July 30, 1960) The tracking dogs then worked their way back, picking up the scent. "Baying, they led Langin on through the brush," reported *The Detroit News*, "to the Schermerhorn cottage at British Landing. They retraced a walk Mrs. Lacey had taken Saturday." (*The Detroit News*, August 22, 1969)

A ballpoint pen is found. Could it be a clue?
(Courtesy of Wesley Maurer, the Saint Ignace News and Mackinac Island Town Crier)

Michigan State Police Lt. Robert Bilgen led a 26-man investigation, assisted by Mackinac Island State Park police, Mackinac Island Police and Mackinac County Sheriff's officers. Lt. Bilgen, Sheriff Garries, acting

Mackinac Police Chief Bloomfield, and Mackinac Island State Park Police Chief Ron LaCouture were assisted in the search by Deputy Sheriff Max Foss, troopers assigned at the Island and from the St. Ignace post and numerous other area police officers. Local residents volunteered to assist in the search, joined by the U.S. Coast Guard and Boy Scout Troop 66 from Detroit, which was on the island performing guide duty at historic Fort Mackinac. (*Mackinac Island Town Crier*, July 31, 1960, p. 1)

Sgt. Spratto and Trooper Yuill checked the Murray Hotel again. Mrs. Lacey had stayed in room 26, but they checked the adjacent rooms to see if anyone had seen anything that could help. Room 24 was occupied by Eleanor Pyle, 660 Seward Street, Detroit, Michigan, from July 16-24. She was described as a very observant person by Cletus Murray, the hotel owner. Donald P. Horst, 1111 Catherine Street, Ann Arbor, Michigan, checked into room 25 on July 23 and checked out the next day. Charles B. Ivory, Jr., 2529 Manor Road, Honolulu, Hawaii, also occupied the room. Room 27 was occupied by Mr. and Mrs. J.L. Murphy, 654 Catawba Avenue, Muskegon, Michigan from July 23 to 25. Room 28 was occupied by Sandra Taylor, 719 North Walnut, Bay City, Michigan, on July 23 and 24. All of these persons had left the island by the time the police came to interview them. (Michigan State Police Complaint Report 83-862-60, p. 14)

Spratto and Yuill interviewed Marvel Cruzan, F/W/18/ of Route 1, Fremont, Michigan. Ms. Cruzan was a chamber maid at the Murray and told investigators that she and Mary Pearson, F/W/18/ of Anamose, Iowa, cleaned Mrs. Lacey's room #26 on Sunday, July 24 after 12:30 p.m. (1230 hours). Trooper Yuill reported (calling the victim "Mrs. Stacey") that Mrs. Lacey "was not in the room but there must have been clothing or a suitcase in the room as they did not make up the bed with clean linen, just straightened bed and room up." Cruzan also told the officers that Mary Pearson had mentioned to her that "a friend of hers who is a cab driver on the Island told her about taking a woman to British Landing Sunday and leaving her there." Pearson was not available on the island to be interviewed, so the name of the cab driver was not known. (Michigan State Police Complaint Report 83-862-60, p. 14) Contrary to this information was the belief that Mrs. Lacey had checked out of the Murray and removed her luggage before 10:00 a.m. Another report said that it was Margaret McCloud that was hotel maid who made up the bed in room 26 on Sunday morning. She reported that the bed had been slept in, the room was not occupied when she cleaned it at about 11:30 a.m. (1130 hours), and she found nothing in the room. (Michigan State Police Complaint Report 83-862-60, p. 32)

Dr. Robert J. Girod, Sr.

The Old Beacon House
(Courtesy of Wesley Maurer, the Saint Ignace News and Mackinac Island Town Crier)

A woman matching the description of Mrs. Lacey was reportedly seen alone on Sunday, July 24, 1960, near a boat house that was, at the time, on the southwest shore of the island nearest to the Mackinac Bridge which connects the upper and lower peninsulas of the Michigan mainland. (*The Detroit News*, p. 1A, July 30, 1960) Mrs. Gloria Davenport, Jr., a year-round resident of the Mission section of Mackinac Island, reported to Trooper Yuill that she and her children were at Bandy Beach, just northwest of the Grand Hotel beach, between 2:00 and 3:00 p.m. (1400-1550 hours) on Sunday when they noticed a woman resembling Mrs. Lacey standing by the beach with her arms folded as in the photograph of Lacey. (Michigan State Police Complaint Report 83-862-60, pp. 16 and 31) "We aren't sure," Lt. Bilgen told reporters, "But it is confirmed in some ways and it may have been her." The boat house housed a radio beacon and was the only building on the lake side of the shore road at the time. In the background is the Mackinac Bridge and ferries from Mackinac City and Saint Ignace (the county seat) passed by on the lake throughout the day. If accurate, the lead placed Mrs. Lacey on the shore road just a few hundred yards from where her body was found and just a few minutes before the time at which the murder was speculated to have occurred. (*The Detroit News*, pp. 1B and 2A, July 30, 1960)

The Crime Scene is Discovered

A few hundred yards past the boathouse was one of the gates to the then, 60-year old (now more than 106 years old) Stonecliff estate. At that time it was owned by the Moral Re-Armament society. Today this is a beautiful resort Inn, where my family and I stayed during one of our visits while we investigated this case. In the 1920s Stonecliff was an opulent showplace of the North, staffed by many servants and offering two ballrooms and a private bowling alley. The huge grounds included an expansive lawn, a rock garden, a stone fountain, a barn and stables, an icehouse on the beach, a pumping station for water, and nearby smaller living quarters. (*Mackinac Island Town Crier*, August 7, 1960, p. 1) The search would lead to Stonecliff's gates.

The mansion was the only stone home on the island and was the summer home of Mr. and Mrs. Alvin T. Hert of Louisville, Kentucky. Mr. Hert amassed a fortune in the creosote business and Mrs. Hert was the vice-chairman of the Republican National Committee until 1935. In 1927 and

Dr. Robert J. Girod, Sr.

1928 she offered Stonecliff to President Calvin Coolidge as a summer White House. In 1929 she was considered for a Cabinet position, which would have made her the first woman in the Cabinet. Instead she directed her attention to re-electing Herbert Hoover in 1932. In 1942 the Mackinac Island State Park Commission tried to purchase the estate for a summer residence for Michigan governors, but Mrs. Hert declined the sale. She gave the property to the Episcopal Diocese of Washington, DC, after her death and it was later sold to the Moral Re-Armament (MR-A) society which was using it as a lodge in 1960. (*Mackinac Island Town Crier*, August 7, 1960, p. 1)

The Gate to Stonecliff
(Courtesy of Wesley Maurer, the Saint Ignace News and Mackinac Island Town Crier)

On Thursday, July 28, 1960, Corporal Conrad and the U.S. Coast Guard again checked the shoreline around the island. Trooper Broderson checked all around Lakeshore Road (M-185) and Sergeant George Burnette, Corporal Conrad, Trooper Grosse and Trooper McKeever made numerous inquiries

Infamous Murders and Mysteries

around the island. Divers were called to check the area of the beach near the Grand Hotel swimming pool rest rooms. Troopers Feldhauser, Parolari, Fersberg and Scott arrived but found nothing. (Michigan State Police Complaint Report 83-862-60, p. 17)

The dog track was not successful. State Police Corporal Conrad said, "The reason that the bloodhounds called in didn't find the body was because of the rain which washed away the scent and this confused the dogs." (*Mackinac Island Town Crier*, July 31, 1960, p. 1) "As it happened," Sheriff Garries said, "we transported them right past the spot where she apparently was killed." (*The Detroit News*, p. 1B, July 30, 1960)

The roadway (M-185) where the dentures were found.
(Courtesy of Wesley Maurer, the Saint Ignace News and Mackinac Island Town Crier)

But Mrs. Lacey's dental plates were found in the center of the road beyond the gate to the Stonecliff estate. The dentures had apparently been shattered by a carriage. Her purse was also found on the shoulder of the road. Scuff marks on the edge of the road led police to the conclusion that she may have been killed or knocked unconscious there, even though the spot is clearly visible from the cliffs above or from boats off shore in Lake Huron. (*The Detroit News*, p. 1B, July 30, 1960) Captain Van Landegend advised that he was sending Lt. Bilgen and D/SGT Spratto by plane with Trooper Albright back to the island. (Michigan State Police Complaint Report 83-862-60, p. 17)

Sergeant George Burnette and Trooper Albright were checking the area near Stonecliff. When they looked beneath an abandoned boat that had been pulled into the woods about thirty feet from the road they discovered a pair of black ladies shoes – one in a plastic bag and the other on the ground. A short distance away Trooper Albright found the body of Mrs. Frances Lacey "partially hidden under the foliage of two fallen cedar trees." Bits of dental plate were found along the road. D/SGT Spratto and Trooper Albright took measurements. Lt. Bilgen took notes describing the body and the location. Martin Rose, a local photographer, was called to take twenty-four (24) photographs of the scene. The District Commander was notified and advised the investigators that five men from the crime laboratory were on the way. He also sent Detective McCluer from Station 32 and Detective Sergeant Bloomquist from Station 71, along with two more detectives from the Second District, to assist in the investigation. (Michigan State Police Complaint Report 83-862-60, p. 17)

The body of Frances Lacey was found about twenty feet inland from the Lake Shore Road and 212 feet from the gate to Stonecliff at about 7:18 p.m. (1918 hours) on July 28, 1960. The press reported that her body was hidden under a fallen balsam tree and another account reported "a windfall of cedar trees." It may have been dragged feet first or carried there and then covered by brush. Mrs. Lacey's clothing was in disarray, leading to speculation of a sexual motive, but tests would be required to confirm this. Her knotted underwear was around her throat. Robbery was also a suspected motive. She is thought to have had about $50-$100 in her purse. Lacey's gold wristwatch was also missing. The perpetrator may then have fled on a nearby footpath ironically named Tranquil Lane. (*The Detroit News*, pp. 1A and 1B, July 30,

1960 and August 22, 1969) (*Mackinac Island Town Crier*, July 31, 1960, p.1) (*Mackinac Island Town Crier*, August 14, 1960, p. 2)

Mrs. Lacey's body was found face down on a down grade, head toward the lake on the right side of her face. Her right arm was folded behind her back, palm up, and her left arm along her left side. She was wearing stockings, but no shoes. Her knees were slightly bent. Her short-sleeved white blouse was "pulled up in a bunch to a line above the shoulder blades." Her dark green skirt was pulled up to the hip line and she was wearing a girdle with the garters still attached to the stockings. The body was 20'7" from the MR-A fence line to the west. A pair of plastic-rimmed glasses was found about two inches from her left upper arm. At 7:35 p.m. (1935 hours) Corporal Conrad was sent in the jeep to get the coroner and a photographer. (Michigan State Police Complaint Report 83-862-60, July 28, 1960, p. 24)

The area, just north of Devil's Kitchen, was roped off and guarded by two state troopers. (*Mackinac Island Town Crier*, July 31, 1960, p. 1) Cpl Conrad returned with Police Chief Bloomfield and George Rose, the photographer from the Grand Hotel. Rose used a 3x4 press camera to take 24 photos of 12 scenes. The photos were completed at 8:18 p.m. (2018 hours). Conrad then brought Robert Davis, a funeral home director from St. Ignace, to the scene. (Michigan State Police Complaint Report 83-862-60, July 28, 1960, p. 24) Clothing, fibers and hair samples were collected from various artifacts at the crime scene. This would constitute significant trace evidence in this case and was sent to the Crime Detection Laboratory of the Michigan Department of Health. (Michigan Department of Health, Division of Laboratories memo, August 9, 1960)

A pair of Lacey's shoes was found, carefully wrapped in a plastic bag, under an abandoned boat in the woods. At first this puzzled investigators. (*The Detroit News*, pp. 1A and 1B, July 30, 1960 and August 22, 1969) The post-mortem (autopsy) later confirmed that the death was a result of strangulation, even though minor bruises were noted on her face. Coroner George W. Davis authorized the autopsy, which was performed at the Davis Funeral Home in St. Ignace. The Sigma and the King Armstrong methods were used and examined at Little Traverse Hospital. J.H. Webster, M.D., conducted the post at 3:00 p.m. (1500 hours) on July 29. (Autopsy Number A-49-60, Mackinac County Coroner's Office)

The Plot Thickens and the Investigation Begins

Sheriff Charles Garries had just taken office two months before the murder. (*The Detroit News*, p. 1A, July 30, 1960) Mackinac Island Police Chief Bernard Gough had resigned just thirteen days earlier because he was dissatisfied with his salary for the 70-hour work week he performed 345 days per year. One of the island's two patrolmen, Myron Bloomfield, Jr., was acting chief until Mayor Robert Hughey made a decision between Bloomfield and Officer John Brenzie to take Gough's place permanently. A new patrolman would then be hired too, at $105 a week. Veterans and island residents would be given preference. (*Mackinac Island Town Crier*, July 17, 1960, p. 1)

The Michigan State Police led an investigation, assisted by the Mackinac Island State Park Police, the Mackinac County Sheriff's Department and the Mackinac Island Police Department. The *Mackinac Island Town Crier* called the investigation "The greatest manhunt in Mackinac's history" as police continued to "make a tedious, thorough check of all Island employees for questioning…" Lt. Bilgen and Chief LaCouture were pictured beneath the headline reading "MANHUNT BLANKETS MACKINAC" in the Week of August 7th, 1960, edition of the *Mackinac Island Town Crier*. (*Mackinac Island Town Crier*, August 7, 1960, p. 1) The article reported:

> *Detectives conferred with every Island employer in gathering a list of all employees and their home addresses, and Michigan State police made a state-wide investigation on employees who quit their summer jobs between Sunday when Mrs. Lacey disappeared, and Thursday, when her body was discovered.*
>
> *(Mackinac Island Town Crier, August 7, 1960, p. 1)*

Troopers began questioning summer employees, most of whom were college students, and residents of the island. Michigan State Police Lt. Bilgen told *The Detroit News*, "We've had only about a dozen tips to work with, so far," opining that, "Someone from Detroit or elsewhere might have seen something while he was here last Sunday that could lead us to a suspect." Detectives were stationed at the islands two ferry docks to observe people leaving for the mainland. A few were questioned. "We're looking for something that might indicate the killer is still on the island," Lt. Bilgen said. He continued, "A tourist could have left by the next ferry." (*The Detroit News*, p. 1A, July 30, 1960)

Sergeant Spratto and Trooper Yuill interviewed the desk clerk while conducting their investigation at the Murray, but neglected to record his name in the initial report. He was 19 year-old Jack Donaldson of Findlay, Ohio. The day clerk told the officers that he came to work at about 7:15 a.m. (0715). The suitcase was not in the lobby at that time but "he is quite sure it was placed there sometime around 10:30 a.m. while he was out of the room." He did not recall putting the key to room 26 away, but must have "placed it back in (the) cupboard without realizing it as many customers just leave their room keys on the desk." The afternoon desk clerk from 4:00 p.m. to 12:00 midnight was Thomas Murray (another report refers to him as Chuck Murray). He remembered registering Mrs. Lacey into room 26 and recalled that she left and returned to the hotel at least three times before 10:30 p.m. (2230 hours). Each time she left the key at the desk and picked it up when she returned. The last time she said that "she guessed she wouldn't be bothering him anymore for the night." Murray closed the desk at about 1:00 a.m. and no employees were on duty in the lobby until 7:15 a.m. (0715). Hotel owner Cletus Murray said that he did not remember Mrs. Lacey, but did notice her suitcase in front of the desk at about 2:00 p.m. (1400) on Sunday and moved it to another location in the lobby. (Michigan State Police Complaint Report 83-862-60, pp. 15 and 31-32)

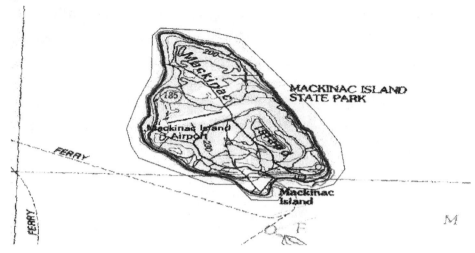

A map of Mackinac Island
(Public Domain map)

Mrs. Lacey's car was still parked on the mainland at Mackinaw City where she and Mr. and Mrs. Sutter had left it on Saturday. (*Mackinac Island Town Crier*, July 31, 1960, p. 1) State police detectives revealed that they had made a "cursory check" of Mrs. Lacey's finances. Lt. Bilgen noted to reporters, "We are going into them further." (*The Detroit News*, p. 1B, July 30, 1960) As mentioned before, Frances' husband, Ford Lacey, had died two years before and he had left her well-provided for financially. Even so she mowed the grass and frugally did repair jobs around her neat brick Dearborn home herself. (*The Detroit News*, August 22, 1969) Lt. Bilgen also noted, "Although we have no reason to believe that her death is due to anything more than a chance encounter, we are checking everything. We are getting started in our inquiry in this and other fields." (*The Detroit News*, p. 1B, July 30, 1960)

The Purse, Wallet, and Walking Shoes

Police checked and rechecked the stories and alibis of 378 persons who were on the island the morning of the murder. They believed that the murderer was right-handed and husky enough to carry Lacey's 118 pounds, while acting without consideration that he might be easily observed. (*The Detroit News*, pp. 1A and 1B, July 30, 1960 and August 22, 1969)

The first break came when a couple, also from the Detroit area, returned home from the weekend at Mackinac Island. They contacted the police and reported that they had found Lacey's purse and brought it home with them. On July 28 a D/LT Howard Whaley was contacted by a friend of his from the Detroit Police Department. The Detroit officer told LT Whaley that a retired police officer was approached by a man who said that he had found the purse. The man did not want to "get involved" because one of them was married and they were not supposed to be at the island together at the time of the murder. They had known each other for about four years. (Michigan State Police Complaint Report 83-862-60, p. 21- 22)

They had stayed the night in their car in Flint part of the night on Friday and in a motel on Saturday night. They reported that they had arrived on Mackinac Island on the first ferry from Mackinac City at 9:30 a.m. on Sunday morning. After strolling through the village they rented a tandem bicycle at Schwinn's near the dock and pedaled east. They went "toward the hospital and past the state police station." They passed the U.S. Coast Guard station. When they reached the end of the pavement, they reversed directions and went back toward the village. They stopped to look at the Grand Hotel and then continued on Lake Shore Road. (*The Detroit News*, August 22, 1969) When they came to a "spring by a cave" they stopped and the woman waded out into the lake. The man took a few photos of her. They rode on and the man saw the purse. He said, "There's somebody's purse," but kept going. The woman said "Stop, there might be something in it." (Michigan State Police Complaint Report 83-862-60, pp. 17, 21- 23)

Detective Sgt. Anthony Spratto inspects the abandoned boat under which Mrs. Lacey's shoes were found.

(Courtesy of Wesley Maurer, the Saint Ignace News and Mackinac Island Town Crier)

The purse was just north of a gateway drive that ran at an angle from the main carriage trail. The gateway was described as having two large stone or concrete posts with an iron grill between them and a sign that read "No Trespassing. Private Property." The police determined that the purse was about four feet off of the island side of the blacktop and about twenty feet north of the gateway to where the purse was found about twenty feet north of Stonecliff. This was about 2.3 miles from the Coast Guard station and

1.3 miles from British Landing. (Michigan State Police Complaint Report 83-862-60, pp. 17, 21 and 22)

If the couple had not stopped at Devil's Kitchen, they may have overtaken Mrs. Lacey before she too stopped just beyond the curve near the entrance to Stonecliff. They reported hearing a "snapping sound" coming from the wooded estate. As the man picked up the purse, he heard "a rustling noise" near the gate "such as might be made by an animal of some size running through the bush or grass." (Michigan State Police Complaint Report 83-862-60, pp. 17, 21, and 22) The man looked into the wooded brush but saw nothing. This turned out to be the spot where Mrs. Lacey's body was found.

The couple looked into the black leather purse with large bamboo handles and found Mrs. Lacey's identification, listing her home address. There was no money in the purse, though it is believed that she had about $100 when she left the hotel. (*The Detroit News*, August 22, 1969) They found a checkbook with Mrs. Lacey's name on it and a hotel circular from the Chippewa Hotel in the purse. When they returned to the village they went directly to the hotel to see if she was registered there, but she was not. They decided to take the purse home with them and return it in Dearborn. They left on the 11:30 ferry boat to St. Ignace. On the boat they agreed that they should have turned the purse in to the police on the island. (Michigan State Police Complaint Report 83-862-60, pp. 21-22 and 23)

Another couple, who were boating, discovered a woman's walking shoe and a pair of men's tennis shoes floating in the water about 200 feet from where Mrs. Lacey's body was found. (*Mackinac Island Town Crier*, August 7, 1960, p. 1) Little more evidence was discovered at the time. Several hair and fiber samples were also collected as trace evidence at the scene.

Dr. Robert J. Girod, Sr.

Lt. Robert Bilgen, who is directing the hunt for the killer, examines the spot where widow's body was found.

(Courtesy of Wesley Maurer, the Saint Ignace News and Mackinac Island Town Crier)

Seventeen days after the murder a gardener at the Grand Hotel grounds found Lacey's empty wallet in a hedge near a gravel lane. (Barfknecht, p. 115) John McKay found a blue "Lady Buxton" wallet at about 1:30 p.m. on August 10, 1960. It was "in a clump of shrubbery adjacent to (a) path" that ran to the Grand Hotel's tennis court and about fifteen feet from the edge of the sidewalk. McKay took the wallet to his boss, Jacob de Blecourt, the Hotel's head gardener. There was no money in the wallet. It contained a birth certificate, driver's license, and AAA card in the name of Frances Lacey. (Michigan State Police Complaint Report 83-862-60, Report on Property)

In 1962 the Michigan Attorney General's Office forwarded a letter to Captain Howard Whaley, who was then the MSP Chief of Detectives. He was the Lieutenant that received the tip from Detroit PD on finding the purse. The letter was from a reader of *True Detective* magazine in Sulphur, Oklahoma. The magazine ran an article on the Lacey murder and mentioned "Harrison Adams" (who was really John McKay) finding the wallet. Follow-up investigation revealed that John Edison McKay was a male, white, 5'2" and 145 pounds, born February 26, 1900, which made him sixty-years old at the time of the murder. McKay, who was considered elderly and in poor health, needed glasses to read and was unable to determine who owned the wallet. That is why he took the wallet to head gardener Jacob de Blecourt. Although Sault Saint Marie Police revealed that McKay had several arrests for "drunk and disorderly" and two minor traffic offenses, he was considered a possible suspect. (Michigan State Police Complaint Report 83-862-60, pp. 297-298)

The Missing Watch and the Safety Deposit Box

The purse and wallet had been found, but there was a watch missing which had been taken from Mrs. Lacey at the time of the murder. Lt. Bilgen told the press, "We are not stymied. We are checking many tips which seem minor on the surface, but any one could develop into the lead we need to break this case." The detectives were looking for a gold, oblong Benrus wristwatch with a gold chain bracelet. Police were checking jewelry repair shops in the

Detroit area, looking for the watch with the correct serial number. (*Mackinac Island Town Crier*, August 7, 1960, p. 1)

Until this writing the details of the watches description have been unpublished for more than 46 years. Detective Sergeant Robin D. Sexton is the MSP detective assigned to this on-going investigation. During the course of this writing D/SGT Sexton decided that the time had come to make this information public in hopes that even today someone will find and report the possession of this watch. The missing watch is a 14-Karat yellow gold, 19-jewel, Benrus Watch Company, Lady Elgin Model 619, serial number E804949 with jewelers repair number L8933. *If any reader discovers a watch matching this description, please report this immediately to the Michigan State Police.*

Meanwhile, on August 5, 1960, officials and relatives of Mrs. Lacey gathered near Detroit, at the Dearborn branch of the Manufacturer's National Bank. A safety deposit box belonging to Mrs. Lacey was opened in hopes of finding a clue. It contained:

- personal papers,
- 951 shares of stock,
- Mrs. Lacey's will, dated February 17, 1954,
- a codicil to the will, dated April 24, 1959,
- a divorce decree, dated May 3, 1932, and
- Another divorce decree, dated September 14, 1933.

William Lacey, Mrs. Lacey's son, declined comment to the press about the divorce decrees, merely stating that they did not concern his mother. (*Mackinac Island Town Crier*, August 14, 1960, p. 1)

Suspects Developed and Questioned

More than 8,000 tourists and 2,000 itinerant workers were on the island on the day of the murder. Most of the visitors had departed by the time the investigation was well under way. Detectives theorized that the killer must have spent the night on the island, as the first ferry arrived at 8:00 a.m., not more than two hours from the estimated time of the murder. The crime scene was about two miles from the ferry docks. (Barfknecht, p. 116) Yet, Mrs. Lacey is believed to have left the Murray Hotel between 9:00 and 10:00 a.m. and walked about half of her three and half mile trek. Walking at 4 M.P.H. someone could walk from the docks to the crime scene in about a half hour, arriving at about 8:30 a.m. (0845). This merely asserts that the perpetrator *could* have arrived that same day and *may not* have stayed on the island the night before.

Detectives investigated every visitor who checked out of a hotel and every employee who had quit their job on either July 24 or 25. They also checked on everyone who had rented a bicycle, saddle horse or horse-drawn carriage during the hours immediately preceding the murder. (Barfknecht, p. 116) Among the persons being sought for questioning were four carriage drivers who left their jobs immediately before Mrs. Lacey's body was found. One of these was an AWOL sailor. (*Mackinac Island Town Crier*, August 7, 1960, p. 1)

Another suspect was a 40-year-old island resident who had been taken to the Federal Correctional Institution at Milan, Michigan, on Friday, July 29, to begin a one-year sentence for check theft. Guards became suspicious when he seemed to have excessive interest in the murder case. He even noted that he had taken part in the search for Mrs. Lacey while he was out on bond. Island residents who knew the man discounted him, asserting that he lost his job as a stableman because he was too small to handle 80-pound bales of hay. The theory was speculated that if he could not carry 80-pound bales then it was unlikely that he could drag a 117-pound woman more than 200 feet up the steep hillside trail from one of the gates to the Stonecliff estate. (*The Detroit News*, p. 1B, July 30, 1960)

Local island residents had their own theory for the murder. Many opined that an "unstable" member of the several hundred weekend guests of the Moral Re-Armament conference was the culprit. MRA leaders were questioned, but produced nothing (Barfknecht, p. 116) and a few days later a 22-year-old hitchhiker was arrested near East Tawas. He told state police that he had been staying at the Moral Re-Armament headquarters on the island. (*Mackinac Island Town Crier*, August 7, 1960, p. 1) On August 5, 1960, state and local police went to Stonecliff and checked the scene for a quarter mile in each direction. (*Mackinac Island Town Crier*, August 14, 1960, p. 1) None of this produced new leads.

The week of August 14, 1960, the headline of the *Mackinac Island Town Crier* read, "HUNT SPREADS TO OTHER STATES," with a banner reading, "Police Check Out 129 Leads." The force investigating the murder was reduced from three state police and eight officers from outside agencies to three. Lt. Robert Bilgen, still leading the investigation, returned to Marquette after business in Lansing. Sgt. George Burnette and Detective Ed Hill from the St. Ignace post of the Michigan State Police remained on-scene. Sgt. Burnette was the officer in charge of the Saint Ignace Post and the fifteen troopers assigned there. A native of Detroit, he joined the Michigan State Police in 1941 and was assigned to the Mount Pleasant Post. In 1942 he transferred to East Lansing and then to East Tawas. In 1955 he was promoted to corporal and sent to Ypsilanti until he promoted to sergeant and transferred to Saint Ignace in July of 1959.

Sgt. Burnette reported that 129 leads had been followed up but "the case is wide open." More than 2,500 phone calls between Mackinac Island and Saint Ignace were checked and polygraphs (lie detectors) were used to check the alibis of suspects throughout the Midwest. "We have nothing definite," Sgt. Burnette told the *Town Crier*. "The other officers have compiled a vast amount of information and we are checking it out although nothing looks like it would have a connection." Police still searched for the whereabouts of the gold Benrus watch. (*Mackinac Island Town Crier*, August 14, 1960, p. 1)

Leaving nothing to chance, the detectives attempted to determine the identity of a nude bather seen two weeks before the murder at the abandoned beach house north of Stonecliff where the body was discovered. A group of friends saw the nudist sitting on a log and one approached him and asked him to put some clothes on. Despite being scolded for bathing naked so near the road, the witness said that the "tall and thin" nudist "was not belligerent" and "said he did not realize he was so near the road." He was nearly six-foot-tall, 165-pound, and had a "definite English accent." (*Mackinac Island Town Crier*, August 14, 1960, pp. 1-2)

The Barber and the Man with the Key

On February 27, 1961, the police contacted Peter Gerald Elkins, who was then twenty-three years old. Elkins was originally from Coopersville, Michigan, and had moved from Oscoda, Michigan, to Mackinaw City in 1956 to live with his uncle, Morris Darrow. He opened a barber shop at 321 Central Avenue in Mackinaw City on the south peninsula of the mainland in 1958. (The year the Mackinac Bridge was built and the ship *Edmund Fitzgerald* was launched). Since his initial questioning in February, the detectives wanted to talk to him again. They called him at Seneca 9-5594 and told him they would be by to see him. (Michigan State Police Complaint Report 83-862-60, pp. 814)

What brought the sleuths back to see this barber may have been the key to this mystery. In fact, that's exactly what they wanted to talk about – the key to room 26 of the Murray Hotel. Elkins said that he had been thinking about this since the police were to see him in February. He said he now recalled that the key came into his possession when it was left with him at his barber shop by an "older man" who he believed was in his 50s. The man was about 5'10 and had graying hair, but he did not think he would be able to identify the man if he saw him again. He remembered the man handing him the key and asking him to mail it back to the Murray Hotel. He did not specifically recall the man having a car, but had the impression that he had a car parked in front of the shop. He believed that this occurred before the Lacey murder, otherwise he would have connected the two events. Elkins said that he threw the key into a drawer that he kept odds and ends in, such as parts for model cars that he built in his spare time. He ran across the key from time to time and would tease his friends that it belonged to the murdered woman and that he could prove that they were the murderer. (Michigan State Police Complaint Report 83-862-60, pp. 814)

Paul Joseph Michael Strantz

On July 28, 1960, a maintenance man at one of the resort hotels was "held for questioning" because of red stains on his clothing, which later was found to be red paint. Newspaper reports said, "He was arrested after the finding of the body because an officer recalled that he had scratches on his face." (*The Detroit News*, p. 1B, July 30, 1960) Shortly after the discovery of the corpus delicti, the State Police arrested the suspect on July 28, 1960, but details on this were withheld from the media "pending results of laboratory tests being conducted by the State Police in Lansing." (*Mackinac Island Town Crier*, July 31, 1960, p. 1)

Paul Joseph Michael Strantz, also known as Paul Strandz, M/W/ date of birth July 29, 1929, was arrested the day after his 31st birthday. He was 5'11" / 160 pounds / brown hair and brown eyes. He listed his residence as the YMCA in South Bend, Indiana, but was now staying at the Island House Hotel. He arrived on the island at 5:00 p.m. (1700) on Saturday, July 23, 1960, and he planned to work at different jobs in kitchens, washing windows, etc. The police report says that he "was interrogated because of his tendencies to be around the streets at all times of the day and night." He told the police that he was at the Murray Hotel on both Saturday and Sunday nights for drinks at the bar. When Sgt. Spratto and Trooper Yuill questioned him about the missing woman, Strantz became belligerent, but allowed them to check his hotel room. (Michigan State Police Complaint Report 83-862-60, p. 15)

Strantz worked for Hardy Stebins at the YMCA in South Bend, Indiana. Strantz said that he had started from South Bend about two weeks ago with $100. He went to Petoskey to get a job at Little Traverse Hospital, but was unsuccessful. By the time he arrived at Mackinac Island, he had $1.50 in change in his pockets when the police questioned him. The officers opined that Strantz "appears to be mentally retarded and there is a possibility this is a good suspect..." (Michigan State Police Complaint Report 83-862-60, p. 16)

In Stantz's room the officers found "several books and newspaper clippings on medical knowledge, such as the complete anatomy of a human being, women and their babies." The report read, "He had his own sketches of many women's faces and bodies and many sketches had meaningless poetry wrote below them." Additionally, officers found about twelve feet of small rope in his suitcase and two ladies pocket mirrors. His wardrobe consisted of one light weight gray suit with blue pin stripes, one pair of khaki pants, one green cotton pull-over short sleeve sport shirt, one red, white and blue pin striped dress shirt, a light tan trench coat, one pair of black oxfords, and one pair of tan canvas, crepe soled shoes. (Michigan State Police Complaint Report 83-862-60, p. 15) The officers took note of the fact that Strantz's gray suit, green sport shirt, and socks were very wet. He told them that he had gotten them wet in the rain Saturday evening. The suit pants had several pine needles and small stones in the cuffs, even though Strantz said he had just retrieved the suit from the cleaners Saturday night. He said the suit was at the cleaners for about a year or since he had left the island the previous summer. (Michigan State Police Complaint Report 83-862-60, p. 15)

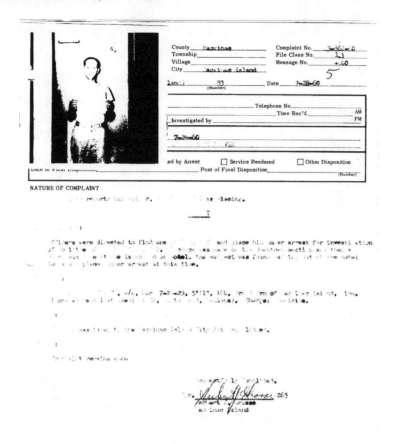

Rap Sheet and only available Photo of Paul Joseph Michael Strantz
(Courtesy of the Michigan State Police)

Strantz told investigators that he got up around 9:00 a.m. on Sunday morning and had breakfast. He said that he went to mass at 10:30 a.m. until 11:30 a.m. He then returned to the Island House and had lunch. He worked at the National Photo shop until 7:00 p.m. when he returned to the island house. His alibis for Sunday morning and afternoon were substantiated, but the red, white and blue shirt had red on the right arm that resembled blood. The shirt was taken to Dr. Joseph Solomon's office on the island. Dr.

Solomon determined that the red was paint and not blood. (Michigan State Police Complaint Report 83-862-60, p. 15 and 31)

Officers' follow-up reports say that Strantz "didn't seem to want to talk about the murder," but he agreed to take a polygraph (lie detector) test. It was tentatively set up for September 9, 1964. On September 11, 1964, D/SGT William S. Simmons of the 8th District Headquarters Detective Bureau examined Strantz. Simmons' report begins:

> PAUL J. STRANTZ, w/m, 35 yrs. of 806 Michauwaukee Ave., South Bend, Indiana. This subject appears to be some-what of a mental, and has been going to Mackinac Island for the past fifteen years, however in 1961 he went to Petoskey, Michigan instead of the Island. (Michigan State Police Complaint Report 83-862-60, p. 157)

Tests were conducted and there were "significant emotional disturbances in this subject's polygraph records on the relevant and irrelevant questions. Simmons concluded that the test was too ambiguous to determine Strantz's guilt or innocence, noting that his "true mental status is some-what of a question." Simmons also remarked:

> After the subject had left the polygraph room, he later appeared in the wash room where this examiner was washing the polygraph pens and wanted a bar of soap and stated that he wanted to remember this momentous occasion.
> Later after he had gone down-stairs he re-appeared in the polygraph room and wanted this examiner to autograph the pamphlet concerning the School Bus law, which he had obtained from the pamphlet rack in the lobby of the post. (Michigan State Police Complaint Report 83-862-60, p. 157)

Nationwide Search for Bartender: Harold Richard Asp

A nationwide alert went out to locate a former bartender from the island. The bartender, Harold Richard Asp, age 40, worked at a local hotel until July 26, just two days after Mrs. Lacey was reported missing. On Wednesday,

July 27, he checked into a hotel in Detroit, paying a week in advance. After spending only one night without returning, the hotel manager became suspicious of the man and entered his room. There the manager found a sports coat with a pay-stub from a Mackinac Island hotel in the pocket. The manager also found a baggage claim check indicating that Asp had left his bag at the Union Terminal Piers dock on Tuesday, July 26. (*Mackinac Island Town Crier*, August 21, 1960, p. 1) The hotel manager notified the police, who considered the bartender a new suspect.

The Michigan State Police crime lab at East Lansing compared hair found on the victim's skirt with hair found on Asp's sports jacket. Both were human hair and demonstrated a "similarity." The suspect had not been seen since July 27. An island resident reported that he had seen Asp at an island bar on Sunday night, July 24, the day of the murder. He said that the suspect was involved in an argument and got into a fight outside of the bar. He was also reportedly seen in the bar on Monday afternoon, July 25. (*Mackinac Island Town Crier*, August 21, 1960, p. 1)

Harold Richard Asp, who listed his home as Minneapolis, was hired by the island hotel through an Indianapolis, Indiana, employment agency. The Detroit Police Department received a tip on the suspect on August 8, but did not want to risk hampering the investigation by releasing the information until a Detroit newspaper discovered the manhunt and made it known. (*Mackinac Island Town Crier*, August 21, 1960, p. 1)

Michigan police alerted the Indianapolis Police Department, Chicago and Los Angeles Police Departments, and the Saint Paul Police Department to be on the lookout for the bartender. While Asp had no record in Michigan, he had been arrested in other states for check fraud, defrauding an innkeeper, and for being drunk and disorderly. Meanwhile another murder was thought to have a connection. Mrs. Bertha DeCourval, 69, a well-to-do widow from Flint, Michigan, was robbed and murdered after midnight on August 16, 1960, after returning from Mackinac Island with her 13-year-old granddaughter, Christine DeCourval. The Flint murder was discounted by police as having any connection to the Lacey murder. (*Mackinac Island Town Crier*, August 21, 1960, p. 1)

At about 9:30 a.m. (0930 hours) on August 18 Asp called the Indiana State Police and said that he had heard they were looking for him. He said that he would make himself available if they wanted to see him. When Indiana authorities arrived at his address at 919 Pennsylvania Avenue, Apartment W,

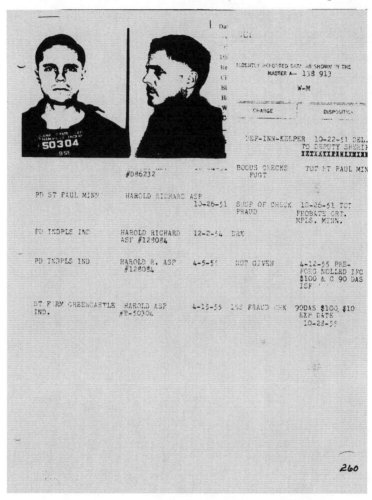

Rap Sheet and only available Photo of Harold Richard Asp
(Courtesy of the Michigan State Police)

he was not there. He often stayed with his girlfriend, Evie Foley, age 48, at 3031 English. When Asp returned about a half hour later, he was taken to ISP headquarters and detained without questioning until the Michigan authorities arrived. (Michigan State Police Complaint Report 83-862-60, p. 236-239)

LT Howard Whaley, SGT Anthony Spratto and Trooper Nottage flew via a state police plane from Traverse City, Michigan, to Indianapolis to question the suspect and bring him back to Mackinac Island. They arrived at Stout Field at 4:00 p.m. (1600 hours). ISP Sergeants Robert Gray and Stan Young met them at the air field. Asp was questioned by the MSP officers and examined on a polygraph ("lie detector") by ISP LT Davis. Officers collected samples of Asp's head and pubic hair. Dr. Kivela later reported that "they did not compare closely with recovered hair specimens." His trousers were also taken for examination. Asp told the officers that they were the same ones he had been wearing since he left the island. He had not cleaned them, so not surprisingly they had several stains and "accumulations" in the cuffs. (Michigan State Police Complaint Report 83-862-60, p. 236-239)

Sgt. Spratto told the press, "The suspect was very cooperative and we cleared him in Indianapolis but he consented to return to Mackinac to clear himself further." Spratto said, "He submitted to a complete investigation including a lie-detector test. There's no question that this particular individual is cleared." (*Mackinac Island Town Crier*, August 28, 1960, p. 1)

The detectives questioned Asp about others who were on a list of Grand Hotel employees who were of interest. Asp told the officers that Lemuel Roy Kemper was a "big guy" – over six feet tall and 200 pounds. He was in his late 40's with long, wavy, gray hair. Kemper, from 2241 Beverly Court, Anderson, Indiana, worked as a bartender at the Grand from July 8-25, 1960. He also left the island just after the murder. Asp told the detectives that he had seen Kemper at the Step Inn Bar in downtown Indianapolis since he arrived back in Indy. (Michigan State Police Complaint Report 83-862-60, p. 239)

The intrepid sleuths also talked with Asp about Clark (Whitey) Sutherland of 2936 Central, Indianapolis, Indiana. Whitey Sutherland was an employee at the Grand from July 9-25, 1960. He came to the island with Roy Kemper the day after Asp arrived because they could not get ready and catch the bus as soon as Asp and had to wait until the following day. Whitey was in his early 40s, about 5'9, 155 pounds, with blue eyes. He was called

"Whitey" most of his life because his hair had been very blond, but was now long gray-white and slicked back. Asp, Roy Kemper and Whitey Clark were all bartenders and roomed together on the fifth floor of the Grand Hotel. (Michigan State Police Complaint Report 83-862-60, p. 239)

At this point the investigation seemed to come to a standstill. The Michigan State Police renewed their resolve by adding to the investigative team once again. Detectives Arthur Stock and Rudolph Lundi from State Police Headquarters and Detective Joe Zimmer from the Marquette Post joined the investigation.

Calvin Kenneth Land

Calvin Kenneth Land, born April 24, 1935 (age 25) was 5'10" and 150 pounds with gray hair and blue eyes. He had been arrested a few times for misdemeanors and for statutory rape when he was 17. He was given probation for that offense. When his father-in-law telephoned him and said the police were checking on him, he returned to the island. Now he was staying at Archie Horn's Apartment on the island with his wife and children. Investigators wanted to talk to Land because they found that he had told J. K. Gallacher that he had committed murder for $500 dollars down and that he was to receive more. He displayed "a considerable amount of money in his wallet." (Michigan State Police Complaint Report 83-862-60, p. 760)

Land admitted to the police that he had told Gallacher that he had killed Lacey by strangling her with her own "Maidenform" panties. He described how she rolled her eyes as she was being strangled and that he had gone out to Lakeshore Drive looking for her. Land said that he grabbed Gallacher around the throat from behind, but that this was all a joke that started when they were working at the Neary home around August 10. (Michigan State Police Complaint Report 83-862-60, p. 760)

Land said that on Sunday, July 24, 1960, he left his home with his step-daughter, Sharon Bagbey, between 10:00 and 10:30 a.m. (1000-1030 hours). They rode saddle horses out to the island cemeteries and down the old State Road to British Landing. At British Landing they visited his mother-in-law,

Mrs. Early, for two hours or more, returning by Lakeshore Road at about 2:00 p.m. (1400 hours). Samples of head and pubic hairs were collected from Land and sent to CPT Grant with the officers' reports. (Michigan State Police Complaint Report 83-862-60, p. 760)

Officers then questioned Land's wife. She said that he was her second husband and they had been married for six years. She said that he had never physically abused her and she did not think he was capable of such a crime. She said that he had white hair that he kept quite short. She had heard that he had made remarks about killing Mrs. Lacey. When she asked him about it, he admitted that he had said this, but didn't know why he would say such a thing. She said that she could not remember for sure, but thought that Land had gone saddle horse riding with her 13 year-old daughter, Sharon Bagbey, on July 24. Sharon Bagbey could not remember if she went riding with her step-father on Saturday or Sunday. (Michigan State Police Complaint Report 83-862-60, p. 760-761)

John (J. K.) Gallacher, who was employed at Francis Contracting, told detectives that Land had told him that he had killed Mrs. Lacey by choking her with her panties. He said that they were "Truefit" or "Formfit" panties and that he wouldn't have killed her if she hadn't screamed. Land told Gallacher that he had been hired to kill Mrs. Lacey, that he had been paid $500 down, and that he would get his next payment in one month. He showed Gallacher a lot of money in his wallet, including a $50 Traveler's check, but would not let him count it. Land kept coming up behind Gallacher and grabbed him around the throat as if to choke. Gallacher said that Land had told him this in front of Clyde Neary, at whose house they working at the time (two weeks earlier). (Michigan State Police Complaint Report 83-862-60, p. 761)

Conclusions

Investigators explored the possibility that murder may have been connected to the triple-murder of three Evanston, Illinois, women who were found beaten to death in Starved Rock State Park in Illinois. The speculation was based upon the similarities that the victims were all middle-aged women and the murders took place in popular resort parks. The Starved Rock case is detailed in another chapter in this book.

While several names were on a long suspect list, Strantz, Asp and Land were prominent. As of this writing, more than forty-six years later, no one has been brought to trial for this crime and many questions remain unanswered as most of those involved have passed on. Neither the 1910 nor the 1960 cases have been solved and the latter remains under investigation by the Michigan State Police.

CHAPTER TWO

TRIPLE MURDER AT STARVED ROCK STATE PARK (1960)

My dear Watson, there we come into those realms of conjecture where the most logical mind may be at fault.

~ Sherlock Holmes ~
Sir Arthur Conan Doyle

An Outdoor Adventure

Starved Rock State Park is a beautiful outdoor adventure for those who love to hike along nature trails, picnic, go boating, fishing, camping, or horseback riding or just enjoy the view of spectacular overlooks along the Illinois River. The eighteen canyons, formed by glacial melt-water and stream erosion, are also the scenes of winter sports and adventure. In January, writers and actors gather to pit their minds against each other at murder-mystery theater weekends. As you will soon read, these are not the only mysteries that have unfolded in these canyons and winter wonderlands.

Located along the south side of the Illinois River, a mile south of Utica and between the cities of Ottawa and LaSalle-Peru, the wooded sandstone bluff stretches for four miles through Starved Rock. The park attracts many visitors to its unique rock formations and is popular with sportsmen due to the rivers and tributaries. Flat, gently rolling plains, remote caves, and glacier-formed canyons characterize the forest area between the Illinois and Vermilion Rivers, located a hundred miles or so southwest of Chicago. It is a beautiful get-away spot or vacation destination.

In 1673, Father Marquette and Louis Jolliet discovered the village of Kaskaskia on the north bank of the Illinois River while they were on en expedition to find a shortcut to China. In 1678-1680, other Frenchmen followed and in1682-1683 Fort Saint Louis was built on top of Starved Rock. By 1763, the French had left and the English dominated the region and when Chief Pontiac of the Ottawa Indians went to the southern part of Illinois to negotiate trade agreements with the French, a member or members of the Illinois Indians of the area murdered him. Sub-tribes of the Ottawa banded together, paddled down river, and attacked the Illinois tribe's village near Starved Rock.

The Illinois Indians realized that they needed to leave the area and climbed atop the 125-foot rock in hopes that the Ottawa would by-pass them on their way back south. The plan failed and the Illinois were surrounded and besieged. As the defenders tried to get water by lowering buckets to the river, the Ottawas cut the ropes and destroyed their buckets with arrows, which they also rained atop the defenders from above on Devil's Nose. As the Illinois became desperate, some were killed while trying to sneak down from the rock. Those who remained on top starved to death and the rock has since been known as "Starved Rock." The rock was dormant until 1805 when a legend held that the explorer Tonti had buried gold on top of the rock, leading to area residents searching for the gold. In 1911, Starved Rock became a state park and remains so to this day. However, this murder is not the true subject of this chapter. Rather, it is interesting background for our real story.

Dr. Robert J. Girod, Sr.

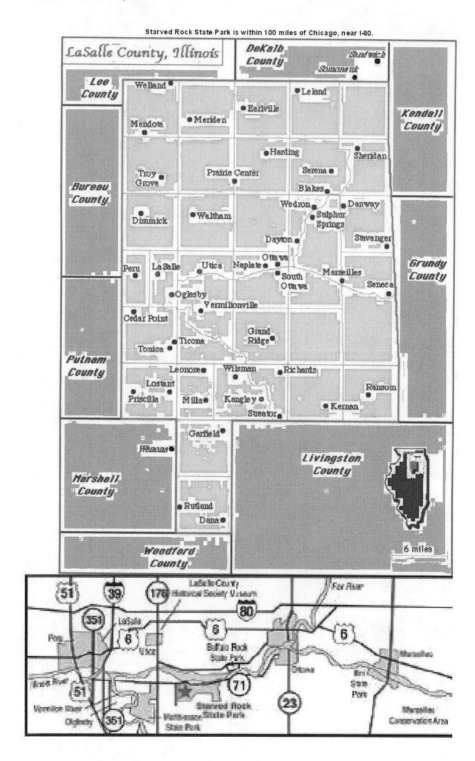

Triple Murder at Starved Rock

On Monday, March 14, 1960, Lillian Oetting, Mildred Lindquist, and Frances Murphy checked into the lodge at Starved Rock State Park in LaSalle County, Illinois, for a four-day stay. The three friends lived only blocks apart in Riverside, a Chicago suburb. All three were active members of the Presbyterian Church of Riverside. Two other members of the Presbyterian Church Women's Association had planned to join the trio, but had changed their minds. (Stout, pp. 49-50) Lillian Oetting was age fifty. Mildred Lindquist was also fifty. The youngest, Frances Murphy, was forty-seven. Mrs. Oetting's husband, George Oetting, was general supervisor of audits for Illinois Bell Telephone. She belonged to several clubs and was planning to lead a dialogue on Shakespearian plays later that week. Mr. and Mrs. Oetting had one son and two daughters. Mrs. Lindquist was president of the Women's Association and a member of the Riverside grade-school board. Her husband, Robert Lindquist, was vice-president of public relations for Chicago's Harris Trust and Savings Bank. They had two daughters. Mrs. Murphy, a former society editor of the Moline Illinois Dispatch, also served on the Riverside grade-school board. Her husband, Robert Murphy, was vice-president and general counsel for the Borg-Warner Corporation and an organist at their church. They had one son and three daughters. (Stout, pp. 49-50)

Lillian Oetting

Frances Murphy

The victims: Lillian Oetting (50), Mildred Lidquist (50), and Frances Murphy (47).

(Reprinted with permission from Steve Stout)

Dr. Robert J. Girod, Sr.

Starved Rock State Park Lodge as it appears today.
Esther Eickhoff, the desk clerk at the Lodge, said that she came on duty

at 12:30 p.m. (1230 hours) and checked the trio in shortly thereafter. The registration time clock said it was 12:28 p.m. (1228 hours). She recalled asking the women if they were going to eat lunch and they said that they were. Esther told them that the dining room was open until 2:00 p.m. (1400 hours). (Petition for Executive Clemency, April 2005, p. 43) (Stout, p. 48)

John Pagels, the bell hop, said that he thought that he checked the women into rooms 109 and 110 at about 2:00 p.m. (1400 hours), but that it could have been earlier. About fifteen minutes later they came back to the desk for their meal tickets and went into the dining room. Virginia Pelszynski, a waitress at the Lodge, said that she did not recall when she waited on the women, but that it was before the dining room closed at 2:00 p.m. (1400 hours). She said that one of the women was wearing a light blue suit with a light blue hat and another was wearing a dark dress. When they were registered and went to lunch, they were not dressed for a hike, so it is inferred from Eickhoff's and Pelszynski's statements that they would have changed after lunch. "No, if they were going on a hike I think they would have changed clothes," she later reported at the Coroner's inquest. (Petition for Executive Clemency, April 2005, p. 44) (Stout, p. 48)

Emil Boehm, the Lodge custodian, said that he saw the three women at the front doorway on March 14 as they were leaving the lodge. It was just before 1:00 p.m. (1300 hours) and he heard one of the women say that it was a beautiful day for a hike. He said that one of the women was wearing "bluish slacks and a little hat." He could not recall what the others were wearing, but said, "I couldn't swear to that either, but I thought she had dark blue slacks on." (Petition for Executive Clemency, April 2005, p. 44) When Boehm went to the employees' restroom beneath the Lodges kitchen, he saw Stanley Tucker, a busboy at the Lodge, talking with dishwasher Chester Weger, who was washing his face. "I'm going to LaSalle," Tucker said. "How 'bout a ride," Weger's voice asked from the sink. "I'm not coming back until five," Tucker replied. "It doesn't make no difference," Weger said, "I have no place to go. I might as well go with you." Boehm didn't see either of the men leave after he went to stoke the furnace. (Stout, p. 48)

Mrs. Murphy and Mrs. Lindquist: Photograph from the film recovered from the victim's camera.

(Reprinted with permission from Steve Stout)

Arnold Day, a truck driver, was driving by the opening of Saint Louis Canyon at about 1:45 p.m. (1345 hours) on March 14 and saw three women at the west end of the park looking at a cliff. He said one was wearing a tan jacket with a skirt and another was wearing slacks, which may have been plaid. He later picked Frances Murphy out of a set of photos that a state police investigator showed him. (Petition for Executive Clemency, April 2005, pp. 44-45)

Lillian Oetting's brother-in-law, Herman Oetting, called the Lodge on the evening March 14, but he was told that the women were not in their rooms. Eickhoff left a message in the key box, where a letter that the women had received late that Tuesday afternoon was. The following night, Lillian's husband called the Lodge, but he was also told that the women were not in. He was (mistakenly) told that the women had been at breakfast on March 15, but had not been seen since. On March 16 Herman Oetting called again, but none of the three women answered their phones. He asked that their rooms be checked and was told that their baggage was in their rooms. A bellboy left a card on the door for the guests. George Oetting called the other women's spouses to see if they had been contacted, but none of them had. (Petition for Executive Clemency, April 2005, p. 43) Mr. Oetting contacted his long-time friend, Virgil W. Peterson, operating director of the Chicago Crime Commission. A friend of all three families, Peterson called his contacts with the Illinois State Police, who, in turn, notified Sheriff Ray Eutsey of the LaSalle County Sheriff's Department. (Stout, pp. 50-51)

Crime Scene Discovered

That Tuesday night a winter storm dumped more than six inches of snow on the area and tall drifts in Saint Louis Canyon concealed what would soon be discovered. On Wednesday, March 16, 1960, a local youth camp supervisor, Henry Wolford, and four teenagers, who had formed a search party to find the missing women, discovered the bodies of the three women in a cave in Saint Louis Canyon. After viewing the macabre scene for several minutes, Wolford and the boys reported the murder to a newsman that they encountered near the entrance to the pathway into the canyon. Bill Danley, of the Daily News-Tribune in LaSalle, called his editor, Herb Hames, to update him on this late-breaking story. The news was soon transmitted around the world through the Associated Press office in Chicago. (Stout, pp. 50-51)

The women were found bound with string or cord. A tree limb, binoculars, and a camera were found with bloodstains on them. This lead investigators to surmise that these were either the murder weapon(s) and/or defensive weapon(s) used by one or more of the victims. The women were found close together in a small cave. They were all face up, the heads of two facing into the cave and the third facing out. Their heads were bloody and battered. Two were naked from the waist down and the third was wearing a girdle. (*Daily Republican Times*, March 17, 1960, pp. 1 and 10) A comb was discovered along the canyon about eight-hundred feet west of the cave where the police opined that the victims first encountered their assailant. (*Daily Republican Times*, March 28, 1960)

Investigators roped off the crime scene. The bodies were not removed for about seven hours as the scene was viewed by the Sheriff of LaSalle County and several of his deputies, investigators from the Illinois State Police, representatives of the LaSalle County State's Attorney and Coroner's Offices, Ottawa Civil Defense workers, a park custodian, and at least one news reporter. (Petition for Executive Clemency, April 2005, pp. 44-45) The Illinois State Police claimed possession of all of the physical evidence and took it to their lab at the National Guard Armory in Springfield. The FBI offered the use of their crime lab facilities, but the offer was refused. Daniel Dragel, of the Chicago Police Department crime lab also offered their assistance, but this was also declined. (Stout, pp. 54 and 73)

As dawn broke, county employees brought in weed-burning equipment to help melt the snow. These were soon replaced by plastic shelters and oil heaters, which eventually revealed a broken piece of an ornamental comb, a gray button, a set of keys, a broken piece of dental plate, and a bloody icicle in the wet mud. Copious amounts of blood up to twelve feet away from the bodies led to the deduction that the bodies were moved following the initial attacks. (Stout, p. 61)

Crime scene preserved with plastic tents erected to melt snow and protect evidence.

(Reprinted with permission from Steve Stout)

Infamous Murders and Mysteries

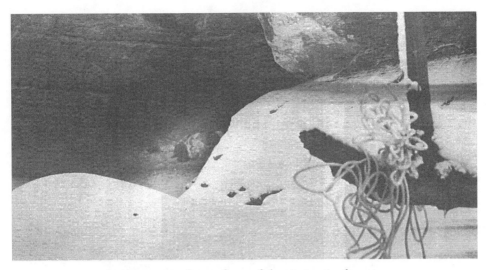

A crime scene photo of one of the victims in the cave.
(Reprinted with permission from Steve Stout)

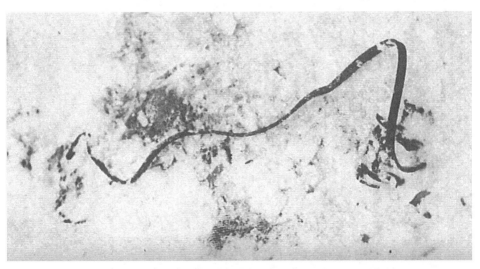

A battered camera and broken binoculars were found among the blood-covered evidence at the scene.
(Reprinted with permission from Steve Stout)

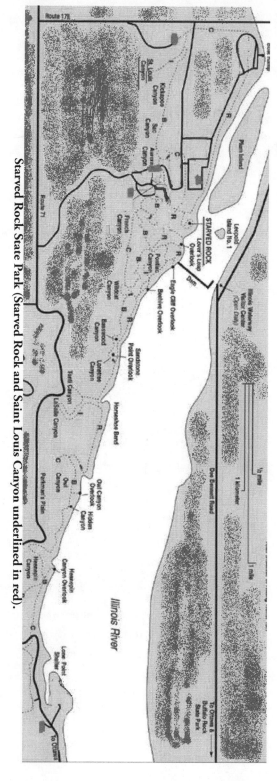

Starved Rock State Park (Starved Rock and Saint Louis Canyon underlined in red).

The Investigation Begins

Prosecutors believed that robbery was the motive when the three women were killed after leaving the park lodge to go for a walk through Saint Louis Canyon. Illinois State Police troopers began reporting in at the Starved Rock Lodge on Wednesday, March 16, 1960. They started by interviewing the lodge employees. One of the lodge employees was Chester Weger, a twenty-one-year-old dishwasher at the lodge. He was married with two children. State police detectives interviewed him at the Kaskaskia Hotel about a month after the murders. Allegedly, Weger was questioned on and off for about two hours of the time he was with the troopers from that afternoon until 1:00 a.m. (0100 hours) the next morning. (Petition for Executive Clemency, April 2005, p. 5)

With no evidence of a robbery or attempted robbery, the investigators decided that a sexual motivation was the only explanation for the murder. Because Weger was married and age 21 and the victims were all married and about age 50, State Police investigators concluded that the young Weger would have no sexual interest in the older victims. Therefore, after his questioning, he was dismissed as a suspect. (Inbau, Reid, Buckley and Jayne, p. 12)

The first photo slide recovered from the victim's camera showed Mrs. Murphy and Mrs. Lindquist near the lodge. Another was a triple-exposed photo slide of Mrs. Lindquist in the shadow of the Saint Louis Canyon icefall, apparently minutes before the murders. Police officials believed a man's image appeared in the background and made an announcement to the media. An expert from Eastman-Kodak in Rochester, New York, discounted this inference. Meanwhile, State Police Superintendent William Morris personally directed the interviews of more than fifty guests and employees at the Lodge. Each was asked to take a polygraph examination and submit a hair specimen for examination. When investigators tried contacting guests at their homes, they were told by several wives that their husbands were away on business trips and could not possibly have been at Starved Rock that week. (Stout, pp. 63-64)

The cave where the bodies were discovered.

Sheriff Tom Templeton leads Laurie Slaughter, the author's son Bobby and the author (not pictured) into the canyon along the crime scene trail.

There were others who theorized that Chicago gangsters may have had a hand in the murders as some sort of revenge upon Chicago Crime Commissioner Peterson who was friends with all three families. This theory was generally discounted. The companies of the three victims' husbands offered a reward of $30,000 for information leading to the arrest and capture of the killer or killers. Dr. M. Kruglik, a psychiatrist at Joliet State Prison, opined that one person committed the act and that it was an impulsive act, executed to demonstrate sexual prowess, without necessarily ejaculating. (Stout, p. 65)

Six months after the murder, a glove was discovered among the victims clothing. Inside the glove that had been worn by one of the victims were two rings – an engagement ring and a wedding ring. County investigators opined that the theory of a sexually motivated murder, set forth by State investigators, may have been incorrect and that the victim may have discarded the rings inside the glove to prevent their loss in a robbery. (Inbau, Reid, Buckley and Jayne, pp. 12-13)

State's Attorney Harland Warren laid down some ground rules for the investigation, based upon court decisions. When a suspect was developed, the fewer interrogators, the better, he insisted. "It would be well to have a photograph taken of the defendant just prior to taking the confession (and) another photograph taken during the time of the confession is being taken showing him smoking a cigarette or drinking a cup of coffee," Warren told the investigators. He gave them advice to help avert an insanity defense and told them that after an initial statement, the defendant should give a statement to an assistant state's attorney in the presence of a court reporter. "As state's attorney," Warren said, "I cannot be present at the taking of a confession and then prosecute the defendant later in open court." This should be followed, he urged, by a re-enactment of the crime recorded on film, a quick arraignment before a judge, and an intense psychiatric examination. The State Police officials resented the directives and continued their investigation. (Stout, p. 66)

Dr. Robert J. Girod, Sr.

Sheriff Templeton shows Bobby and Laurie the end of the canyon.

Illinois State Crime Division Chief James Christensen personally interviewed Chester Otto Weger during one of four interviews. From a statement given by lodge caretaker Emil Boehm, the detectives took note of his overhearing Weger talking to Stanley Tucker about getting a ride to Oglesby. Weger told Christensen that he did not leave the Lodge with Tucker or anyone else. Christensen also questioned Tucker, who said that he did not leave with Weger, but left the kitchen alone and that he had friends to verify his whereabouts. He also recalled that waitresses teased Weger about the marks on his face coming from "a wildcat." Weger and Tucker were both considered suspects. (Stout, p. 71)

Chester Otto Weger Becomes the Prime Suspect

Chester Otto Weger / male / white / 320-32-8217 / DOB March 3, 1939 / 5'8" / was born in Derby, Iowa. His family moved to Utica, Illinois, in 1942 and later to Oglesby, both in LaSalle County. Family members referred to Chester by his middle name, Otto, but he was also known by the nickname "Rocky." He was the only son of Herschell Wayne Weger and Juanita Louise Weger. He had five sisters: Elvita Weger (1933) of Utica, Illinois; Rosa Mae Popplewell (1936) living in Kentucky; Mary Ann Pruett (1942) of Smithville, Missouri; Patsy Lou Nieves (1948) living in South Carolina; and Linda Jean Kelley (1950) of Ostero, Florida. (Petition for Executive Clemency, April 2005, p. 21)

Sometime between 1951 and 1952 when "Rocky" Weger was twelve or thirteen years old, he was arrested on a statutory rape charge in Oglesby. Weger denied committing any wrong-doing. His account was that he recalled placing a "piece of white cloth inside the vagina of a girl who had been raped by someone else." Apparently he was released the night of his arrest and was never incarcerated as a result of this juvenile arrest. The record shows that he was adjudicated a delinquent minor at the age of twelve for rape and sexual molestation of an eight-year-old girl. (Petition for Executive Clemency, April 2005, p. 21)

In 1955 Weger was a bellhop at the Starved Rock Lodge until he enlisted in the United States Marine Corps on July 24, 1956, and was sent to San Diego, California. His serial number was 1615835. From mid-1956 to 1957 Weger performed a variety of duties with the Marines. He was assigned to Military Police duty, worked in an officers' dining room, bartended at an officers' club, was a desk clerk at a military game room, was an assistant supply sergeant at a supply warehouse, and received training to drive a bucket-operated trench digger and bulldozer – all in an eighteen-month career. He was arrested twice in 1957 for being AWOL (absent without leave). His girlfriend, Jo Ann Orth, was pregnant at the time and they were married in September of 1957. On December 13, 1957, a court martial hearing gave Weger a general discharge under honorable conditions, apparently as a result of the "hardship" of his wife's pregnancy. (Petition for Executive Clemency, April 2005, p. 22)

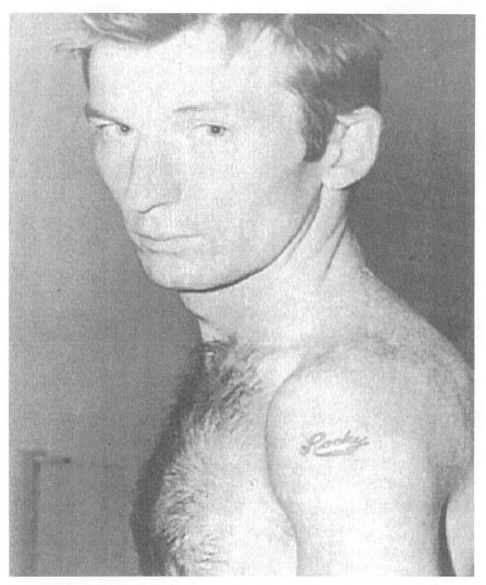

Chester Otto Weger with a tattoo on his left arm of his nickname, "Rocky."
This photo was taking following his interrogation and medical examination, showing no injuries.
(Reprinted with permission from Steve Stout)

Infamous Murders and Mysteries

Investigators were interested in the similarity between Weger's tattoo and this carving, later found in Saint Louis Canyon.
(Reprinted with permission from Steve Stout)

Following his discharge, the Wegers returned to Oglesby, Illinois. Weger had two children: Rebecca Jo Weger (December 23, 1957) and John Weger (November 19, 1959). In 1958 Chester lived in Joliet for two months where he worked at the Joliet Tractor Company. He then lived in Minooka, Illinois, for five months before going back to Oglesby. In 1959 Weger and his family moved to nearby LaSalle where he worked for the IC Railroad. In 1960 Weger was again employed at the Starved Rock Lodge, this time as a dishwasher, and also worked as a part-time painter. (Petition for Executive Clemency, April 2005, p. 22)

The Interrogation of Chester Weger

State's Attorney Warren was not satisfied with the expertise of the Illinois State Police lab and contacted the John Reid Institute in Chicago to conduct a polygraph tests. Stephen Kindig, a Reid associate, was sent to LaSalle County. On September 22, 1960, Kindig started examinations of several lodge employees. Most were cooperative, but one cook seemed apprehensive. Warren wondered if the fat chef was the killer. Kindig laughed, revealing that the man was just afraid of being found out to be a homosexual. None of the employees appeared to be involved in any way. At 9:15 a.m. (0915 hours) on September 26, 1960, Kindig examined Chester Weger. As he observed and recorded Weger's answers and responses the specialist's heart started pounding, but he concealed his emotions until Weger left. "That's him," he told Warren. (Stout, pp. 79-80)

Weger had taken two previous polygraph tests by state police examiners and passed both. Warren called John Reid, known as the "father of polygraph," to personally examine Weger. Reid, whose institute is known for training the best interviewers and interrogators (including the author), had conducted more than 25,000 polygraph examinations. (Stout, p. 80)

Chester Weger was picked up by LaSalle County Sheriff's Deputy William Dummett on September 27, 1960. Deputy Dummett found Weger at his father's home in Oglesby at about 7:00 a.m. (0700) and drove him to John Reid & Associates, 600 South Michigan Avenue, in Chicago, arriving at about 9:00 a.m. (0900). Weger had previously been given a polygraph test at one of the cabins at the Starved Rock Lodge and was now asked to undergo further testing. Reid & Associates was then and remains today one of the leading authorities on interviewing and interrogation, polygraph, and the detection of deception. I have attended their basic and advanced interview and interrogation schools many times over the past twenty-five years and have several books written by John Reid and members of his staff. Reid & Associates are professionals who enjoy a great reputation within the law enforcement community.

John Reid, himself, met with Weger at about 11:00 a.m. (1100) and they discussed the case for about an hour and a half. The polygraph was then administered for the next one or two hours. When Reid concluded that Weger was lying, he admonished him for the next two or three hours to tell the truth. Throughout the afternoon, Reid periodically interrogated Weger and called in an assistant on three occasions. Chester Weger testified at trial that Reid told him during the interrogation that he could obtain a court order to compel him to take "truth serum." Reid admitted that he told Weger that if Weger did not believe the polygraph was correct, that he could take truth serum. Reid denied telling Weger that he could be forced to take the serum. Reid's interrogation of Weger concluded sometime between 10:00 and 11:00 p.m. (2200-2300 hours) that night, after eleven to twelve hours. (Petition for Executive Clemency, April 2005, p. 5)

Captain William Dummett, LaSalle County Sheriff's Department, was the lead investigator in this case.

(Reprinted with permission from Steve Stout)

Dr. Robert J. Girod, Sr.

Reid told Warren that his examination disclosed that Weger was not telling the truth about his knowledge of the murders. He cautioned Warren that his experience suggested that he should not push Weger too far too soon and to have as much physical evidence as possible before confronting him further. "Open up too soon or too late," Reid said, "and he'll button up forever." (Stout, p. 80)

On the return trip to LaSalle County, Deputy Bill Dummett and Chester Weger were joined by Assistant State's Attorney Craig Armstrong. It was late – sometime after midnight – and the drive along the streets of Chicago bore a strange contrast to those back home. Weger asserts that during the return trip Dummett told him several times that if he did not sign a confession, he would be sentenced to the electric chair. At both a pre-trial hearing and at trial Dummett denied having made either promises or threats during that trip.

The LaSalle County Courthouse, Ottawa, Illinois

Weger maintains that Dummett repeatedly threatened that Weger was going to "ride a thunderbolt" if he did not confess. In a disturbing twist, it was Assistant State's Attorney Armstrong, the third party on the return trip from Chicago, who testified at both pre-trial and at the trial that, in fact, Dummett did tell Weger that he was "going to ride a thunderbolt." Armstrong not only refuted Dummett's testimony, but also testified that he "was positive that the word 'thunderbolt' was used by Dummett more than once on the ride back to Ottawa." Armstrong said that the word "chair" was also mentioned during the trip, but did not recall if Dummett had mentioned it or if Weger had mentioned it in response to Dummett. He did recall that Weger told Dummett that he would not get the electric chair because he did not kill the women. (Petition for Executive Clemency, April 2005, p. 6)

After a long, nineteen-hour day, the party arrived back in Ottawa. Instead of taking Weger back to his father's house, Dummett drove to the LaSalle County Courthouse. It was 2:00 a.m. (0200 hours), September 28. Assistant State's Attorney Armstrong started the interrogation again, questioning Weger in the presence of a court reporter. This interrogation lasted another three and a half to four hours. Afterwards, Weger agreed to stand in a lineup, where a suspect stands with other individuals for possible identification by witnesses. The records do not note whether Weger actually stood for a lineup or what the outcome was, if he did. Armstrong and Deputy Sheriff Wayne Hess took Weger back to his father's house in Oglesby and then to his own apartment in LaSalle. There Weger allowed Armstrong and Hess to collect some of Weger's personal property, including his buckskin jacket. They then drove Weger to his father's home, arriving at about 7:30 a.m. (0730), more than twenty-four hours after he was picked up by Dummett. (Petition for Executive Clemency, April 2005, p. 6)

State Police Surveillance

In October 1960, the Illinois State Police assigned a team of troopers to surveill Chester Weger. The investigation was definitely focused on him by this time. Weger, who lived with his wife and children in an apartment in LaSalle, was continuously followed by the state police. Weger was photographed at Libby-Owens Ford, where he was employed as a painter. They followed him to a job painting a church steeple in Peru, to a bowling alley in LaSalle, and to local taverns. So overt was the surveillance that, because Weger did not have a vehicle, the troopers sometimes gave him rides to work.

The State Police investigators, looking through the reams of reports, ran across a lead from Chicago attorney Herbert Barsey, who reported that two of his clients were accosted by a suspicious young man in Deer Park on March 12, 1960, just two days before the murders. They identified Weger, from a photo, as that man. Dummett remembered a rape and robbery report in Matthiessen State Park (Deer Park) on September 13, 1959. He and Hess interviewed Jean Kapps and James Supan. When Kapps studied the stack of mug shot photos the detectives showed her, she suddenly screamed when she saw the photo of Chester Weger. Supan also identified Weger as the man who robbed him and raped his girlfriend. (Stout, pp. 83-84)

State's Attorney Warren decided it was time to bring Weger in for another interrogation and to be arrested. But he wanted the LaSalle County detectives to bring him in without telling the State Police detectives of the pending arrest. After almost two months of nearly constant State Police surveillance, LaSalle County Sheriff's Deputies Bill Dummett and Wayne Hess picked up Chester Weger at his apartment at 1022 ½ Third Street in LaSalle at 6:00 p.m. (1800 hours) on November 16, 1960. Weger agreed to go with them to the LaSalle County Courthouse in Ottawa for more questioning. As he left with the county detectives, Weger smiled and waived to the state police plainclothesmen who were surveilling his house. (Petition for Executive Clemency, April 2005, p. 7) (Stout, pp. 92-93)

The Justice of the Peace

Dummett and Hess were met by a court reporter who was brought in to record Weger's statement of his whereabouts on March 14, 1960. The detectives interrogated Weger until about 7:30 p.m. (1930 hours). Meanwhile, Sheriff Ray Eutsey brought in Justice of the Peace Louis Goetsch, who was also a local grocer. The sheriff answered the justice's questions, under oath, about the allegations and complaint against Weger. Not being a court of record, there is no record of what the sheriff told the justice to determine probable cause. But, based upon this, Justice Goetsch prepared complaints against Weger, Sheriff Eutsey signed them, and warrants were issued for Weger's arrest for the murder of the three women. (Petition for Executive Clemency, April 2005, p. 7)

After Deputies Dummett and Hess read the warrants to him, Weger stood in a lineup for a robbery and a rape that occurred in 1959 at Deer Park. At about 9:30 p.m. (2130 hours) Justice of the Peace Goetsch joined Dummett and Hess at the State's Attorney's Office. Goetsch explained his rights and the charges to Weger, who then requested a preliminary hearing. (Advisement of rights under *Miranda v. Arizona* was not dictated by the U.S. Supreme Court until 1966). Assistant State's Attorney Peter Ferracuti made a motion by telephone for a ten-day continuance, which Goetsch granted. Justice Goetsch later recalled that Chester Weger was "wringing wet under the armpits." (Petition for Executive Clemency, April 2005, p. 8)

LaSalle County Sheriff's Deputy Wayne Hess was Dummett's partner in this investigation.
(Reprinted with permission from Steve Stout)

Dummett and Hess continued the interrogation. Weger asserts that, while the officers did not physically abuse him, they threatened him throughout this interrogation. Weger maintained that Dummett told him that, if he confessed, he would get a life sentence and be out in fourteen years; otherwise he would be sentenced to the electric chair. Weger said that Dummett made remarks about his wife to the extent that he was afraid he would hit Dummett and make his situation worse. Justice Goetsch brought food and drinks in for Weger and the officers. Weger had coffee but did not eat. It was close to midnight when the deputies finished and Weger asked them if he could see his wife. (Petition for Executive Clemency, April 2005, p. 8)

Family Meeting

Between 1:00 and 1:30 a.m. (0100-0130) on November 17, Wayne Weger, Chester's father, arrived with Chester's mother and wife. Wayne said that before seeing Chester, Sheriff Eutsey told him that Chester had been arrested for the Starved Rock murders. The sheriff told Wayne that he had brought up his own children to tell the truth and asked Wayne if he had done the same. When Wayne said that he had, the sheriff said, "You don't want him to go to that little green room," referring to the electric chair. The sheriff told Wayne to tell Chester to tell the truth to save him from the "little green room." Chester Weger again stated that Sheriff Eutsey said in front of both Chester and Wayne that if Chester confessed, he would get a lighter sentence. The sheriff denied making any statements of this type. (Petition for Executive Clemency, April 2005, pp. 8-9)

When Weger's family was brought near the room where Chester was being questioned, Wayne Weger said that he heard Dummett tell Chester at least twenty times, "You know you did it. Why don't you come clean and say you done it? Why do you want to treat your wife and children like that and why do you want to treat your father and mother like that? Come clean and tell us about that." The elder Weger did not hear Dummett threaten Chester or mention the electric chair. When Weger's father asked him if he had committed the murder, Chester sat without saying a word. When they were alone Wayne asked his son again and Chester replied, "Daddy, I did not." Chester did not seem afraid. His father asked the sheriff if they could "let it go until the morning" when they could retain an attorney. The sheriff did not answer, but said that the state's attorney had enough evidence to convict Chester of the murders. He said that if Chester would confess, the sheriff would do everything in his power to keep him from "the little green room." (Petition for Executive Clemency, April 2005, p. 9)

Weger's family left just before 2:00 a.m. (0200 hours). Chester's mother hugged him and told him to tell the truth. His wife gave him a kiss. Chester Weger then gave Dummett and Hess a confession to the murders. The initial confession was not recorded, but later a court reporter was summoned to the room. Weger said, "All right. If you want a confession, I'll give you one." Dummett allegedly showed him photographs of the crime scene, pointing out various details. He then gave Weger his version of how the events transpired. Weger said that most of the details given in his confession were provided by Dummett. When Court Reporter Josephine Thompson arrived, the interview was repeated. (Petition for Executive Clemency, April 2005, p. 10)

The Confession: Weger's Account of the Murders

Weger said that on March 14, 1960, he was walking along the Bluff Trail toward the Saint Louis Canyon. He was between his afternoon and evening shifts at the lodge. At about 3:15 p.m. (1515 hours) he encountered the three women. Deputy Hess asked Weger which direction the women headed – in or out of the canyon. He did not recall for certain, but was, "pretty sure they must have been coming out." He said that he grabbed a strap from one of the women, thinking it was a purse. The strap was attached to a pair of binoculars and it broke when he pulled it. (Petition for Executive Clemency, April 2005, p. 10-11)

Bobby (left) and Laurie with Sheriff Tom Templeton (lower right).

Weger said that the "white haired woman" (Lillian Oetting) hit him with something, either a camera or binoculars, so hard she gave him a bruised eye. (Petition for Executive Clemency, April 2005, p. 27) The "youngest woman" (Frances Murphy) yelled that her husband was on the police force and that he would not get away with it. The third woman hit him with something sharp, possibly a comb or something similar. Despite their defenses, Weger was able to get all three women to walk back down into the canyon where he agreed to let them go free. Weger later explained to Assistant State's Attorney Craig Armstrong that he did not have to force the women to go into the canyon, because he promised them that he would let them go if they did so. He said, "I told them to walk down by the waterfall. I promised I would leave them, and they promised, and this and that." (Petition for Executive Clemency, April 2005, p. 27)

He walked behind them as they proceeded down the path. Once they were deep into the cold, snowy canyon with eighty-foot walls, the three women agreed to allow Weger to tie them up if he promised not to hurt them. Weger said that the small, white-headed woman (Lillian Oetting) continued trying to hit him, so he tied her up first, using string in his pocket from the lodge kitchen. "At any rate," Weger said, "then I tied up these other two women, I think, each one, their hands together, and I think I tied their other hand to their ankle if I am not mistaken, and I started to leave." Weger later said, "What I meant to say was I tied Mrs. Oetting's hand to Mrs. Lindquist's left hand and ankles in the same order." (Weger later testified that Deputy Dummett instructed him to make this correction). (Petition for Executive Clemency, April 2005, pp. 27-28)

Weger said that once he had the women bound with the string, he checked to make sure their circulation was not cut of on their wrists. He then walked away taking nothing from the three victims. Suddenly Lillian Oetting, the "white-headed woman," freed herself and again attacked Weger from behind. He picked up a club and hit her with it, knocking her out. (Petition for Executive Clemency, April 2005, p. 27) He said, "I seen a club sticking out from a bunch of brush and I just picked that club up… and I lost my head. I hit her with it." He picked up his victim's limp body and threw it over his shoulders in a "fireman's carry" and carried her back to the cave in front of the other two stunned victims. (Stout, p 108)

"This here other woman kept trying to kick me with her free leg. Both women were trying to stand up," Weger said. "I walked over there… I thought they got loose, and one tried to scratch me, she did. That's where I got a lot of them scratches." He sighed and continued, "I turned around and looked at the woman I hit and she was laying there still. I thought I killed her. She had her eyes closed and that… and the next thing I knew this other woman was hitting me and everything. She kept hitting me. I had this club in my hand and I hit them." (Stout, p. 108)

Fearing that he had killed Oetting, Weger decided that it would be necessary to kill the other two women, who could identify him. He repeatedly struck the other two bound women in the head with the club. (Petition for

Executive Clemency, April 2005, p. 27) Deputy Hess asked Weger if the women were facing him when he was beating them with the club. Weger told Hess, "Yes, they were facing me, if I am not mistaken." Hess pressed for more, asking, "But not in a sitting-down position?" Weger responded, saying, "They stood up, and then I hit this one woman and knocked her down. The other one set back down...." (Petition for Executive Clemency, April 2005, p. 12)

Bobby observes the canyon walls.

Weger then asserted that Frances Murphy regained consciousness, stood up, and hit him with her binoculars with enough force to shatter them. He grabbed them from her and hit her with them, chased the screaming woman across the canyon, hit her with his fist, knocking her into a small snowdrift and then hit her with the club. "I kept hitting her," Weger said, "I felt these other two women's pulse; both of them were dead. I killed them. I had to kill this other woman." (Stout, p. 109) Then Weger observed a red and white Piper Cub flying overhead and thought it was a police plane. Fearing the plane might see the women, he "dragged them up in the cave and made it look like a rape" by pulling their skirts up and tearing their undergarments. His transcribed confession said, "Then I took this here lady's coat off, if I am not mistaken, and put in front of this one here and just made it look like rape, is all I can say." When the investigators asked him if he took one of the victim's pants and stuck them up under her underskirt he simply said, "I do not know." (Petition for Executive Clemency, April 2005, p. 12)

The top of the canyon. Bill Dummett, the lead investigator, was Sheriff Templeton's training officer when he was a new officer. Dummett told Templeton all about the case.

Weger began to search the pockets of the three victims, looking for money. Feeling something in one's pocket, he found a glove, a handkerchief and a comb. Looking only for money, Weger left everything else behind that

The approach to the cave where the victims were bound.

The cave openings where the victims were bound and killed (from the outside).

Infamous Murders and Mysteries

Looking at the crime scene from inside the cave.

The cave opening where the victims were bound and killed (from inside the cave).

may be easily identifiable. After washing his hands in the creek and snow he fled the murder scene and went back to the lodge. "I washed my hands again," he said, "I washed them downstairs. I went upstairs; it was almost 5:00 in the afternoon. Glen Camatti, he's the chef, he told me to check the furnace. I told him, 'I've been checking it, but I'll go back down and check it again anyway.' So I walked downstairs and played the pinball machine in the Pow-Wow Room for awhile. Then I threw some coal in the furnace and came back upstairs." (Stout, p. 110)

Chester Weger's confession to Deputy's Dummett and Hess ended at approximately 2:30 a.m. (0230 hours) on November 17. Weger refused to be photographed naked, but Dummett photographed him bare-chested to show that he had no injuries. (Stout, p. 111) A physician, Dr. Harold Lane, examined Weger until approximately 3:00 a.m. (0300 hours) and later testified that Weger had no evidence of bruises, discoloration, lacerations, or trauma of any kind. Dr. Lane further testified that Chester Weger had no complaints during his examination. Following the examination, at about 3:00 a.m. (0300 hours) Weger was transported to the Ottawa County Jail.

Police and newsmen watch and listen on November 17, 1960, as Chester Weger reenacts the details of his confession-account of the March 14 murders.
(Reprinted with permission from Steve Stout)

Returning to the Crime Scene

The Lodge was overtaken by reporters and the curious who had rented every room and taken up cots in every available space. They waited each day for any new angle to keep the story going. When news intentionally leaked that Chester Weger had confessed to the murders and was going to walk officials through a re-enactment, media excitement was at a fever pitch.

At about 7:30 a.m. (0730 hours) Sheriff Ray Eutsey, Deputies Dummett and Hess, and a court reporter transported Chester Weger from the Ottawa County Jail to the crime scene in Saint Louis Canyon at Starved Rock State Park. Weger re-enacted the events described in his confession for the county officials in the presence of several Illinois State Troopers and news reporters. At about 12:40 p.m. (1240 hours) Assistant State's Attorney Craig Armstrong interviewed and took an official statement from Weger in the presence of the court reporter.

Chester Weger Goes to Trial

On November 18, 1960, the Grand Jury of LaSalle County, Illinois, indicted Chester Otto Weger on five felony counts. The state psychiatrist, M. Kruglik, M.D., examined Weger, saying that he was definitely not psychotic, that he was capable of understanding what he was doing, comprehended the nature of his acts, and had an appreciation of the effects of his acts (the elements necessary to withstand an insanity defense). Dr. Kruglik opined that "Weger possesses the personality characteristics of one who could be considered capable of committing the acts in question." (Stout, p. 115)

In one count Weger was charged with the July 24, 1959, larceny and robbery of Virginia Funfsinn. Mrs. Funfsinn was at Matthiessen State Park with her son and a friend with her three children on that date. Their husbands were fishing near the Vermilion River outside of Lowell. Also known to locals as Deer Park, the 175-acre park is just two miles east of Oglesby in the middle of LaSalle County. A young man approached the group, frightening them, then disappeared. He reappeared as suddenly as he had gone, this time snatching their two purses, which Virginia had under each arm. The perpetrator again disappeared into the woods (Stout, pp. 11-13) but was later identified as Chester Otto Weger.

Weger was also indicted for and charged with committing larceny, armed robbery and assault with a deadly weapon emanating from a complaint filed by James Supan and for rape, assault with intent to rape, and assault with a deadly weapon from a complaint filed by Jean Kapps for an incident that occurred on September 13, 1959. Supan, then 18, and Kapps, then 17, were on a date and walking through Deer Park (Matthiessen State Park). They were approached by a young man with a .22 caliber rifle and a sheathed knife. The perpetrator accosted them, forcing them down the trail and into the woods, where he told the girl to tie the boy's hands with fishing line. He then tied the boy's feet and "hog-tied" his hands and feet together. The attacker bound the girl's hands with fishing line and, cutting the boy's t-shirt away, gagged them both with pieces of Supan's shirt. After taking Supan's wallet, he raped Kapps and told them that his partner would be by in a half hour to release them, but he would kill them if they called the police. The perpetrator then fled into the woods. (Stout, pp. 15-33) The perpetrator was later identified as Chester Otto Weger.

On March 12, 1960, two days before the murders, another woman, her daughter and sister were accosted by a suspicious young man. His description and "drawl" matched that of the perpetrator of the previous two incidents, but these women were fortunate enough to escape harm, as they were near the parking lot of the Starved Rock State Park lodge. But, instead of calling the police, they hurriedly packed and left with their friends. (Stout, pp. 34-37)

In the most serious counts, Weger was indicted for the March 14, 1960, murders of Lillian Oetting, Frances Murphy and Mildred Lindquist. The Defense filed an unsuccessful motion to suppress the statements given in his interrogations and a jury trial was set to begin in January 1961. Weger was charged, at trial, with only one count of murder – that of Lillian Oetting. None of the other indicted charges were included at trial either. Perhaps the prosecution felt that if they were unsuccessful in this count, precluding it from

Infamous Murders and Mysteries

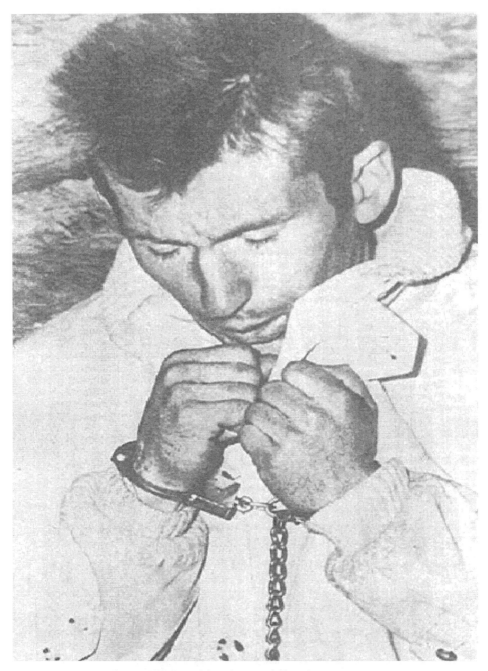

Chester Weger, cold and manacled at the crime scene.
(Reprinted with permission from Steve Stout)

being retried under double-jeopardy, the other two murders and remaining charges could be brought at another time.

The courtroom is full as the trial of Chester Weger begins.
(Reprinted with permission from Steve Stout)

The State of Illinois presented photographs and testimony depicting and describing the crime scene. All three victims were wearing skirts. The scene depicted the copious amounts of blood shed by the victims. Lillian Oetting was nearly decapitated.

One of the decedents was in a corner of the cave with her legs toward the cave opening (toward the canyon) and her skirt was pulled up. A boot was lying below the head. There appeared to be drag marks and there was blood around the head where it crushed from the blows. A pair of broken binoculars was next to her left arm.

A second corpse was next to the first. The decedent's legs were also facing out of the cave toward the canyon. Her legs were spread apart with her panties off and stuck up under her underskirt.

The third decedent was at the other side of the cave with her feet pointing out as the first two. Her feet were also spread apart and her girdle had been cut. Between her legs was a jacket. Her head and face had also been crushed by the bludgeoning.

A wood artifact (from a log) and camera was found in the snow in front of the cave. Afterwards a broken leather strap from the camera was discovered, by a corporal from the Illinois State Police, about 150 feet from the cave between two footbridges. The leather was examined and determined to match that of the camera strap. Deputy Bill Dummett found a pair of gloves and a handkerchief in Lillian Oetting's pockets. These were the images and descriptions presented to the jury. (Petition for Executive Clemency, April 2005, p. 13)

Testimony Begins

Several employees of the Starved Rock Lodge were called to testify that they saw scratches and bruises on Chester Weger's face on the evening of March 14, 1960, or later that same week. Some of these witnesses said that they did not report scratches and bruises on Weger's face until specifically questioned about them by Assistant State's Attorney Craig Armstrong in October 1960 – seven months after the murders. The Defense called several Illinois State troopers as witnesses to testify that during the course of their investigation they came into contact with Chester Weger several times and none of them recalled noticing any suspicious scratches, bruises or other marks on his face.

The transcript of Weger's confession to Deputies Dummett and Hess, as recorded by Court Reporter Josephine Thompson at 2:00 a.m. (0200 hours) on November 17, 1960, was entered into evidence and presented to the jury. Dummett and Hess also testified about statements purportedly made by Weger prior to the court reporter arriving at the courthouse.

Harland Warren (R) was LaSalle County State's Attorney from 1952-1960. Warren, a U.S. Naval Reserve veteran of WWII, was defeated in the 1960 election amid allegations of incompetence for not bringing the murderer to justice. He waited to file charges against Weger until after the election to avoid accusations of political motivation. His opponent, Robert Richardson (D), considered asking Warren to assist in the prosecution, as he had never tried a murder case.

(Reprinted with permission from Steve Stout)

The transcript of Weger's confession and account given at Saint Louis Canyon, as recorded by Court Reporter Thomas Hanrahan at 8:00 a.m. (0800 hours) on November 17, 1960, was entered into evidence and read to the jury. Hanrahan's transcript of Weger's confession to Assistant State's Attorney Craig Armstrong at the LaSalle County Jail at 12:40 p.m. (1240 hours) on November 17, 1960, was also read to the jury. Finally, a brief statement given by Defendant Chester Weger and recorded by Court Reporter Hanrahan at 3:00 p.m. (1500 hours) on November 17, 1960, was entered into evidence and read to the jury.

Former FBI agent and newly-elected LaSalle County State's Attorney Robert Richardson (D) confers with his first assistant Tony Raccuglia, who was a recent law school graduate.
(Reprinted with permission from Steve Stout)

Deputies Dummett and Hess also testified that they escorted Weger back to the LaSalle County Jail after the trip to Saint Louis Canyon on November 17, 1960. They testified that Dummett asked Weger if he thought he would ever get caught and Weger said something like, "No, after this long I did not think I would get caught." Dummett said that he asked Weger if he was glad that it was all over and Weger replied that he should have done it (confessed) before. He said that Weger told him that he thought about telling Dummett about when they went to Chicago (to John Reid & Associates), but decided not to. (Petition for Executive Clemency, April 2005, pp. 14-15)

Dummett and Hess also testified that on the same afternoon they were present at the LaSalle County Jail with Chester Weger when his father told Chester that he could not believe that Chester had committed these murders on his own and that there must have been an accomplice. Dummett and Hess testified that Chester replied to his father that he did it alone and that if it would ease his father's mind, he would take a "lie detector test" in Chicago. They testified that Chester also said, "I beat the State test, but you cannot beat those fellows in Chicago." (Petition for Executive Clemency, April 2005, p. 15)

The State also called Homer Charbonneau, a local recreational pilot, who testified that he flew a red and white plane in the vicinity of Starved Rock State Park's Saint Louis Canyon on March 14, 1960, sometime between 3:05 and 4:05 p.m. (1505-1605 hours). The pilot said that he was first asked about the flight by Deputy Dummett near the end of November, 1960. (On appeal, the Illinois Supreme Court ruled that the details about the plane corroborated Weger's confession. *Weger*, 185 N.E. 2d 189). The Defense opined that because Dummett had previously been a member of the Ottawa Airmen's Club that he could have checked the sign-out sheet on the wall at the airport prior to November 16, 1960, speculating that he knew that it was Charbonneau who checked the plane out the day of the murders.

Expert Testimony

A psychiatrist who interviewed Chester Weger at the LaSalle County Jail on November 17, 1960, said that Weger told him that he had slept for the first time in a long time after he confessed. He testified that Weger told him that he confessed willingly after his mother kissed him and told him to tell the truth. He said that he had been concerned about his mother's health and felt the best thing to do was to confess and let the court take whatever course it decided. Weger told the psychiatrist that his motive was robbery, but he did not take any valuables that could be identified. He said that he arranged the bodies to appear as if they had been raped because he thought it would be more difficult to prove than a robbery. (Petition for Executive Clemency, April 2005, p. 15)

The State presented expert testimony. A pathologist who performed the autopsy of Lillian Oetting testified that she died of brain injury from multiple fractures. He opined that the camera recovered from the crime scene may have been the weapon causing the fatal injuries. The pathologist inferred, based on her stomach contents, that Lillian Oetting died within two hours of having consumed a meal consisting of meat, mushrooms, celery, and a cereal grain. (Petition for Executive Clemency, April 2005, pp. 15 and 45)

The wood artifact (from a log) found in the snow in front of the cave was examined by two experts. A wood expert testified shards of wood found in Oetting's skull were from the wood artifact (piece of log) found at the cave opening.

Edgar Kivela, of the Michigan Crime Lab, testified that he examined the wood artifact and found hair fragments consistent with that of or similar to the hair of Mildred Lindquist. He testified that he examined the camera found at the scene and discovered skin tissue on it indicative of forcible contact with skin. Blood stains were splashed across camera and the nose of the camera case. Kivela opined that the camera was used to deal at least three or four blows against a bloody surface. He examined the binoculars and found blood stains on it, as well as hair fragments consistent with that of or similar to the hair of Lillian Oetting. (Petition for Executive Clemency, April 2005, pp. 13-14)

Chester Weger's jacket, which was seized in September 1960, was submitted as an exhibit into evidence. The State presented expert testimony that minute blood spatter stains on the jacket were human blood stains. The Defense observed, however, that the testimony did not specify that the blood was the same blood type as any of the victims, instead indicating that the samples were too small for such a determination. (Petition for Executive Clemency, April 2005, p. 15)

Finally, the State presented witnesses who testified that the string used to bind Lillian Oetting was 20-ply string, similar to that used by employees in the kitchen area of the Starved Rock Lodge. (Petition for Executive Clemency, April 2005, p. 16)

Hair samples were also recovered from Lillian Oetting's hand and from Frances Murphy's glove at the crime scene. This evidence was not introduced at trial. Newspaper accounts suggested that law enforcement officials believed the samples may have been indicative of two perpetrators – one with "distinctive brown hair and one with blonde hair." (Petition for Executive Clemency, April 2005, p. 19) The prosecution may have declined to introduce this evidence because it conflicted with Weger's "lone perpetrator" confession or simply because there were no other suspects or evidence to present at trial.

Chester Weger Testifies on His Own Behalf

When Chester Weger took the stand on his own behalf, he denied killing the three women. His alibi was that during the time in question he was writing a letter in the Pow Wow Room at the Lodge and tending the boiler downstairs. He admitted that there were marks on his face but explained that they were from cuts from shaving with a straight razor that afternoon and from hitting his head on a towel cabinet in the bathroom in the basement of the Lodge. Other witnesses were called by the defense to testify that they did not notice any unusual marks on Weger's face the week of March 14, 1960. (Petition for Executive Clemency, April 2005, pp. 16-17)

Weger asserted that his confessions were a result of threats to be sentenced to the electric chair and that he believed the only way to save his life was to give the deputies the confession they sought. He alleged that during his interrogations he was threatened with having "truth serum" injected into him.

Infamous Murders and Mysteries

Artist conception of Chester Weger on the witness stand.
(Reprinted with permission from Steve Stout)

He said that Deputy Dummett promised that he would get a life sentence if he confessed. He said that he was concerned for the safety of his wife, who, he said, had been raped in LaSalle in September, and that Dummett had told him that it would be better for his wife and children if he confessed. Weger said that after his wife and parents left the jail prior to his confession, Dummett told him that his wife had not really been raped and began calling her indecent names. At this Weger told Dummett and Hess, "All right! If you want a confession, I'll give you one." (Petition for Executive Clemency, April 2005, pp. 16 and 32)

Weger testified that prior to the court reporter's arrival, Dummett gave him the details of the confession-story of what occurred at Saint Louis Canyon by showing him pictures of the crime scene and pointing things out in the photos. Weger said that in addition to Dummett's coaching, he knew details of the crime from newspaper and TV accounts, rumors at the Lodge, and comments made to him by a state police sergeant when Weger showed him a shortcut to the canyon. He said that the state police officers showed him photos of the crime scene during his interrogation at the Kasakaski

Hotel in April, 1960, and again at John Reid's office in Chicago. Finally, Weger asserted that it was Dummett who told him about the red and white plane flying over the park's canyon at the time of the murders. (Petition for Executive Clemency, April 2005, pp. 16-17)

Cross-Examinations and Rebuttal

In a rather unusual move the Defense called Assistant State's Attorney Craig Armstrong, as result of investigative role in this case. Armstrong corroborated Weger's assertion that Dummett had told Weger that he was going to "ride a thunderbolt" during the trip to Chicago in September. This called into question Dummett's credibility, not only on this issue, but, as a result, his truthfulness in general. Dummett's supporters maintain that he was a man of the highest integrity and are not, to this day, shaken in their belief in him. Others find the testimony by the assistant State's attorney to the contrary to be very damaging to his credibility. (Petition for Executive Clemency, April 2005, p. 17)

In rebuttal, Dummett testified again, asserting that he did not provide Weger with the details of the crime or of having made any promises or threats to Weger. Dummett denied showing Weger any photos of the crime scene prior to the arrival of Court Reporter Josephine Thompson. Dummett acknowledged that he was a friend of the manager of the Ottawa Airport, but that the first time he heard about the red and white plane flying over Saint Louis Canyon on March 14, 1960, was when Chester Weger told him about it on November 17, 1960. Dummett also acknowledged that he knew a lot of the pilots and even co-owned an airplane at the airport about four years earlier. (Petition for Executive Clemency, April 2005, p. 17)

The manager of the Ottawa Airport also testified that Dummett did not question him about the red and white plane flown over Starved Rock State Park on March 14, 1960, until sometime in late November 1960. It was then that the manager told Dummett that there was an Aeronca 7FC flying day, which belonged to the Ottawa Airmen's Club. The manager testified

A *Aeronca 7FC* similar to the one flying over Starved Rock State Park's Saint Louis Canyon on March 14, 1960.

that, although the club had 50 members and any one of them could fly the plane, he was able to determine who was flying the plane at that time from a schedule sheet and a log book at the airport.

The Illinois State Police officers who interrogated Weger at the Kaskaskia Hotel also denied showing Weger photographs of the crime scene. A LaSalle County Jail officer testified that Weger told him after his arrest that he had made two mistakes. He said the first mistake was taking six "lie detector" tests in Chicago and the second was going out to Starved Rock and "putting all the pieces together for the dumb cops." (Petition for Executive Clemency, April 2005, p. 18)

The Verdict

On March 3, 1961, Chester Otto Weger was convicted of the March 14, 1960, first-degree murder of Lillian Oetting. The jury declined to impose the death penalty and on April 3, 1961, the judge formally imposed a sentence of life in imprisonment. Weger, currently at Menard Correctional Center, has been denied parole more than two dozen times, thus far, since 1972.

LaSalle County Sheriff Thomas J. Templeton shows the author the manacles used on Chester Weger on his trip to Saint Louis Canyon with the police and news media in 1960.

Post-Conviction Appeals

In a post-conviction affidavit (incorporated as an appendix to his Petition for Executive Clemency) Chester Otto Weger gave a new story and an explanation for why he now offered a new version. This later alibi has been questioned as inconsistent with his alibi at trial, but is the story he maintains to this day.

Weger asserts that on the afternoon of March 14, 1960, he received a ride to Oglesby, Illinois, at about 2:40 p.m. (1440 hours) from a man named Stanley Tucker. He and Tucker left the Starved Rock Lodge for their afternoon break and Tucker drove him to Oglesby and dropped him off near the Times Theater. Tucker told Weger that he would return to Oglesby later that afternoon and take him back to the Lodge. After being dropped off, Weger attests that he received a haircut from a barber named Ben Franklin. Ben Franklin corroborated this in a like affidavit. Franklin could not recall giving Weger a haircut on that day, but did remember Weger leaving the shop and pointing to an airplane in the sky at about 3:30 or 4:00 p.m. (1530-1600 hours). Ben Franklin passed away in December 2004. (Petition for Executive Clemency, April 2005, pp. 18 and 47)

Weger then asserts that he left the barbershop at about 3:50 p.m. (1550 hours), walking towards Swords' Pool Hall, and when he was near Marty's Café he asked a paperboy if Eddie Swords was still at the pool hall, because Eddie also drove a taxi. Swords was not around, so Weger went into the café and bought a cheeseburger and a Coke, leaving there just after 4:00 p.m. (1600 hours). He then walked to Biama's Tavern to get a beer and a pack of cigarettes. When he left the bar, Weger said that he received a ride back to the Starved Rock State Park Lodge from a man by the last name of Higgins (who is otherwise unidentified) and that he returned to work for his evening shift. (Petition for Executive Clemency, April 2005, pp. 18 and 47)

Weger claims that he was told by state troopers that his story matched that of Stanley Tucker's and that he could return to work. Weger said that later, when the police focused their investigation on both Weger and Tucker, their investigation and techniques caused friction between the two men. He said that the police told each of the suspects that the other was not corroborating their story. Weger said that the police told him that Tucker had confessed and had implicated him also and told Tucker that Weger had confessed and implicated him. Both men became afraid that the other was going to cause them to be charged with murder, so Chester asserts that he fabricated the story of writing a letter in the Pow Wow Room of the Lodge and tending the furnace. That is the version that he told Assistant State's Attorney Craig Armstrong and John Reed in September 1960 and then at his trial in 1961. Weger contends that he lied at his trial because Tucker testified that he did not recall having seen him that afternoon and that his attorney did not call any of his other alibi witnesses. (Petition for Executive Clemency, April 2005, p. 48)

Weger also claims that years after his trial he spoke to Stanley Tucker's brother, Earl Tucker, who was then incarcerated at Stateville, and Earl told him that Stanley had tried to come to the trial and testify on his own, but that the bailiffs would not let him enter the courtroom. Weger also claims that he did not testify that the sheriff and his deputies beat him because his attorney told him that the judge would not believe him. (This may be because of the photographs and medical examination to the contrary). Upon Weger's petition for clemency, Steven Spearie, and investigator for the Illinois State Appellate Defender's Office, interviewed Stanley Tucker in 2004 at his home in Georgia. Tucker said that when he and Weger were taken to Chicago for "lie detector" (polygraph) tests, they were placed in a room where crime scene photos were spread out on the table. Tucker said that he did drive Weger to Oglesby and drop him off at the pool hall, but could not remember the day of the week, month, or even the year. Tucker also refused to sign an affidavit because he was reluctant to raise the possibility of having to testify in court. (Petition for Executive Clemency, April 2005, pp. 48-49)

In April 2004 Chester Weger filed a motion in Circuit Court for DNA testing, which was not available in 1960. The Defense wanted testing of the blood found on Weger's jacket, however, the sample was so slight that it was only used to confirm that it was human blood and even blood group typing was not possible in 1960 due to the insufficient sample. In 2004 the sample would not have been adequate to allow DNA testing. The defense also wanted testing of the hair samples from Lillian Oetting's hand and Frances Murphy's glove. This would confirm whether or not one or the other samples belonged to Chester Weger, if the sample contained adequate DNA, but would not identify possible co-perpetrators, assuming that Weger's "lone perpetrator" confession was not accurate.

Infamous Murders and Mysteries

Chester Weger at Stateville in Joliet, Illinois.
(Reprinted with permission from Steve Stout)

Author, Dr. Robert Girod (also a career detective), and Sheriff Thomas Templeton at the LaSalle County Sheriff's Office. The two lawmen discuss their experiences in murder investigation and as adjunct professors.
That same day Dr. Girod accompanied Sheriff Templeton to the scene of a shooting at a nearby police station in which an officer was seriously injured and a prisoner shot and killed himself.

But that bridge was not to be crossed. In May 2004 the State filed a response to this motion for DNA testing asserting that the crime scene and the evidence may have been contaminated by any of a number of individuals having access over the past forty- years. In short, the State admitted that the chain-of custody had been inadequate over the four and a half decade period to establish that it had not been "substituted, tampered with, replaced or altered in any material aspect…" The Defense withdrew its request for DNA testing. (Petition for Executive Clemency, April 2005, p. 20)

Weger has come up for parole every three years since 1972, but has been denied every time. La Salle County State's Attorney Joseph P. Hettel and two of Oetting's grandchildren from Alabama spoke to board officials. Hettel said he asked the board to deny parole and to not hold another hearing for at least three years. Hettel pointed out that Weger expressed no remorse, but also denies guilt. Weger was not present at this meeting. Instead, Weger appeared at a separate meeting before officials, along with Steven Spearie, an investigator with the Third District Appellate Defender's Office in Ottawa, and a few of Weger's relatives. The attorney who worked for Weger's clemency, Donna Kelly, is no longer representing Weger. She left the Third District Appellate Defender's Office and took a job with the McHenry County State's Attorney's Office. The Appellate Defender's Office still represents Weger. (*The Times,* August 18, 2005)

Chester Weger has again been denied parole and won't be reconsidered for three years. "The crime itself in this case is reason enough not to give consideration to this man," said Prisoner Review Board member Barbara Dye before she and the rest of the board rejected Weger's request. The board has repeatedly denied Weger parole since 1972. (*Small Newspaper Group*, September 27, 2005)

Other Theories

In his 2005 Petition for Executive Clemency, Weger's Defense presented an affidavit from Sergeant Mark Gibson of the Chicago Police Department. SGT Gibson attested that in 1982 or 1983 he was dispatched to Rush Saint Luke's Presbyterian Hospital in Chicago where he and his partner were met by a nurse who informed them that a female patient who was on her deathbed wanted to "clear her conscience" and wanted to speak to the police. When Gibson and his partner entered the woman's room, she grabbed his hand and told him that when she was younger she had been with her friends at a state park when "something happened." She said the park was at "Utica" and that things "got out of hand" and they "dragged the bodies." The woman died leaving SGT Gibson "with the impression" that she and her friends had been involved in the murder of multiple victims at the state park near Utica, Illinois. (Petition for Executive Clemency, April 2005, p. 42)

George N. Spiros, whose family operated the lodge at the park from around 1927 to about the mid-1980s, talked to State Police investigators at least five times between March and October 1960. Spiros' father, Nicholas, offered a $5,000 reward for information in the case when it was still unsolved. A police report dated April 26, 1960, reported that a State Police polygraph test had been done on Spiros because he was suspected of being untruthful about having said he saw Chester Weger and Stanley Tucker talking to three women at the park the day of the slayings. However, the State Police polygraph examiner, William Abernathie, wrote that Spiros was telling the truth. Abernathie also said he believed Spiros told the truth when Spiros denied having killed the women or knowing who did. Abernathie also reported that after testing Weger three times, he thought Weger too was innocent of the murders. A private polygraph examiner from Chicago (John Reid) later tested Weger and said Weger showed guilt. (*The Times*, May 4, 2005) George Spiros, age 73, had missed a doctor's appointment, on Monday, May 2, 2005, which prompted the doctor's office to call the Sheriff's Office to check on his well-being. The Sheriff's Office asked Conservation Police at the park to check on Spiros. Officers arrived at Spiros' home at 10:25 a.m. (1025 hours) and could not get a response from inside the home. After about 10 minutes, officers entered through an open door and found Spiros' body, dead of an apparently self-inflicted gunshot wound. He was pronounced dead at 11:15 a.m. (1115 hours) by the La Salle County Coroner's Office. It is believed that no one else lived at the Spiros' house. Illinois Conservation Police and LaSalle County Sheriff's Department officers said no note was found. (*The Times*, May 4 and May 6, 2005) Donna Kelly of the Appellate Defender's Office in Ottawa, Weger's attorney, questioned the timing of Spiros' death, saying, "I feel it's suspicious that this man was a suspect in this highly publicized case, and I filed documents two weeks ago that named him as a suspect, and now he's dead." It is unknown whether Spiros was aware of the documents, but the Spiros family had a house at the park, about 200 yards from the murder scene, where Spiros was living at the time of his death. (*The Times*, May 6, 2005)

Anthony Raccuglia of Peru (Illinois), who prosecuted Weger in 1961, said "Everyone was a suspect who worked or was at Starved Rock. There was nothing that remotely connected Mr. Spiros to the murders." Harland Warren, who was the LaSalle County State's Attorney from 1952 to 1960 and brought the case against Chester Weger, said, "We did a complete investigation and George (Spiros) was not involved." The current State's Attorney, Joseph P. Hettel, said, "He (Spiros) was suffering from cancer and that was the apparent motive for the suicide," Hettel said. "It's coincidental that it happened now. There is no evidence linking him to the murders. He had an alibi." Spiros had a sales receipt from an Evanston store indicating that he was there at the time prosecutors said the slayings were committed, according to a 1960 investigative report. (*The Times*, May 6, 2005) Sheriff's Office Investigator Dave Guinnee testified that Spiros' body was found sitting at a desk with a bullet wound. His dog also was found shot to death, presumably by Spiros. There was no suicide note, but Marc Maton of State Police District Five in Lockport said that computer forensic investigators with his district have possession of computers that were in Spiros' home and planned to check them for an electronic suicide note. Spiros was last seen alive a few days before his body was found. Coroner Jody Bernard said Spiros had recently been diagnosed with oral cancer, had undergone surgery and in the week before his death had learned his cancer had spread. His death was ruled a suicide. (*The Times*, June 18, 2005)

Epilogue

A team from Chicago-based 77 Films filmed interviews with figures connected to the case. Production of the documentary began around June 2004 and is being directed by David Raccuglia, son of Anthony Raccuglia of Peru, who prosecuted Weger in 1961. David said he is approaching the project with an open mind. The film, planned to run almost two hours, will be shown at the annual Sundance Film Festival for independent films and possibly the HBO cable channel. The producers are unsure when the film will be completed. (*The Times*, April 4, 2006)

Chester Otto "Rocky" Weger remains incarcerated at Menard Correction Center, in Menard, Illinois, at the time of this writing. He earned his G.E.D. in 1985. The only disciplinary infraction he has recorded on Prison Review Board record is a 2001 ticket for "disobeying a direct order" and a 1996 ticket for "drugs and drug paraphernalia" allegedly from his cell mate's possession of homemade wine. He is in poor health, suffering from an ulcer, asthma and pulmonary emphysema, and in 2001 he suffered from a gross hematuria (blood passing through the urethra). (Petition for Executive Clemency, April 2005, p. 51)

Having served forty-four years of a life sentence, sixty-five year old Weger petitioned for a pardon or commutation of his sentence to Governor Rod Blagojevich in 2005. He and his Appellate Attorney, Donna Kelly of the Illinois State Appellate Attorney's Office, criticized not only the evidence in the case, but the primary investigator of the crime, Captain William Dummett, who, allegedly, displayed the murder weapon (the log piece) on his mantelpiece "as some type of macabre trophy." This story is largely based upon documents provided by Ms. Kelly and the Illinois State Appellate Attorney's Office.

Chester Weger's five sisters are still living at the time of this writing. His father passed away in 1990 and his mother passed away in 2001. His wife, Jo Ann, initiated divorce proceedings in 1967 following Chester's imprisonment. She remarried another man and remained married for about ten years. Afterwards Chester and Jo Ann wrote letters to each other and talked by phone. They did not remarry and Jo Ann died in 1996. Weger had two children: Rebecca Jo Weger (December 23, 1957) and John Weger (November 19, 1959). Becky Real (the daughter) lives in LaSalle, Illinois with her family. If he is ever released, Weger plans to live with his daughter.

Deputy Wayne Hess, one of the sheriff's investigators on this case, died in 1980. Captain Bill Dummett, the sheriff's office investigator who largely handled the case, died in the spring of 1982. His protégé, Tom Templeton, is the Sheriff of LaSalle County, Illinois, and helped piece this story together from Dummett's account. Dummett and Hess received citations from the

National Police Hall of Fame in 1966 for the capture and arrest of Chester Weger. Harland Warren served as LaSalle County State's Attorney from 1952-1960 when he was defeated in the election and returned to private law practice. Robert Richardson defeated Warren in the election and succeeded him as State's Attorney. (Stout, pp. 206-207)

Mildred Lindquist's daughter, Nancy Temple, said, "They would have been great grandmothers because they were great mothers." Mildred's granddaughter, Patti Temple Rocks, of Geneva, Illinois, said Weger's petition for parole is a painful reminder to the family. Dr. George Oetting, Lillian's son, is a retired educator. Diane Oetting, who wears a button with a photo of grandmother, was born three years after her grandmother's murder. LaSalle County State's Attorney Joseph Hettel has repeatedly stated that he will oppose Weger's appeal for clemency. Former prosecutor Anthony Raccuglia told the Prisoner Review Board, "One of the biggest disappointments of my professional career is that Chester Weger did not get the electric chair… he will face his final justice when his soul burns in hell." (*The* Times, April 14, 2005) Lillian Oetting, Mildred Lindquist, and Frances Murphy have been deceased since 1960.

On June 10, 2006, Dan Churney of *The Times* (Ottawa, Illinois) wrote the following:

Detective to write about Starved Rock Slaying

An Indiana sleuth plans to include a chapter on the 1960 Starved Rock slayings in his forthcoming book.

Robert J. Girod Sr., a detective supervisor with the police department in Fort Wayne, Ind., and an adjunct professor of criminal justice and public management, is gathering information on the La Salle County case that held national headlines 46 years ago and still generates controversy.

"I think they got the right guy, but I can see why people might question it," Girod said.

Chester O. Weger, 67, has been in custody since November

1960 in connection with the March 1960 killings of Mildred Lindquist, Frances Murphy and Lillian Oetting, all of Riverside, at Starved Rock State Park. He confessed, but then recanted.

Weger asked Gov. Rod Blagojevich to release him from prison last year, but Blagojevich, who is under no statutory requirement to respond, has not responded.

The working title for Girod's pending book is "Infamous Murders" and will include about 12 to 14 chapters, each chapter detailing murder cases between 1907 and 1969 that involved either famous people or places. He hopes to finish the work this year and then shop for a publisher.

Girod has written a textbook, "Profiling the Criminal Mind."

Girod said he first learned of the Starved Rock case while researching a still-unsolved slaying that occurred in July 1960 on Michigan's Mackinac Island. At that time, Girod noted, investigators suspected a connection to the Starved Rock murders -- a suspicion Girod said he doesn't share.

In spring 2005, Girod contacted La Salle County Sheriff Tom Templeton and arranged to visit the county. When Girod came, Templeton accompanied him on a trip to the scene of the murders at St. Louis Canyon and explained the case, as well as showing Girod souvenirs at the sheriff's office that included the handcuffs used on Weger.

Girod, who has been in law enforcement 26 years, said he has also read the court papers filed by Weger's appellate attorney and might visit La Salle County again.

"There is a lot of circumstantial evidence and the confession, but I see the appeals side. They raised questions you have to look at," Girod observed. "It puzzles me somewhat how Weger killed three women, but I've seen the strangest things turn out to be true. I never rule anything out."

(*The Times*, June 10, 2006)
Used by permission of Dan Churney of *The Time*, Ottawa, Illinois.

PART II

GHOSTS, CURSES, AND SPIES WHO KILL

*Ambereley excelled at chess –
one mark, Watson, of a scheming mind.*
~ Sherlock Holmes ~
Sir Arthur Conan Doyle

CHAPTER THREE

THE GHOSTS OF MANSFIELD PRISON: MURDER BEHIND BARS

Chance has put in our way a most singular and whimsical problem, and its solution is its own reward.

~ Sherlock Holmes ~

Sir Arthur Conan Doyle

Ohio State Reformatory: Mansfield, Ohio

The Ohio State Reformatory at Mansfield, Ohio, closed in 1990 after 104 years of operation. It was reportedly the scene of more than 217 deaths, including both murders and executions. Executions were carried out by public hanging in the county where the crime was committed since Ohio became a state in 1803. But in 1885 the state legislature passed a law requiring executions to be carried out at the Ohio Penitentiary in Columbus. A Morrow County resident, 56-year-old Valentine Wagner, was the first person to be executed at the Ohio Penitentiary. He was hanged for the murder of Daniel Shehan of Mount Gilead, Ohio. Twenty-seven other convicted murderers were eventually hanged at the penitentiary in Columbus. (Internet: http://www.ohiodeathrow.com/)

Mansfield Prison: Ohio State Reformatory.
(Photo courtesy of www.mansfieldtourism.com)

By 1897 a more "humane" form of execution replaced the gallows - the electric chair. The first prisoner to be executed by electrocution was 17-year-old William Haas, from Cincinnati (Hamilton County), Ohio, for the murder of William Brady. From 1897 to 1963, 315 convicts were executed in the electric chair, including three women. The last person to be executed by electrocution in Ohio was 29-year-old Donald Reinbolt, from Columbus (Franklin County), Ohio, for the murder of Edgar L. Weaver, a Columbus grocer. He was executed on March 15, 1963.

(Internet: http://www.drc.state.oh.us/Public/capital.htm)

Infamous Murders and Mysteries

Scary night as lightning strikes near the guard tower (left). Spooky days, too, at the main entrance to Mansfield prison (right).
(Photos courtesy of www.mansfieldtourism.com)

When the United States Supreme Court declared the death penalty to be unconstitutional in 1972, the sentences of sixty-five Ohio convicts were reduced to life in prison. Death Row was moved to the newly opened Southern Ohio Correctional Facility (SOCF) at Lucasville, Ohio. In 1981 the Ohio legislature enacted a new law giving prisoners the option to choose between death by electrocution or lethal injection. If the prisoner did not choose, the default method of execution was death by electrocution.

In 1995 Death Row was relocated to the Mansfield Correctional Institution in Mansfield, Ohio, even though the "Death House" remained at the Southern Ohio Correctional Facility at Lucasville, Ohio. On February 19, 1999, inmate Wilford Berry, known as "The Volunteer," became the first inmate to be executed in Ohio since 1963. He voluntarily waived all of his appeals and selected lethal injection as the method of execution. He was serving a death sentence from Cleveland (Cuyahoga County), Ohio, for the 1989 murder of Charles Mitroff. (Internet: http://www.ohiodeathrow.com/)

To date, Ohio has executed a total of 362 convicted murderers. The electric chair was eliminated in Ohio in 2001, making lethal injection the only method of execution in Ohio. On February 26, 2002, Ohio's electric chair, nicknamed "Old Sparky" (as it is in most states) was decommissioned and disconnected. The original electric chair was donated to the Ohio Historical Society in 2002 and a replica electric chair was donated to the Mansfield Reformatory Preservation Society. (Internet: http://www.drc.state.oh.us/ Public/capital.htm) The old Ohio State Reformatory (OSR) attracts paranormal investigators from around the country and is located at 100 Reformatory Road, Mansfield, Ohio. To experience its mysteries for yourself, take I-71 to the U.S. 30 West exit, then follow State Route 545 north for about ½ mile and turn west (left) onto Reformatory Road.

Opening Day at OSR

A headline in the *Richland Shield & Banner* proclaimed November 4, 1886, as "Mansfield's Greatest Day" when ceremonies marked the laying of the cornerstone for the Ohio State Reformatory (Mansfield Prison). The city was decked out in flags and bunting for the celebration, which opened with a parade from downtown Mansfield to the prison grounds. An estimated 15,000 people turned out for the ceremonies, including numerous dignitaries such as former President Rutherford B. Hayes, Senator John Sherman, Governor J.B. Foraker and General Roeliff Brinkerhoff, who was the chief proponent for building the prison there. (*Mansfield News Journal*, December 9, 1990)

The prison officially opened on September 17, 1896. Large crowds gathered between Columbus and Mansfield to watch 150 prisoners as they were transferred to the new prison from the Ohio State Penitentiary at

Columbus, Ohio. Almost as if a circus paraded by, the crowds watched as the inmates, dressed in prison stripes, marched from the penitentiary to the train station in Columbus. *The Columbus Evening Press* wrote about the prisoners as if they were celebrities and a Mansfield newspaper reported that the train was greeted by a large crowd when it stopped in Galion before continuing on to Mansfield. Crowds along the tracks outside of the reformatory watched, as if at a carnival attraction, as the prisoners were unloaded at the northwest corner of the prison and marched to their new cells. (*Mansfield News Journal,* December 9, 1990)

The reformatory was not finished when it opened, so the first inmates were put to work on the prison sewer system and the 25-foot stone wall that surrounded the 15-acre complex. The east cell block was not completed until 1908. The massive medieval looking six-tier prison is noted in *The Guinness Book of World Records* as having the largest freestanding steel cellblock in the world. (Internet: http://www.drc.state.oh.us/ web/inst/ohioref.htm)

A few of the prison's former inmates became infamous, such as Henry Baker, one of the perpetrators convicted of the infamous Brink's robbery of 1950. Another former OSR inmate "changed his stripes" (pun intended) and to pursue a career in baseball. Gates Brown of Crestline, Ohio, served a sentence at the prison for burglary from 1958 to 1959. He went on to play with the Detroit Tigers from 1963 to 1975 and became one of baseball's best pinch-hitters. Another athlete who was already well-known in sports when he entered OSR was Kevin Mack, a star running back for the Cleveland Browns, who served one month at the prison on drug charges in 1989. (*Mansfield News Journal,* December 9, 1990)

The Ghosts of Mansfield Prison

By the mid 1900's the deteriorating prison no longer met the standards required for state correctional facilities. The prisoners were gradually transferred to other prisons over a period of decades until the OSR was entirely closed in 1990. Since the closing of the Reformatory, numerous legends of violence, suicides, murders, and other unexplained deaths have circulated. The prison is said by some to be filled with "restless spirits" of inmates, guards, and prison officials whose spirits were never able to leave their prison. Paranormal enthusiasts assert that the macabre tragedies of the past trap the spirits of those involved in these events within the prisons cold walls and rusting cell bars. These "ghost-busters" suggest that the architecture of the prison itself draws paranormal energies to the prison. The pyramid shaped towers atop the prison pointing toward the large central pyramid tower of the Reformatory are thought to create a catalyst for paranormal activty. Many visitors opine that the halls of the long-closed Mansfield Reformatory are not as quiet as they seem at first glance.

The Chapel is one area of the prison where strange events have been reported. Camcorders and other electrical equipment reportedly fail to operate without apparent cause and witnesses suggest that shadows seem to move through the darkness. Other visitors claim that they have seen spirits peering around doors into the room and "pulling away" after being noticed. Still others report taking strange photographs and recordings in the Chapel. One legend asserts that inmates were hung from the rafters and tortured in the Chapel (before it was a Chapel) and rumors allege that it was even used as an execution chamber. Some ghost hunters report stories of a small boy, appearing to be about ten years old, who goes by the name of Paul. They say that he seems to be contented to haunt and play on and around the stage in the chapel.

The hospital infirmary is directly above the chapel. Inmates were treated for injuries and illness and some reportedly died from diseases like influenza and tuberculosis. Many visitors believe that many of the inmates who died in the infirmary may still haunt the Reformatory as ghosts. Some report feeling "strange energies" and "invisible entities" that rush past them and down the stairs from this area.

The library is the site of an alleged female ghost haunting. Some speculate that this ghost is either Helen Glattke, the Warden's wife, or the ghost of a young nurse who was supposedly killed by an inmate. Many psychics claim to experience the vision of a young woman inside the prison, while other visitors

Infamous Murders and Mysteries

to the library report feeling sick and light headed. Recording and photographic equipment reportedly fails to properly function here and photographs often show strange lights or "orbs" (spheres of light which some assert are spirits).

The east and west cellblocks are like caverns of rusting bars, chipping paint, and piles of old musty mattresses. In the lower bowels of the prison, the basement level is a maze of dark, twisting hallways. Legends suggest that prisoners were taken to be tortured and beaten. Some visitors have reported seeing the ghost of a small boy, appearing to be about 14 years old, standing in the dark hallways. The boy vanishes or runs away seconds after being noticed. Another tale tells of an old ghost named George, a former employee, haunting the basement of the Reformatory.

Cell block area.
(Photos courtesy of www.mansfieldtourism.com)

Nearby is a small graveyard with 215 numbered markers marking the graves of the inmates who were unclaimed after they died. They are buried there with a number instead of a name. The graveyard is off limits to visitors because it is owned by the new prison facility, but it can be seen from the guard tower, where some visitors say that they have seen objects "mysteriously" fall or move without explanation.

Murders and suicides in the cellblocks are not uncommon in prisons. Inmates often tied bed sheets around their necks and the bars to hang themselves to death. Others were thrown off of the higher tiers - murdered for something as trivial as a pack of cigarettes or a perceived insult. Some speculate that these ghosts roam their old "haunts" because they continue to struggle with the tragedies that haunted them during their lives.

Some "ghost busters" say that an indication of nearby paranormal "ghost energy" is the quick and noticeable drop in temperature in a relatively small portion of air or space. They say that "ecto-mist" is not as common as orbs when energy materializes, but they too can be seen in photographs or materializing on video. Various visitors report experiences of this type. Another story is told of a prisoner who was confined in a cell in the East Cell Block on the fourth tier. He poured turpentine on himself and ended his life by setting himself on fire. Some investigators report the smell of burnt flesh or turpentine when investigating his cell. Two other prisoners were reportedly involved in a fight on the top tier of the West Cell Block. One of them pushed the other over the railing, sending him to his death below. These are only a few of the many legends of deaths in the prison.

Killed in the Line of Duty

Two corrections officers were victims of murder in the line of duty at the Ohio State Reformatory in Mansfield. The first was on November 2, 1926, when a paroled inmate returned to the prison and shot Officer Urban Wilford with a .38 caliber pistol outside the west gate in an botched attempt to help a friend escape. The 72-year-old guard had moved from Jefferson (Ashtabula County),

Ohio, to Mansfield almost seven years earlier. He was survived by his wife. The gunman, Philip Orleck, was arrested two months later and was executed the following year (July 18, 1927) in the Ohio Penitentiary electric chair.

Philip Orleck: Executed 07-18-1927
(Ohio Department of Corrections)

Merrill Chandler: Executed 11-24-1933
Chester Probaski: Executed 11-24-1933
(Ohio Department of Corrections)

The second murder occurred on Sunday, October 2, 1932. Officer Frank Hanger, age 48, was beaten to death with a three-foot iron rod in "the Hole" (solitary confinement) during an escape attempt by a dozen prisoners. Officer Hanger's fatal injuries were sustained when an inmate struck him on the head with the iron bar. He died four days later on, Thursday, October 6, 1932. Inmates Merrill Chandler and Chester Probaski were charged with and found guilty of the guard's murder and were executed in the electric chair in 1935.

The Prison Farm Murders

Murl Robert Daniels (also known as Robert Murl Daniels) was born on April 8, 1924, at Nelsonville, Ohio. By the age of 19 Murl was already in trouble. On September 22, 1943, he, two other young men, and three girls were joy-riding in a stolen car. When their gasoline and money ran low, one of the girls mentioned a store in the town of Waverly where the grocer was known to keep a good bit of money. The three couples got some guns and held up the store, tying the storekeeper up in the back room. They got about fifty miles away when they encountered a sheriff's roadblock and were arrested. Murl was an adult and was sentenced to one to twenty-five years for robbery. He was incarcerated at OSR in Mansfield on January 28, 1944. (Martin, p. 333)

Many inmates and former inmates complained of cruel beatings by the guards at the prison. Superintendent Arthur L. Glattke denied this, saying, "I won't say the guards never hit a boy. That's why the boys are here – they don't conform." The former high-school coach added though, "But the guards aren't brutal. Every time they use force they have to report it." Complaints were common – this was prison after all. (Martin, p. 335)

It was at OSR that Daniels met John Coulter West. West was from the river town areas near Parkersburg, West Virginia. He had been a truck driver and was of below average IQ and described as "a moron." He had been on probation for a store burglary that he committed in April, 1946. He was also described as a twenty-one year old, small, and fox-faced, with big ears and nose and glasses that sat crooked on his crooked face. He was incarcerated at OSR on January 16, 1947, almost three years after Daniels had arrived. (Martin, p. 337)

Dr. Robert J. Girod, Sr.

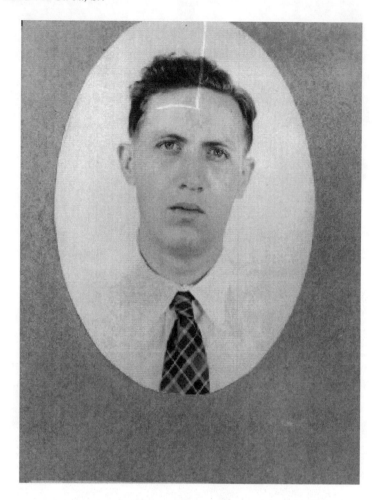

Robert Murl Daniels - Executed: 01/03/1949
(Ohio Department of Corrections)

The head farmer at OSR was John Elmer Niebel, a six-foot, 230 pound man, who had been at the prison eighteen years, since 1928. Niebel had little contact with either Daniels or West. But Willis Harris was one of the guards at the farm and Daniels complained that Harris often mistreated him and other prisoners. Harris had been a guard at the prison since 1923, but quit in 1941 to manage a private farm. A Reformatory inmate was paroled to him and when they had an argument, the parolee told Harris he was going to leave. Harris was bedfast with a broken back and unable to stop him from leaving, so he shot him. Harris was charged and plead guilty to the felonious shooting and sentenced to twenty-one years in the Ohio State Penitentiary, but was released after serving two years. On March 5, 1944, about four days after he was paroled, he was re-hired as a guard at Ohio State Reformatory at Mansfield. Superintendent Glattke said, "He is not criminally inclined. He had a very good record here. I needed a man." It was during World War II and men were hard to come by for guards at the prison. (Martin, p. 337)

Murl Robert Daniels was paroled on September 25, 1947, after serving less than four years of his sentence. John Coulter West was paroled on March 12, 1948, after just over one year. That night West telephoned Daniels on his way back to West Virginia. Daniels mother asked where he knew Murl from and West said, "At Mansfield." Mr. Daniels told his wife, "Forget it; don't tell Murl nothing concerning nobody at Mansfield." West later wrote to Daniels and invited him for a visit. "Keep away from that boy, Murl," his father warned. Murl made a fist and hit his bed. "Pop, he is a smart ___ __ _ _____. The smartest man I ever saw," Murl said. (Martin, pp. 339-340)

In July of 1948, the two former inmates released, from the Reformatory for "good behavior," went on a killing spree. Murl Robert Daniels and John Coulter West, were later called "Mad Dog Killers" by the papers. When they met up, West was waiting in a two-tone gray Pontiac stolen from a parking lot. They got a gun and started drinking. They started by robbing a gas station. As Daniels walked the attendant down the steps, West hit the attendant with a black-jack and started beating him in the head. West said that he wanted to prove that he had the guts. The next robbery was easier. They just took the attendants money and left. They ran into a State Highway Patrol roadblock near Columbus, but they were waived on. They stopped in Indianapolis to make change and Daniels was accidentally locked in the bank at closing time. They finally made their way to Saint Louis, Missouri, and Nashville, Tennessee. They got drunk a missed a radio production at the "Grand Ole Opry," before returning to Columbus, Ohio. (Martin, pp. 341-343)

Back in Columbus by July 10, they went out with a couple of girls, but ditched them and bought some guns. They went to Joe's Grill on West Broad Street. The bar was crowded and when the customers saw the robbers' guns, several of them ran out the back door. Daniels ran after the customers and, when the bar tender took his hands off the bar, West fired a .45, but did not hit anyone. They cleaned out the safe and cash register and made their get-away. They came upon another tavern at Fifth Avenue. Daniels and West went in through the rear door, stepped to the bar and ordered beers. The tavern owner, Earl Ambrose, went toward the phone booth when the hoods announced the robbery. West shot him three times and the pair fled with $8,000. They saw a by-stander write down their license plate number – L4190." On Tuesday, July 20, they decided to drive to Mansfield, Ohio. They arrived on July 21, 1948, at about 1800 (6:00 p.m.). They stopped at a bar then headed for OSR and the honor farm, looking for Willis Harris. (Martin, pp. 343-344) There they kidnapped the 54-year-old OSR farm superintendent John Elmer Niebel, his wife, and his twenty-year-old daughter.

John Elmer Niebel, a six-foot, 230 pound man, had been at the prison eighteen years, since 1928. His wife, Nolana Niebel, was a heavy woman. Their daughter, Phyllis Niebel, was a twenty-year-old blond and was also heavy. She worked at a local factory in clerical work and lived with her parents in the white frame house on the honor farm on the North Main Street Road just outside of Mansfield. Their house was dark when Daniels and West pulled up outside just after midnight. When they came to the door, Mr. Niebel dressed and answered the front door. Daniels said that their car had broken down and they wanted to call a garage. Niebel pointed to the phone. Niebel seemed to recognize West and asked his name. West used an alias that he had used before and said that his name was "John Le Vond," as he and Daniels moved to get Niebel between them. (Martin, pp. 346-347)

Mr. Niebel went upstairs to get his glasses and when he came back down, Daniels pulled his gun. They asked where he kept his guns and decided to take them. They asked who else was in the house. Niebel said that his wife and daughter were upstairs. He didn't know if they were asleep or not. Daniels told him to call to them. When they answered, the three went up and took Mrs. Niebel into Phyllis' room. The men smashed their cigarettes on the floor and West threw a gun at Mr. Niebel's feet, daring him to reach for it. Daniels wanted Willis Harris' address and Niebel wrote it on OSR stationary;

it was the next house up the road. After ransacking the house, Daniels and West told the three Niebels to come along. They couldn't find any rope in the basement to tie them up, so they ordered the three into the back seat of their stolen car and drove off into the dark, quiet night. (Martin, p. 347)

They drove into Mansfield and circled the court house a few times. A sign read "Cleveland 74 Miles." They turned and drove north on Route 42 until they came to a gravel road and turned right. They drove a mile and turned around at a "T" intersection and came back a few yards before stopping next to a cornfield just off Fleming Falls Road. The moonlight was now bright as it reflected on the sycamore trees. It was a hot July night as they herded the Niebel family across a shallow ditch and sixty feet or so into a corn field. "Take your clothes off," Daniels ordered, Phyllis standing between her parents. He told West to gather them up and take them to the car and bring some rope to tie them up. "There ain't no rope," West said. Daniels said that they would have to hit them all in the head with the blackjack. "Daddy can't help it that he works for the State," Phyllis protested. "Well he doesn't have to be such a _____ about it," Daniels retorted. Mr. Niebel told her to be quiet. "Tip your head forward just a little bit," Daniels said, "This won't hurt you; otherwise it might kill you." The Niebels all complied and they all just stood there for several moments. Then West pulled his .25 auto and pulled the trigger, but nothing happened. Daniels pulled his gun and walked down the line, right to left, beginning with Mr. Niebel, shooting him twice on the top of the head. Phyllis looked up slightly as Daniels shot her in the top of the head. Then he shot Mrs. Niebel and, as she fell, West shot her in the abdomen "for good measure." (Martin, pp. 348-349)

The Manhunt for Daniels and West

Following the murders Daniels and West drove to Cleveland and stopped to rest. From there they went to Akron, where they bought a .30 caliber rifle and slept some more. The next day, July 22, they headed for Findlay, but stopped in Tiffin at about 1300 (1:00 p.m.). There they rented a room and rested until about 2100 (9:00 p.m.) and went out looking for a different car to steal. The newspapers had already given the description of the two-tone gray Pontiac. After two unsuccessful car-jacking attempts, they spotted a car-hauler with five new Studebakers atop the trailer. The driver, Orville Taylor, was asleep and West shot him. He was a young man with a wife and four small children. At about 2300 hours (11:00 p.m.) they stopped, climbed into the front car atop the hauler and went to sleep. In the morning they drank some whiskey and headed toward Saint Louis. They encountered a couple of police roadblocks, but were waved through. (Martin, pp. 349-350)

On July 23, the two ex-cons were encountered a roadblock at the intersection of Routes 637 and 224 outside of Van Wert, Ohio, and near the Ohio-Indiana state lines. Sheriff Roy Shaffer stepped from his car a flagged down the truck. West was driving and stopped the truck. Sheriff Shaffer asked West where he was from. "Tiffin," he said. He asked if he was alone and West said that he was. The sheriff walked along the car-hauler and was becoming suspicious. These cars were Studebakers and the haul-away was heading the wrong way, back to the factory. Sheriff Shaffer told Sergeant Leonard Conn to cover him with a sub-machinegun as he climbed atop the truck and walked along the catwalk. The cars were covered with canvass, but the one in front had a slit in the canvass. The sheriff pulled the canvass back and saw Daniels with the .30 caliber rifle in his lap and a pistol in each hand. Sheriff Shaffer ordered Daniels to drop the guns. He did, saying, "You have got me. Don't kill me; I'll do anything you tell me." The sheriff found a .25 automatic in his hip pocket and threw it into the ditch below. (Martin, p. 350)

Suddenly shooting started below. West, using the truck door as a shield, shot Sergeant Conn in the abdomen. Conn, though wounded, cut loose with the machinegun, spraying the cab of the truck. West fell to the pavement dead. A game warden who happened along was slightly wounded, but helped Sheriff Shaffer get Daniels down from the truck. The sheriff then radioed for help. (Martin, p. 352) West was killed in the shoot-out with police but Daniels was captured. The Niebel murders were part of a two-week crime spree during which the pair killed six people. Daniels confessed to the honor-farm killings, claiming they were an act of revenge.

Daniels seemed to enjoy his notoriety. When the sheriff took him before a crowd of news reporters, photographers, and citizens, Daniels said, "Give me credit for the Niebels." The crowd went wild, chanting and yelling, "Kill him! Lynch him!" His bragging soon came to and end and he regretted saying that he told the Niebels, "I'll give you three minutes to get right with the Lord." He asked to have that comment taken out of his statement. "Lieutenant, I don't want that in there," he said. "The Lord's name is in vain there; I would like to have you take that out." Several counties wanted him, but Richland County got him and he was taken to the jail in Mansfield and charged with the murders of John Elmer, Nolana, and Phyllis Niebel. The local citizens wanted him executed and they made this clear to Prosecutor Theodore Lutz. (Martin, p. 351)

Judge G.E. Kalbfleisch would hear the case and he appointed Attorney Lyndon Beam as the defense council. Daniels waived a jury trial, so the Ohio Supreme Court appointed judges Chester Pendleton and H.E. Culbertson as the other two members of a three-judge panel to hear the case. The trial started on September 13, 1948. The court room was crowded and Daniels would wink at young bobby-soxers as he swaggered by them in the courtroom. (Daniels, pp. 351-353)

Daniels had bragged about the possibility of dying in the electric chair. His prediction was about to come true at the State Pen in Columbus. After a week-long trial Robert Murl Daniels (or Murl Robert Daniels, as he was named at birth) was found guilty of the three Niebel murders. The judge read the sentence:

> It is the sentence, order and judgment of this Court, that the defendant, Robert Murl Daniels, on the third day of January, A.D. 1949, within the walls of the Ohio Penitentiary, Columbus, Ohio, be executed by causing a current of electricity, of sufficient intensity to cause death, to pass through the body of the said Robert Murl Daniels, and application of such current continued until the said Robert Murl Daniels is dead." (Martin, pp. 326-327)

On December 30, 1948, the governor of Ohio refused to commute Daniels sentence. On Monday, January 3, 1949, Daniels brother and two sisters came to see him at 1230 (12:30 p.m.) and stayed for three hours. His parents were not there. At 1705 (5:05 p.m.), the guards unlocked his Death Row cell and led him across the prison yard to the Death House. There were two rooms – a cell for him and the room where the electric chair was. He ordered his last meal: grape juice, orange juice, coffee, fried chicken, fried oysters, chili, potatoes, limburger cheese, bread and butter, and vanilla ice cream with chocolate syrup. His last guest was another prisoner. (Martin, pp. 356-357)

The witnesses gathered at 1930 (7:30 p.m.). There were guards, reporters, and police officers, including Sergeant Leonard Conn, who had recovered after being shot by John Coulter West, Daniels crime partner. There were about two dozen witnesses in all. After strapping him into the chair securely, Daniels voice could be heard, low and rapid from beneath the mask, "Our father who art…" The blue light went off and the red light went on. Daniels body jerked hard and the red light went off at 2002 (8:02 p.m.), a blue wisp of smoke curling up from his right leg. A priest and two physicians checked him. At 2009 (8:09 p.m.) one of the doctors said, "I think he's dead." The other turned to the warden and said, "Warden Alvis, sufficient electricity has passed through the body of Robert Murl Daniels, 87057, to have caused death at 8:01 p.m." The warden turned to the witnesses and said, "That's all gentlemen," and they walked out leaving only the guards to turn the body over to a waiting ambulance. Murl Robert Daniels was buried by his parents in secret. (Martin, pp. 357-359)

The Warden and His Wife

The administration wing of the prison was a home and office to Superintendent (Warden) Arthur L. Glattke and his wife Helen, age 41. Both of them died in this section of the prison. Helen Glattke's death has been controversial and the subject of one of OSR's legends. (Internet: http://www.zerotime.com/storefront/ghosthunter/sample3.htm)

Four families lived in the residential area of the upper-floor Administrative Wing in the front of the large facility and through the center wing. Mr. and Mrs. Allen and Mr. and Mrs. Allarding, the associate superintendents, were two of the families that shared the residence. They lived on the second and third floors, respectively, above the West wing offices. Reverend Wapner and his family also lived on the second floor rooms between the East and West wings, around the corner from the stairwell on the second floor from where the Glattke Family lived.

The Wapner's Living Room is the room in the Reformatory that was used as the Probation Hearing Room in the *Shawshank Redemption*. Sometime around 1961-1962, Reverend Wapner was fatally injured in an automobile accident. His son, David, who was raised in the Reformatory, grew up to become a physician. The Reformatory's physician, Dr. John Horst, and his family lived on Route 13. His neighbor was Mr. John Neibel, the Farm Manager. In 1948, Mr. Neibel, his wife and daughter were murdered by two paroled ex-prisoners who were later recaptured and tried for the murders.

Ohio State Reformatory, Mansfield, Ohio.
(Photos courtesy of www.mansfieldtourism.com)

Dr. Robert J. Girod, Sr.

Arthur, Sr. and Helen met in 1930 while working on an editorial campaign for the Governor of Ohio, Martin Davey. Because Helen was Catholic and Superintendent Glattke was Jewish when they married in the 1930s, few guests attended the wedding. Governor Davey appointed Arthur, Sr. as Superintendent of OSR. Arthur, Jr. (Art) is the older son and Theodore (Ted) Glattke is the younger son of Superintendent Glattke and his wife, Helen. They lived in the Mansfield Reformatory during the period from 1930 to the late 1950's.

On November 6, 1950, Helen apparently knocked a .32 automatic pistol off a high closet shelf while attempting to remove a jewelry box from the shelf. The gun went off when it hit the floor and the bullet went through the left lung. Some accounts say she was killed instantly while others say she died the next day in the Mansfield hospital. Some have speculated that it is possible that the superintendent shot her in order to spare himself the messy legal work and political stigma of a divorce. In an e-mail with Professor Theodore (Ted) Glattke, Arthur and Helen's younger son, he told me that he recalls the essential details of that day.

The room connecting from Art, Junior's bedroom was used as a guest room by the Glattke Family for visitors who stayed, like the Governor of Ohio. The bathroom near the Guest Room was shared by the guests as well as Art, Jr. The bedroom, located at the front of the living quarters on the southeast corner of the hallway, was Superintendent and Mrs. Glattke's bedroom. The Glattkes preferred separate beds, so Arthur Glattke Sr.'s bed was next to the closet door and Mrs. Glattke's was near the front of the bedroom. It is in this bedroom where Helen Glattke's met her unfortunate death.

The family was preparing for Sunday morning mass at approximately 0700 (7:00 a.m.) on November 5, 1950. When Helen reached up in her closet she apparently knocked a loaded gun off of the top shelf. When the gun hit the floor, Helen was accidentally shot. She called for Art, Jr., whose bedroom was directly across from Arthur, Sr. and Helen's bedroom. Art ran to find his Father. Helen was taken by ambulance to Mansfield General Hospital. Two days later, on November 7, Helen passed away due to internal bleeding and loss of blood.

In February 1959, almost decade later, Warden Glattke died of a heart attack in his office. Many believe that the ghosts of both Warden Glattke and his wife Helen continue to haunt the Reformatory. At certain times, visitors say that they can feel cold rushes of air move over their bodies and "strange anomalies" are regularly recorded in the administration wing. "Orbs" are photographed and equipment failures are common. The now infamous pink bathroom is also in the administration section. Visitors to the pink bathroom reportedly smell fresh flowers and perfume scents. (Internet: http://www.zerotime.com/storefront/ghosthunter/sample3.htm) Some observers claim that argumentative voices of a man and woman have been heard from somewhere within the Administrative Wing. The voice of a woman, they report, is heard in the living quarters. While there is much speculation, no one really knows who these voices belong to or from where they are heard.

Again, in an e-mail with Professor Theodore (Ted) Glattke, Arthur and Helen's younger son, he told me that this is essentially what happened that day. On February 10, 1959, Ted was returning home from school and was told to go to his father's office. Hurrying there he found his father and older brother, Art, Jr. Arthur Glattke, Sr. had suffered a heart attack. While Art, Jr. accompanied Superintendent Glattke in the ambulance, Ted followed in a car, bringing some personal items he thought his father might need. Shortly after arriving at the Mansfield General Hospital, Superintendent Arthur Glattke, Sr. passed away.

Before his death, Superintendent Glattke gained responsibility that took him to Columbus every day from 1949 through 1953. After Mrs. Glattke's death in 1950, the inmates who staffed the residence got Ted up for school, helped him with his homework, and practiced his music lessons with him after school until Superintendent Glattke returned from his offices in the Department of Correction in Columbus. One inmate taught him to play the guitar and another gave him cooking lessons. The trustee who managed the garage took Ted to and from school each day.

Neither Mr. nor Mrs. Glattke passed away in the Mansfield Reformatory, as is commonly believed and reported. Arthur Jr. (Art) is retired in Modesto, California. Theodore (Ted) is a professor at the University of Arizona in the

Speech, Language and Hearing Departments and plans to retire at the end of 2007. Arthur and Helen Glattke were buried in a small Catholic cemetery in Toledo, Ohio. Arthur, Sr.'s parents, two of his brothers and other family members are buried in a Jewish cemetery across the Maumee River, east of Toledo, Ohio.

The Riot of 1957

By the late 1950s conditions at the prison were extreme. An inmate hung himself in his cell in 1955. One burned himself to death in his cell with turpentine and paint thinner stolen from the prison furniture shop. Two convicts were left in a cramped single-occupancy solitary confinement cell overnight. The next morning only one walked out. The other, according to legend, was stuffed under the bunk. This led to rumors and legends of this being a common occurrence. (Internet: http://www.forgottenoh.com/OSR/osr.html)

The prison's most violent events happened in 1957. A riot put an estimated 120 inmates in "The Hole," the 20 solitary confinement cells in a basement level of the prison, for 30 day stints. The Hole is a place that has witnessed the darkest side of human nature. The legend became "two men enter and only one came out alive." The bodies of the murdered inmates were allegedly secreted away under the beds. Visitors to The Hole report being impressed with "experiences of intense residual negative energy."

Mansfield Prison from a distance.
(Photos courtesy of www.mansfieldtourism.com)

Many visitors tell the same stories. Some say that they have recorded strange sounds and scary voices on EVP recorders and other medium. Other visitors say that they have become sick to their stomachs and hear ghostly footsteps following them. Still others have reported a feeling of being watched, some even claiming to see glowing eyes peering at them through the darkness. Visitors and investigators exploring the entire prison report being "physically and mentally exhausted." There seem to be few reasonable or logical explanations for some of these occurrences, leading paranormal investigators to travel to the old prison in hopes of discovering macabre mysteries from the past.

Dr. Robert J. Girod, Sr.

Ghost image in cell? Filmed by a TV-10 reporter.
(Courtesy of Jackie Waite)

Ghost Busters: Paranormal Investigators

Whether one believes in such phenomenon or not, most people are intrigued by a good ghost story. Several groups of paranormal investigators or "ghost busters" have conducted investigations during one of the scheduled ghost hunts that take place each year. Some of these teams include police investigators, psychologists, professors from various disciplines, theologeans, technicians and scientists. On one evening the weather was overcast with light sprinkles and a temperature of 70 degrees at the start of an investigation. By the end of their tour it was raining heavily and the temperature had dropped to the upper 50's. The investigators started their research in the west administration building shortly before 2100 hours (9:00 p.m.). The lights are normally turned off during such inquiries, so a flashlight was necessary to avoid the many hazards inside the prison.

Legend says that the "ghosts" of two young boys, aged 16 at the time of death, who were inmates at the Reformatory during the 1940s, appear in the basement. Ghost-hunters claim that, using "dowsing rods" as a form of communication and an EVP on a cassette tape recorder they have been able to communicate with these apparitions. Ghost-hunters say that the L-shaped "dowsing rods" (similar to the divining rods used for "witching water") are used to seek ghosts by adjusting to the magnetic fields radiating from the targeted paranormal energy. The rods conform to a cross or "X" and move together to point in the direction of paranormal energy.

Ohio State Reformatory, Mansfield, Ohio.
(Photos courtesy of www.mansfieldtourism.com)

Though no distinct voices have been reported, high and low pitched squealing sounds are thought by researchers to be direct communications with the "spirits." These investigators say that they are able to look at the LCD screen on an infrared-capable camcorder and see orbs flying around the area. Orbs are transparent spheres thought to carry the circles of energy and that are sometimes caught on film or video. These are also attributed to "backscatter" of chromatic aberrations (the reflection of normally invisible particles). Moving orbs, paranormal investigators say, can also resemble a mist or a ball of fire.

The investigators found no signs of paranormal activity in the west administration building, so they headed to the east administration wing. On the second floor of the wardens living quarters the investigators reported that their camcorder had recorded several orbs in motion inside a large room at the front of the prison. Their "dowsing rods" also indicated that paranormal energy was present.

A continuous counter-clock-wise spinning of the left rod occurred at the same time the orbs were videotaped. The second floor hallway, just outside of the large room, also indicated paranormal activity to the ghost busters, who started to experience unexplained equipment failures. The investigators were excited when several orbs were captured on the camcorder with activity lasting for more than 25 minutes. Fear was predominated by the excitement of their discoveries. Most of the orbs could be seen coming down the stairs leading to the third floor and shooting over their heads. Their camcorder suddenly turned off while they were filming the orbs in motion. A ghost hunter from another group also had camcorder and camera malfunctions at the same time.

During the time they were filming the orbs they recorded several spikes on an EMF detector (an electromagnetic field meter used for measuring electromagnetic radiation), most jumping to between 3 and 4 on the meter. One spike nearly buried the needle at the upper range. The dowsing rods and the EMF meter also indicated paranormal energy was present in a family bedroom across from the large room they were in earlier.

The investigators left the administrative wings and continued in the prisoner holding areas. As they ascended a set of stairs in the west wing, one investigator reported feeling a pressure like someone was holding them back with the palms of their hands. The dowsing rods began another counter clock wise spinning motion half way down the row of cells in the isolation wing.

At the end of the east cell block, in a small room that is filled with toilets that appear to have never been used, the left dowsing rod was spinning counter clock wise just inside the door to this room. The investigators said that the "evidence" they gathered included EMF readings, dowsing-rod activity, and orbs filmed in motion on the camcorders. They said that there was a lot of dust in the air, so the investigators sought to determine the difference between the dust and the paranormal orbs. When researchers review video tape of the orbs, many report that the paranormal orbs do not show the same movement patterns as the dust. These orbs reportedly change direction and dart up or down across the screen, only briefly remaining still. Many research teams and investigators report strange phenomenon which most of us cannot explain. Many of these ghost busters have their own explanations and theories.

Ohio State Reformatory today.
(Photos courtesy of www.mansfieldtourism.com)

Dr. Robert J. Girod, Sr.

Ohio State Reformatory Today

Today the Ohio State Reformatory at Mansfield attracts tourists, moviemakers, and paranormal investigators who seem to appreciate not only the ancient, imposing prison structure, but the history and mystery that the old institution still holds within its walls. The architecture lured Hollywood to OSR to film portions of *Harry and Walter Go to New York* in 1975 and *Tango and Cash* in 1989, bringing major stars to Mansfield, including James Caan, Elliot Gould, Diane Keaton and Michael Caine (*Harry and Walter*) and Sylvester Stallone and Kurt Russell (*Tango and Cash*). Hollywood blockbuster movies like *Shawshank Redemption* and *Air Force One* have also been filmed on the grounds of the Mansfield Reformatory.

Today the Mansfield Reformatory Preservation Society (MRPS) holds the deed to the prison and leases the land from the State of Ohio. MRPS conducts Hollywood tours and public ghost hunts inside the gothic prison for a specified donation to the society. During the hunts, volunteer guides roam the former prison to answer questions and tell visitors about the history of the 120-plus year-old building. Visitors are urged to bring flashlights (for things that go bump in the night) and are encouraged to explore on their own. Hunts are open to 100 visitors each night and the admission includes a late-night pizza dinner. Participants must be 21 or older. For more information contact: www.mansfieldtourism.com. Happy haunting!

CHAPTER FOUR

THE CURSE OF THE HOPE DIAMOND

Watson, if it should ever strike you that I am getting a little over-confident in my powers, or giving less pains to a case than it deserves, kindly whisper "Norbury" in my ear, and I shall be infinitely obliged to you.

~ Sherlock Holmes ~

Sir Arthur Conan Doyle

To Catch a Thief

The image of art thieves and jewel thieves conjures visions of "cat burglars" (so called because of their stealth). A classic illustration is the 1955 movie *To Catch a Thief* starring Cary Grant as a former thief suspected of a new series of crimes and Grace Kelly as the woman who romances him. The movie portrays Cary Grant as a former resistance hero and gentlemanly cat burglar who is retired from the trade. But there's someone out there who's using all his old cat burglar tricks and putting him in the trick bag. Unlike a lot of Alfred Hitchcock films this one doesn't have all that much mystery to it, but the backdrop of the French Riviera makes the romance of this adventure alluring. Grace Kelly met her future husband, Prince Rainier, on the set of the movie and the road where she takes Cary Grant for a speeding car ride in the film. It is the same road where the automobile accident occurred which took her life a years later.

Real life cat burglars aren't as romantic as those in the cinema, at least not always. Take for example petty thief Russell Grant-McVicar, who walked into England's Lefevre Gallery in March, 1997, and asked an employee if the painting he was viewing was a Picasso. After the employee confirmed that it was the "Tete de Femme," the thief pulled out a sawed-off shotgun and stole the million-dollar masterpiece, fleeing in a taxi cab waiting for him outside. He may have gotten away with it, but for the fingerprints left on the frame which he left behind in the cab.
(Internet: http://www.courttv.com/news/hiddentraces/heist/stupid_crimes.html)

In 1978, three Cezanne paintings, then valued at $3 million, were stolen from the Art Institute of Chicago. A museum employee who had been there just a month had been asking the curator about their value and left that day carrying "packages." When the police searched his home, they found an essay that the thief wrote about his thefts. (Internet: http://www.courttv.com/news/hiddentraces/heist/stupid_crimes.html)

A burglar broke into the Budapest Kiscelli Museum and absconded with $400,000 worth of art treasures until he slipped on the wet grass outside. Awakening the vagrants who were camped nearby, the burglar was not only robbed of the artwork, but his wallet and clothes. More than thirty hours later he was found lying outside the crime scene. (Internet: http://www.courttv.com/news/hiddentraces/heist/stupid_crimes.html)

Somewhat more consistent with the image of the sophisticated art thief was art smuggler Jonathan Tokeley-Perry, who bought an Egyptian sculpture for $7,000, hoping to fence it for $50,000 from a New York art dealer. He smuggled it out of Egypt by dipping it in melted plastic and painting it black to appear as "junk." Art dealer Frederick Schultz actually paid him $915,000 for the piece – a tidy profit until he was arrested and sentenced to three years

FACTS ABOUT THE HOPE DIAMOND

Diamonds are commonly judged by the "**four Cs**" - **C**arat, **C**larity, **C**olor, and **C**ut.

Carat: 45. 52 carats. The *carat weight* measures the mass of a diamond. One carat is defined as a fifth of a gram or exactly 200 milligrams (approximately 0.007ounce).

Clarity: VS1 – *Very Slightly Imperfected* is the upper grade in this range and the hallmarks of this very desirable grade of diamond; extremely minor imperfections that are impossible to see with the unaided eye and are even difficult to locate under 10X magnification.

Color: Dark blue (after exposure to ultraviolet light it phosphoresces red, while most other blue diamonds phospheresce light blue)

Cut: The *cut* of a diamond describes the manner in which a diamond has been shaped and polished from its beginning form as a rough stone to its final gem proportions. The cut of a diamond describes the quality of workmanship and the angles to which a diamond is cut. Often diamond cut is confused with "shape."

Size: 21.78 millmeters wide, 25.60 millimeters long, and 12.00 millimeters deep.

The Hope Diamond is surrounded by sixteen white diamonds and another 45 white diamonds making up the necklace chain.

But what is the real story behind art and jewel thieves, the Hope Diamond and the mysteries behind the deaths of those who possessed her?

The Legend of Hope

According to the legend, a curse befell the large, blue diamond when it was stolen from an idol in India. The curse promised bad luck and death not only for the owner of the diamond but for anyone who touched it. Whether or not you believe in the curse, the Hope diamond has intrigued people for centuries. Its perfect quality, large size, and rare color make it unique and uncommonly beautiful.

The Hope Diamond is a brilliant, deep-blue faceted, ovoid diamond that measures 25.60 millimeters by 21.78 millimeters by 12.00 millimeters and weights 45.52 carats. It is set in a pendent, which is encircled by sixteen white diamonds. Its color is a combination of blue (which is caused by boron, as in all blue diamonds) and gray. From different angles vivid reds, yellows, and greens can also be seen. The Hope Diamond is characterized by its depth, intensity of its color, and the highlights that flash from its facets, which observers find are truly unique.

Where has the Hope diamond been and is there really a curse? This jewel has an intriguing and varied history. It was owned by King Louis XIV, stolen during the French Revolution, sold to earn money for gambling, and worn to raise money for charity. The diamond's known history dates to 1830 when David Eliason, a noted gem dealer, sold the stone to Henry

Thomas Hope. After numerous owners and mysterious mishaps, the Hope diamond was donated to the Smithsonian Institution and remains a truly a unique centerpiece of the Museum's gem collection. The Hope Diamond was presented to the Smithsonian by Harry Winston, a New York gem merchant, on November 10, 1958, after being acquired in 1949 from the estate of Mrs. Evelyn Walsh McLean. She received it from her husband, Edward B. McLean, in 1911.

Catch Me If You Can: It Takes a Thief

You may have already deduced that the Hope Diamond gets stolen and that some of the would-be possessors have met untimely and mysterious deaths. But does this story really reflect the "who-dunnit" of traditional literary jewel thieves? Are there such thieves in today's society and under-world? Art theft is big business and the National Criminal Intelligence Service estimates that raids on British collections net up to £100 million worth of art works each year. Interpol suggests that art theft may be the fourth largest criminal activity in the world, after drugs, money laundering and arms dealing. Scotland Yard officials suspect that many new art theft gangs originate in the Balkans and Eastern Europe. Rare treasures are often stolen to order by gangs who use them to launder money or as payment for drugs and arms. Stolen art is used in illicit exchanges because no cash is required, either in hand or through bank accounts.

Charles Sobhraj was a jewel thief, con man, drug dealer and murderer, who lived a life of adventure and intrigue which brought him near-celebrity status in the media. A Vietnamese-Indian by birth and French national by adoption, his illicit operations brought him enough money to provide him with whatever he wanted during his incarceration, including the drugs and food that he used to entertain and control fellow inmates in the prison that was reputedly the harshest in India. Sobhraj was implicated in more than 20 murders in various countries, including Thailand, Nepal and India. His *modus operandi* was to befriend the victims, then drug them, rob them, and strangle or even burn them. (Internet: http://www.rediff.com/

news/2003/oct/06spec1.htm) He turned a homicide sentence in India into a life of comparative leisure and evaded prosecution for a dozen murders in jurisdictions that might have resulted in a death sentence. At 52 years old, Sobhraj left Delhi's Tihar prison, signed a $15 million contract for his life story and charged $5,000 an interview in Paris. (Internet: http://en.wikipedia.org/wiki/ Charles_Sobhraj)

More along the lines of *It Takes a Thief*, the 1968-1970 TV series in which suave cat burglar Alexander Mundy (Robert Wagner) plies his trade for the U.S. Government, is the movie *Catch Me If You Can* (2002, starring Leonardo DiCaprio), the true story about Frank Abagnale Jr. who, before his 19th birthday, successfully conned millions of dollars worth of checks as a Pan Am pilot, doctor, and legal prosecutor. The story-line of thief-turned-bounty-hunter runs true in the world of art and jewel theft as well. David Duddin is a convicted art thief who lives in Newcastle-upon-Tyne (England). He was approached in 1999, while he was serving time, by former policeman Charles Hill to use his underworld contacts to recover stolen art for a bounty or fee. (Internet: http://news.bbc.co.uk/1/hi/england/2029166.stm)

An even more accurate portrayal of the "cat burglar" jewel thief is the story of the Hyde Park burglar who, described as a "smartly dressed young man," was caught on CCTV video in the Bayswater apartment block of Paddington (England) where three burglaries netted the thief nearly $100,000 worth of jewelry. A Russian oil consultant had just left her flat when the burglar found his way into her bedroom and absconded with her family heirlooms of gems and five watches. A commissioned set of jewelry, which consisted of a ring, earrings and a necklace by Italian designer Carlo Luca from Guerzia Giooelleri, comprised nearly half of the nights haul. There were no signs of forced entry, leading the police to believe the burglar used lock picks. For a "glamorous jewel thief" he exhibited the characteristics of a common petty thief, taking purses and handbags, credit cards and other petty larceny objects.(Internet: http://www.thisislocallondon.co.uk/ specialreports/ameliemurder/display.var.576848.0.0php)

Today's typical art thief is less the "cat burglar" and more the "businessman." A case in point is Edward Forbes Smiley III, of Martha's Vineyard, Massachusetts. Smiley was caught in June 2005 leaving Yale University's Beinecke Library with five rare maps in his briefcase and tweed jacket. After being taped on surveillance video removing the maps, valued at $150,000, from a book, Smiley admitted in court in New Haven to having stolen 97 maps, worth at least $3 million, from seven institutions over a seven-and-a-half year period. Following the announcement of the once respected map dealer's arrest, Harvard University's Houghton Library discovered eight of the their collection's rare maps missing, including a 1524 A.D. map of the New World by conquistador Hernan Cortes. (Harvard Magazine, p. 72)

Smiley, age 50, studied church history and classics at Hampshire College and spent a year at Princeton Theological Seminary before becoming a map dealer. He sold most of his stolen treasures to private collectors and other dealers. Authorities have recovered 86 stolen maps, six others have been located but not returned, and five were reported to be "unrecoverable." The thief established a restitution fund from the sale of property in Maine and his "half interest" in the home on Martha's Vineyard. His ill-gotten gains cost him a mere 57 to 71 months in prison. (Harvard Magazine, p. 72)

So who were the thieves of the Hope diamond? Well, they were many, as were those who possessed the treasure and are said to have been cursed by its possession.

Taken from the Forehead of an Idol

The diamond is believed to have come from the Kollur mine in Golconda, India. The legend is said to begin with a jewel theft several centuries ago. It is known that around 1631A.D. gem merchant Jean Baptiste Tavernier made the first of his six trips to the Orient. In 1642 the French jeweler visited India and bought a large 112 3/16 carat blue diamond, which had reputedly been stolen from the forehead or eye of a statue of the Hindu goddess Sita. This diamond was much larger than the present weight of the Hope diamond but it is also known that the Hope diamond has been cut at least twice in the past three centuries.

Tavernier returned to France in 1668, twenty-six years after he acquired the magnificent blue diamond. It was then that he revealed what was then called "the Tavernier Blue," weighing 112 carats (nearly the size of a man's fist), but he never explained how he acquired the gem. King Louis XIV of France purchased the large, blue diamond from Tavernier, along with forty-four other large diamonds and 1,122 smaller diamonds. According to legend, Tavernier was torn apart by wild dogs (purportedly for his theft) while he was on a trip to Russia after he had sold the diamond. This was the first of several macabre deaths attributed to the curse. Records indicate that Tavernier was made a noble and, in fact, did die in Russia at the age 84, but it is not known for certain how he died.

Experts suggest that the shape of the diamond was unlikely to have been an eye or on the forehead of an idol. (Patch, pp. 44 and 55) In 1673, King Louis XIV decided to re-cut the diamond to enhance its brilliance. The previous cut had been to enhance size, but not the brilliance. The newly cut gem was 67 1/8 carats. Louis XIV officially named it the "Blue Diamond of the Crown" and would often wear the diamond on a long ribbon around his neck.

Revolution and Jewel Theft

In 1749, Louis XV, was king and ordered the crown jeweler to make a decoration for the Order of the Golden Fleece, using the blue diamond and the Cote de Bretagne (a large red spinel thought at the time to be a ruby). The resulting decoration was extremely ornate and large. (Patch, pp. 44 and 55) When Louis XV died, his grandson (Louis XIV's great-grandson), Louis XVI, became king with Marie Antoinette as his queen. According to the legend, Louis XVI and Marie Antoinette were beheaded during the French Revolution because of the blue diamond's curse. Although both King Louis XIV and King Louis XV had possession of and wore the blue diamond a number of times neither suffered any consequences attributed to the curse.

Though it is true that Louis XVI and Marie Antoinette were beheaded, it seems likely that it had more to do with the French Revolution than a curse on the diamond, as they were not the only ones beheaded during the Reign of Terror.

During the French Revolution, the crown jewels (including the blue diamond) were taken from the royal couple after they attempted to flee France in 1791. The jewels were placed in the treasury at the Garde-Meuble but were not well guarded. The repository was usually well guarded and tightly sealed, but sometime between September 12 and 16, 1791 (or September 1792, depending upon which account you read) it became the scene of an infamous spree of burglaries. When bands of men came to steal its valuable contents, one of the metal bars that were supposed to keep the windows shut was unsecured, granting the men easy access. The thefts went without notice by officials until September 17 and, though most of the crown jewels were soon recovered, the blue diamond was not. With that, the French Blue disappeared from history because no blue diamond of its weight and appearance was ever recovered.

Why it is called the "Hope diamond"?

There is some evidence that the blue diamond resurfaced in London between 1812 and 1813 after being missing for about twenty-two years. John Françillion wrote a memorandum documenting the presence of a large blue diamond weighing over forty-five carats. By 1823 it had come into the possession of a jeweler named Daniel Eliason. (Patch, p. 18) At about the same time an illustrated prospectus for the sale of the diamond was discovered, signed by the gem's owner, Daniel Eliason. It was speculated that the diamond was cut from the French Blue.

No one is sure that the blue diamond in London was the same one stolen from the Garde-Meuble because the one in London was of a different cut and the blue diamond that surfaced in London was about 44 carats. Most experts, however, opine that because of the size, unusual color, and rare perfection of the French blue diamond and the blue diamond that appeared in London, it is likely that someone re-cut the French blue diamond in the hopes of concealing its origin.

There is some evidence that shows King George IV of England bought the blue diamond from Daniel Eliason and upon King George's death, the diamond was sold to pay off debts. Henry Philip Hope was one of the heirs of the banking firm Hope & Company, which was sold in 1813. He was a collector of fine art and gems and sometime around 1939 he came to acquire the large blue diamond that came to be known as the Hope diamond. Legend tells that the Hope family was afflicted with the diamond's curse and that the once-rich Hopes went bankrupt because of the Hope diamond.

Since he had never married, Henry Philip Hope left his estate to his three nephews when he died in 1839. The Hope diamond went to the oldest of the nephews, Henry Thomas Hope. Henry Thomas Hope married and had one daughter. She married and had five children. When Henry Thomas Hope died in 1862 at the age of 54, the Hope diamond stayed in the possession of Hope's widow, but when she died, she passed the Hope diamond on to her grandson, the second oldest son, Lord Francis Hope, who took the maternal name of Hope in 1887.

Records indicate that Francis Hope was only given access to the life interest on his grandmother's estate. History reveals that in 1898, because of gambling and excessive debt, Francis petitioned that the court sell the Hope diamond for him or aloow him to do so. His request was denied and in 1899 he appealed the case, but was again denied. In both cases, Hope's siblings opposed selling the diamond. But in 1901, on an appeal to the House of Lords, Francis Hope was finally granted permission to sell the diamond for $148,000. Three generations of Hopes were unaffected by the curse and it seems most likely that Francis Hope's gambling and spending habits, rather than the curse, caused his bankruptcy.

Evalyn Walsh with her parents and brother.
(Public domain photo)

Evalyn Walsh (age and year unknown)
(Public domain photo)

The McLean family.
(Public domain photo)

The Hope Diamond as a Good Luck Charm

Simon Frankel, an American jeweler from New York, bought the Hope diamond in 1901. He kept the Hope Diamond in the business safe of Joseph Frankel & Sons for six years. After this, possession changed hands several times over the next several years, until it came into the possession of jeweler Pierre Cartier. Cartier believed he had a wealthy buyer, Evalyn Walsh McLean. Mrs. McLean, wife of *Washington Post* owner Edward McLean, first saw the Hope diamond in 1910 while visiting Paris with her husband. She had previously told Cartier that artifacts which were usually considered bad luck by others seemed to turn into good luck for her, so Cartier made sure to emphasize the Hope Diamond's mysterious history. The legend of the curse on the diamond did not appear in the press, however, until the twentieth century, leading to some speculation that Cartier may have extrapolated the concept of a curse to impress Mrs. McLean. (Patch, p. 58) But Mrs. McLean did not like the diamond in its current mounting and she did not buy it at that time.

Evalyn Walsh McLean (date unknown).
(Public domain photo)

Infamous Murders and Mysteries

A few months later, Pierre Cartier arrived in the U.S. and asked Mrs. McLean to keep the Hope Diamond for the weekend. Having reset the diamond into a new mounting, Cartier hoped she would grow attached to it over the weekend. His plan must have worked and Evalyn McLean bought "The Hope." She constantly wore the diamond and, reportedly, only took it off after a great deal of cajoling by her doctor for a goiter surgery to be performed. (Patch, p. 30)

Evalyn Reynolds and Evalyn Walsh McLean.
(Public domain photo)

Evalyn Walsh McLean with Hope Diamond
(Public domain photo provided by: http://en.wikipedia.org/wiki/Image:Evalyn_Walsh_McLean_with_Hope_Diamond.jpg)

Before she owned the Hope Diamond, mining heiress Evalyn Walsh McLean lived in an ornate mansion at 2020 Massachusetts Avenue. This building, now the Indonesian Embassy, was McLean's first East Coast address. Her life seemed to change for the worse after she married *Washington Post* owner Edward McLean and acquired the infamous jewels. Having heard some of the stories associated with the curse, Evalyn McLean reportedly had a priest bless the diamond before she ever wore it, but this did not abate her family's tragic destinies. Though Evalyn wore the Hope diamond as a good luck charm, others came to believe that the curse afflicted her and her family too.

Evalyn and Edward McLean had a large staff, but even surrounded by servants they were not able to protect the McLean's older son, Vinson, from a freak automobile accident. Vinson died in a car crash when he was only nine. Not long afterward, the McLeans underwent a bitter divorce and in 1933 Evalyn persuaded the court to commit her husband to an asylum. Edward was declared insane and confined to a mental institution until his death in 1941 of a heart attack.

In 1946, their only daughter, Evalyn Reynolds, died of an overdose of sleeping pills at age 25, possibly the result of a suicide. Mrs. McLean outlived her daughter by just one year. She died of pneumonia and was buried in Rock Creek Cemetery, Washington D.C., in the Walsh family tomb. For the McLean's, if it was real, the curse was complete.

Though Evalyn McLean had wanted her jewelry to go to her grandchildren when they were older, her jewelry was put on sale in 1949, two years after her death, in order to settle debts from her estate. New York jewelry broker Harry Winston acquired the Hope Diamond and sent it to the Smithsonian Institution on "permanent loan." Reputedly, a female spirit, believed by some to be Evalyn McLean, is occasionally sighted at the old 2020 Massachusetts Avenue house, roaming the halls and stairways. Witnesses claim that the female figure that glides down the great staircase of the mansion appears in the nude.

J. Edgar Hoover Gets the Hope Diamond

During the Warren G. Harding administration (1921-1923), Harry Daugherty ran the U.S. Department of Justice as Attorney General. Critics believed that this was like sending the fox to guard the henhouse, but President Harding was indebted to Daugherty for helping him to win the U.S. presidency.

So Daugherty was appointed to the highest law enforcement position in the land as U.S. Attorney General. Heading up the Bureau of Investigation within the Justice Department was William J. Burns, founding head of the William J. Burns International Detective Agency. Billy Burns allegedly secured his new job appointment at the Bureau of Investigation (BI, later the FBI) by sending one of his underlings, Gaston B. Means, to blackmail key people into supporting Burns. If this is true, it apparently worked.

FBI Director J. Edgar Hoover and Associate FBI Director Clyde Tolson.
(Public domain photo provided by: http://en.wikipedia.org/wiki/J._Edgar_Hoover)

Attorney General Harry Daugherty made Ned McLean, then-owner of the *Washington Post* newspaper, a "dollar a year" agent of the Justice Department. His "agent" status gave some legitimacy to McLean's participation in his spying and any "black bag" operations that he undertook. Agent McLean owned several properties, including a house at 1509 H Street, located only two blocks from the White House and just one block from the Justice Department. It was connected by a "secret" passage to another house owned by McLean, which was allegedly the unofficial headquarters for Daugherty's associates.

Gaston Means reputedly took orders from both Billy Burns and Jess Smith, but also worked for Ned McLean, Evelyn McLean (Ned's wife and then-owner of the Hope Diamond), and First Lady Florence Kling Harding. Means wrote in his book, ***The Strange Death of President Harding***, that Florence Harding had ordered him to investigate Harry Daugherty, but never reveals the results of his investigation or why. Means is said to have kept many secrets which gave him an advantage when Daugherty's organization disbanded.

Evalyn Walsh McLean (age and year unknown)
(Public domain photo)

After the suspicious death of President Warren G. Harding in 1923, the shady network operating at the house on H Street disbanded. Walter Thayer, another Burns Agency detective, Bureau of Investigation agent, and Secret Service agent during the Harding presidency, spent seven years researching a three-volume manuscript called **The Harding Poison Murder Case**. This manuscript asserted that Harding had been assassinated. The new B.I. director, J. Edgar Hoover, countered that Thayer was mentally unbalanced and ordered that the manuscript be destroyed.

The Hope Diamond, carrying the legendary curse, reputedly found its way into the possession of FBI Director J. Edgar Hoover when Evalyn McNeal died in 1948. The diamond was given to Hoover and upon receiving the gem, wrapped in brown paper (according to legend). Hoover reportedly went into a "frantic fit." The FBI Director unloaded the diamond in a hurry and the Hope Diamond now resides at the Smithsonian Institution. (Neither the FBI nor the Smithsonian will verify this legend).

Hope Donated to the Smithsonian

It is a fact, however, that when the Hope diamond went on sale in 1949, it was bought by Harry Winston, a New York jeweler. On numerous occasions Winston offered the diamond to be worn at balls to raise money for charity. While some postulate that Winston donated the Hope diamond to rid himself of the curse, but it is also a known fact that he had long hoped to help in creating a national jewelry collection. Winston donated the Hope diamond to the Smithsonian Institution in 1958. He wanted "The Hope" to be the focal point of the new gem exhibit and to inspire others to donate to the collection as well. On November 10, 1958, the Hope Diamond was sent in a plain brown box by registered mail to the Smithsonian, where it was met by a crowd of people who celebrated its arrival.

The weight of the Hope diamond for many years was reported to be 44.5 carats. In 1974 it was removed from its setting and found to weigh 45.52 carats. It is classified as a type IIb diamond, which are semi-conductive and usually phosphoresce. The Hope diamond "phosphoresces" a strong red color, which will last for several seconds after exposure to short wave ultraviolet light. The diamond's blue color is attributed to trace amounts of boron in the stone, as is characteristic of all blue diamonds.

The Hope diamond has been on display as part of the National Gem and Mineral Collection in the National Museum of Natural History at the Smithsonian Institution since 1998. After extensive remodeling of the display area, the Hope Diamond was exhibited in the new Harry Winston Room in the Hall of Geology, Gems and Minerals, where thousands of visitors crowd slowly by to view this mysterious jewel every day. Better just look, and don't touch!

CHAPTER FIVE

THE CAMBRIDGE FIVE: CLOAK AND DAGGER MURDER

All my instincts are one way, and all the facts are the other, and I much fear that British juries have not yet attained that pitch of intelligence when they will give the preference to my theories over Lestrade's facts.

~ Sherlock Holmes ~

Sir Arthur Conan Doyle

Trinity College, Cambridge University

The Cambridge Apostles

Great spies are more interesting in fact than in fiction and more fascinating in reality than in the legends that grow up around them. Through their treachery these spies are some of the most efficient of killers. Their murder victims are usually never seen by the intelligence agents who author their deaths. This was true enough on a chilly winter evening in 1950. The police radio sputtered a static sounding call to a police car cruising in Manhattan. A body was found shot twice in the head and one of NYPD's finest, walking a beat, was already on the scene. The squad arrived and detectives were called to the scene. The victim, Mr. Wilkerson, was a night watchman in Manhattan, New York City. He was walking to a subway to catch a train home for the night. What the detectives would not discover was who had killed him or why. The "why" was what the watchman had seemingly discovered and that would remain a secret now. The "who" was someone who did not want the secrets to be revealed by the man who may never have known what his discovery really meant. Mr. Wilkerson's place in history would barely be a punctuation mark in this story.

Dr. Robert J. Girod, Sr.

Kim Philby Donald Maclean
(Public domain photot: http://upload.wikimedia.org/wikipedia/en/c/c2/Kim_philby.jpg) (Public domain photo: http://en.wikipedia.org/wiki/Image:Maclean.jpg)

The *Cambridge Five* (sometimes known as the *Cambridge Four* or the *Ring of Five*) was a ring of British double-agents who spied for the Soviet Union during World War II and into the Cold War in the 1950s. Some intelligence experts believe that they may also have passed Soviet disinformation to the Nazis first, then betrayed their own country later. No novel by Ian Fleming or Tom Clancey creates the brilliance of this group of English spies. No James Bond film, with all of its gadgets and action, or Jack Ryan epic, with its characteristic realism, captures the real-life drama of the Cambridge spies. The four were not characters in a spy novel, but were real spies – Philby, Burgess, Blunt, and Maclean. Some say that the fifth spy has never been officially identified, though John Cairncross (code named "the Carelian") is commonly associated as "the Fifth Man." Others say that the only speculation is how many others were actually involved.

There has never been a more successful group of spies than this group who all met at Trinity College, Cambridge University, in the 1930s. They were traitors who betrayed their country and revealed many of the most important secrets of the free world to the communists. Their thirty years of spying for the Soviet Union was highly successful for their spymasters. They have been attributed as the most effective double agents against American and British interests in the Twentieth Century. All four were eventually exposed but none was ever caught.

Guy Francis de Moncy Burgess (cryptonyms [code names]: Hicks, Paul and Madchen, which is German for "girl") was a flamboyant, alcoholic homosexual who was born in Devonport, Devon, England, in 1911. He was begat from at least two generations of military officers. Evelyn Burgess married a naval officer, Lieutenant Commander Malcolm Kingsforth Burgess, son of Colonel Burgess of the Royal Artillery. Guy Burgess entered the Royal Naval College at Dartmouth at an early age but left abruptly for Eton, graduating in 1930. He went on to Cambridge and, at Trinity College, associated with the sons of wealthy men. He and his comrades got drunk at elite clubs nightly, toasting the lower classes and praising the virtues of Communism.

Guy Francis De Moncy Burgess
(Public Domain photos)

Anthony Blunt (cryptonyms: Johnson, Tony and Yan), was a little more discrete, but was also a homosexual. He was a foppish man who rose to knighthood as the Royal Curator of Art and used his post to make influential contacts.

Donald Duart Maclean (cryptonyms: Homer, Lyric, Wise and Stuart), was described as a tense and insecure diplomat of ambiguous sexual persuasion, though he was later married to wife, Melinda, and had children.

Perhaps the most intriguing of the group was Harold Adrian Russell Philby, known to most as "Kim" (cryptonyms: Stanley, Tom, Stanley, and Sohnchen, which is German for "Sonny"). He was a heterosexual who has been referred to as the "Spy of the Century." He was a Soviet mole who had infiltrated the British Secret Intelligence Service (SIS) or MI-6 and served the KGB for almost fifty years.

The Missing Man

In October of 1949 a farmer saw something floating in the sea near the Essex marshes and discovered that it was a torso with its hands tied, head and legs sawed off, and stab wounds in the chest. The chief superintendent of the London Metropolitan Police asked the assistant commissioner of the Criminal Investigation Department at Scotland Yard to send detectives to investigate. In addition to detectives from the Forensic Science Lab, detectives from the Criminal Intelligence Branch, the Flying Squad, and Special Branch went to the scene. The Special Branch detectives worked in protection and counter-intelligence, but their presence at the murder scene was due to information they received from MI5s C Branch (protective security and vetting).

While Scotland Yard and MI5 were not known for sharing much at that time, there was mutual interest in this case. The victim was determined to be an auto dealer who had been carrying a large sum of cash when he was reported missing two weeks earlier. He received the cash after selling a car to two unknown men. The manager of the nearby United Services Flying Club at Elstree reported to Scotland Yard that he had rented a plane to a man who had left the plane at another airport. A plane mechanic also reported that he remembered seeing the man carrying a heavy bundle to the aircraft. Still another witness told the detectives that he saw the man with two bundles tied with cord.

The Scotland Yard detectives picked up and questioned Brian Donald Hume. Two MI5 officers listened over a microphone in the next room. He admitted that he had rented the plane, but denied everything else. He finally admitted that he had dumped the bundles into the sea. He said that three men, calling themselves Mac, Green, and Boy, paid him to dump the bundles. Shyest was likely one of these men. Hume also admitted that he saw blood on the bundles, but that the men told him that they contained forging plates. Scotland Yard and MI5 looked for the three men, but they were never found. Meanwhile, Hume left London after a jury was unable to decide his guilt. He was acquitted, later confessed (but was unable to be recharged because of double-jeopardy), and made his way to Switzerland where he was arrested for another murder. He was sentenced to life in prison, but never revealed the identity of Shyest or the whereabouts of the three mystery men.

"The Fifth Man"

The term "friends" was spy trade jargon popularized by John leCarr`e, a former MI5 officer, in his popular novels. The "Five" comes from KGB defector Anatoli Golitsyn (Golitsin), who named Philby, Maclean and Burgess as part of a "Ring of Five." He said that he did not know who the other two agents were, but all three agents named by Golitsin had already defected to the Soviet Union. Of all the information provided by Golitsin, the only thing that was ever confirmed by independent sources was the exposure of John Vassall. Vassall was a relatively low-ranking spy who some believe may have been sacrificed to protect the identity of more important operatives.

Golitsin's information also suggested that Philby may be a member of the "Five," but Philby was already a suspect. He had been publicly accused in newspapers but he was in a country with no extradition agreement with Britain. Golitsin also provided information that is generally considered as highly improbable, such as the claim that Harold Wilson (then Prime Minister of the United Kingdom) was a KGB mole. To this day Golitsin's reliability remains in question and there has always been a great deal of controversy about the actual number and identities of double-agents in the Cambridge spy ring. When Blunt confessed he named several completely different people as those he had recruited into the spy ring, only adding to the confusion and mystery. At least a dozen suspects have been implicated as possible members of Golitsin's "Ring of Five" but none have ever been confirmed.

Due to Golitsin's information or disinformation, speculation as to the identity of "the Fifth Man" has been a mystery for decades now. It is now widely accepted that the spy ring probably had more than five members. Three other persons have confessed, several more were identified in confessions and credible circumstantial evidence implicates still others. The extent to which the following suspects can be regarded as members of "the Ring" depends upon the degree to which they knew and cooperated with each another. This remains largely unknown because even Philby, Burgess and Maclean primarily operated alone.

Some of the prime suspects include John Cairncross (1913-1995) who, it was publicly revealed in 1990, confessed in 1951. Most experts agree that Cairncross was, in fact, one of the Five. Cairncross had worked for the Treasury and during the war for the Government Code and Cipher School. He was also part of MI6 for a time. Additional KGB spies recruited at Cambridge were Leo Long, Dennis Proctor, Michael Witney Straight, and Alister Watson but most investigators believe that they were relatively independent rather than actual members of the Cambridge Spy Ring.

Sir Roger Hollis, at the time Director of MI5, was accused by Arthur Martin, head of MI5's Soviet counter-intelligence section at the time of being a member of the ring. Peter Wright, the MI5 officer assigned to investigate Hollis and Chapman Pincher, an investigative journalist who produced several exposés of failures in British counter-intelligence, has also been speculated as a possible, yet unlikely, suspect.

Guy Liddell (1892 - 1958), a close friend of Burgess and Goronwy Rees, was accused of being a spy by an anonymous informer in 1949. This was eventually written off as Soviet disinformation, but the accusation detroyed Liddell's career. He was accused of being a member of the Cambridge Spy Ring in the 1979 death-bed confession of Goronwy Rees, a close friend of both Guy Burgess and Guy Liddell. Rees admitted in an interrogation in

1951 that he had known Burgess was a spy and that he himself was a spy. But he also accused Guy Liddell of having been a member of the Ring.

Victor Rothschild (1910 to 1990), also known as the third Baron Rothschild, was accused of being yet another member of the ring by Roland Perry in his book *The Fifth Man*. Rothschild was a member, along with Blunt and Burgess, of the Cambridge Apostles. (Perry)

Anthony Blunt himself named four other suspects during his confession in 1964: Peter Ashby, John Cairncross (again, considered by most experts as the most likely suspect), Leo Long, and Brian Symon. Thus, there is substantial information leading to an inference that there were more than five members of the ring from Cambridge, many of whom held high positions in both British government and the intelligence services. Perhaps this issue is somewhat obscured further by the fact that some of the suspects were, in fact, spies, but operated independently and not as part of the "Ring of Five."

More Than Five: Other Members

The rooky KGB officer sat at a table in a windowless room in KGB Headquarters while a filing clerk piled stacks of files in front of him. The files were marked in red Cyrillic print: *"Transmission to Control, to Beria, to Stalin."* As he went through the dossiers, the young KGB officer was stunned as he read the history of five agents who had penetrated the highest levels of British intelligence community. Everything that Churchill, Roosevelt, or Truman discussed was immediately revealed to the Soviets. Their information was too important and reliable to be impeded by the usual vetting. Even the young intelligence officer did not know the true identity of Shyest, who at that moment was leaving a body on the Canadian side of the U.S.-Canadian border. The RCMP officers who were called once the man was found would note that the ferry boat skipper had been shot twice in the head, but there was no known motive. This would be another seemingly random, unsolved murder with an unknown motive. But Shyest knew that his presence after crossing the border undetected several times and with the help of the well-paid skipper, must remain undetected. Shyest was a member of the "Ring of

Five," but is actually a pseudonym for the other unconfirmed members of the spy ring – a composite of several possible members.

They were originally known as the Cambridge Spy Ring because all known members of the ring were recruited at Trinity College, Cambridge University, while members of the Cambridge Apostles, a secret, elite debating society based around Trinity and King's Colleges. It is believed they were recruited by Anthony Blunt, who was a Fellow at Trinity while the others were undergraduates, and who had also been an Apostle.

Another Apostle, Victor Rothschild, has also been suspected by many counter-intelligence experts of being another member of the group. Rothschild was recruited to work for MI5 during World War II in roles including bomb disposal, disinformation and espionage. Michael Whitney Straight was another known Soviet spy and a Cambridge Apostle who was suspected of being a member of "the Five."

Michael Whitney Straight was an American magazine publisher, novelist, and a patron of the arts. Born in New York City, as a member of the prominent Whitney family, Straight later relocated to London after his mother's remarriage. He attended the London School of Economics and, while a student at Cambridge University in the mid-1930s, he became a member of the Communist Party and a secret intellectual society known as the Cambridge Apostles.

After returning to the United States in 1937, Straight worked as a speechwriter for President Franklin Roosevelt and the Department of the Interior. In 1938 Straight worked with Iskhak Akhmerov, the KGB head of illegal operations. His family ties are also intriguing. In 1939 he entered into a relatively uneventful marriage with Belinda Crompton. His second wife, Nina G. Auchincloss Steers, was a half-sister of the writer Gore Vidal and a stepsister of Jacqueline Kennedy Onassis. In 1940 Straight secured a position in the Eastern Division of the U.S. State Department. He served in the United States Army Air Forces in 1942 as a B-17 Flying Fortress pilot, but remained in the U.S. for his service.

When the war ended Straight took over as publisher of his family-owned The New Republic magazine but left the magazine in 1956 and began writing novels. In 1963, Straight told family friend and Presidential special assistant, Arthur Schlesinger, Jr., about his communist connections at Cambridge. This admission confirmed that Anthony Blunt was the recruiter of the Cambridge Five spy ring. Straight later served as the deputy chairman of the National Endowment for the Arts from 1969 to 1977. In 1983, Michael Straight detailed his communist activities in a memoir titled After Long Silence. Michael Whitney Straight died of pancreatic cancer at his home in Chicago, Illinois, at the age of 87.

Master Spy: Harold Adrian Russell (Kim) Philby

Harold Adrian Russell (Kim) Philby has been called "the spy of the century" and is considered by most scholars and intelligence experts to be one of the most intriguing and successful of the Cambridge Five spy masters. Philby was born in 1912 in Ambala Haryana, India, the son a British Army officer, diplomat, explorer, and author. He was nicknamed "Kim" after a character in Rudyard Kipling's novel Kim about a young Irish Indian boy who spied for the British in India during the 19th century. It has been suggested that his father, while not a spy himself, was opposed to the British establishment. His father died in 1960.

SECRET INTELLIGENCE SERVICE
Her Majesty's Secret Service – MI6

Philby entered Cambridge University's Trinity College between 1928-1929, at the age of 16, and studied history and economics. He met Guy Burgess when he arrived at Cambridge in 1930. Philby joined the Cambridge University Socialist Society in 1931 and became its treasurer in 1932.

A confirmed communist, he went to Vienna in 1933 to aid refugees who were fleeing Nazi Germany. He met and married his first wife Alice (Litzi) Friedman-Kohlmann, a Jewish Communist, in 1934 and returned to England with her following their marriage on February 24. In 1936, he was directed by his Russian handlers to assume a pro-fascist cover and in 1937 he went to Spain as a journalist to cover the Spanish Civil War.

In 1940, Guy Burgess, who was working in Section D of SIS (later MI6) introduced him to Marjorie Maxse, another SIS officer. Philby was recruited as a British intelligence officer and became an expert in the art of "black propaganda." He became an instructor in methods of sabotage, subversion, and under-cover work and in 1941 he transferred to Section V (five) in MI6 where he trained American CIA counter-intelligence legend James Jesus Angleton.

In 1942 Philby married his second wife, Aileen Furse. Philby performed his training duties so successfully that he was promoted to a key position as head of the new Section IX (nine): counter-espionage against the Soviet Union 1944. This was a significant accomplishment for a Soviet double-agent.

In August, 1945, Konstantin Volkov, an officer of the NKVD (later KGB) defected to Britain, promising to reveal the names of Soviet agents in SIS and the Foreign Office. When the report reached Philby's desk, he made sure that he received the assignment and flew to Istanbul by way of Cairo. Philby's plane was delayed by storms and the ambassador was on his yacht in the Bosporus. This gave the Russians time to snatch Volkov and prevent his revelations. Meanwhile, Philby returned to London after a close call. The Russian agents who kidnapped Volkov took him to the Lubyanka in Moscow for interrogation and execution. This may not have been Philby's first involvement in a murder, but it certainly would not be the last.

In 1946, a Soviet officer, Lieutenant Skripkin, contacted British Naval Intelligence and offered to defect. Two Naval Intelligence Department (NID) reports, one in May and one July, 1946, were sent from the joint MI5-MI6 Security Intelligence Far East (SIFE) office in Singapore to MI5 headquarters in London. These reports are believed to have made their way into the hands of Kim Philby, who passed them on to the KGB. When Skripkin returned from the Far East to Moscow to get his wife, he was approached by two KGB officers who presented themselves as MI6 officers. Skripkin gave himself away and was eventually tried and shot. Philby later denied any involvement in Skripkin's murder or execution. (Wright, pp. 286-7)

After the war, Philby was sent as Head of Station to Istanbul, Turkey, under the cover of First Secretary to the British Embassy. While there, he received a visit from Guy Burgess. In 1949, Philby's next and last assignment was as First Secretary to the British Embassy in Washington, where he acted as the MI6 liaison between the British Embassy and FBI and the newly formed CIA.

Guy Francis De Moncy Burgess

The "Crown Jewels" was the title used by the KGB for the transcript reports of the infamous Cambridge spy ring. This reportedly included the report of Guy Burgess's offer to murder his fellow conspirator Goronwy Rees. A remorseless traitor, notorious drunk and flamboyant homosexual, Guy Burgess was far from being the ideal Soviet agent. Yet he was undeniably one of the Soviet's most effective spies during the Cold War. But he also had considerable help in his treacherous activities from others sharing his lifestyle of vice and corruption, including his friends Donald Maclean, Kim Philby and the foppish British art historian Anthony Blunt.

Burgess' father had been an officer in the Royal Navy and the lore and legend of the sea made Guy Burgess want to follow the family tradition to join the Navy. He attended the Royal Naval College at Dartmouth until he dropped out, claiming that it was because an eye problem disqualified him from Navy service. The real reason was that he had reputedly attempted to seduce some other youths at the institution. Burgess went on to Cambridge University and graduated from Eton in 1930. At Trinity College he and the sons of well-to-do men got drunk at clubs almost every night while toasting the lower classes and the virtues of Communism. In reality, none of these decidedly homosexual young men ever had anything to do with the working class and their "brand" of Marxism came in bottles of expensive, imported brandy. His roommate and the fellow classmate, Anthony Blunt, recruited him into the ranks Soviet double-agents.

In 1934, Guy Burgess, Donald Maclean, Kim Philby, and the others from Cambridge took a trip to Moscow, more for social than political reasons. The experience in the reality of socialist society did not agree with Burgess who found the Soviet city dreary and depressing. He stayed drunk during most of his holiday in Russia and was found drunk in the Park of Rest and Culture by the Moscow police. In his coat pocket the police found letters of introduction to prominent Russian scholars and politicians. Burgess and his weak-moraled clique lived and prospered through their social and academic connections.

Burgess got a job, through a friend, as a writer for the *London Times*. Through his connection with historian G. M. Trevelyan, he went to work for the British Broadcasting system in 1936. He produced a BBC political program called *The Week at Westminster*. Again, Burgess used his position to further his career, befriending politicians along the way who were able help in advancing his career. Among his political connections was Hector McNeil, who would become the Minister of State at the Foreign Office.

Throughout his time with the BBC, Burgess continued spying for the KGB, receiving information from John Cairncross of the Foreign Office and passing these secrets to the Soviets. He went to France in 1937 and in 1939 to meet with Kim Philby, who was then working as a journalist and reporting on the Spanish Civil War (1936-1939) and reporting to his Moscow masters all that he observed. When Philby returned to England at the end of the Spanish Civil War, he was interviewed by his friend, BBC correspondent Guy Burgess.

In January 1939, Burgess secured a post through his high-placed connections and went to work for MI6 in Department D, a growing section assigned to recruit new agents for SIS (MI6). In 1940 Burgess recruited his old Cambridge friend Kim Philby, whose impartial reporting on the Spanish Civil War had impressed many government officials. Once Philby was securely entenched at MI6, Burgess quit the secret service in 1941 to go back to the BBC where he could more easily communicate with his KGB masters. In 1944, Burgess joined the Foreign Office with the job of handling the news.

He had access to a great deal of classified secrets for the six years he was with this department and he passed them on to the Russians with ease.

Treachery in Washington, D.C.

Peter Wright, a senior MI5 officer, was in Hugh Winterborn's office. "The Third Man business is brewing up again," his boss said. "MI6 are interrogating one of their officers – chap named Philby. They want us to provide the microphone." Wright had met Philby before and immediately liked him. He had charm, style, and the two men shared the affliction of a chronic stutter. Philby had just been appointed MI6 Head of Station in Washington when he made his way around MI5 saying goodbye to friends and receiving briefings before departing for the new post. Philby had developed close ties with MI5 during the war, which Wright observed few MI6 officers bothered to take the trouble to do. (Wright, p. 43)

In January 1949, the British Government was informed that *Venona project* intercepts showed that nuclear secrets were passed to the Soviet Union from the British Embassy in Washington in 1944 and 1945 by an agent code-named "Homer." Philby received *Venona* material which the U.S. was sharing with the U.K., but he did not have information about the source, since *Venona* was top secret.

In October, 1949, Philby arrived in Washington as British intelligence liaison to the U.S. intelligence agencies. He was the MI6 (SIS) liaison to the Federal Bureau of Investigation (FBI) and the newly created Central Intelligence Agency (CIA), which was established under the National Security Act of 1947. The American and British governments planned an attempted revolution in Soviet-influenced Albania. The exiled King Zog had offered his troops and other volunteers to help, but for three years every attempted landing in Albania was met with a Soviet or Albanian Communist ambush and the Soviets knew the emergency radio call routine. Kim Philby is attributed with the betrayal which cost 300 Albanian lives and a similar betrayal which occurred in the Ukraine. Couriers would travel to Soviet territory and disappear, leading many intelligence professionals to accuse Philby and his associates of out-right murder.

In 1950 several teams of agents parachuted into the Soviet Union. Two of these missions disappeared without a trace. In March, 1951, Philby reportedly gave Guy Burgess the names and arrival points of three groups of six men who were to parachute into Ukraine. Anthony Blunt received this information and passed it directly to KGB officer Yuri Modin. None of these teams ever reported back. (Dorril, pp. 244-5)

Philby is also believed to have passed information on the United States' small stockpile of atomic weapons and its capacity to produce new atomic bombs to the Soviets. This likely influenced Stalin's decision to blockade West Berlin in 1948 and instigate a large-scale offensive armament of Kim Il Sung's North Korean Army and Air Force that would lead to the Korean War. That conflict would cost the lives of over one million Koreans and about 30,000 Allied soldiers and marines.

Donald Maclean (aka Homer) was also posted in Washington. His wife, Melinda, used the embassy as her official address, but went to New York with her first son, Fergus. They lived with her mother, Mrs. Dunbar, and stepfather. Homer's handler was in Manhattan and this made a convenient excuse for him to visit a couple of times per week. He also traveled back and forth to London where he kept Guy Burgess up-to-date on the information that he had collected. (Modin, pp. 117-118)

It was during this time that Klaus Fuchs, a nuclear physicist working on the Top Secret Manhattan Project, gave Alexandre Feklisov, his KGB case officer, the principal theoretical outline for creating a hydrogen bomb and initial drafts for its development. Fuchs met with Feklisov six times, making a connection between him and the infamous Ethel and Julius Rosenberg "atom bomb" espionage conspiracy. In 1947 Fuchs attended a conference of the Combined Policy Committee (CPC), created to facilitate exchange of atomic secrets between the highest levels of government of the United States, Great Britain and Canada. Donald Maclean also attended as British co-secretary of CPC. The information which Fuchs gave to Soviet intelligence in 1948 was confirmed by Donald Maclean's reports to his spy-masters.

Meanwhile, back in London, Burgess and Blunt were providing their case officer with weekly drops of secret documents. They brought so many that they exchanged suit cases. The KGB officer would copy the documents and return them by again exchanging cases. On one occasion KGB officer Yuri Modin, the handler, was walking with Burgess in an empty square. Burgess was carrying the suit case, which they habitually did not exchange until the last moment. Suddenly two policemen appeared and detained the two men. Modin was shocked, thinking that they had been careful not to attract suspicion. Burgess remained calm and held up the suit case. "Is this what concerns you, Officer?" he asked the Bobby. One nodded as Burgess stepped up to him and boldly opened the suit case, showing the Bobbies the contents. After a cursory search, the policeman said, "Sorry, Sir. Everything's quite in order." The two Bobbies saluted and walked away. Burgess explained to Modin that the burglars in London used similar cases to carry burglar tools and skeleton keys and this is what prompted the officers' suspicions. (Modin, pp. 175-7)

In January, 1950, Klaus Fuchs confessed to spying to MI5 officer William Skardon and was prosecuted by Sir Hartley Shawcross. He was convicted on March 1, 1950, and was sentenced to fourteen years in prison for passing military secrets. The Soviets denied that Fuchs was a Soviet spy, but Fuchs' admissions to British and American intelligence agencies was used in the Julius and Ethel Rosenberg spy investigation.

In August, 1950, Guy Burgess arrived in Washington as Second Secretary and Philby invited him to live at his home at 4100 Nebraska Avenue, N.W for the year. Mrs. Eleanor Philby hated the sight of Burgess. On many occasions she complained to her husband that Burgess was supercilious, loud, habitually drunk. She also knew and despised Burgess' reputation as a flagrant homosexual. Philby said nothing and Burgess stayed.

Shyest, who was working in Washington to agitate communist sentiments for Puerto Rico's independence, was also concerned about Burgess and his behavior. He knew that the time was near for him to leave Washington. But Shyest had other interests to facilitate. He let thoughts of "The Five" pass as he walked past the Blair House on Halloween night of 1950. The next day would make headlines. On Wednesday, November 1, 1950, White House Police Force Officer Leslie William Coffelt, age 40, was shot and killed when two Puerto Rican nationalists attempted to shoot their way into Blair House, the temporary residence of President Harry S. Truman, in Washington, DC.

White House Police Force Officer Leslie William Coffelt
(Public domain photo: http://upload.wikimedia.org/wikipedia/commons/7/7c/Coffelt.jpg)

Officer Leslie William Coffelt's funeral procession and service.
(Public domain photos)

Though mortally wounded by three 9 mm bullets, Coffelt killed one of the suspects, Griselio Torresola, with a single shot to the head. The other suspect was caught, arrested and sentenced to prison. He was pardoned after serving only 25 years and was deported to Puerto Rico, where he died in 1994. Officer Coffelt was a WWII veteran and had served with the White House Police Force for 15 years. He was survived by his wife and daughter.

Leslie William Coffelt's grave marker.
(Public domain photos)

Leslie William Coffelt's grave marker.
(Public domain photos)

Philby was asked to help track down the agent known as "Homer." Knowing from the start that "Homer" was his old friend, Second Secretary Donald MacLean, Philby warned MacLean in 1951, but Philby's luck was about to run out. The cryptonym *Homer* was discovered to be Donald Maclean in the Venona decrypts when a Soviet code clerk used a one-time pad twice. Also, Burgess's alcohol problem led to Ambassador Franks' decision to remove him and send him back to England. Soon afterwards both Maclean and Burgess disappeared from Britain with the help of Philby who was summoned back to England for interrogation.

The Get-away

A code breaking success uncovered evidence that someone was revealing nuclear secrets to the enemies of the West and Maclean came under suspicion. Though Philby tried to deflect suspicion on someone else, he discovered that Maclean was to be interrogated the following Monday, on May 28, 1951. Maclean had also worked at the British Embassy in Washington until being transferred back to London. By then Burgess and Maclean were both the subjects of a secret investigation. MacLean was identified in April and surveillance commenced to obtain evidence independent of *Venona*, because neither the U.S. nor the U.K. wanted to reveal the existence of *Venona*.

Philby warned Burgess that if Maclean was questioned he (Burgess) would be next. It was time to warn Maclean and then disappear. Burgess went on a rampage of drunkenness and reckless driving at high speeds. When the police stopped him Burgess cursed them, ripping up the speeding tickets and throwing them in the air, shouting, "I have diplomatic immunity from such nonsense!" The British Ambassador dismissed Burgess and ordered him to return to London. This was part of the plan to get Burgess back to England to warn Maclean.

Back in London on May 7, 1951, Burgess took the simple approach on how best to warn his friend. He dropped by the Foreign Office to see Maclean and simply handed him a slip of paper with a coded message telling

Maclean that he was about to be questioned, probably arrested, and that it was time for him to escape. Burgess returned to his apartment, packed a bag and called Maclean at home. It was Maclean's 38th birthday and he was about to sit down to a birthday dinner on the Friday evening of May 25, 1951. But he had no time to celebrate. Burgess drove to Maclean's suburban home in Surrey in a rented car where Maclean waited for him with his bag already packed. Saying his good-byes to his wife and three children, he hopped into the car with Burgess and drove off, making their way to a ferry for France.

Their escape route had already been worked out by a KGB spymaster who had been contacted by Anthony Blunt. The two men drove to Southampton, arriving in time to catch the 11:45 p.m. cross-Channel boat *S.S. Falaise* which was sailing to St. Malo, France. A dockside attendant shouted to both men as they scrambled up the gangplank, "Hey, what about the car?" Burgess called back with a slight smile, "Be back Monday." He knew that neither of the traitors would ever be back.

Burgess and Maclean went to their cabin, locked themselves in, and did not leave the cabin when the rest of the passengers disembarked in St. Malo to take the train to Paris. They remained in their cabin consuming a case of beer they had ordered from the steward. Later they staggered from the cabin and hired a taxi to drive them fifty miles to Rennes, where they caught a later train to Paris. Their false papers allowed them to travel to Vienna. The KGB arranged for them to fly to Czechoslovakia, then on to Moscow.

MacLean and Burgess made international headlines after their very public defection to the Soviet Union a month later in May of 1951. Burgess, reportedly, took with him nothing more than his dinner jacket, an overcoat belonging to Jackie Hewit (Anthony Blunt's boyfriend at that time) and his collection of Jane Austen.

Beirut

After Burgess and Maclean defected, Philby came under instant suspicion as the man who had tipped off Maclean and Burgess. He was asked to resign from SIS under a cloud of suspicion and his pension was withheld until an internal investigation was unable to confirm his guilt. He spent the next several years being questioned by MI5 and MI6 (SIS). Since he did not confess he was finally cleared in 1955 of being the "Third Man" by Foreign Secretary Harold Macmillan in the House of Commons. Although the new SIS chief suspected Philby of being a double-agent, Philby was re-hired as an MI6 secret service agent in 1956, with the cover as a correspondent in Beirut for The Observer and The Economist. In 1957 his second wife, Aileen, died and Philby married his third wife, Eleanor Brewer in 1958.

Investigators immediately realized that Burgess and Maclean had been tipped off and Philby was the prime suspect. The investigation of Philby revealed circumstantial evidence of suspicious activities, but not enough to prosecute the spy. Philby was forced to resign and in 1955 the news media named him as the chief suspect for "the Third Man." He was allowed to call a press conference to deny his involvement, but after being forced to leave MI6, Philby began working as a journalist in the Middle East. In 1956 Philby was re-hired by MI6 as an "informant on retainer" and was allegedly involved in the British, French, and Israeli plan to attack Egypt and depose Gamal Abdel Nasser.

In December 1961, Anatoli Golitsin (or Anatoliy Golitsyn, depending upon the transliteration), a KGB agent working in Finland, defected. The CIA had him flown to the United States and lodged in a safe house called Ashford Farm near Washington. He was interviewed by James Jesus Angleton and Arthur Martin, head of MI5's D1 Section. Golitsin supplied information about a large number of Soviet agents working in the West. In these interviews Golitsin said that as the KGB would be extremely concerned about his defection and would attempt to convince the CIA that the information he was giving them was unreliable. He predicted that the KGB would send false defectors with false information that contradicted what he was saying.

Golitsin claimed that Kim Philby, Donald Maclean and Guy Burgess were members of a Ring of Five agents based in Britain. However, he did not have the names of the other two agents. Martin came to believe that the Director General of MI5, Roger Hollis or his deputy, Graham Mitchell, could be spies and possibly members of the ring. Angleton believed that

Golitsin was telling the truth but most senior CIA officials did not. After the initial debriefing, the CIA sent MI5 a list of ten "serials," each one itemizing an allegation Golitsin had made about a mole in the British intelligence community. Martin initially held the complete list, then Patrick Stewart, the acting head of D3 (Research), conducted a preliminary analysis of the serials and constructed a list of suspects to fit each one. The individual serials were apportioned to different officers in the Dl (Investigations) section for detailed follow-up investigations and Peter Wright was asked to provide technical advice as the investigations required.

Sometime in late 1962, a British-Jewish woman, Flora Solomon, was attending a cocktail party in Tel Aviv and made a comment about how Philby, the journalist in Beirut, displayed sympathy for Arabs in his articles. She made the accusation that his masters were the Soviets and said that she knew that he had always worked for them. The comment was overheard by someone at the party and was relayed to MI5 in London, which then sent Victor Rothschild to interview her. Mrs. Solomon said that she would never testify against Philby, but admitted that he had told her he was a spy and had tried to recruit her for the Communists.

In January 1964 Yuri Nosenko, who wanted to defect to the United States, contradicted Golitsin's information. Nosenko also claimed that he had important information about the assassination of President John F. Kennedy. He told the CIA that he had been the KGB official who had handled the case of Lee Harvey Oswald. After interviewing Oswald, Nosekno asserted, it was decided that Oswald was not intelligent enough to work as a KGB agent. The KGB, Nosenko said, was also concerned that he was too mentally unstable to be of any value to them.

Infamous Murders and Mysteries

Anatoliy Golitsyn, KGB   Alexandr Feklisov, KGB

James Jesus Agleton, CIA   J. Edgar Hoover, FBI
(Public domain photos)

James Jesus Angleton, chief of the CIA's counter-intelligence section (Associate Deputy Director of Operations for Counterintelligence/ADDOCI), believed that Anatoli Golitsin was a genuine double-agent but that Nosenko may be a part of a Soviet disinformation campaign. However, CIA Director Richard Helms and FBI Director J. Edgar Hoover believed Nosenko and thought Golitsin was a liar. Peter Wright, MI5 Counter-intelligence officer, found Hoover to be an ordeal to deal with, but was impressed by Angleton's intensity and keen mind. He believed that Angleton was not just fighting the Cold War, but was determined to win it. He described Angelton as having a fascination for every "nuance and complexity of his profession" and "a prodigious appetite for intrigue." (Wright, p. 102) Yuri Nosenko was eventually released and was given a false identity. He became an adviser to the CIA and the FBI.

There seemed to be a leak of classified information and it was alleged that there was a high-level mole in the Security Service (MI5) at that time. Novelist Graham Greene, a close friend of Philby, reportedly left MI6 rather than become involved in exposing Philby. Although MI5 and MI6 could not agree at first on how to deal with Philby, it was eventually agreed that a personal friend of Philby from his MI6 days, Nicolas Elliott, would be sent to confront him in Beirut. It is not known whether Philby was aware of the accusations against him by Flora Solomon or whether he knew about the defection of Anatoly Golitsyn. When George Blake, a fellow MI6 officer and Soviet double-agent, was discovered as a spy in 1962, Philby was confronted by evidence brought to him by his old SIS friend, Elliott. Shortly afterwards Blake was arrested, escaped, and defected to Moscow. There is evidence that in the last few months of 1962 Philby began to drink heavily and his behavior became increasingly erratic.

The British Security Service MI5 agent reported that Philby knew he was coming and that the first thing that Philby said upon meeting with Elliott was that he was "half expecting" to see him. Many sources claim that he confessed immediately when confronted with the evidence, while others, including Philby himself, have maintained that he continued to downplay the accusations. Philby may have also been warned by Yuri Modin, a Soviet spy-master who had served in the Soviet embassy in London, when he traveled to Beirut in December of 1962. Modin was the reputed handler of the "Cambridge Five" spy ring.

Constantly only a step ahead of the danger that his cover would be blown by the next Soviet defector, Philby finally defected to the Soviet Union in

1963. Further interrogation was scheduled in the last week of January 1963, but Philby disappeared in Beirut on January 23. Records later revealed that the *Dolmatova*, a Soviet freighter, was called to port in Beirut on this date and had left so quickly that its cargo remained scattered on the dock. On March 3 Mrs. Philby received a telegram from her husband postmarked from Cairo, Egypt.

Sir Anthony Blunt: Surveyor of the Queen's Pictures

Sir Anthony Blunt was the Surveyor of the Queen's Pictures, an international art historian and a former MI5 Security Service officer. In 1963 MI5 was informed by the FBI that U.S. citizen Michael Whitney Straight had admitted that Blunt had recruited him for the Soviets while they were both at Cambridge University in the 1930s. MI5 sent Arthur Martin to interview Straight, who confirmed the information and agreed to testify in British court if necessary. In April, 1964, Blunt confessed to spying for Russia. (Wright, p. 213)

Peter Wright and other MI5 officers met with Blunt. "It's quite clear to me, reading the transcripts, that you have not been telling us the full truth...," Wright told Blunt. Blunt flinched as if struck. "I have told you everything which you have asked, Blunt replied, looking Wright straight in the eye. "That's nonsense, and you know it is too. You say you only know about Long and Cairncross, those were the only ones. I don't believe you!" Wright fired back. Blunt was not impressed, knowing they had nothing more on him. "Have you ever thought about the people who died?" Wright asked. "There were no deaths. I never had access to that type of thing..." Blunt smoothly replied. "What about Gibby's spy?" Wright asked, referring to an agent run inside the Kremlin by MI6 officer Harold Gibson. He was betrayed by Blunt and was executed. "He was a spy. He knew the game; he knew the risks," Blunt said coldly, letting down his guard for a moment (Wright, pp. 219-220) but apparently forgetting that he now stood in the same position.

As the investigation progressed, those associated with it began to die, some allegedly by natural causes and others by alleged suicide. Sir Andrew Cohen, who had also been at Cambridge with the others, had recently died of a heart attack. Peter Floud was already dead and his brother, Bernard Floud, allegedly committed suicide with a gas poker and a blanket. Phoebe Pool, a message runner, allegedly threw herself under a tube (public transit system) and was dead. (Wright, pp. 265-6)

Moscow: The Final Days of the Five

Mrs. Melinda Maclean and her three children disappeared in Switzerland on a holiday more than two years after her husband fled to Russia. They were taken into the Soviet Union to live with Maclean in Moscow, where he secretly continued with his work for the Soviet Foreign Ministry alongside his fellow spy and traitor Guy Burgess. The Russians paraded their prize double-agents before Western journalists in a 1956 press conference. Both Burgess and Maclean denied ever having spied, asserting that they were merely "peace lovers" who had become disillusioned with the West. Both men continued to work in the espionage business in Russia. Maclean appeared to adapt to the communist culture, but Burgess continued to drink heavily. His once handsome facial features became bloated as he gained weight. He spoke often of his native country and of missing his British culture. Miserable, Guy Francis de Moncy Burgess drank himself to death in Moscow, Russia, on August 30, 1963. That same year, Kim Philby, the most influential spy the Russians had in the West, finally fled to the Soviet Union.

Kim Philby surfaced in Moscow, quickly discovering that he was not a colonel in the KGB as he thought, but was still just an agent. It was ten years before he was permitted to walk through the doors of KGB headquarters. A traitor to his own country was looked upon with skepticism and distrust even by his own handlers. Philby, as his friends had, also suffered severe bouts of alcoholism. In Moscow, he seduced MacLean's American wife, Melinda, and abandoned his own wife, Eleanor, who left Russia in 1965. His autobiography,

My Silent War, was published in 1968. In 1972 Philby married a Russian woman, Rufina Ivanovna Poukhova, who was twenty years younger than he was. They lived together in Moscow until his death at age 76 in 1988. He was awarded a hero's funeral and numerous posthumous medals by a grateful USSR.

By 1979 investigative journalist Andrew Boyle publicly accused Anthony Blunt of being a Soviet agent in his book *Climate of Treason*. In November 1979 Prime Minister Margaret Thatcher announced to the House of Commons that Blunt had confessed to being a Soviet spy fifteen years earlier. Blunt had secretly been granted formal immunity by the Attorney General in exchange for allegedly revealling everything that he knew about the spy ring. He provided a considerable amount of information and, by preventing the Soviets from knowing that he had confessed, he had increased value as a "double-double-agent."

James Jesus Angleton (December 9, 1917 - May 12, 1987), known to friends and colleagues as Jim and nicknamed "the Kingfisher," was the long-serving director of the CIA's counter-intelligence division. Angleton's internal CIA code was KU/MOTHER and his cover name was Hugh Ashmead. An occasional poetry aficionado, avid fly-fisherman and orchid-grower, it has also been speculated that Angleton was either homosexual or bisexual who was himself under the control of the KGB, who were blackmailing him. Angleton died of lung cancer in Washington's Sibley Hospital on May 12, 1987. He was survived by a son, James Charles Angleton, and two daughters, Guru Sangat Kaur and Lucy d'Autremont Angleton.

Spy novelists Ian Fleming and John LeCarre had also worked in MI5 and were contemporaries of "The Cambridge Five." Ian Fleming was educated at Eton and Sandhurst Military Academy, studied languages and, during World War II, became a senior naval intelligence officer. He was first commissioned as a Royal Naval Volunteer Reserve lieutenant, promoted to Lieutenant Commander, and then Commander. When he worked for MI5 his known codename was 17F. Fleming's first novel, *Casino Royale* was published in 1953. The main character, James Bond, Secret Service Agent 007, was the hero in twelve spy novels by Fleming. Initially Fleming's Bond novels were not bestsellers in America, but when President John F. Kennedy included *From Russia With Love* on a list of his favorite books, sales quickly jumped.

In March 1956 Fleming wrote in the "Author's Note" of *From Russia With Love*:

Not that it matters, but a great deal of the background to this story is accurate.

> SMERSH, a contraction of *Smiert Spionam* – Death to Spies – exists and remains today the most secret department of the Soviet government.
> At the beginning of 1956, when this book was written, the strength of SMERSH at home and abroad was about 40,000 and General Grubozaboyschikov was its chief. My description of his appearance is correct.
> Today, the headquarters of SMERSH are …at No. 13 Sretenka Ulitsa, Moscow. The Conference Room is faithfully described and the Intelligence chiefs who meet round the table are real officials who are frequently summoned to that room for purposes similar to those I have recounted.

(Fleming, Author's Note)

Nearly six hundred books from Fleming's collection are in the Lilly Library at Indiana University, in Bloomington, Indiana. Fleming died of a heart attack on August 12, 1964, in Canterbury, Kent, England, at the age of 56, and was buried in the churchyard of Sevenhampton village, near Swindon. Upon their deaths, Fleming's widow, Ann Geraldine Mary Fleming (1913–1981), and son Caspar Robert Fleming (1952–1975), were buried next to him.

The number of deaths that resulted from the direct and indirect operations of the Cambridge Five will never be known. The treachery perpetrated by this ring will hold bitter memories for the professional intelligence officers who remember their deeds. Their activities will have a place in history as among the greatest betrayals and most effective spy rings of all time. The murders that were committed in the process will remain largely unknown and little more than a footnote in the chronicles of murder.

CHAPTER SIX

THE KENNEDY ASSASSINATION: DECLASSIFIED (PART I)

Perhaps when a man has special knowledge and special powers like my own, it rather encourages him to seek a complex explanation when a simpler one is at hand.

~ Sherlock Holmes ~

Sir Arthur Conan Doyle

Lone Gunman or Conspiracy: The Warren Commission

"You ask too many questions, kid," the agent told the young reporter as he intentionally bumped into him as he brushed by. At least he looked like an "agent" with his close cut hair and sun glasses that seemed out of place for the weather. He didn't look like the street-wise city or county police detectives that he knew in Dallas or even the Texas Rangers he had seen with their distinctive Texas dress and style. Was he FBI or Secret Service the reporter wondered? And he resented being called a "kid;" he was in his early thirties and had been a reporter for more than seven years. Besides, how could a member of the "fifth estate" ask "too many questions" when the President of the United States had been murdered only weeks before. The young reporter, like many Americans of the time, would never live to see the answers to his questions which would not be released for more than thirty-five years.

The assassination of President John F. Kennedy has been called "the crime of the century" and will continue to be one of the most speculated mysteries of all time. Whether one believes in the "lone gunman theory" or one of many conspiracy theories, the fact remains that the many unanswered questions shroud this event in secrecy and mystique. Only recently have some of the documents in the Kennedy assassination case become declassified. Perhaps these documents will answer some of the many questions in the enigma that has become the crime of the century. Perhaps all of our questions will never be answered and the entire truth known. Maybe no one living knows the entire truth. Maybe no one ever did. Maybe the puzzle had too many pieces for one person to piece together. Regardless of the how the "big picture" really looks, examining just a few of the pieces is fascinating, even if they only lead to still more questions.

The Presidential motorcade procedes along Main Street in Dallas.
(Public domain photo: http://en.wikipedia.org/wiki/Image:Motorcade_on_Main.jpg)

Infamous Murders and Mysteries

The President's Commission on the Assassination of President Kennedy, known as the "Warren Commission," was established by President Johnson on November 29, 1963, one week after President Kennedy was assassinated and five days after alleged assassin Lee Harvey Oswald was killed while in police custody. Almost ten months later, the Commission delivered the 888-page report that found that Lee Harvey Oswald killed President Kennedy, alone and unaided, and that Oswald's killer Jack Ruby was a "lone nut." This Report was followed up a couple of months later by the publication of 26 volumes of Hearings and Exhibits and was hailed as an exhaustive investigation of the assassination. It was widely accepted by the public, until a few years later when several books and magazine articles questioned many of the findings. The Warren Report remains the definitive statement of the "lone gunman" theory of the assassination of President Kennedy. Transcripts of the Commission's secret meetings were to remain classified as Top Secret for seventy-five years and sealed from the public until the year 2039. However, these transcripts have gradually been declassified, some available now for the first time.

Warren Commission presents report
(Public domain photo: http://en.wikipedia.org/wiki/Image:Lbj-wc.jpg)

Dr. Robert J. Girod, Sr.

Lyndon B. Johnson hoped that the Warren Commission would convince the American public that President John F. Kennedy had been killed by a single gunman, Lee Harvey Oswald. However, polls indicate that the majority of Americans believe that the President died as a result of a conspiracy. This belief proliferated during the investigations of Frank Church and his House Select Committee on Intelligence Activities, followed by the House Select Committee on Assassinations (HSCA).

The Kill Zone and the Shadow of Death

Just before 12:30 p.m. CST, President Kennedy's limousine entered Dealey Plaza and slowly approached the Texas School Book Depository and then turned left 120-degrees directly in front of the Depository, 65 feet away.

COMMISSION EXHIBIT 369

The Presidential limosine passing the Texas School Book Depository. An arrow points to a man who resembles Lee Harvey Oswald in the doorway of this Warren Commission Exhibit.
(Public domain photo: http://commons.wikimedia.org/wiki/Image:HSCA-z161-Croft-6-44.jpg)

When the Presidential limousine passed the Depository and continued down Elm Street, shots were fired at Kennedy. The majority of witnesses recalled hearing three shots. There was little reaction in the crowd to the first shot. Some witnesses later said that they thought it was a firecracker or the backfire of a vehicle. Both President Kennedy and Governor John Connally turned abruptly from looking to their left to looking to their right. Governor Connally recognized the sound of the high powered rifle and exclaimed, "Oh, no, no, no!" President Kennedy raised his clenched fists up to his neck and leaned forward and to his left. Connally yelled, "My God, they are going to kill us all." Film and photos reveal that as the final shot rang out, a fist-size hole exploded out from the right side of President Kennedy's head, covering the interior of the car and a nearby motorcycle officer with blood and brain tissue.

Presidential limosine just before the shots were fired.
(Public domain photo: http://commons.wikimedia.org/wiki/Image:CE369.jpg)

Secret Service agent Clint Hill was riding on the left front running board of the car immediately behind the Presidential limousine. Sometime after the first shot hit the President, Hill jumped off and ran to overtake the limousine. After the shot that hit the President in the head, Mrs. Kennedy climbed onto the rear of the limousine, as if to retrieve something, though she later had no memory of doing so. Hill believed she was reaching for something, perhaps a piece of the President's skull. He jumped onto the back of the limousine, pushed Mrs. Kennedy back into her seat, and hung on to the car as it sped away from Dealey Plaza toward Parkland Memorial Hospital.

The Presidential limosine viewed from the rear.
(Pubic domain photo: http://commons.wikimedia.org/wiki/Image:Hudson_Exh1-Willis20-183.jpg)

Infamous Murders and Mysteries

The Moorman photo; just after the first shot.
(Public domain photo: http://en.wikipedia.org/wiki/Image:Moorman.jpg)

Looking at the grassy knoll as it looks today from across Elm Street (approximately where the Presidential limosine was during the fatal shots).

Looking up Elm Street toward the Texas School Book Depository where the motorcade passed. (The sniper nest window is marked).

Lee Harvey Oswald was reported missing to the Dallas police by his supervisor at the Depository. He was arrested an hour and twenty minutes after the assassination for killing a Dallas police officer, J.D. Tippit, who had spotted Oswald walking along a sidewalk. Oswald was arrested in a nearby movie theatre and resisted arrest by attempting to shoot the arresting officer with a pistol. He was charged with the murders of Tippit and Kennedy later that night. Oswald denied shooting anyone and claimed he was a "patsy." Oswald's case never came to trial because two days later, while being transferred to an armored car for transfer from Dallas Police Headquarters to the Dallas County Jail, he was shot and killed by Jack Ruby.

Dr. Robert J. Girod, Sr.

Squad car of Dallas Police Officer J. D. Tippit (1924–1963) (left), on East 10th Street in the Oak Cliff section of Dallas, Texas, on November 22, 1963. Tippit was shot and killed as he exited the car, about 45 minutes after the assassination of U.S. President John F. Kennedy. Photograph from the *Warren Commission Hearings and Evidence*, volume 17, p. 228, Commission Exhibit 522.
(Public domain photo: http://commons.wikimedia.org/wiki/Assassination_of_John_F._Kennedy)

Infamous Murders and Mysteries

Dallas Police Officer J. D. Tippit's ID Photo (right)
(1924–1963). According to the Warren Commission Report, Tippit was shot and killed by Lee Oswald about 45 minutes after the assassination of U.S. President John F. Kennedy, on November 22, 1963. Photograph, originally from Tippit's 1952 police identification card, is from the *Warren Commission Hearings and Evidence*, volume 29, p. 304, Carlin Exhibit No. 1.

Photo of Officer J.D. Tippit (left) in Dallas police uniform (left).
(Public domain photos: http://commons.wikimedia.org/wiki/Image:CarlinBruce-Exh2.jpg)

Assassination Theories and Official Investigations

Theories about the motive and conspiracies for the assination abound. Some are quickly and easily despensed with, while others are an enigma. Some conspiracy theorists believe that Oswald was not involved at all, while others believe that he was the fall guy for an elaborate conspiracy. Shortly after his arrest, Oswald insisted he was a "patsy" and that he had no part in the assassination at all. He never admitted any involvement and he was himslef murdered two days after being taken into police custody. In the decades following the assassination many theories have been proposed, pondered and published detailing organized conspiracies to kill the President. These theories include as possible conspirators:

The KGB – this is discounted by most researchers, although that organization may have had advance knowledge of relevant information.

Fidel Castro – Most of the evidence for this theory came from the CIA's Mexico City station. Witnesses claimed to have seen Oswald take money for the assassination and tapped phone lines produced sinister, though vague, information about his connections. A defector from Cuba's intelligence service claimed that Oswald had met with agents on multiple occasions. These connections have been viewed by many as a false and deliberate setup to throw off other investigations.

Photo of Oswald (left) taken in October 1959 shortly after his arrival in the Soviet Union. Oswald signed the back of the photo his future wife's aunt and uncle in 1961. It was discovered in Minsk in 1992. Marina Prusakova (right), Oswald's future wife, taken in Minsk in 1959.
(Public domain: http://en.wikipedia.org/wiki/Lee_Harvey_Oswald)

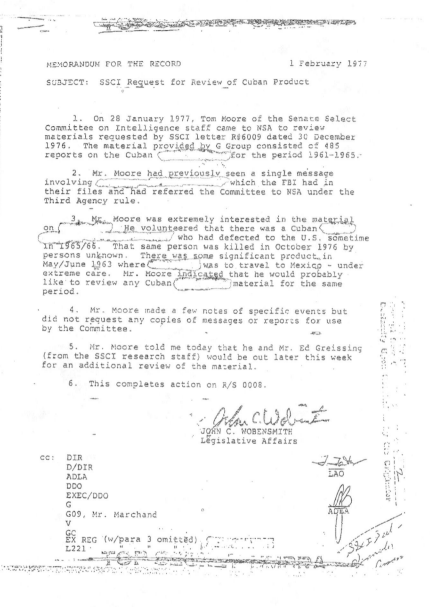

Request for Secret Special Compartmented Information (SSCI) for Cuban Product.

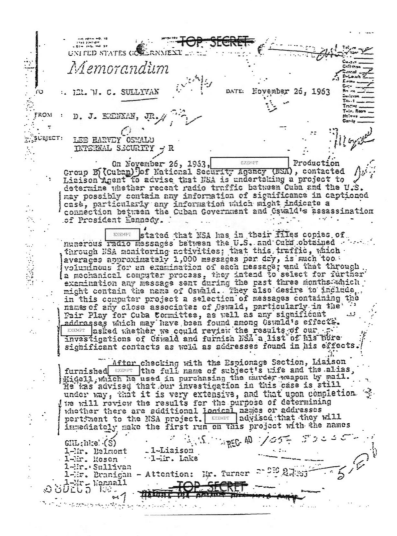

Communications with Cuba. (Memo to FBI Counter-Intelligence Chief W.C. Sullivan, who was shot and killed about a decade later).

Cuban statement on Oswald's 27 September 1963 request for a transit visa to the Soviet Union.

Anti-Castro Exiles - Another group with an alleged motive to kill President Kennedy were the anti-Castro exiles, who Kennedy failed to provide support for during the Bay of Pigs invasion. Oswald was reportedly in contact with members of these groups in the summer of 1963 in New Orleans. These groups were reputedly working under the direction of their CIA handlers, allegedly including David Phillips or Howard Hunt.

The Right-Wing - In the Warren Commission's only interview with Jack Ruby, he alluded to the possible involvement of the John Birch Society and right-wing ex-general Edwin Walker.

The Mafia – Though there is evidence implicating certain mobsters and the mob ties of Jack Ruby, it appears to be mostly circumstantial. Others point to a nexus of the CIA-Mafia plots to kill Castro and Ruby's involvement in gunrunning to Cuban exiles. Still others opine that rather than an organized crime hit, it is more likely that a new use of an existing relationship between the CIA officers and their mob connections may have been mutually advantageous.

Jack Ruby.
(Public domain photo: http://commons.wikimedia.org/wiki/Image:CE5301C.jpg)

> Legislative Affairs
>
> 9 Dec 77
>
> To: DIR
> THRU: D/DIR
> SUBJECT: Correspondence from House Assassinations Committee
>
> 1. The Deputy Chief Counsel of the Assassinations Committee, Mr. J. Wolf called to say he is sending a letter to DIR. Letter, to be drafted Monday, will request certain information (unspecified) of NSA.
>
> 2. Committee is investigating assassinations of President Kennedy & Mr. King.

Subject: Correspondence from House Assassinations Committee (to National Security Agency)

Serial: N1380
24 November 1975

~~TOP SECRET~~

MEMORANDUM FOR THE SPECIAL ASSISTANT TO THE SECRETARY AND DEPUTY SECRETARY OF DEFENSE

SUBJECT: Senate Select Committee Request for Information on Matters Related to President Kennedy's Assassination

Inclosed is our response to the request of the Senate Select Committee on Intelligence dated 14 November 1975.

DAVID D. LOWMAN
Special Assistant
to the Director
for Congressional Reviews

Incl:
a/s

Memo #1: National Security Agency (NSA) to Special Assistant to the secretary and Deputy Secretary of Defense.

Dr. Robert J. Girod, Sr.

NATIONAL SECURITY AGENCY
CENTRAL SECURITY SERVICE
FORT GEORGE G. MEADE, MARYLAND 20755

Serial: N1404
3 December 1975

~~TOP SECRET~~

MEMORANDUM FOR THE SPECIAL ASSISTANT TO THE SECRETARY AND DEPUTY SECRETARY OF DEFENSE

SUBJECT: Senate Select Committee Request for Additional Information on Matters Related to President Kennedy's Assassination

1. Please refer to my Memorandum, Serial: N1380 dated 24 November 1975 which forwarded our initial response to the subject request.

2. Mr. Peter Fenn of the Select Committee Staff has requested copies of the four messages referred to in our initial response. They are inclosed for your review and forwarding to Mr. Fenn.

DAVID D. LOWMAN
Special Assistant
to the Director
for Congressional Reviews

4 Incls:
a/s

ATTACHED DOCUMENTS CONTAIN
CODEWORD MATERIAL

DECLASSIFY UPON REMOVAL
OF ENCLOSURES

~~TOP SECRET~~

Memo #2: National Security Agency (NSA) to Special Assistant to the secretary and Deputy Secretary of Defense.

Infamous Murders and Mysteries

NSA Record of Event: 22 November 1963.

The CIA and/or FBI – Many suspect that Oswald was an agent of the U. S. intelligence community, though no documentation actually confirms this. If Oswald was some kind of intelligence agent, this does not necessarily make him a CIA killer. The CIA as an immense organization is hardly a credible suspect in the assassination, though individual officers or even a powerful conclave of "rogue agents" could have been part of a plot.

COMMISSION EXHIBIT 346

The interior of the Presudential limosine following the assignation.
(Public domain photo: http://commons.wikimedia.org/wiki/Image:CE346.jpg)

The Military and/or the "Military Industrial Complex" - The U. S. military has never been the focus of any of the investigations. The autopsy which has generated so much controversy over the years was controlled by the military at the Bethesda Naval Medical Center. One of the autopsy doctors, Dr. Pierre Finck, told jurors at the Clay Shaw trial that an Army General was in charge of the Kennedy autopsy, and that he had failed to dissect the neck (necessary to track the bullet's path) because he had been told not to. Autopsy participants were issued orders not to speak of what they had seen under penalty of court martial. The Army had maintained a file on Lee Oswald, but it was "routinely destroyed" in 1973. Colonel Robert Jones of the 112th

Infamous Murders and Mysteries

Military Intelligence Group told the HSCA that Army intelligence personnel were in Dealey Plaza the day of the motorcade. Motives for this theory have included Cuba, Russian, and Vietnam policies.

President Kennedy's Air Force One (26000) is on display at the USAF Museum at Wright-Patterson Air Force Base.

Lyndon Johnson – Those who subscribe to this theory point out that Johnson not only had the most to gain by the assassination, but that it was no secret that a great deal of animosity existed between Johnson and the Kennedy brothers. These theorists assert that President Johnson played an active early role in the cover-up, but the assertion that he was involved in a murder plot remains speculation.

Dr. Robert J. Girod, Sr.

Lyndon B. Johnson takes the oath as President of the United States aboard Air Force One (tail number 26000).
(Public domain photo: http://en.wikipedia.org/wiki/Image:Lyndon_B._Johnson_taking_the_oath_of_office%2C_November_1963.jpg)

Infamous Murders and Mysteries

The **Dallas Police investigation** focused on the interrogation of Oswald, who was held at the police headquarters. He was questioned intermittently for approximately twelve hours between 1430 (2:30 p.m.), on November 22, and 1100 (11:00 a.m.), on November 24, about both the Tippit shooting and the assassination of President Kennedy. Oswald denied any involvement with either the assassination of President Kennedy or the murder of Officer Tippit. Captain Fritz, of the Homicide and Robbery Bureau, led the questioning, but there were no stenographic or taped recordings. Afterwards he wrote a report of the interrogation from notes that he had made. Agents from the FBI and the U.S. Secret Service, were also present, as well as investigators from other law enforcement agencies. Some of them also took notes of the interrogation. Oswald provided little information though and, when confronted with evidence which he could not explain, he allegedly made statements which were verifiably false.

On the evening of November 22, 1963, the Dallas Police Department performed paraffin tests on Oswald's hands and right cheek in an effort to scientifically determine whether Oswald had recently fired a firearm. The results were positive for the hands and negative for the right cheek, although the Warren Commission dismissed the reliability of the results in their findings. Dallas police never completed their investigations due to the murder of Oswald by Jack Ruby and alleged interference by the FBI.

The **FBI investigation** was completed on December 9, 1963, just seventeen days after the assassination. The FBI issued its report, which was given to the Warren Commission, and stayed on as the primary investigating authority for the Commission. The FBI concluded that only three bullets were fired during the assassination and the Warren Commission agreed but disagreed with the FBI report on which shots hit Kennedy and which hit Governor Connally. The FBI report concluded that the first shot hit President Kennedy, the second shot hit Governor Connally, and the third shot hit Kennedy in the head, killing him. The Warren Commission concluded that one of the three shots missed, one of the shots hit Kennedy and then struck Connally, and a third shot struck Kennedy in the head, killing him.

The FBI's investigation was reviewed by the House Select Committee on Assassinations in 1979. The Committee concluded that the FBI adequately investigated Lee Harvey Oswald's background prior to the assassination, properly conducted a threat assesment of his potential to endanger the public safety, and conducted a thorough and professional investigation into Lee Harvey Oswald's participation in the assassination. However, the Committee also concluded that the FBI had failed to adequately investigate the possibility of a conspiracy to assassinate the President and was "deficient" in the sharing of information with other agencies and departments.

Another big question mark has been the actions of FBI agent James Hosty, who appeared in Oswald's address book. The FBI provided the Warren Commission with a typewritten transcription of Oswald's address book, in which Hosty's name and phone number were omitted, even though it is known that two days before the assassination, Oswald went to the FBI office in Dallas to meet with Hosty. When he found that Hosty was not in the office at the time, Oswald left an envelope with a letter inside for him. After Oswald was murdered by Jack Ruby, Hosty's supervisor ordered him to destroy the letter, which he allegedly did by tearing it up and flushing it down the toilet. When Hosty testified before the Warren Commission, he failed to disclose this connection with Oswald, but this information became public when it was investigated by the U.S. House Select Committee on Assassinations.

The **Warren Commission investigation** of the assassination, called the Warren Commission because it was chaired by U.S. Supreme Court Chief Justice Earl Warren, was established by President Johnson on November 29, 1963, a week after the assassination. In late September 1964, after a ten month investigation, the Warren Commission Report was published and concluded that it could find no persuasive evidence of a domestic or foreign conspiracy involving any other persons, groups, or countries. The Commission concluded that Lee Harvey Oswald had acted alone in the murder of Kennedy (the "lone gunman theory") and that Jack Ruby acted alone in the murder of Oswald.

The Commission also concluded that only three bullets were fired during the assassination and that Lee Harvey Oswald fired all three bullets from the Texas School Book Depository from behind the motorcade in a time period of approximately 4.8 to 7 seconds. It noted that three empty shells were found in the sixth floor in the book depository, along with a rifle, identified as the one used in the shooting. The rifle was allegedly Oswald's Italian military surplus Carcano 6.5x52 mm Model 91/38. The Commission concluded that the same bullet that wounded Kennedy also caused all of Governor Connally's wounds, then came out of Connally's left thigh and was found on a stretcher in the hospital. This theory has become known as the "single bullet theory" or the "magic bullet theory."

PRESIDENT'S COMMISSION
ON THE
ASSASSINATION OF PRESIDENT KENNEDY
200 Maryland Ave. N.E.
Washington, D.C. 20002
Telephone 543-1400

September 24, 1964

The President
The White House
Washington, D. C.

Dear Mr. President:

    Your Commission to investigate the assassination of President Kennedy on November 22, 1963, having completed its assignment in accordance with Executive Order No. 11130 of November 29, 1963, herewith submits its final report.

Respectfully,

Earl Warren, Chairman

Richard B. Russell

John Sherman Cooper

Hale Boggs

Gerald R. Ford

Allen W. Dulles

John J. McCloy

Warren Commission cover letter.
(Public domain document: http://commons.wikimedia.org/wiki/Image:Warren_commission_cover.jpg)

Infamous Murders and Mysteries

Assessment of the Middle East and the Elections

The **Ramsey Clark Panel** investigation was commissioned in 1968 by Attorney General Ramsey Clark and appointed a panel of four medical experts to examine the photographs, x-rays, documents and other evidence in the murder of President Kennedy. The Clark Panel determined that Kennedy was struck by two bullets fired from above and behind him. The chain of custody of the evidence was questioned and Clark brought this to the attention of President Johnson. A complete accounting of the number of photographs and a proper chain of custody for the autopsy materials have been criticized in the investigation. However, the House Select Committee on Assassinations subjected the photos and x-rays from the autopsy to scientific investigation by a panel of experts, which concluded that the materials were authentic.

The **U.S. President's Commission on CIA Activities within the United States** was set up under President Gerald Ford (a former Warren

Commission member) in 1975 to investigate the activities of the Central Intelligence Agency within the United States. The commission was led by Vice President Nelson Rockefeller and is commonly referred to as the Rockefeller Commission Investigation. Part of the commission's work dealt with the Kennedy assassination. One of the issues included the "head snap" as seen in the Zapruder film (which was first shown to the public in 1975) and the possible presence of CIA officers E. Howard Hunt and Frank Sturgis in Dallas. The Commission concluded that the "head snap" did not conclusively indicate that a shot was fired from the front and that neither Hunt nor Sturgis were in Dallas at the time of the assassination.

Fifteen years after the Warren Commission issued its report, the Congressional House Select Committee on Assassinations investigation reviewed the Warren Commission report and the FBI reports to the Commission. The Committee was critical of both the Warren Commission and the FBI for failing to adequately investigate whether other people may have conspired with Oswald to murder President Kennedy. The Committee concluded, as had the Warren Commission, that Lee Harvey Oswald fired three shots at the President, that the second and third shots struck the President, and that the third fired killed him. The HSCA agreed with the "single bullet theory" but concluded that it occurred at a time during the assassination that was different from what the Warren Commission had concluded. Their theory was based on evidence from the Dictabelt recording. The Committee came to the conclusion that President Kennedy was probably assassinated as a result of a conspiracy. They opined that four shots had been fired during the assassination. Their theory suggests that Oswald fired the first, second, and fourth bullets. The Committee further theorized that, based on the acoustic evidence, it is probable that a second assassin fired the third bullet from President Kennedy's right front, while concealed behind a picket fence on the grassy knoll, but missed.

For Your Eyes Only: Files Declassified

Many conspiracy theories have been suggested over the years and many Americans say they believe in at least one of these theories. Following the release of Oliver Stone's film *JFK*, public pressure resulted in Congress passing the President John F. Kennedy Assassination Records Collection Act of 1992, which required the gathering and opening of declassified records concerned with the death of the President. Two main categories of documents and related materials are now available. The first are records directly relating to the assassination of President Kennedy and subsequent investigations. The second relates to foreign policy concerning The Soviet Union, Cuba, and Vietnam during the Kennedy administration. Most of the files remain classified.

The Assassination Records Review Board was not commissioned to make any findings or conclusions, but only for the purpose of releasing documents to the public in order to allow them to draw their own conclusions. From 1992 until 1998, the Assassination Records Review Board gathered and unsealed about 60,000 documents, consisting of more than 4 million pages. All remaining documents are scheduled to be released by 2017.

President's Motorcade and Route

There were concerns about security, because as recently as October 24, 1963, United States Ambassador to the United Nations, Adlai Stevenson, had encountered violent protesters during a visit to Dallas. President Kennedy had mentioned the danger of snipers on the morning he was assassinated, as had the Secret Service agents when they were fixing the motorcade route. Winston Lawson of the Secret Service, who was in charge of planning for the visit, told the Dallas Police not to assign its usual squad of experienced homicide detectives to follow immediately behind the President's car. The car in which the President was traveling was a modified 1961 Lincoln Continental open-top limousine. (It is now on display at the Ford Museum near Detroit). No presidential car had used a bulletproof top as of 1963, though plans for such a top were presented just a month earlier in October 1963. The motorcade route was made public in both Dallas newspapers on November 19, 1963, and a map of the route was published on November 21, 1963. The route and order of the procession of the President's motorcade helps to understand the events of 22 November 1963.

Photo of Dealey Plaza (annotated), from the Warren Commission report.
(Public domain photo: http://en.wikipedia.org/wiki/Image:Dealey-plaza-annotated.png)

The motorcade consisted of numerous cars, police motorcycles and press buses:
- The pilot car, a white Ford sedan:
    - oDallas Police Deputy Chief George L. Lumpkin,
    - oDallas homicide detectives Billy L. Senkel and
    - oF.M. Turner, and
    - oLTC George Whitmeyer, commander of the local Army Intelligence reserve unit.
- Three two-wheel Dallas police motorcycle officers under the command of SGT S.Q. Bellah.
- Five two-wheel motorcycle officers under the command of SGT Stavis "Steve" Ellis.
- The lead car, an unmarked white Ford police sedan:

- o Dallas Police Chief Jesse Curry (driver),
- o Secret Service Agent Winston Lawson (right front),
- o Sheriff Bill Decker (left rear),
- o Agent Forrest Sorrels (right rear).
- The presidential limousine, known to the Secret Service as **SS-100-X** (with District of Columbia license plate **GG 300**), a dark blue 1961 Lincoln Continental convertible:
  - o Agent Bill Greer (driver),
  - o Agent Roy Kellerman (right front),
  - o Nellie Connally (left middle),
  - o Texas Governor John Connally (right middle),
  - o First Lady Jacqueline Kennedy (left rear),
  - o President Kennedy (right rear).
- Four Dallas Police motorcycle escorts, two on each side of the presidential limousine, flanking the rear bumper:
  - o Billy Joe Martin and
  - o Robert W. "Bobby" Hargis (left), and
  - o James M. Chaney and
  - o Douglas L. Jackson (right).
- **Halfback** (a Secret Service code name), a black 1955 Cadillac convertible:
  - o Agent Sam Kinney (driver),
  - o Agent Emory Roberts (right front),
  - o Agent Clint Hill (left front running board),
  - o Agent Bill McIntyre (left rear running board),
  - o Agent John D. Ready (right front running board),
  - o Agent Paul Landis (right rear running board),
  - o Presidential aide Kenneth O'Donnell (left middle),
  - o Presidential aide David Powers (right middle),
  - o Agent George Hickey (left rear),
  - o Agent Glen Bennett (right rear).
- 1961 light blue Lincoln four door convertible:
  - o Hurchel Jacks of the Texas Highway Patrol (driver),
  - o Agent Rufus Youngblood (right front),
  - o Senator Ralph Yarborough (left rear),
  - o Lady Bird Johnson (center rear),
  - o Vice-President Lyndon Johnson (right rear).
- **Varsity** (Secret Service code name), a yellow 1963 Ford Mercury hardtop:
  - o Joe H. Rich of the Texas Highway Patrol (driver),
  - o Vice Presidential aide Cliff Carter (front middle),

- oSecret Service agents Jerry Kivett (right front),
- oWarren W. "Woody" Taylor (left rear), and
- oThomas L. "Len" Johns (right rear).
- White 1963 Ford Mercury Comet convertible:
    - oTexas Highway Patrolman Milton T. Wright (driver),
    - oDallas Mayor Earle Cabell and
    - ohis wife Elizabeth, and
    - oCongressman Ray Roberts.
- National press pool car (on loan from the telephone company), a blue-gray Chevrolet sedan:
    - otelephone company driver;
    - oassistant White House press secretary Malcolm Kilduff (right front);
    - oMerriman Smith, UPI (middle front);
    - oJack Bell, AP;
    - oRobert Baskin, Dallas Morning News;
    - oBob Clark, ABC News (rear).
- First camera car, a yellow 1964 Chevrolet Impala convertible:
    - oa Texas Ranger (driver);
    - oDavid Wiegman Jr., NBC;
    - oThomas J. Craven Jr., CBS;
    - oThomas "Ollie" Atkins, White House photographer;
    - oJohn Hofan, an NBC sound engineer;
    - oCleveland Ryan, a lighting technician.
- Second camera car:
    - oFrank Cancellare, UPI;
    - oCecil Stoughton, White House photographer;
    - oHenry Burroughs, AP;
    - oArt Rickerby, Life magazine;
    - oDonald C. "Clint" Grant, *Dallas Morning News*.
- Dallas Police motorcycle escorts
    - oH.B. McLain and
    - oMarion L. Baker.
- Third camera car, a Chevrolet convertible:
    - odriver from the Texas Department of Public Safety;
    - ophotographer Robert H. Jackson, The Dallas Times Herald;
    - ophotographer Tom Dillard, *Dallas Morning News*;
    - oJimmy Darnell, WBAP-TV, Fort Worth;
    - oMal Couch, WFAA-TV/ABC [4];
    - oJames R. Underwood, KRLD-TV.

- First car of Congressmen.
- Second car of Congressmen.
- Third car of Congressmen.
- VIP staff car carrying
  - a governor's aide and
  - the military and
  - Air Force aides to the president.
- Dallas Police motorcycle escorts
  - J.W. Courson and
  - C.A. Haygood.
- First White House press bus:
  - Mary Barelli Gallagher, Jacqueline Kennedy's personal secretary;
  - Pamela Turnure, Jacqueline Kennedy's press secretary;
  - Marie Fehmer Chiarodo, the Vice President's secretary;
  - Liz Carpenter, staff director for Lady Bird Johnson;
  - Jack Valenti, in charge of press relations during President Kennedy's visit to Texas;
  - Robert MacNeil, NBC News;
  - and a few others.
- Local press car with four *Dallas Morning News* reporters.
- Second White House press bus.
- Dallas Police motorcycle escorts
  - R. Smart and
  - B.J. Dale.
- Chevrolet sedan:
  - Evelyn Lincoln, the President's personal secretary;
  - Dr. George Burkley, the President's personal physician.
- 1957 black Ford hardtop: Two representatives from Western Union.
- 1964 white Chevrolet Impala:
  - White House Signal Corps officer Art Bales;
  - Army Warrant Officer Ira Gearhart.
- 1964 white-top, dark-body Chevrolet Impala.
- Third White House press buss: staff and members of the Democratic Party.
- 1963 black and white Ford police car.
- Solo three-wheel Dallas Police motorcycle escort.

Report in immediate aftermath: 26 November 1963.

Film and Recordings of the Assassination

Most media crews were not even with the motorcade but were waiting instead at the Dallas Trade Mart in anticipation of Kennedy's arrival. Those members of the media that were with the motorcade were riding at the rear of the procession. The Dallas police were recording their radio transmissions over two channels. Channel One was used for routine police communications and Channel Two, an auxiliary channel, was dedicated to the President's motorcade. Up until the time of the assassination, most of the broadcasts on this channel consisted of Police Chief Jesse Curry's announcements of the location of the motorcade as it wound through the streets of Dallas. Recordings are said to exist from both police channels.

President Kennedy's last seconds traveling through Dealey Plaza before, during, and immediately following the assassination were recorded for the 26.6 seconds on a silent 8 mm film, taken by Abraham Zapruder, and has come to be known as the Zapruder film. Mr. Zapruder was not the only one who recorded some part of the assassination. At least thirty-two photographers were in Dealey Plaza and several amateur motion pictures were filmed, although at greater distances than Zapruder's.

Thomas Atkins, F. Mark Bell, Charles Bronson (not the actor), Mal Couch, Elsie Dorman, Robert Hughes, John Martin Jr., Marie Muchmore, Orville Nix, Patsy Paschall, Tina Towner, James Underwood, and Dave Wiegman, and an unknown woman in a blue dress on the south side of Elm Street were among the many who captured films of the infamous events that unfolded before them. Still photos by Hugh W. Betzner, Jr., Wilma Bond, Robert Croft, Mary Moorman, Phillip Willis, and many others captured these tragic moments in history. The only press photographer in Dealey Plaza who was not in the press cars in the motorcade was Ike Altgens, a photo editor for the Associated Press in Dallas. An unidentified woman, nicknamed "the Babushka Lady" (Russian for "grandmother") by researchers, might have been filming the presidential motorcade during the assassination. She was apparently seen doing so on film and photographs taken by the others. Previously unknown, color footage filmed on the assassination day by George Jefferies was released on February 20, 2007, by the Sixth Floor Museum, in Dallas, Texas. It does not document the actual shooting, as it was taken about ninety seconds before the shots, but captures a few moments of history in its frames.

Dr. Robert J. Girod, Sr.

Chaos in Dealey Plaza

Historic footage and stills recorded the Presidential limousine as it was passing a grassy knoll on the north side of Elm Street at the moment of the fatal head shot. As the motorcade sped away from the plaza, police officers and spectators ran up this "grassy knoll." Others ran toward the knoll from a railroad bridge over Elm Street (the Triple Underpass) to the area behind a five-foot high stockade fence atop the knoll. No sniper was found. S. M. Holland, who had been watching the motorcade on the Triple Underpass, testified that "immediately" after the shots were fired, he went around the corner where the overpass joined the fence but did not see anyone running from the area.

The railroad control tower as it appears today.

Lee Bowers, a railroad switchman sitting in a two-story tower, reported that he had a clear view of the rear of the stockade fence atop the grassy knoll during the shooting. He said that he saw four men in the area between his tower and Elm Street. One was a middle-aged man and another was a younger man. They were standing ten to fifteen feet (three to five meters) apart near the Triple Underpass. Bowers did not think that they appeared to know each other. One or two other men appeared to be uniformed parking lot attendants. Bowers testified that one or both of the men were still there when motorcycle officer Clyde Haygood ran up the grassy knoll to the back of the fence. Bowers clarified his original statements in a 1966 interview by reporting that the two men he saw were on the opposite side of the stockade fence from him and that no one was behind the fence at the time the shots were fired.

Howard Brennan, a steamfitter, was sitting across the street from the Texas School Book Depository. He told the Dallas police that as he watched the motorcade go by, he heard a shot come from above. When he looked up he saw a man with a rifle take another shot from a corner window on the sixth floor. He had seen the same man minutes earlier looking out the window. Brennan gave a description of the shooter, which was broadcast to all Dallas police at 12:45 p.m., 12:48 p.m., and 12:55 p.m.

Looking up Elm Street toward the Texas School Book Depository from the grassy knoll.

As Dallas police interviewed Brennan in front of the building, they were joined by Harold Norman and James Jarman, Jr., two employees of the Texas School Book Depository who had watched the motorcade from windows at the southeast corner of the fifth floor. They reported that they were with another employee, Bonnie Ray Williams, when they heard three gunshots from directly over their heads. They said that they saw plaster fall from the ceiling. Norman also heard what sounded like a bolt action rifle and cartridges dropping on the floor above them. Dallas police sealed off the entrances to the Texas School Book Depository sometime between 12:33 to after 12:50 p.m.

Of the 104 "ear-witnesses" who gave testimony as to the direction from which the shots came, 56 (53.8%) thought that they came from the direction of the Texas School Book Depository, 35 (33.7%) thought that they came from the area of the "grassy knoll" or the Triple Underpass, 8 (7.7%) thought the shots came from a location other than from the knoll or the Depository, and 5 (4.8%) thought they heard shots from at least two locations.

Conspiracy Theorists, Witness Accounts and the Tellers of Tales

What is the truth? Many witnesses have made claims that are both plausible and skeptical in nature. Which are true and which are not is a matter to be pondered, but are also a part of the history of this enigma.

Norma Jean Lollis Hill (February 11, 1931–November 7, 2000) was with her friend, Mary Moorman, across from the grassy knoll. She was one of the closest witnesses to President Kennedy when the shots were fired. She reported seeing a shooter on the Grassy Knoll and of seeing Jack Ruby in Dealey Plaza. Moorman can be seen in the Zapruder film taking pictures, which Hill claimed were taken by men purporting to be "Secret Service agents" just minutes after the assassination.

Gordon Arnold reported that he too had been on the Grassy Knoll during the shooting, to have heard a shot whiz past his left ear, and to have been confronted by a man who confiscated his camera.

Beverly Oliver was another witness who took photos of the assassination which were also allegedly confiscated by the FBI. She also claimed to have seen Oswald and Ruby together in the Carousel Club. In 1970 Oliver married the reputed mobster George McGann, but soon afterwards he was murdered by fellow of the underworld.

Tom Tilson claimed to have seen a man with a gun running down the slope behind the Knoll in the minutes following the assassination.

Virgil E. (Ed) Hoffman reported seeing a shooter on the "grassy knoll." He went to the FBI and made a report. A Justice Department memorandum and follow-up memo read:

Dr. Robert J. Girod, Sr.

UNITED STATES DEPARTMENT OF JUSTICE
FEDERAL BUREAU OF INVESTIGATION

Dallas, Texas
June 28, 1967

ASSASSINATION OF PRESIDENT
JOHN FITZGERALD KENNEDY
DALLAS, TEXAS, November 22, 1963

On June 26, 1967, Mr. Jim Dowdy, 725 McLenore, Texas, advised a deaf mute, Virgil E. Hoffman, who is employed at Texas Instruments, had indicated he wanted to furnish information to Agents of the Federal Bureau of Investigation regarding the assassination of President John Fitzgerald Kennedy. It was pointed out to Mr. Dowdy that Hoffman should put in writing in detail everything he saw the day of the assassination.

On June 28, 1967, Virgil E. Hoffman appeared at the Dallas Office of the FBI and advised he resided at 424 Grand Prairie Road, Grand Prairie, Texas, and was employed at Texas Instruments, Dallas. He said he parked his automobile near the railroad tracks on Stemmons Freeway and Elm Street, about 12:00 noon on November 22, 1963.

Hoffman said he was standing a few feet south of the railroad on Stemmons Freeway when the motorcade passed him taking President Kennedy to Parkland Hospital. Hoffman said he observed two white males, clutching something dark to their chests with both hands, running from the rear of the Texas School Book Depository building. The men were running north on the railroad, then turned east, and Hoffman lost sight of both of the men.

This document contains neither recommendations nor conclusions of the FBI. It is the property of the FBI and is loaned to your agency; is and its contents are not to be distributed outside your agency.

[p.2]

ASSASSINATION OF PRESIDENT
JOHN FITZGERALD KENNEDY

Approximately two hours after the above interview with Hoffman, he retuned to the Dallas Office of the FBI and advised he had just returned from the spot on Stemmons Freeway where he had parked his automobile and had decided he could not have seen the men running because of a fence west of the Texas School Book Depository building. He said it was possible that he saw these two men on the fence or something else.

Hoffman said the only description he could furnish of the men was that one of them wore a white shirt. He stated he had discussed this matter with his father at the time of the assassination, and his father suggested that he not talk to anyone about this, but after thinking about what he saw, Hoffman stated he decided to tell the FBI.

Dr. Robert J. Girod, Sr.

UNITED STATES DEPARTMENT OF JUSTICE
FEDERAL BUREAU OF INVESTIGATION

Dallas, Texas
July 6, 1967

ASSASSINATION OF PRESIDENT
JOHN FITZGERALD KENNEDY
DALLAS, TEXAS, November 22, 1963

Virgil E. Hoffman was not interviewed prior to June 28, 1967.

On July 6, 1967, Roy S. Truly, Manager, Texas School Book Depository, advised there is a fence approximately 6 feet tall running from the parking lot west of the Texas School Book Depository for about 150 feet to the north of the Texas School Book Depository. This fence was constructed approximately two years prior to the assassination and has not been moved to date.

On July 5, 1967, Mr. E. Hoffman, father of Virgil E. Hoffman, and Fred Hoffman, brother of Virgil Hoffman, were interviewed at 428 West Main Street, Grand Prairie, Texas. Both advised that Virgil Hoffman has been a deaf mute his entire life and has in the past distorted facts of events observed by him. Both the father and brother stated that Virgil Hoffman loved President Kennedy and had mentioned to them just after the assassination that he (Virgil Hoffman) was standing on the freeway near the Texas School Book Depository at the time of the assassination. Virgil Hoffman told them he saw numerous men running after the President was shot. The father of Virgil Hoffman stated that he did not believe that his son had seen anything of value and doubted he had observed any men running from the Texas School Book Depository and for this reason had not mentioned it to the FBI.

NOTE:

Virgil E. Hoffman, a deaf mute employed by Texas Instruments, Dallas, Texas, advised Agents of our Dallas Office that immediately following the assassination, he observed two white males running from the rear of the Texas School Book Depository building. Males were allegedly clutching something dark. Two hours after furnishing this information, Hoffman returned to our Dallas Office and advised he had reobserved the area where he allegedly saw the two men and decided he could not have seen the men running because of an intervening fence.

Bureau files contain no identifiable information with Virgil E. Hoffman and Dallas is being instructed to fully resolve this matter. Upon completion of the investigation the results will be furnished to the Criminal Division of the Department and to Secret Service.

Looking onto Elm Street from behind the stockade fence above the grassy knoll.

Infamous Murders and Mysteries

Looking up Elm Street from the stockade fence overlooking the grassy knoll.

```
                        UNCLASSIFIED
                  *** BEGIN MESSAGE   20 ***
SERIAL=   UDN=W00(9347)
CLASS=UNCLASSIFIED
LZY042
REULB
R A
  BC-USA-ASSASSINATION    11-19 0618
BC-USA-ASSASSINATION
  EX-CIA AGENT CLAIMS HE BOUGHT RIFLES FOR KENNEDY KILLING
      BY DAN COX
     NEW YORK, NOV 19, REUTER - A MAN CLAIMING TO HAVE BEEN
LINKED TO THE U.S. CENTRAL INTELLIGENCE AGENCY SAYS IN A NEW
BOOK THAT HE BOUGHT AND CUSTOMIZED FOUR RIFLES HE SAYS WERE USED
BY THE CIA AND THE MAFIA TO KILL PRESIDENT JOHN F. KENNEDY.
     IN
FIRST HAND KNOWLEDGE: HOW I PARTICIPATED IN THE
CIA-MAFIA MURDER OF PRESIDENT KENNEDY,:: ROBERT MORROW CLAIMS
THAT UNDER ORDERS, WHILE ON CONTRACT TO THE CIA, HE BOUGHT FOUR
7.35 MM MANNLICHER RIFLES AND SUPPLIED SEVERAL CIA HIT MEN WITH
SOPHISTICATED ELECTRONIC EQUIPMENT TO HELP KILL THE PRESIDENT.
     IN A LECTURE AT NEW YORK UNIVERSITY ON THURSDAY, MORROW SAID
HE WAS NOT AWARE AT THE TIME THAT THE EQUIPMENT HE SUPPLIED WAS
TO BE USED TO KILL KENNEDY.
  I THOUGHT THEY WERE TO BE USED AGAINST A HEAD OF STATE IN
CENTRAL AMERICA,:: HE SAID.
     ALTHOUGH TWO WEEKS BEFORE THE NOVEMBER 22, 1963 SHOOTING HE
HEARD A RUMOUR THAT A KENNEDY ASSASSINATION WAS IN THE WORKS AT
THE CIA, HE SAID HE DISREGARDED IT UNTIL HE SAW ONE OF THE
RIFLES HE HAD BOUGHT SHOWN ON TELEVISION THE NIGHT OF THE
SHOOTING.
  I DIDN:T PAY ANY ATTENTION UNTIL THE RIFLE WAS SHOWN ON
THE AIR THAT NIGHT,:: HE SAID, REFERRING TO BROADCASTS OF LOCAL
DALLAS POLICE HOLDING UP A RIFLE REPORTEDLY SEIZED FROM LEE
HARVEY OSWALD.
  THEN I WENT INTO A STATE OF PANIC. I WENT TO MY
(CIA) CASE OFFICER AND HE SAID :SHUT UP.:::
     MORROW:S CLAIMS ARE PART OF A LONG LINE OF CONSPIRACY
THEORIES ABOUT KENNEDY:S ASSASSINATION AND THE EARL WARREN
COMMISSION THAT INVESTIGATED IT. THESE THEORIES CLAIM KENNEDY
WAS KILLED BY SEVERAL ASSASSINS, SOME CONNECTED TO THE CIA.
     SUCH THEORIES WERE THE SUBJECT OF OLIVER STONE:S FILM
JFK,:: WHICH FOCUSED ON ATTEMPTS BY THE LATE NEW ORLEANS
DISTRICT ATTORNEY, JIM GARRISON, TO CONVICT A NEW ORLEANS
BUSINESSMAN AS A CONSPIRATOR IN KENNEDY:S DEATH.
     A CIA SPOKESMAN CONTACTED ON THURSDAY SAID:
THERE IS NO
RECORD THAT ROBERT D. MORROW WAS EVER A CONTRACT AGENT OF THE
CENTRAL INTELLIGENCE AGENCY.::
     BUT MORROW CLAIMED THE AGENCY WAS USING A LINGUISTIC TRICK
TO AVOID NAMING HIM.
  I WAS A CONTRACT EMPLOYEE, NOT AN AGENT,
AND I WAS PAID BY THE U.S. ARMY,:: HE SAID.
     MORROW REFERRED TO OSWALD, LONG THOUGHT TO BE KENNEDY:S
                        UNCLASSIFIED
```

Release on Morrow claim to have provided rifle for CIA.

Robert Morrow claimed to have been a CIA agent and to have supplied weapons for the shooters in Dealey Plaza. He named the alleged conspirators and explained that the motive was the U.S. intelligence community conclusion that President Kennedy was soft on communism, a threat to the

Mafia status quo and a traitor to the freedom fighters in Cuba. He alleged that he was a part of a CIA network of assassins and Mafia enforcers, personally participated in the assassination plot, and acted under direct orders from the head of CIA Covert Operations.

James Files claimed to have been the grassy knoll shooter in Dealey Plaza. Files claims that after fourteen months of military service he was about to be court-martialed for killing two of his own men to "save face" with the Laotian Army. He claimed that he was instead recruited by CIA officer David Atlee Phillips, who introduced him to Lee Harvey Oswald. He, like Morrow, said that he was contacted by CIA and Mafia assassins to participate in the assassination. Files claimed that when President Kennedy came into view, he was aiming for the President's right eye through his rifle scope as he came down Elm St. He had been instructed to count the shots and to take the shot if no headshot was made. When no headshot had been made, he made the fatal shot that took President Kennedy's life. He packed the gun into a suitcase and simply walked away.

Gordon Novel, also claimed to be a CIA agent and worked with the Jim Garrison investigation in New Orleans until he became a Garrison suspect.

Richard Case Nagell claimed to have worked for both the CIA and the KGB and to have had "foreknowledge" of the JFK assassination. In1957 Nagell reportedly worked for the U.S. Army Counter Intelligence Corps (CIC), 441st Counter Intelligence Corps Group, in Tokyo. He alleged supervised classified Military Intelligence files and confidential informants for the CIA. Nagell claimed that he and Lee Harvey Oswald met shortly after Oswald allegedly visited the Soviet embassy in Tokyo in November 1957 and that they were both involved in CIA operations. On September 20, 1963, (two months before the assassination) Richard Case Nagell walked into a bank in El Paso, Texas. He fired two shots into the wall near the ceiling, walked back out to his car, and waited to be arrested. Nagell claimed he was a double (or triple) agent for the U.S. and the KGB. He said that he knew Lee Harvey Oswald and that he was monitoring the JFK assassination plot which involved Cuban exiles. He declared that he had been ordered to kill Oswald to prevent the plot from being carried out and that he had mailed a registered letter to FBI Director Hoover, warning him of the assassination conspiracy.

John Elrod claimed that he had shared a jail cell in Dallas with Lee Oswald. Allegedly, he and Oswald saw a prisoner with a battered face being escorted by the jailers. Elrod asserted that Oswald told him that he had been with the same man in a motel room a few days before the assassination. He said that they discussed a transaction involving stolen weapons and that Jack Ruby was there with them. Many observers, however, question whether the time line of Elrod's story is even possible.

Judyth Vary Baker, a fellow employee of Oswald's at the Reily Coffee Company in the summer of 1963, claimed that she had been Oswald's girlfriend. She also claimed that she was involved with him in a secret biological weapons project intended to kill Castro but instead it resulted in the assassination of President Kennedy. Her story is one of the least believed, even among conspiracy theorists.

Dallas County Deputy Sheriff Roger Craig
(Public domain)

7 January 1965

Captain W.P. Gannaway
Special Service Bureau
Dallas Police Department

Thru:
Lieutenant Jack Revill
Criminal Intelligence Section
Special Service Bureau
Dallas Police Department

SUBJECT: CRIMINAL INTELLIGENCE (4)
MICHAEL R. PAINE

Sir:

The following automobiles were observed at SUBJECT'S residence, 2515 W. FIFTH STREET, IRVING, TEXAS.

A 1959 Citroen, 4 door, color black and yellow, Texas 64 license PU-4474. This vehicle is registered to SUBJECT at the above address. (parked in driveway)

A 1955 Chevrolet, station wagon, Texas 64 license PU-4475. This vehicle is registered to RUTH PAINE, SUBJECT'S wife, at the above address. (parked in driveway)

A 1954-56 Oldsmobile, color blue and white, Texas 64 license NY-9880. Registration on this vehicle is not available at this time. (parked in front of the house)

Respectfully submitted,

R.W. Westphal, Detective
Criminal Intelligence Section

OFFICERS COMMENT: MARINA OSWALD was living with SUBJECT and RUTH PAINE at the time of President Kennedy's assassination.

An inquiry has been sent to the Texas Department of Public Safety to determine the owner NY-9880.

Dallas Police report about Ruth Paine's station wagon, allegedly seen by Deputy Sheriff Roger Craig fleeing the assassination scene.

Roger Craig, a Dallas County Deputy Sheriff, testified that he saw Oswald flee the scene of the assassination in a Rambler station wagon with an accomplice and that he saw a Mauser rifle recovered in the sixth floor of the Depository. He also said that he "witnessed a confrontation" in Dallas Police headquarters that implicated Ruth Paine in the assassination. Allegedly

Oswald told him that the Rambler station wagon was Ruth Paine's. (While he could have been mistaken on the make, as is common, even for police witnesses, the Dallas Police report, below, is often used to contradict this). Roger Craig died, allegedly by suicide, in 1975 at age 39. Many believe that it was not suicide, but part of the conspiracy to silence him.

Marita Lorenz made several public assertions that she travelled with a "caravan" of assassins from Miami to Dallas on the night before the assassination. Lorenz made many dramatic claims. She said that she had an affair with Fidel Castro while in Cuba in February of 1959 and that she had a child by the Cuban dictator. She claimed that she was recruited by Frank Sturgis to work for the Central Intelligence Agency and took part in a 1960 failed attempt to poison Castro. She also alleged that the Federal Bureau of Investigation recruited her to spy on Soviet diplomats. In 1977 Lorenz was interviewed by a journalist and claimed that a group of anti-Castro operatives called "Operation 40," which included Lee Harvey Oswald and Frank Sturgis, were involved in a conspiracy to kill both John F. Kennedy and Fidel Castro.

Dr. Charles Crenshaw, a resident physician at Parkland Hospital, asserted that there was an entance wound from the front of President Kennedy's throat and that the back of his head was blown out – both inferring a frontal shot. He futher claimed that the body was altered between Parkland and Bethesda and that Parkland medical staff feared speaking about an apparent conspiracy. Finally, Dr. Crenshaw has insisted that President Johnson called the operating room while Lee Harvey Oswald was being treated and demanded that a confession be obtained from Oswald. Dr. Crenshaw died of natural causes in 2001 at the age of 68, still insisting that his assertions were correct.

Robert LeRoy Knudsen claimed to have photographed Kennedy's autopsy. He was a White House photographer from 1946 until 1974. He died of a heart attack at the Bethesda Naval Hospital in Maryland at 61 years old.

Madeleine Duncan Brown claimed to have been Vice President Lyndon Baines Johnson's lover and to have attended a very suspicious party on the eve of the assassination. The night before the Kennedy assassination, Brown asserted, LBJ met with some wealthy Dallas businessmen, FBI officials and organized crime bosses. After the meeting Johnson allegedly told Brown that "After tomorrow those SOB's will never embarrass me again." She further claimed that, on New Year's Eve 1963, LBJ confirmed to her that there was a conspiracy. Like Beverly Oliver had, Brown also claimed to have seen Oswald and Ruby together at the Carousel Club in Dallas.

Acoustical Evidence of Gunshots: One or More Shooters?

A 6.5 x 52 mm Italian Carcano (incorrectly called a Mannlicher-Carcano) M91/38 bolt-action rifle was found on the 6th Floor of the Texas Book Depository by Deputy Sheriff Eugene Boone and Deputy Constable Seymour Weitzman shortly after the assassination. The recovery was filmed by Tom Alyea of WFAA-TV. A bullet found on Governor Connally's hospital stretcher was ballistically matched to the found rifle and Oswald's palm print was found on the barrel. The rifle had allegedly been purchased in March by Lee Harvey Oswald under the name "A. Hidell" and delivered to a post office box in Dallas.

In 1979 the House Select Committee on Assassinations concluded that President John F. Kennedy's murder in 1963 was "probably . . . the result of a conspiracy." The conclusions were that there was a shot from the grassy knoll and a shot from the grassy knoll inferred that two gunmen must have fired at the President. As a result of acoustic evidence, G. Robert Blakey, the HSCA's chief counsel, concluded that four shots, over a total period of 7.91 seconds, were fired at the President. It is believed that the first, second and fourth came from the Depository, while the third came from the grassy knoll. The Committee concluded on the basis of the available evidence that President John F. Kennedy was probably assassinated as a result of a conspiracy.

A panel of the National Academy of Sciences (NAS) later disputed the evidence contained on a police dicta-belt of the sounds of a fourth shot in Dealey Plaza. The panel insisted it was simply random noise may have been static recorded as much as a full minute after the shooting while Kennedy's limosine was on the way to Parkland Hospital.

Infamous Murders and Mysteries

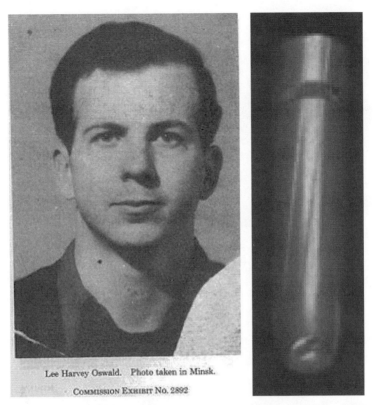

Lee Harvey Oswald (left), taken during his time in Minsk. CE 399, the "magic bullet" (right). Lee Harvey Oswald's Carcano M91/38 Fucile Corto (short rifle) 6.5 x 52 mm (below).
(Public domain photos: http://en.wikipedia.org/wiki/Lee_Harvey_Oswald)

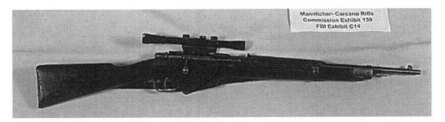

The NAS study, disputing the HSCA findings, was in turn disputed by a peer-reviewed article in *Science and Justice*, a quarterly publication of Britain's Forensic Science Society. The article asserted that the NAS panel's study was flawed and failed to take into account the recorded words of a Dallas patrolman that demonstrate that the gunshot-like noises occurred "at the exact instant that John F. Kennedy was assassinated." The article said it was more than 96 percent certain that there was a shot from the grassy knoll to the right of the president's limousine, in addition to the three shots from a book depository window above and behind the President's limousine.

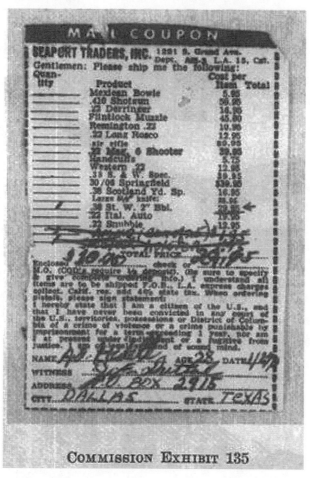

Mail order form for Lee Harvey Oswald's Carcano M91/38 Fucile Corto (short rifle) 6.5 x 52 mm rifle.

Infamous Murders and Mysteries

<del>TOP SECRET — EYES ONLY</del>

March 1, 1963

MEMORANDUM FOR MR. BUNDY

SUBJECT: Mr. Donovan's Trip to Cuba

Bob Hurwitch tells me that Donovan is still waiting to hear from Castro regarding a meeting this weekend in Havana. If there is a meeting, it will probably be devoted solely to the release of the prisoners; there will probably be no talk of U.S./Cuba relations.

Optimumly, Bob sees two stages in the process. The first stage is to release the prisoners, while the second stage is to have Donovan talk to Castro about broader policy questions. It would not be good to take the second stage until the prisoner issue is settled. It might indicate to Castro that he can use the prisoners as leverage; he has not yet tried to do so.

Once the prisoner deal is laid on, Donovan will be given ~~further~~ instructions when he prepares to go down to Cuba for his week-long walk on the beach with Castro. While he has not yet cleared such instructions, Bob thinks we should instruct Donovan to tell Castro that "As far as I understand U.S. policy, only two things are non-negotiable, (1) Cuba's ties with the Sino-Soviet Bloc and (2) Cuba's interference with the hemisphere." Bob visualizes Donovan's role as primarily a transmitter to the U.S. Government of any proposals Castro might make in response to this line. Care would be exercised to avoid any connection with this trip and the U.S. Government.

There is a slim chance that Castro may force the policy issue this weekend. We should know the answer to this when Castro's man calls Donovan about the appointment. If Castro does insist on talking about policy, we will have to instruct Donovan carefully.

Gordon Chase

<del>TOP SECRET — EYES ONLY</del>   2/5/97

Top Secret White House memo, "Mr. Donovan's Trip to Cuba," March 1, 1963

Dallas police were using two radio channels that day. Routine radio traffic was on Channel One and recorded on a dicta-belt at police headquarters. Channel Two was dedicated to the President's motorcade and used primarily by Dallas Police Chief Jesse Curry. Channel Two transmissions were recorded on a separate Gray Audiograph disc machine. The sounds of assassination were recorded at Dallas police headquarters when a motorcycle patrolman microphone was accidentally left in the "keyed" (transmitting) position. The shooting took place within an 18-second interval that began with Chief Curry in the lead car announcing on Channel Two that the motorcade was approaching the triple underpass and ended with the chief stating urgently: "Go to the hospital." What seemed to be the gunshots were picked up on Channel One during that interval. Dallas County Sheriff Bill Decker came over both channels saying, "Hold everything secure" seemingly about a half-second after the last gunshot on Channel One.

Audio filtering techniques have produced "audible events" within a 10-second time frame that is believed may be gunfire. The Warren Commission concluded in 1964 that only three shots (all from behind and all from Oswald's rifle) were fired in Dealey Plaza. But the HSCA experts found ten "echo patterns" that matched sounds coming from the grassy knoll, carrying to nearby buildings and then reflecting to the open microphone of the motorcycle's transmitter. These patterns also placed the unknown gunman behind a picket fence at the top of the grassy knoll, in front of and to the right of the presidential limousine. The Committee concluded that this shot missed and that Kennedy was killed by a final bullet from Oswald's rifle. Some experts, however, believe that it was a shot from the knoll, seven-tenths of a second earlier, which killed the president.

The NAS panel concluded that the supposed gunshot noises came "too late to be attributed to assassination shots." Other experts believe that Chief Curry issued his "go to the hospital" order right after the first shots were fired, wounding Kennedy and Governor John Connally, and that the final bullet was fired almost the same moment that Chief Curry gave his command. A minute later, Sheriff Decker, riding in the same car with Curry, grabbed the mike and issued his orders to, "hold everything secure."

The NAS experts may have erred in using Sheriff Decker's words to line up the two channels. Other experts say that a much clearer instance of "cross talk" was when Dallas Police Sergeant S. Q. Bellah could be heard on both channels asking, "You want me to hold this traffic on Stemmons until we find out something or let it go?" This came 179 seconds after the last gunshot on Channel One and 180 seconds after Chief Curry's order to "go to the hospital" on Channel Two. When Bellah's words are used to line up the two channels, the gunshot sounds match the exact instant that John F. Kennedy was assassinated. Sheriff Decker's remarks on Channel One seem to come a full minute after Chief Curry's on Channel Two, yet a half-second after the last gunshot on Channel One. Some experts assert that a bump on the recorder may have caused an "over-dub" and may account for the discrepancy.

This story continues to become more interesting as more facts and theories are unfolded. It also becomes more mysterious. Is it any wonder that the most pondered murder mystery in our generation is such an enigma? Thus far we have merely set the stage and looked at a few of the declassified files on the murder of President John F. Kennedy. This story fills volumes, so packing the story of only the declassified documents into a single chapter is impossible. In the next chapter we will look more at the theories and declassified documents of this tragic drama.

REFERENCES:

NOTE: The sources for the information in this chapter are from public archives and sources, many of which are common knowledge. The declassified documents are from the National Archives, released to the public by the Assassination Records Review Board. The photos are public domain photos.

CHAPTER SEVEN

THE KENNEDY ASSISSINATION: DECLASSIFIED (PART II)

My dear Watson, there we come into those realms of conjecture where the most logical mind may be at fault.

~ Sherlock Holmes ~

Sir Arthur Conan Doyle

Kennedy and Castro: The Cuban Policy

A few days before his assassination, President Kennedy was allegedly planning a meeting with Cuban officials to negotiate the normalization of relations with Fidel Castro. Those who suggest this assertion say that a newly declassified tape and White House documents prove this to be true. It is asserted that an audio tape of the President and his national security advisor prove that they were discussing the possibility of a secret meeting in Havana with Castro. The tape, dated only seventeen days before the assassination, records a briefing on Castro's invitation to William Attwood, a deputy to United Nations Ambassador Adlai Stevenson, to come to Cuba for secret talks on improving relations with the U.S. The tape purportedly proves that President Kennedy approved the meeting if there could be plausible deniability of official U.S. participation.

The possibility of a meeting in Havana allegedly resulted from the President's changing his view on "an accommodation with Castro" following the Cuban Missile Crisis. Top Secret White House memos allegedly record the President's position that "we should start thinking along more flexible lines." Castro also seemed to be interested. In a May 1963 ABC News special on Cuba, Castro told correspondent Lisa Howard that he considered negotiations with the United States "possible if the United States government wishes it." He said, "In that case, we would be agreed to seek and find a basis" for improved relations. Howard's became an intermediary as a result of her contact with Ambassador Stevenson at the United Nations and a message was sent back to Castro through her from the White House. This opportunity ended following the assassination of President Kennedy and there are indications that Castro viewed the assassination as a setback. When Castro tried to re-open dialogue with the Johnson administration, LBJ was concerned about appearing soft on communism and later became too distracted by Vietnam.

Dr. Robert J. Girod, Sr.

~~TOP SECRET~~
~~EYES ONLY~~

March 4, 1963

MEMORANDUM FOR THE RECORD

SUBJECT: Mr. Donovan's Trip to Cuba

At Mr. Bundy's request I passed to Bob Hurwitch the following Presidential reactions to the attached memorandum:

    1. The President does not agree that we should make the breaking of Sino/Soviet ties a non-negotiable point. We don't want to present Castro with a condition that he obviously cannot fulfill. We should start thinking along more flexible lines.

    2. Donovan should resist taking his week-long walk along the beach with Castro until we have had a chance to give Donovan a very good briefing. We may want to give Donovan some flies to dangle in front of Castro.

    3. The above must be kept close to the vest. The President himself, is very interested in this one.

Gordon Chase

~~TOP SECRET - EYES ONLY~~

Top Secret White House memo, "Mr. Donovan's Trip to Cuba," March 4, 1963

THE WHITE HOUSE
WASHINGTON

~~TOP SECRET~~
~~SENSITIVE~~
~~EYES ONLY~~

November 19, 1963

MEMORANDUM FOR

MR. BUNDY

SUBJECT: Approach to Castro

Bill Attwood called to report the following:

1. Lisa Howard called Vallejo and then put Bill Attwood on the line. Vallejo repeated his invitation for Bill to come to Cuba, adding that the visit would be very secure. Bill replied that this was impossible for the present, that preliminary talks were essential, and that Vallejo might consider coming to New York.

2. Vallejo said he could not make it to New York at this time. However, a message would be sent to Lechuga instructing him to discuss an agenda with Bill. Bill agreed that this might be a good way for the Cubans to convey what was on their mind. He added that we are prepared to listen.

3. The ball is now in Castro's court. As soon as Lechuga calls Bill to set up an appointment for the discussion of an agenda, Bill will get in touch with us.

GC
Gordon Chase

~~TOP SECRET - SENSITIVE~~
~~EYES ONLY~~

COPY LBJ LIBRARY

Top secret White House Memo on trip to Cuba, November 19, 1963.

S-E-C-R-E-T
NO FOREIGN DISSEM/CONTROLLED DISSEM/NO DISSEM ABROAD/BACKGROUND USE ONLY
CENTRAL INTELLIGENCE AGENCY
WASHINGTON 25, D. C.

1 May 1963

MEMORANDUM FOR: The Director of Central Intelligence

SUBJECT: Interview of U.S. Newswoman with Fidel Castro Indicating Possible Interest in Rapprochement with the United States

1. On 30 April 1963 Liza Howard, U.S. newswoman associated with the American Broadcasting Company, returned to Miami from Cuba where she had interviewed a number of high-ranking Cuban officials, including Fidel Castro, Raul Castro, Ernesto "Che" Guevara, Vilma Espin de Castro, Raul Roa, and Reno Vallejo. Her conversations with Fidel Castro totaled about ten hours and included one session on 22 April which lasted from 12:45 a.m. to 5:30 a.m. Following is an account of those conversations and Liza Howard's observations concerning the present Cuban situation.

2. It appears that Fidel Castro is looking for a way to reach a rapprochement with the United States Government, probably because he is aware that Cuba is in a state of economic chaos. The October blockade hurt the Cuban economy. Liza Howard believes that Castro talked about this matter with her because she is known as a progressive and she talked with him in frank, blunt, honest terms; Castro has little opportunity to hear this type of conversation. Castro indicated that if a rapprochement was wanted President John F. Kennedy would have to make the first move. In response to the statement that Castro would probably have to make the first move, Castro asked what the U.S. wanted from him. When a return to the original aims of the revolution was suggested, Fidel said that perhaps he, President Kennedy,

S-E-C-R-E-T
NO FOREIGN DISSEM/CONTROLLED DISSEM/NO DISSEM ABROAD/BACKGROUND USE ONLY

Part of CIA Director's interview with ABC's Liza Howard, May 1, 1963.

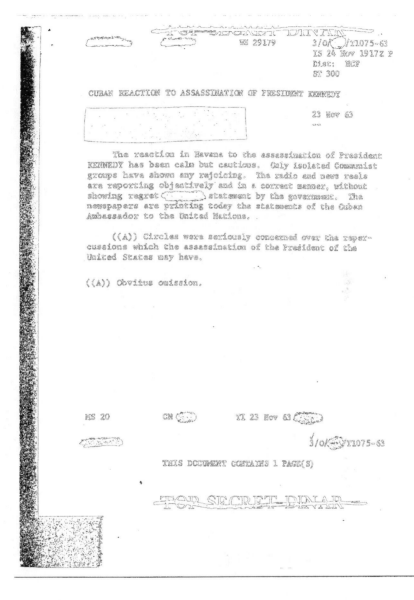

Intelligence report on the Cuban reaction to assassination.

```
                                            2X/O/   /T2421-63
                                            IS 24 Nov 1713Z P
                                            Dist: HCF
                                            ST 300

                    SECRET              O/27208-63

    OFFICIAL CUBAN STATEMENT ON DEATH OF PRESIDENT KENNEDY

                                    23 Nov 63


        In spite of the antagonism existing between the Government
    of the United States and the Cuban Revolution, we have received
    the news of the tragic death of President KENNEDY with deep
    sorrow. All civilized men always grieve about such events as
    this. Our delegation to the Organisation of the United Nations
    wishes to state that this is the feeling of the people and of
    the Government of Cuba.

    GROUP 1                    SECRET      PAGE  1  of  2  PAGE(s)
    EXCLUDED FROM AUTOMATIC
    DOWNGRADING AND DECLASSIFICATION



    MS 36         CN        TI 24 Nov 63
                            WS 17263        2X/O/   /T2421-63
                                            O/27208-63
                                            PAGE  1  of  2  PAGE(s)

                    SECRET SABRE
```

Intelligence report on the official Cuban statement on the death of President Kennedy.

TOP SECRET DINAR

WS 9776   3/O/_/T1463-63
           IS 05 Dec 2135Z P
           Dist: HCF
           - ST 300

COMMENT ON CASTRO'S REACTION TO DEATH OF KENNEDY

27 Nov 63

Late Friday afternoon and through the night a large movement of troops began here. They were sent to take up positions and reinforce strategic positions around Havana and the northern coast of the island because of the assassination of President KENNEDY. Saturday evening FIDEL CASTRO appeared on television and spoke about the death of KENNEDY and tried to refute charges which had already appeared in the United States that the assassin was a Marxist and a Communist Castroite. Although it was only the third time that I had witnessed a speech by FIDEL, I got the immediate impression that on this occasion he was frightened, if not terrified. _____, however, confirmed that impression and indicated surprise at this hasty jump into the arena to denounce insinuations which were merely from news and nongovernmental agencies. In fact, it is the general opinion in _____ circles that CASTRO feared that the assassination would be the spring which would unleash passions and violent and blind hysteria of the American people against Cuba and Russia and provide the excuse which up to now was lacking to justify internationally an invasion of Cuba. There is talk again about the coincidence of rumors concerning a crisis at the end of the year (_____).

FIDEL, emotional and uneasy, tried through the same telegrams of the American news agencies to refute the accusations which were then appearing and to twist them so that the assassination would appear as the work of the Ultra Reaction, of the extreme racists of the Pentagon, who are fanatical supporters of war against Cuba and the Soviet Union.

3/O/_/T1463-63

THIS DOCUMENT CONTAINS 2 PAGES(S)

TOP SECRET DINAR

Intelligence report on Castro's reaction to the assassination.

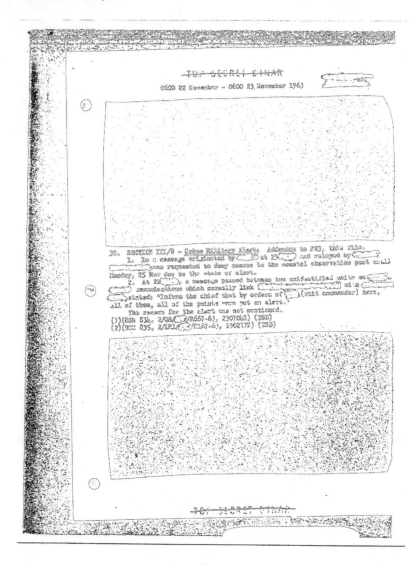

Cuban Military alert.

Cuban Naval alert.

REPRODUCTION/FURTHER DISSEMINATION PROHIBITED
WITHOUT PRIOR DIRNSA CONCURRENCE

ISHTAR
3/O/....R26-63
ELECTRICAL RELEASE
23 Nov 63 2103Z
DIST: O/ZK
ST 022; 052, 072, 102,
141, 221

NATIONAL SECURITY AGENCY
Fort George G. Meade, Maryland

COMINT REPORT

WARNING

This Document Contains Information affecting the National Defense of the United States within the meaning of the Espionage Laws, Title 18, U.S.C., Sections 793, 794 and 798, the transmission or revelation of which in any manner to an unauthorized person is prohibited by law.

This document is to be distributed to and read by only those persons who are officially indoctrinated in accordance with communications intelligence security regulations and who need the information in order to perform their duties.

No action is to be taken on information herein reported, regardless of temporary advantage, if such action might have the effect of revealing the existence and nature of the source.

THIS DOCUMENT CONTAINS CODEWORD MATERIAL

Cuban military and Naval alert.

Infamous Murders and Mysteries

2/O/ R96-63
05 Dec 63 2303Z
DIST: O/WG
ST 250

NATIONAL SECURITY AGENCY
Fort George G. Meade, Maryland

COMINT REPORT

Western Army alert.

The Soviet Policy Declassified: From Russia with . . .

The Kennedy assassination was as closely a guarded secret for the Soviet, Russian and satellite states as it was for the Unites States and Western intelligence services. But decades later the Eastern intelligence community began to declassify some of their information as well. The more documents that become available, the more questions arise. Whether declassified documents come from the Western or Eastern intelligence communities, more mysteries seem to emerge and more fascination results.

On June 20, 1999, the Office of the White House Press Secretary released a statement while in Cologne, Germany, that Russian President Boris Yeltsin had given the United States with a very interesting presentation. Yeltsin said that he had asked all of the agencies of the Russian government to declassify any and all material related to President Kennedy and President Kennedy's assassination. More than eighty documents, including reports by Soviet intelligence officers operating in the U.S. at the time, on the Kennedy assassination and on Lee Harvey Oswald were given to then President Bill Clinton. The revelations in these files, however, remain mostly unknown to the public at large.

Yuriy Nosenko, Lee Harvey Oswald, and the "Family Jewels"

Lieutenant Colonel Yuriy Nosenko was a KGB defector who became a figure of significant controversy within the U.S. intelligence community. He helped expose John Vassall, a British civil servant charged with spying in 1962 (see The Cambridge Five Spy Ring). His case was documented in the "Family Jewels" documents and handled by CIA officer George Kisevalter (1910-1997). Kisevalter was a CIA operations officer who also handled both Soviet GRU Major Pyotr Popov and Colonel Oleg Penkovskiy. The "Family Jewels" refers to the reports that detailed activities of the CIA that were considered illegal or inappropriate between the 1950s through the mid-1970s. Most of the documents were publicly released on June 25, 2007, after more than three decades of secrecy. The non-governmental National Security Archive had filed a Freedom of Information Act request fifteen years earlier.

According to a briefing provided to the Justice Department by CIA Director William Colby on December 31, 1974, the "Family Jewels" reports describe numerous activities including eighteen issues which were of legal concern:

1. The confinement of a Russian defector, Yuri Ivanovich Nosenko, which "might be regarded as a violation of the kidnapping laws."

2. The wiretapping of two syndicated columnists, Robert Allen and Paul Scott, which was approved by Attorney General Robert Kennedy and Secretary of Defense Robert McNamara.

3. The surveillance of investigative journalist Jack Anderson and his associates, including Les Whitten of the Washington Post and future Fox News Channel anchor and managing editor Brit Hume. (Jack Anderson had written two articles on CIA-backed assassination attempts on Cuban leader Fidel Castro).

4. The surveillance of then-*Washington Post* reporter Michael Getler.

5. The warrantless entry into the apartment of a former CIA employee.

6. The break-in at the home of another former CIA employee.

7. The break-in at the office of a former defector.

8. The opening of mail to and from the Soviet Union between 1953 and 1973 (including letters associated with Jane Fonda).

9. The opening of mail to and from the People's Republic of China from 1969 to 1972.

10. The funding of behavior modification research on unwitting U.S. citizens, including "unscientific, non-consensual human experiments concerning LSD" experiments).

11. Surveillance of dissident groups between 1967 and 1971.

12. Surveillance of a Latin American female and of U.S. citizens in Detroit.

13. Surveillance of former CIA officer and Agency critic, Victor Marchetti, author of the book, *The CIA and the Cult of Intelligence,* published in 1974.

14. Amassing of files on more than 9,900 Americans involved in the antiwar movement.

15. Polygraph experiments with the sheriff of San Mateo County, California.

16. Forged CIA identification documents that might violate state laws.

17. Testing of electronic surveillance equipment on U.S. telephone circuits.

18. The assassination plans against
- Cuban president Fidel Castro (authorized by Attorney General Robert Kennedy);

- Congolese leader Patrice Lumumba (killed in 1960);

- President Rafael Trujillo of the Dominican Republic (killed in 1961); and

- René Schneider, Commander-in-chief of the Chilean Army (killed in 1970).

Records reveal that Yuri Ivanovich Nosenko started working as a double agent for the CIA in 1962. In 1964 Nosenko reported that he had been discovered by the KGB and needed to defect immediately. Tennent H. Bagley was Nosenko's case officer when they met in Geneva in 1962 and when he defected in 1964. George Kisevalter, who was fluent in Russian and well respected for his handling of Major Pyotr Popov, was assigned to assist Bagley. To persuade the CIA to accept his defection, Nosenko claimed that the KGB in Geneva had received a cable recalling him to Moscow and he was fearful that he had been found out. The National Security Agency (NSA) determined that this was not true.

Nosenko claimed that he could provide important information about the assassination of President John F. Kennedy, affirming that he personally handled the case of Lee Harvey Oswald. Nosenko said that Oswald was not useful to the KGB because he was "mentally unstable." He said that the KGB had never questioned Oswald about information he had gained as an aviation electronics operator at Naval Air Facility Atsugi in Japan.

Two polygraph (lie detector) tests conducted by the CIA asserted that Nosenko was lying about Oswald. The polygrapher who conducted the first two tests determined that Nosenko lied on the first test, though not about Oswald, and that he had lied on the second test on two of the Oswald questions. Another polygrapher conducted a third test and concluded that Nosenko was telling the truth. In the 1970's, the CIA reviewed the handling of the Nosenko case and concluded that the first two polygraph tests should be considered "invalid or inconclusive" due to deficiencies in the way they were conducted.

```
                      CONFIDENTIAL
                   *** BEGIN MESSAGE    2 ***
SERIAL=MOSCOW72-92    UDN=VOO(1670)
CLASS=CONFIDENTIAL
                        CONFIDENTIAL  NSA0017
PAGE 01         MOSCOW  00072  030826Z
ACTION EUR-01
INFO  LOG-00    AID-01    AMAD-01   CIAE-00   C-01      DODE-00   EAP-01
      E-01      CSCE-01   HA-09     H-01      INRE-00   INR-01    L-03
      ADS-00    EOFM-01   MOF-03    M-01      MPI-01    NRRC-01   NSAE-00
      NSCE-00   OMB-01    PA-01     PM-01     PRS-01    P-01      SCT-03
      SDEL-01   SNP-01    SP-01     SSO-00    SS-01     TRSE-00   T-01
      USIE-00   /041W
                       ------------------BD8534  030826Z /38
O 030823Z JAN 92
FM AMEMBASSY MOSCOW
TO SECSTATE WASHDC IMMEDIATE 5686
BT
C O N F I D E N T I A L  MOSCOW 000072
SERIAL: MOSCOW00072-92
FOR P, C/E, H, EUR/SOV AND EAP/VLC
E.O. 12356: DECL: OADR
TAGS: PREL, PINR, MOPS, UR
SUBJECT:  EX-KGB GENERAL KALUGIN ON AMERICAN POW
-         INTERROGATIONS IN VIETNAM
REF: STATE 871
1. CONFIDENTIAL -- ENTIRE TEXT.
2. EMBOFF CONTACTED EX-KGB GENERAL OLEG KALUGIN
(PROTECT) ON JANUARY 2 TO INQUIRE ABOUT HIS PLANS TO
TRAVEL TO WASHINGTON TO MEET WITH SENATE
INVESTIGATORS. KALUGIN CONFIRMED THE REPORT WHICH

APPEARED IN A JANUARY 2 ASSOCIATE PRESS STORY THAT
HE WOULD BE MEETING WITH SENATE INVESTIGATORS TO
DISCUSS FURTHER HIS OFT REPEATED CLAIM THAT THE KGB
INTERROGATED THREE AMERICAN POWS IN VIETNAM IN 1978.
3. KALUGIN EXPRESSED SURPRISE THAT WASHINGTON IS
GIVING SO MUCH ATTENTION TO HIS ASSERTIONS --
PARTICULARLY SINCE HE HAS NOT SAID ANYTHING NEW OR
DIFFERENT ABOUT THE CASE SINCE HE FIRST SPOKE OUT
PUBLICLY ON THIS ISSUE SEVERAL MONTHS AGO.
NEVERTHELESS, HE TOLD EMBOFF THAT HE WANTED TO BE AS
HELPFUL AS POSSIBLE.
4. KALUGIN SAID THAT HE HAD RECENTLY BEEN IN TOUCH
WITH ONE OF THE FORMER KGB INTERROGATORS WHO
QUESTIONED THE AMERICAN POWS IN VIETNAM IN 1978.
THE INTERROGATOR, KALUGIN TOLD EMBOFF, HAS RECENTLY
DECIDED TO GO PUBLIC IN THE NEAR FUTURE WITH WHAT HE
KNOWS ABOUT THE INCIDENT. KALUGIN SAID THAT HE
PLANNED TO SPEAK WITH HIS FORMER COLLEAGUE ON
JANUARY 3 TO DISCUSS HIS INTENTIONS FURTHER.
KALUGIN ALSO SAID THAT THE FORMER INTERROGATOR
CLAIMED TO HAVE OTHER INFORMATION OF INTEREST TO THE
                       CONFIDENTIAL
```

KGB interviewed Oswald, page 1.

```
                    -CONFIDENTIAL-
                *** BEGIN MESSAGE    2 ***
SERIAL=MOSCOW72-92   UDN=VOO(1870)
CLASS=CONFIDENTIAL
                     -CONFIDENTIAL- NSA0017
PAGE 01          MOSCOW 00072 030826Z
ACTION EUR-01
INFO   LOG-00   AID-01   AMAD-01  CIAE-00  C-01     DODE-00  EAP-01
       E-01     CSCE-01  HA-09    H-01     INRE-00  INR-00   L-03
       ADS-00   EOFM-01  MOF-03   H-01     WPI-01   HRRC-01  NSAE-00
       NSCE-00  OMB-01   PA-01    PM-01    PRS-01   P-01     SCT-03
       SDEL-01  SNP-01   SP-01    SSO-00   SS-01    TRSE-00  T-01
       USIE-00  /041W
                           ------BD8S34   030826Z  /38

O  030823Z JAN 92
FM AMEMBASSY MOSCOW
TO SECSTATE WASHDC IMMEDIATE 5686
BT
C O N F I D E N T I A L  MOSCOW 000072
SERIAL: MOSCOW00072-92
FOR P, C/E, H, EUR/SOV AND EAP/VLC
E.O. 12356: DECL: OADR
TAGS: PREL, PINR, MOPS, UR
SUBJECT: EX-KGB GENERAL KALUGIN ON AMERICAN POW
-        INTERROGATIONS IN VIETNAM
REF: STATE 871
1.  CONFIDENTIAL -- ENTIRE TEXT.
2.  EMBOFF CONTACTED EX-KGB GENERAL OLEG KALUGIN
(PROTECT) ON JANUARY 2 TO INQUIRE ABOUT HIS PLANS TO
TRAVEL TO WASHINGTON TO MEET WITH SENATE
INVESTIGATORS.  KALUGIN CONFIRMED THE REPORT WHICH

APPEARED IN A JANUARY 2 ASSOCIATE PRESS STORY THAT
HE WOULD BE MEETING WITH SENATE INVESTIGATORS TO
DISCUSS FURTHER HIS OFT REPEATED CLAIM THAT THE KGB
INTERROGATED THREE AMERICAN POWS IN VIETNAM IN 1978.
3.  KALUGIN EXPRESSED SURPRISE THAT WASHINGTON IS
GIVING SO MUCH ATTENTION TO HIS ASSERTIONS --
PARTICULARLY SINCE HE HAS NOT SAID ANYTHING NEW OR
DIFFERENT ABOUT THE CASE SINCE HE FIRST SPOKE OUT
PUBLICLY ON THIS ISSUE SEVERAL MONTHS AGO.
NEVERTHELESS, HE TOLD EMBOFF THAT HE WANTED TO BE AS
HELPFUL AS POSSIBLE.
4.  KALUGIN SAID THAT HE HAD RECENTLY BEEN IN TOUCH
WITH ONE OF THE FORMER KGB INTERROGATORS WHO
QUESTIONED THE AMERICAN POWS IN VIETNAM IN 1978.
THE INTERROGATOR, KALUGIN TOLD EMBOFF, HAS RECENTLY
DECIDED TO GO PUBLIC IN THE NEAR FUTURE WITH WHAT HE
KNOWS ABOUT THE INCIDENT.  KALUGIN SAID THAT HE
PLANNED TO SPEAK WITH HIS FORMER COLLEAGUE ON
JANUARY 3 TO DISCUSS HIS INTENTIONS FURTHER.
KALUGIN ALSO SAID THAT THE FORMER INTERROGATOR
CLAIMED TO HAVE OTHER INFORMATION OF INTEREST TO THE
                    -CONFIDENTIAL-
```

KGB interviewed Oswald, page 2.

However, Associate Deputy Director of Operations for Counterintelligence James Jesus Angleton did not believe Nosenko. When Nosenko told his version of the story about Lee Harvey Oswald and the Kennedy assassination it didn't fit with the agency's "corporate view." Nosenko was sent to solitary confinement in a ten square feet attic at "the farm" for three years. Wires were strapped to his head and agents told him that an electroencephalograph

(EEG) would allow them to read his mind, while it was really a medical instrument for reading brainwave patterns. This was intended to be psychological intimidation to persuade him to "tell the truth."

James Jesus Angleton, CIA Counterintelligence Chief
(Public domain photo)

```
                       UNCLAS 3G
                 *** BEGIN MESSAGE       9 ***
SERIAL=OW0408163592    UDN=V03(39310)
CLASS=UNCLAS 3G
FBIS 05JAUG04
UNCLAS 3G
BYELARUS: KGB CHIEF OPPOSES RELEASE OF LEE HARVEY OSWALD FILES
OW0408163592 MOSCOW INTERFAX IN ENGLISH 1559 GMT 4 AUG 92
  FOLLOWING ITEM TRANSMITTED VIA KYODO
     TEXT  BYELARUS'S KGB CHIEF EDUARD SHIRKOVSKIY HAS HIGHLY
PRAISED THE BYELARUSIAN-UKRAINIAN AGREEMENT ON COOPERATION BETWEEN
THE SECRET SERVICES OF THE TWO COUNTRIES SIGNED IN KIEV ON JULY 31.
HE POINTED OUT THE FACT THAT THE REPUBLICAN KGB CARRIED OUT ONLY
INTELLIGENCE AND COUNTERINTELLIGENCE ACTIVITIES NEEDED FOR A NEUTRAL
STATE.
     EDUARD SHIRKOVSKIY SAID THAT HE HAD PERSONALLY EXAMINED THE CASE
OF LEE HARVEY OSWALD AND ADDED THAT IT WOULD BE DECLASSIFIED ONLY BY
PERMISSION OF PARLIAMENT. THE KGB GENERAL BELIEVES THAT IT SHOULD
NOT BE DONE, FOR THE SIX VOLUMES OF MATERIALS OF THE CASE REVEAL ALL
METHODS OF OPERATION WORK OF THE SECRET SERVICE. THOUGH, EDUARD
SHIRKOVSKIY EXPRESSED CONFIDENCE THAT LEE HARVEY OSWALD WAS UNLIKELY
TO BE INVOLVED IN THE ASSASSINATION OF PRESIDENT JOHN KENNEDY. HE
ADDED THAT LEE HARVEY OSWALD WAS NEITHER KGB, NOR CIA COLLABORATOR,
AND THAT HE WAS NO MARKSMAN.
04 AUG 1641Z KC
NNNN
NNN


                            UNCLAS 3G
```

KGB Chief's opinion – Oswald was not a KGB or CIA operative and not involved in assassination.

```
                              UNCLAS 3D/PNU/SU 291 797
                         *** BEGIN MESSAGE    6 ***
SERIAL=LD1006145792      UDN=VO2(45790)
CLASS=UNCLAS 3D/PNU/SU 291 797
2CECOLC0040
RTTUZYUW RUDKHKA6141 1621519-UUUU--RUETIAV.
ZNR UUUUU ZYN
R 101457Z JUN 92
FM FBIS LONDON UK
TO RUCWAAA/FBIS RESTON VA
RHHHNCY/JICPAC HONOLULU HI
RUCKDDA/SECOND INTEL CD//ITD//
RUDPHAX/FAISA FT BRAGG NC
RUOPWDC/DA AMHS WASHINGTON DC
RUERFGA/VOA WASH DC
RUEBHAA/STORAGE CENTER FBIS RESTON VA
RUEHC/SECSTATE WASHINGTON DC//INR/SES/SI//
RUEKJCS/DEFINTRAGNCY WASH DC
RUEOACC/CDR PSYOPGP FT BRAGG NC//ASOF-POG-SB//
RUESDJ/FBIS OKINAWA JA
RUESFV/FBIS VIENNA AU
RUETIAV/NPC FT GEO G MEADE MD
RUFHPT/AMCONSUL FRANKFURT//FBCIC//
ACCT FBLD-EWDK
BT
UNCLAS 3D/PNU/SU 291 797
SERIAL:  LD1006145792
PASS:    COPY TO CD
COUNTRY: RUSSIA
SUBJ:    EX-KGB CHIEF DENIES COMPLICITY IN KENNEDY ASSASSINATION
SOURCE:  MOSCOW ITAR-TASS IN ENGLISH 1311 GMT 10 JUN 92
TEXT:
     //((BY ITAR-TASS CORRESPONDENT SERGEY SOSNOVSKIY))
     ((TEXT)) BONN JUNE 10 TASS -- KGB TOOK NO PART WHATSOEVER IN THE
ORGANISATION OF THE ASSASSINATION OF PRESIDENT JOHN KENNEDY", EX-
CHIEF OF THE KGB VLADIMIR SEMICHASTNII SAID IN AN INTERVIEW WITH THE
GERMAN MAGAZINE DER SPIEGEL.
     SEMICHASTNII HEADED THE KGB WHEN THE TRAGIC EVENTS UNFURLED IN
DALLAS, TEXAS.
     ASKED WHEN THE KGB FIRST CAME ACROSS LEE HARVEY OSWALD,
SEMICHASTNII SAID: "WHEN OUR COUNTER-INTELLIGENCE CHIEF REPORTED
THAT OSWALD ASKED US FOR POLITICAL ASYLUM". I.E. ABOUT TWO YEARS
PRIOR TO THE ASSASSINATION.
     "HE ARRIVED AT A CONCLUSION THAT OSWALD WAS A COMMON PERSON OF
LITTLE INTEREST".
     OSWALD SPENT SOME TIME IN MOSCOW AND WAS LATER TRANSPORTED TO
MINSK WHERE HE LIVED UNDER LOCAL KGB SURVEILLANCE. THE OSWALD FILE
CONTAINED MAINLY "TRIVIAL THINGS: LOVE AFFAIRS, DANCING SPREES AND
PICNICS WITH A GIRL-FRIEND".
     ACCORDING TO SEMICHASTNII, OSWALD COULD NOT BE THE CENTRAL FIGURE
IN THE ASSASSINATION OF KENNEDY. "HE IS A STOOGE, A SORT OF
LIGHTNING ROD IN A MUCH MORE SERIOUS OPERATION", WHICH "WAS
BRILLIANTLY ARRANGED", SEMICHASTNII SAID.
(ENDALL) 101311 LEWICK PLE2100S.034/WE 10/1517Z JUN
                              UNCLAS 3D/PNU/SU 291 797
```

Former KGB chief calls Oswald a "stooge" in a "much more serious operation" which was "brilliantly arranged."

~~TOP SECRET DINAR~~
************************ NO FOREIGN DISSEM ****************************
XRAY HANDLING REQUIRED

WN N-9004   3/O/X/T84-63
               IS 25 Nov 1839Z P
               Dist: XCF

AMERICAN AMBASSADOR BELIEVES RUSSIA AND CUBA INVOLVED IN KENNEDY'S DEATH

24 Nov 63
Normal

30.

After signing the register which is open in the American Embassy on the occasion of the death of KENNEDY, I saw the Ambassador. He is of the opinion that Russia and Cuba had a finger in the assassination.

MS 36   CN   TI 24 Nov 63

                          3/O/X/T84-63

THIS DOCUMENT CONTAINS 1 PAGE(S)

~~TOP SECRET DINAR~~

Top secret report on a conversation overheard of an American Ambassador opining on Russia's and Cuba's involvement in the assassination of President

Kennedy.

TOP SECRET DINAR

WS 15532

Change 1
3/O/~~~~/T1657-63((A))
IS 13 Dec 63 P
Dist: HCO

~~~~ REPORTS SOVIET REACTION TO ASSASSINATION OF U.S. PRESIDENT

29 Nov 63

Reference repercussions in the Soviet Union to the assassination of President KENNEDY.

Basing the first on personal judgment and the others on reports from reliable ~~~~ sources, I will give the following evaluations:

The deep grief produced here by the assassination was absolutely spontaneous and can be explained by the high culture of the Soviet people, which enables them to rise above world events, and by traditional Russian sentimentality.

The moment the news was received, because of the possibility of international complications the military authorities increased their security measures. These have now returned to normal.

High-ranking Soviet officials are concerned over what international policy the new President will pursue, especially with respect to Cuba, and, although it seems that MIKOYAN's feelings, after speaking with the President and other high-ranking United States officials, were moderately calm, Soviet leaders are waiting to learn how the matter of the purchase of wheat in the United States will be resolved and also for the conclusion of a new Soviet-United States cultural agreement, in order to obtain a more clear idea of the above-mentioned policy.

((A)) Reissue based on better text.

MS 19   CN ~~~~   TI 29 Nov 63 ~~~~
                                    Change 1
                                    3/O/~~~~/T1657-63

THIS DOCUMENT CONTAINS 1 PAGE

TOP SECRET DINAR

A Top Secret report, dated 29 November 1963, on the Soviet reaction to the President's assassination.

```
                              CONFIDENTIAL
                       *** BEGIN MESSAGE    55 ***
   SERIAL=MINSK1220-92    UDN=V05(4718)
   CLASS=CONFIDENTIAL
                           CONFIDENTIAL  NSA3562
   PAGE 01       MINSK   01220  01 OF 02   041530Z
   ACTION EUR-01
   INFO  LOG-00    CIAE-00    C-01      ANHR-01   CISA-02   DS-00    FBIE-00
         INRE-00   INR-01     JUSE-00   L-03      ADS-00    NSAE-00  NSCE-00
         PM-02     P-01       SP-00     SSO-00    SS-00     ASDS-01  /0139
                                        -----76802E  041608Z /43

   O 041421Z NOV 92
   FM AMEMBASSY MINSK
   TO SECSTATE WASHDC IMMEDIATE 0885
   BT
   C O N F I D E N T I A L SECTION 01 OF 02 MINSK 001220
   SERIAL: MINSK 01220-92
   DEPT FOR EUR/ISCA
   E.O. 12356: DECL: OADR
   TAGS: PINR, BO, US
   SUBJECT: THE OSWALD FILES
   REF: A) STATE 353053, B) MINSK 703
   1. C - ENTIRE TEXT.
   2. BEGIN SUMMARY: IN A NINETY-MINUTE
   MEETING NOVEMBER 4 AT THE KGB HEADQUARTERS IN
   MINSK (OTHER ISSUES REPORTED SEPTEL),
   AMBASSADOR MADE REF A DEMARCHE, REQUESTING
   ACCESS TO THE KGB'S FILES ON LEE HARVEY
   OSWALD. BELARUSIAN KGB CHIEF EDUARD
   SHIRKOVSKIY, WHILE EXPRESSING A WILLINGNESS
   "TO MAKE THINGS MORE TRANSPARENT" TO THE

   U.S., SAID HE COULD NOT SIMPLY HAND OVER THE
   DOCUMENTS INASMUCH AS KGB METHODS OF
   OPERATION WOULD ALSO BE REVEALED. HE ADDED
   THAT HE WOULD OPEN HIMSELF UP TO ALL SORTS OF
   ACCUSATIONS IF HE ACTED WITHOUT THE APPROVAL
   OF PARLIAMENT.
   3. SHIRKOVSKIY SUGGESTED AN EXCHANGE OF
   INFORMATION MIGHT BE POSSIBLE, ADDING THAT
   BELARUS HAD MANY LINGERING QUESTIONS ABOUT
   WHO SENT OSWALD TO THE FORMER USSR AND FOR
   WHAT PURPOSE. HE EXPRESSED THE PERSONAL VIEW
   THAT OSWALD HAD NOT ACTED ALONE; OSWALD, HE
   SAID, WAS INCAPABLE OF SHOOTING PRESIDENT
   KENNEDY WITHOUT INSTRUCTIONS FROM SOMEBODY.
   SHIRKOVSKIY PROPOSED THAT THE FBI SUBMIT A
   LIST OF POINTED QUESTIONS WHICH THE KGB
   WOULD SEEK TO ANSWER. UPON RECEIPT AND
   INITIAL RESEARCH OF THE QUESTIONS,
   SHIRKOVSKIY SUGGESTED U.S. EXPERTS MIGHT
   VISIT MINSK TO PARTICIPATE IN A WORKING
   GROUP. SHIRKOVSKIY UNDERSCORED THAT SUCH A
                        CONFIDENTIAL
```

Confidential State Department report: KGB chief in Belarus opines that Oswald did not act alone.

Nosenko was given little food and only allowed to wash once a week during his 1,277 days of interrogation. Later he was tied up, dropped down a laundry chute into a waiting station wagon and taken to a custom-made prison cell for the next two years, until an anti-Angleton faction within the CIA was able to secure his release. On March 1, 1969, Nosenko was acknowledged as a genuine defector and released to accept a job with the CIA.

Oswald Call to the Soviet Embassy in Mexico City

Just hours after President Kennedy was assassinated, FBI agents reportedly listened to a tape of a phone call that had been placed to the Soviet Embassy in Mexico City by a man who identified himself as "Lee Oswald." According to government reports they did not believe the voice on the tape was Oswald's. This tape has been a controversial question in the assassination investigation since 1963. The Agency asserted that it routinely erased and reused tapes of phone intercepts. A message from the CIA's Mexico City station to headquarters on 24 November 1963, reported, "HQ has full transcripts [of] all pertinent calls. Regret complete recheck shows tapes for this period already erased."

Oswald was in Mexico City in September and October 1963 and did contact the Soviet Embassy and the Cuban Consulate about visas to go to the Soviet Union through Cuba. The CIA intercepted telephone calls and took surveillance photos at both the embassy and consulate. The discovery that the voice on the tape was someone other than Oswald, however, is of great concern because the man who impersonated Oswald was still at large.

While Oswald was in Mexico City he had contact with Valeriy Kostikov, a man that CIA reports described as a "case officer in an operation which is evidently sponsored by the KGB's 13th Department responsible for sabotage and assassination." It was the caller who is thought to have impersonated Oswald who links him to this Soviet spy unit known as Department 13.

The CIA said that the tapes on which it recorded the "Oswald" call were erased years ago. Declassified documents indicate that this is not correct and the tapes were not erased. After the President was shot, a Navy plane carried a Top Secret package from Mexico City to Dallas, landing there about 0400 EST (4:00 a.m.), the day after the murder. Former FBI Agent Eldon Rudd, later a Republican congressman from Arizona, was aboard the plane. He has been quoted as saying, "There were no tapes to my knowledge." He said, "I brought the pictures up (from Mexico) and it was my understanding that it was just pictures." Declassified documents contradict Rudd's understanding. A memo dated 27 November 1963 from FBI headquarters to its office in Mexico City, stated:

> *If tapes covering any contacts subject (Oswald) with Soviet or Cuban embassies available, forward to bureau for laboratory examination and analysis together with transcript. Include tapes previously reviewed Dallas if they were returned to you.*

J. Edgar Hoover, Director of the FBI
(Public domain photo)

```
                SECRET DOCUMENTS ON THE ASASSINATION OF U
                    *** BEGIN MESSAGE    3 ***
SERIAL=   UDN=V01(6484)
CLASS=SECRET DOCUMENTS ON THE ASASSINATION OF U
LBY370
REULB
R W
 BC-USA-KENNEDY     05-13 0700
BC-USA-KENNEDY
 CIA RELEASES OSWALD FILE
     BY JIM WOLF
   WASHINGTON, MAY 13, REUTER - THE CIA ON WEDNESDAY RELEASED
SECRET DOCUMENTS ON THE ASASSINATION OF U.S. PRESIDENT JOHN
KENNEDY WHICH IT HOPES WILL CLEAR IT OF SUSPICIONS OF COMPLICITY
BUT RESEARCHERS SAID THE NEW MATERIAL LEFT ALL THE CONSPIRACY
QUESTIONS UNANSWERED.
   THE 34 DOCUMENTS RELEASED BY THE CENTRAL INTELLIGENCE AGENCY
WERE THE FIRST OF WHAT COULD SOON BECOME A VAST FLOW OF
INFORMATION RELATED TO THE 1963 ASSASSINATION TO BE MADE PUBLIC
IN COMING MONTHS.
   PETER EARNEST, A CIA SPOKESMAN, SAID THE SIGNIFICANCE OF THE
MATERIAL WAS THAT IT SHOWED
THE TOTALITY OF WHAT IS CONTAINED
IN AGENCY RECORDS UP TO THE TIME OF THE ASSASSINATION.
SO I THINK THIS SHOULD PUT TO REST A LOT OF THE
SPECULATION ABOUT THE AGENCY:S KNOWLEDGE OR INVOLVEMENT WITH
OSWALD PRIOR TO THE ASSASSINATION,:: HE SAID.
   BUT HAROLD WEISBERG, AN AUTHOR OF SIX BOOKS ON THE KENNEDY
ASSASSINATION, SAID:
THE MOUNTAIN OF LABOUR PRODUCED A
MOUSE.::
   WEISBERG, WHO SAID HE HAS FILED MORE THAN A DOZEN LAWSUITS
SEEKING ASSASSINATION-RELATED MATERIAL, WONDERED WHY THE WARREN
COMMISSION, WHICH INVESTIGATED THE KILLING, HAD NOT RECEIVED THE
MATERIAL RELEASED ON WEDNESDAY.
   THE PRESIDENTIALLY APPOINTED COMMISSION, HEADED BY SUPREME
COURT JUSTICE EARL WARREN, CONCLUDED THAT LEE HARVEY OSWALD
ACTED ALONE IN THE ASSASSINATION. THE DEFUNCT HOUSE
ASSASSINATIONS COMMITTEE SAID IN A 1979 REPORT THAT EVIDENCE
POINTED TO A SECOND GUNMAN.
   EARNEST, THE CIA SPOKESMAN, DECLINED TO COMMENT ON WHICH
DOCUMENTS HAD GONE TO WHICH ASSASSINATION REVIEW COMMISSION.
   ON TUESDAY CIA DIRECTOR ROBERT GATES ANNOUNCED THE VOLUNTARY
RELEASE OF WHAT HE SAID WERE ALL CIA FILES ON OSWALD COMPILED
BEFORE THE ASSASSINATION. THE PACKET, MADE PUBLIC AT THE
NATIONAL ARCHIVES, CONTAINED 34 SANITISED DOCUMENTS, 12 OF WHICH
ORIGINATED WITH THE CIA.
   GATES SAID A PUBLIC AIRING OF WHAT INVESTIGATORS KNOW SHOULD
FREE HIS AGENCY OF SUSPICIONS -- REVIVED BY HOLLYWOOD IN THE
FILM
JFK:: -- THAT IT WAS PART OF A CONSPIRACY TO KILL KENNEDY
IN DALLAS.
   DOCUMENTS RELEASED ON WEDNESDAY SHOWED THAT U.S. AGENTS
TRACKED OSWALD BEFORE THE ASSASSINATION, BUT THE CIA COULD NOT
                SECRET DOCUMENTS ON THE ASASSINATION OF U
```

Reuter's report on CIA file on Oswald (which was included in the file).

A transcript of a telephone call from FBI Director J. Edgar Hoover to President Johnson just six hours after the plane arrived in Dallas suggests that

FBI agents listened to a tape that they believed it was an impersonation of Oswald:

> *We have up here the tape and the photograph of the man who was at the Soviet embassy using Oswald's name... That picture and the tape do not correspond to this man's voice, nor to his appearance. In other words, it appears that there is a second person who was at the Soviet embassy down there.*

Mexico City "Mystery Man," mistakenly identified as Oswald.
(Public domain photo)

Speculation as to the identity of the caller offers various viable explanations. A CIA officer could have impersonated Oswald, calling the Soviet Embassy in hopes of getting details about what Oswald was doing in Mexico City. Someone may have been trying to connect Oswald to the KGB's assassination unit to provide a motive for a fall-guy (patsy) in Kennedy's murder. Someone may have been establishing a theory for Oswald's defection to Cuba and/or Russia. There could be an infinite number of scenarios for someone with a little imagination.

A memo from FBI Director J. Edgar Hoover to U.S. Secret Service Director James Rowley, dated 23 November 1963, read:

> *The Central Intelligence Agency advised that on Oct. 1, 1963, an extremely sensitive source had reported that an individual identified himself as Lee Oswald, who contacted the Soviet Embassy in Mexico City inquiring as to any messages.*
>
> *Special Agents of this bureau, who have conversed with Oswald in Dallas, Texas, have observed photographs of the individual referred to above and have listened to a recording of his voice. These Special Agents are of the opinion that the above-referred-to individual was not Lee Harvey Oswald.*

Another memo, written 23 November 1963, from Alan Belmont, third in command at FBI Headquarters, to Clyde Tolson, Hoover's number-two man said:

> *The Dallas agents who listened to the tape of the conversation allegedly of Oswald from the Cuban Embassy to the Russian Embassy in Mexico and examined the photographs of the visitor to the Embassy in Mexico ... were of the opinion that neither the tape nor the photograph pertained to Oswald.*

And another memo written 24 November 1963 by Director Hoover read:

Oswald made a phone call to the Cuban embassy in Mexico City, which we intercepted. It was only about a visa, however. He also wrote a letter to the Soviet Embassy here in Washington, which we intercepted, read and resealed. This letter referred to the fact that the FBI had questioned his activities on the Fair Play to Cuba Committee and also asked about extension of his wife's visa.

That letter from Oswald was addressed to the man in the Soviet Embassy who is in charge of assassinations and similar activities on the part of the Soviet government. To have that drawn into a public hearing would muddy the waters internationally.

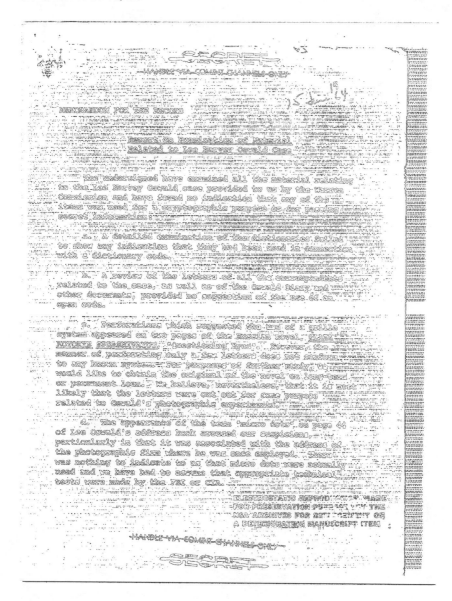

Examination of Oswald materials. (Nearly illegible, but of great significance under close examination).

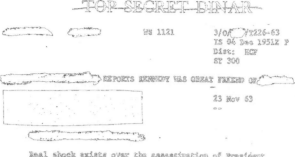

~~TOP SECRET DINAR~~

WS 1121 3/O/ T226-63
 IS 06 Dec 1951Z P
 Dist: RCP
 ST 300

REPORTS KENNEDY WAS GREAT FRIEND OF

23 Nov 63

Real shock exists over the assassination of President KENNEDY. Television, via Telstar, is showing touching demonstrations in Europe.

The Chiefs of State from many countries will attend the funeral services.

It is my personal opinion that your attendance would be advisable in view of the fact that the new martyr to human rights was a great friend of ▮▮▮▮ and was convinced of the grandeur and hopes of the national revolution.

Cordially,

MS 974   CN ▮   TI —

3/O/ T226-63

THIS DOCUMENT CONTAINS 1 PAGE(S)

~~TOP SECRET DINAR~~

Great friend of X? 23 November 1963

Dr. Robert J. Girod, Sr.

~~TOP SECRET DINAR~~

NO FOREIGN DISSEMINATION
REPRODUCTION PROHIBITED

Reproduction of this document in
whole or in part is prohibited
except as specifically authorized
by the DIRECTOR, NATIONAL
SECURITY AGENCY.

WS 373   3/O/W/T1945-63
              29 Nov 63

REACTIONS TO KENNEDY'S DEATH

23 Nov 63 1100
Urgent

For ▓▓▓

Our ▓▓▓ Everything points to the continuation of the internal struggle [B val based] on the political interpretation of KENNEDY's assassination. Immediately after the attempt, the initial commentaries linked it with the racist movement, which assumed the offensive by rallying themselves around the efforts of the Texas police in order to saddle OSWALD, a reputed pro CASTRO activist who two years ago wanted to remain in the USSR, with the responsibility for the attempt. The arrest of Cubans was begun in Dallas. GOLDWATER, who yesterday refused to comment on the assassination, joined the campaign. Radio and television suspended all their programs and — with minor exceptions which included ABC directed among others by the former EISENHOWER press agent HAGHERTY — taking advantage of this background to bring about anti-communist hysteria. The fact that Saturday through Monday are days free of work facilitates reaching the community.

Today's declaration by JOHNSON and the Department of State denying the existence of reputed facts of a conspiracy against KENNEDY's life involving the USSR and Cuba has as its aim the restraint of the campaign of extreme racists, which can create difficulty in overcoming the internal situation and could paralyze the foreign policy of Washington.

Probably in reply to these declarations circulated among the American press (among others in the ▓▓▓) is the theme that the KENNEDY murder could have been inspired by those centers in the USSR which do not want a detente. This theme is also being linked with the attempt to arrest BARGHOORN, the downing of the Iranian aircraft, and Berlin access roads.

3/O/W/T1945-63

THIS DOCUMENT CONTAINS 2 PAGES

~~TOP SECRET DINAR~~

Reaction of XXX? 29 November 1963.

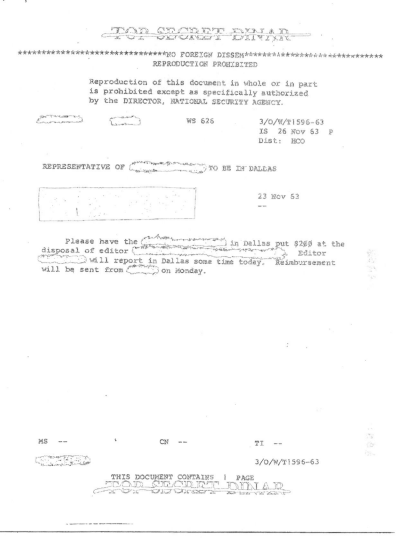

Representative X to be in Dallas. 26 November 1963

The Emergency Room and Autopsy: Parkland and Bethesda

Dr. George Gregory Burkley, the President's personal physician, had been in the motorcade. He arrived at the Parkland Hospital emergency room about five minutes after the mortally wounded President arrived. The staff who treated President Kennedy at Parkland's Trauma Room 1 realized that the President had no chance of survival upon arriving at the hospital. "We never had any hope of saving his life," one physician said. Dr. Burkley observed wounds to both the head and the back and determined the head wound was the cause of death. President Kennedy was pronounced dead at 1300 CST (1:00 p.m.) (19:00 UTC) after all heart activity had ceased and after a priest administered the last rites. The President's death was officially announced by Acting White House Press Secretary Malcolm Kilduff at 1333 CST (1:33 p.m.) (19:33 UTC). The priest who administered the last rites said that the President was already dead by the time he had arrived at the hospital and he had to draw back a sheet covering the President's face to administer the sacrament of Extreme Unction. Dr. Burkley signed President Kennedy's death certificate.

The body was removed before a forensic post-mortem could be conducted by the Dallas County Coroner's Office. This violated Texas state law because the murder was a state crime and occurred under Texas jurisdiction. At that time it was not a federal offense to kill the President of the United States. Yet the late-President's body was quickly taken away to Air Force One to be flown to Washington. Vice-President Johnson (who had been riding two cars behind Kennedy in the motorcade through Dallas and was not injured) became President of the United States upon Kennedy's death. At 2:38 p.m. Johnson took the oath of office on board Air Force One just before it departed Love Field.

Air Force One landed at Andrews Air Force Base. President Kennedy's body was removed to Bethesda Naval Hospital for an immediate autopsy. The autopsy (about 2000 to 2300 EST on 22 November, 1963) led the three examining pathologists to conclude that the bullet wound to the head was fatal. Their report said that the bullet had, "entered Kennedy's head through a small hole in the scalp in the rear of the president's head, on the right hand side.... [with a] final exit of this missile, or fragments of it, through a large lateral defect in the right parietal region of the skull over the right ear." Embalming and cosmetic funeral preparation followed almost immediately after the post-mortem (about 2300 to 0400) in the morgue at Bethesda, a room adjacent to the autopsy theater. This was done by a team of private mortuary personnel, who made a special trip to the hospital for this. The body, prepared for viewing, was then placed in a casket.

National Archives Autopsy Photos and X-rays May Not be of JFK's Brain

Pathologists who conducted the autopsy on President John F. Kennedy may have performed two brain examinations - possibly of two different brains. A staff report for the Assassinations Records Review Board summarized several discrepancies in the medical evidence compiled in its effort to make public as much information about the assassination as it deemed appropriate. The controversy asserted by the report is that brain photographs in the Kennedy records are not of Kennedy's brain and show much less damage than Kennedy sustained when he was shot in Dallas and brought to Parkland Hospital there on 22 November 1963. The doctors at Parkland told reporters then that they thought Kennedy was shot from the front and not from behind as the Warren Commission later concluded.

A former naval officer and physician reported that he was "90 to 95 percent certain that the photographs in the Archives are not of President Kennedy's brain" and that "If they aren't, that can mean only one thing - that there has been a cover-up of the medical evidence." The physician contends that the damage to the second brain reflected a shot from behind. He says the first brain was Kennedy's and reflected a shot from the front.

Among those present at the President's autopsy were:

Dr. James J. Humes. Humes was the lead prosector at JFK's autopsy.

Dr. J. Thorton Boswell. Boswell assisted Dr. Humes.

Dr. Pierre Finck. Finck, an Army ballistics expert, and the third autopsy doctor.

Lt. Cmd. John Stringer was the primary photographer at the autopsy and at a supplemental brain exam.

Floyd Riebe. Riebe was an assistant photographer at the autopsy.

Jerroll Custer took X-rays at the autopsy.
Edward Reed assisted Custer in the taking of X-rays.
James Sibert was one of two FBI agents who witnessed the autopsy.
Francis O'Neill, Jr. was the second FBI agent present at the autopsy.
Saundra Kay Spencer processed JFK autopsy photographs the weekend after the assassination.

Seal of the Assassination Records Review Board, which is separate from and not to be confused with the National Archives.

On October 10, 2007, I contacted the National Archives to inquire about the numerous web sites that display the autopsy photos of President Kennedy. Many of these sites claim copyrights on the photos and others

Infamous Murders and Mysteries

claim to show altered and unaltered photos, suggesting a conspiracy to alter the photographic evidence. Others claim to expose those alterations. The National Archives e-mailed this response:

Dear Dr. Girod:

This is in reply to your October 10, 2007 inquiry regarding the autopsy photographs in the John F. Kennedy Assassination Collection.

I refer you to the National Archives JFK web page "FAQ" regarding the collection: http://www.archives.gov/research/jfk/faqs.html#top

Specifically the FAQ regarding the autopsy photos:

I have seen the autopsy photographs and x-rays in books. Did NARA make them available?

Any photographs that have been published in books throughout the years were not obtained from NARA.

The autopsy photographs and X-rays of President Kennedy were donated to the National Archives by the Kennedy family by an agreement dated October 29, 1966. This agreement limits access to such materials to: (1) persons authorized to act for a Committee of Congress, a Presidential Commission, or any other official agency of the Federal government having authority to investigate matters relating to the assassination of President Kennedy and to (2) recognized experts in the field of pathology or related areas of science and technology whose applications are approved by the Kennedy family representative, Mr. Paul Kirk.

The National Archives and Records Administration can not comment on the images found on the world wide web, not can we comment on any claims regarding copyrights of said images.

Should you have any further questions please feel free

to contact me or any of my colleagues at <u>specialaccess_FOIA@nara.gov</u> or call us at 301-837-3190.

Sincerely,

Joseph A. Scanlon
Archivist
Special Access and FOIA Staff

Photos and drawings were available, but after much deliberation I decided not to include them here. They are inherently graphic and I do not feel that it is beneficial to sacrifice dignity for sensationalism in this case for no apparent purpose.

The report also examines the testimonies of two key witnesses. The first was from former FBI agent Francis X. O'Neill, Jr., who was present at the 22 November 1963, autopsy at Bethesda Naval Hospital. The second was from former Navy photographer John T. Stringer, who said he took photos at a supplementary brain examination two or three days later, probably on the morning of 25 November 1963. O'Neill told the board in a 1997 deposition that at the 22 November autopsy "there was not too much of the brain left" when it was taken out of Kennedy's skull and "put in a white jar." He said "more than half of the brain was missing."

There were four autopsy photographers (and cameras): John Stringer, William Bruce Pitzer, Robert L. Knudsen and Floyd Riebe. Lieutenant Commander Pitzer was reputedly murdered soon after President Kennedy's autopsy. Commander Pitzer was reportedly, at the time of his death, in possession of a 16 mm film of the autopsy which he had taken during the autopsy examination and been working on at the time he was allegedly murdered. The film allegedly disappeared and has never been found or confirmed.

Commander Pitzer was due to retire after twenty-eight years of service to his country. It has been rumored that upon his retirement from the Navy, Pitzer had planned to release a bootlegged copy of the film and photos of the

Kennedy autopsy. On the evening of Saturday, 29 October 1966, Lieutenant Commander William B. Pitzer was found dead at his desk, shot through the head, at his duty station at the Bethesda Naval Hospital, Bethesda, MD. Six hours later, an urgent teletype went from the FBI's Baltimore field office to HQ.

Pitzer was found with a gunshot wound to the right temple. A gun was found in his right hand (one report says a .45 caliber automatic and another says a .38 caliber revolver). He was reputedly left handed, although other sources say that he was right handed. The autopsy report specifies that that there was no evidence of a contact wound, which is nearly always present with self-inflicted gunshot wounds or at close contact. Investigations by the Naval Investigative Service and the FBI later concluded that a gunshot wound to the head had been self-inflicted. FBI files on the investigation, released in 1997 under the Freedom of Information Act, revealed what some analysts opine are "anomalies" in the investigation.

X-ray technician, Jerrol Custer, said the x-rays that became a part of the official investigation were false. (See the declassified document below). Custer lost his job as a supervisory X-ray technician. He then worked as an armed security guard in Pittsburgh. Jerrol Francis Custer died of a massive heart attack in 2000.

When shown the brain photographs deeded to the National Archives by the Kennedy family, O'Neill said they did not represent what he saw. Stringer said the photos he took at the "supplementary examination" conducted by J. Thornton Boswell and James Humes did not resemble those at the National Archives. He said they appeared to be on a different type of film from the one he used. He also said that he took photographs of "cross sections of the brain" that had been cut out to show the damage, but no such photos are in the National Archives collection. He also said that some photos he took at the autopsy itself were missing. He said he "gave everything" from the brain examination to Dr. Humes, who gave the film to Kennedy's personal physician, the late Admiral George Burkley.

Dr. Humes testified in a 1996 deposition that Kennedy's brain was not sectioned in the way Stringer described "because the next thing you know

George Burkley wanted it." He said that Dr. Burkley told him "flat out" that the Kennedy family wanted to inter the brain with the President's body and that Dr. Burkley said he was going to deliver it to Attorney General Robert F. Kennedy.

According to testimony about the autopsy on President John F. Kennedy, a second set of photographs, in addition to the set at the National Archives, was taken of Kennedy's wounds. The second set is believed to have been taken by a White House photographer, Robert L. Knudsen, during or after the autopsy, at the National Naval Medical Center in Bethesda, Maryland. These photographs were never made public and have not been located or confirmed to exist. In 1997, the Review Board located Saundra K. Spencer, who worked at the Naval Photographic Center in 1963, and showed her the archives' autopsy photos. Spencer asserted that they were not the photos that she had helped process. She said that those which she developed had "no blood or opening cavities." She speculated that a second photographer took pictures of a cleaned-up corpse and opined that this was done at the request of the Kennedy family in case autopsy pictures had to be made public.

The president's coffin was buried on the afternoon of 25 Nov1963. However, a third autopsy physician, Dr. Pierre Finck, said in a 1965 report that Dr. Humes called him on 29 November 1963 to "examine the brain" at Bethesda. He said that he, Humes, and Boswell examined the formalin fixed brain and that a Navy photographer was present. He said the photographer took photographs of the brain from below. John Stringer, however, reported that he did not take "basilar, or inferior, views."

Dr. Horne wrote in a memo that this "second hypothesized examination" may have taken place as late as 2 December 1963. The officer in charge of the Pathology Department at Bethesda, Dr. Boyers, told the House Assassinations Committee in 1978 that he processed brain tissue and prepared paraffin blocks of eight or twelve sections of the brain on 2 December 1963.

Dr. Boswell told a reporter that the brain was "examined in detail" at the 22 November 1963 autopsy and again a few days later after it had been "put in form and fixation." He insisted that it was the same brain that was examined on 25 November 1963. He asserts that it was decided that it was destroyed to the extent that sections did not need to be taken. When questioned about Stringer's account of photographing sections, Dr. Boswell said, "He's full of _ _ _ _!"

Missing Autopsy Items and Altered Inventories

Some sources question the accuracy of inventoried items turned over to the Kennedy family. They opine that these discrepancies suggest a conspiracy. On April 26, 1965, Robert F. Kennedy, with the help of Admiral Burkley (the U.S. Navy physician assigned to Presidents Kennedy and Johnson), reportedly arranged to have the autopsy materials transferred from U.S. Secret Service to the Kennedy family. That day an inventory report was completed and signed by Admiral Burkley, Secret Service Agent Roy Kellerman, and others. Item # 1 was listed as a broken casket handle and Item #9 listed numerous body parts and autopsy documents. On October 28, 1966, Burke Marshall's (a Kennedy family representative) Deed of Gift Letter to GSA Knott for transfer of the autopsy materials to the archives listed on an attachment both the clothing and the autopsy materials. Its wording matched the April 26, 1965, transfer inventory (from two days earlier) verbatim, except that Items #1 and #9 had been taken off the list. The list was re-numbered to read Items #1 through #7.

When National Archives personnel open the Kennedy footlocker on the day of physical transfer, October 31, 1966, both of the Kennedy family representatives (Burke Marshall and Angie Novello) reportedly left the room as soon as the footlocker was opened, but before an inventory was taken. Archives personnel noted that Items #1 and #9 on the original April 26, 1965, transfer inventory list were missing. If they had only looked at the Burke Marshall letter, skeptics assert, and not compared it to the April 26, 1965, transfer-list, they would not have noticed that anything was missing.

In 1966 Inspector Thomas Kelley, of the U.S. Secret Service, wrote a memorandum of a meeting with Mr. Van Cleve of the General Services Administration, which several other government officials also attended, at which concerns were expressed about the missing "Item # 9" materials. This, of course, included the autopsy materials, presumably a brain, numerous tissue slides, the original and 7 copies of the autopsy report, and memos on autopsy photographs.

Texas School Book Depository.
(Public domain: http://en.wikipedia.org/wiki/Image:HowardBrennan.jpg)

Infamous Murders and Mysteries

The Texas School Book Depository (the sniper nest window is marked).

The Texas School Book Depository from the grassy knoll.

```
                              UNCLASSIFIED
                         *** BEGIN MESSAGE    21 ***
SERIAL=    UDN=VO1(13785)
CLASS=UNCLASSIFIED
LBY621
REULB
R A
  BC-USA-KENNEDY    05-28 0331
BC-USA-KENNEDY
    JFK AUTOPSY REPORT FALSE, MEDICAL TECHNICIANS SAY
       BY JEANNE KING
       NEW YORK, MAY 28, REUTER - TWO U.S. NAVY MEDICAL TECHNICANS
WHO WITNESSED THE AUTOPSY OF PRESIDENT JOHN KENNEDY SAID ON
THURSDAY THAT AUTOPSY PHOTOGRAPHS AND X-RAYS RECENTLY RELEASED
BY THE GOVERNMENT HAVE BEEN TAMPERED WITH AND FALSIFIED.
       JERROL CUSTER WHO TOOK X-RAYS OF KENNEDY:S BODY AT BETHESDA
NAVAL HOSPITAL IN MARYLAND AFTER HIS ASSASSINATION ON NOVEMBER
22, 1963, TOLD A MANHATTAN NEWS CONFERENCE THAT THE X-RAYS
ARE
WRONG.::
       HE SAID THE RELEASED X-RAYS SHOWED A BLACK HOLE WHERE THE
RIGHT SIDE OF KENNEDY:S FACE SHOULD BE, INDICATING THAT A
PORTION OF THE FACE HAD BEEN DESTROYED.
       BUT HE SAID,
THERE WAS NO DAMAGE TO HIS FACE AND NO PART
OF HIS SKULL WAS MISSING ON THE FORWARD PART OF HIS HEAD. THESE
ARE FAKE X-RAYS.::
       PHOTOGRAPHER FLOYD RIEBE, WHO TOOK PICTURES OF THE BODY
DURING THE AUTOPSY, CLAIMS THAT THE PHOTOGRAPHS RELEASED BY THE
GOVERNMENT ARE
PHONY AND NOT THE PHOTOGRAPHS WE TOOK.::
       AFTER THE AUTOPSY WAS COMPLETED, CUSTER SAID HE WAS SENT TO
AN ADMIRAL:S OFFICE AT BETHESDA WHERE HE WAS WARNED TO
KEEP MY
MOUTH SHUT. NOTHING WAS TO BE SAID OF WHAT I SAW, WHAT I DID AND
THAT IF I WERE TO OPEN MY MOUTH, I WOULD WIND UP IN PRISON.::
       THE NEWS CONFERENCE WAS CALLED TO REBUT ARTICLES PUBLISHED
LAST WEEK IN THE JOURNAL OF THE AMERICAN MEDICAL ASSOCIATION
(JAMA) BY TWO NAVY PATHOLOGISTS WHO PERFORMED THE AUTOPSY ON
KENNEDY AND WHO SUPPORT THE OFFICIAL WARREN COMMISSION FINDINGS
THAT THE PRESIDENT WAS SHOT TWICE FROM BEHIND BY A LONE
ASSASSIN, LEE HARVEY OSWALD.
       ATTENTION HAS BEEN FOCUSED ANEW ON THE KENNEDY ASSASSINATION
IN RECENT MONTHS BECAUSE OF THE FILM
JFK,:: WHICH SUGGESTS THE
FACTS OF THE PRESIDENT:S DEATH WERE NEVERY FULLY REVEALED.
       IN LOS ANGELES A GRAND JURY HAS REFUSED TO PROBE ALLEGATIONS
OF A COVERUP BY LOS ANGELES POLICE IN THE 1968 ASSASSINATION OF
THE PRESIDENT:S BROTHER, SENATOR ROBERT KENNEDY, A CITIZEN:S
COMMITTEEE WHO ASKED FOR THE INVESTIGATION SAID THURSDAY.
       REUTER JK BH
REUT17:38 05-28
NNNN
                              UNCLASSIFIED
```

Copy of a Reuter's report that was declassified from the government's files on the Kennedy assignation. The report says that the x-ray technician, Jerrol Custer, said the x-rays were false.

```
                              UNCLASSIFIED
                          *** BEGIN MESSAGE     2 ***
SERIAL=    UDN=V01(5707)
CLASS=UNCLASSIFIED
LBY590
REULB
R W
BC-USA-KENNEDY    05-12 0620
BC-USA-KENNEDY 1STLD (SCHEDULED)
   CIA, FBI DIRECTORS BACK RELEASE OF JFK MATERIAL
   (EDS: NEW STORY WITH BACKGROUND, DETAIL, QUOTES)
       BY ROBERT GREEN
       WASHINGTON, MAY 12, REUTER - THE CHIEFS OF THE CIA AND FBI
ON TUESDAY URGED THE RELEASE OF STACKS OF CLASSIFIED KENNEDY
ASSASSINATION DOCUMENTS TO HELP RESOLVE THE DOUBT, DEBATE AND
CONSPIRACY THEORIES THAT SWIRL AROUND MODERN AMERICA:S MOST
WRENCHING MURDER.
       CENTRAL INTELLIGENCE AGENCY DIRECTOR ROBERT GATES SAID HE
BELIEVES A PUBLIC AIRING OF WHAT INVESTIGATORS KNOW WILL FREE
HIS AGENCY OF SUSPICIONS -- REVIVED BY HOLLYWOOD IN THE FILM
JFK:: -- THAT IT WAS PART OF A CONSPIRACY TO KILL PRESIDENT
JOHN F. KENNEDY IN DALLAS ON NOVEMBER 22, 1963.
WE ARE HOPING THAT OPENING UP AND GIVING JOURNALISTS,
HISTORIANS AND, MOST IMPORTANTLY, THE PUBLIC ACCESS TO
GOVERNMENT FILES WILL HELP TO RESOLVE QUESTIONS THAT STILL
LINGER OVER 28 YEARS AFTER THE ASSASSINATION,:: GATES SAID IN
TESTIMONY AT A SENATE GOVERNMENTAL AFFAIRS COMMITTEE HEARING.
FURTHER, I BELIEVE THAT MAXIMUM DISCLOSURE WILL DISCREDIT
THE THEORY THAT CIA HAD ANYTHING TO DO WITH THE MURDER OF JOHN
F. KENNEDY.::
       FEDERAL BUREAU OF INVESTIGATION DIRECTOR WILLIAM SESSIONS
ALSO SUPPORTED THE PROPOSED RELEASE OF CLASSIFIED KENNEDY FILES,
SAYING,
I WHOLLY ENDORSE THE PURPOSE OF THIS BILL TO RELEASE
AS MUCH INFORMATION PERTINENT TO THE ASSASSINATION AS WE
RESPONSIBLY CAN.::
       THE SENATE COMMITTEE IS CONSIDERING LEGISLATION TO RELEASE
HUNDREDS OF THOUSANDS OF DOCUMENTS ABOUT THE ASSASSINATION THAT
HAVE BEEN KEPT SECRET SINCE THE OFFICIAL INVESTIGATION CHAIRED
BY SUPREME COURT CHIEF JUSTICE EARL WARREN.
       THE WARREN COMMISSION FOUND THAT LEE HARVEY OSWALD ACTED
ALONE IN SHOOTING KENNEDY FROM THE DALLAS SCHOOL BOOK DEPOSITORY
-- A CONCLUSION QUESTIONED FOR DECADES BY MILLIONS OF AMERICANS
ATTRACTED BY CONSPIRACY THEORIES THAT CAST SUSPICION ON
GOVERNMENT AGENCIES, THE MAFIA, A VARIETY OF FOREIGN GOVERNMENTS
AND OTHERS.
       THE PROPOSED LEGISLATION WOULD CREATE A FIVE-MEMBER
INDEPENDENT PANEL TO DECIDE WHAT KENNEDY INVESTIGATIVE MATERIAL
SHOULD BE MADE PUBLIC.
       DEMOCRATIC SENATOR DAVID BOREN, CHAIRMAN OF THE SENATE
INTELLIGENCE COMMITTEE AND A CO-SPONSOR OF THE LEGISLATION,
TESTIFIED THAT HE HAD CHECKED WITH THE KENNEDY FAMILY AND
RECEIVED ITS APPROVAL FOR THE BILL.
       DEPUTY ASSISTANT ATTORNEY GENERAL DAVID LEITCH SAID THE
                             UNCLASSIFIED
```

CIA and FBI Directors release files.

Sealing of Assassination Records

Several key pieces of evidence and documentation are alleged to have been lost, cleaned, or otherwise become missing from the original chain of evidence (e.g., the Presidential limousine cleaned out at the hospital by order of President Johnson, Governor Connally's suit dry-cleaned, his Stetson hat and gold cufflink missing, Oswald's military intelligence file destroyed in 1973, forensic autopsy photos missing, etc.)

All of the Warren Commission's records were transferred to the National Archives in 1964. The unpublished portion of those records was initially sealed for 75 years (until 2039) under a general National Archives policy that applied to all federal investigations by the executive branch of government. The 75-year rule no longer exists because of the Freedom of Information Act of 1966 and the JFK Records Act of 1992. The remaining Kennedy assassination documents are scheduled to be released to the public by 2017, twenty-five years after the passage of the JFK Records Act.

John F. Kennedy, Jr., was born seventeen days after his father was elected to the presidency. His father was buried on his third birthday. On May 19, 2044, the 50th anniversary of the death of Jacqueline Kennedy Onassis, if her last child has died, the Kennedy library will release to the public a 500-page transcript of an oral history about John F. Kennedy given by Mrs. Kennedy before her death in 1994.

REFERENCES:

NOTE: The sources for the information in this chapter are from public archives and sources, many of which are common knowledge. The declassified documents are from the National Archives, released to the public by the Assassination Records Review Board. Photos are public domain photos.

PART III –

THE LIFE AND CRIMES
OF THE RICH AND FAMOUS

*I play the game for the games own sake.
As to reward, my profession is its reward; but you are at liberty
to defray whatever expenses I may be put to, at the time which
suits you best.*

~ Sherlock Holmes ~
Sir Arthur Conan Doyle

CHAPTER EIGHT

MASS MURDER AT TALIESIN:
THE FRANK LLYOD WRIGHT TRAGEDY

I cannot agree with those who rank modesty among the virtues. To the logician all things should be seen exactly as they are, and to underestimate one's self is as much a departure from the truth as to exaggerate one's own powers.

~ Sherlock Holmes ~

Sir Arthur Conan Doyle

Taliesin: Frank Lloyd Wright's Wisconsin Getaway

Taliesin was the secluded country getaway that Frank Lloyd Wright designed and built for his mistress, Martha Borthwick Cheney and himself. Martha Bouton Borthwick, known as "Mamah" (pronounced "Mayma"), was Mrs. Edwin H. Cheney of Oak Park, Illinois. (*Atlanta Constitution*, August 16, 1914) Cheney and Wright met and began an affair while Wright was designing a house for the Cheneys. Once Wright had abandoned his wife and family for Mrs. Cheney, they went to Europe in 1909 before returning to Wright's home in Wisconsin, where he built Taliesin. Wright's estranged wife refused to grant him a divorce, so Wright and Cheney began co-habitating in

1911, creating a scandalous affair for their time. Edwin Cheney was granted a divorce and remarried in 1912.

In the summer of 1914 Wright and Borthwick-Cheney were at their Wisconsin hide-away of Taliesin. In September, 1914, Mamah's children – Martha (age twelve) and John (age ten) came to visit. One account says that the Cheney children were living with Mrs. Cheney at Taliesin. The same source, however, records the ages of the two children as John Bothwick (spelling not corrected) Cheney as being aged thirteen and Martha Borthwick Cheney as being aged ten. (*Atlanta Constitution*, August 16, 1914, p. 1) All seemed peaceful and normal, though it is said that the Cheney children did not care to be at Taliesin.

Madman Commits Mass Murder

Frank Lloyd Wright was in Chicago working on the Midway Gardens project with his son, John Wright. At Taliesin a work crew of five men and a boy were busy around the house and gardens. Julian Carlton and his wife Gertrude, Wright's houseman and cook, were preparing the luncheon. Julian Carlton did not like the isolation at Taliesin and had often demanded to leave, though he did not seem to be in a hurry to do so.

Frank Lloyd Wright
(Public Domain photo)
(Internet: http://en.wikipedia.org/wiki/Image:Frank_Lloyd_Wright_LC-USZ62-36384.jpg)

Dr. Robert J. Girod, Sr.

Taliesin
(Used by permission of Jeff Dean, en.wikipedia)

Mamah and the children, Martha and John, were sitting at a table in the courtyard overlooking the pond. Other accounts say they were in an enclosed screen porch overlooking the Wisconsin River. In any event, they were separated from the main dining room, where the employees were, by a twelve-foot passageway. Taliesin foreman Thomas Brunker (age 68) and David Lindblom (age 38), the gardener and handyman, were having lunch in the approximately twelve foot square staff dining room on the west side of the house. Carpenter William (Billy) Weston and his son, Ernest Weston (age 13), joined them. Two draftsmen, Herbert Fritz (age unknown) and Emil Brodelle (age 26) of Milwaukee, were also there.

Infamous Murders and Mysteries

Julian Carlton
(Used with permission. The Caribbean Voice, www.caribvoice.org)

Carlton, dressed in a white jacket, served the soup to the men there and then returned to the kitchen. Once they were eating, Carlton came back to Weston for permission to get some gasoline to "clean a rug." Carlton locked the courtyard door and quietly bolted the doors and windows from the outside. He dumped several buckets of gasoline on the rugs inside the house and all around the outside of the house. One of the men saw some "greasy liquid" flowing from the kitchen but for some reason was not particularly suspicious. Carlton warned his wife, Gertrude, to leave then he threw a lighted match into the dining room onto the volatile fluid. The gasoline exploded into flames and set the room ablaze. The locked door trapped the burning men long enough to allow Carlton to kill Mrs. Cheney and her two children with a hatchet.

The Atlanta Constitution reported that each of the victims were attacked as they attempted to escape through the same window. The report read, "The negro displayed fiendish ingenuity in arranging his victims for the slaughter." News accounts were replete with vernacular that would be thought insensitive for contemporary times, but which reflected the social environment of 1914. The article noted that there was but one point of egress from the inferno – a single window. The article continued, "Mrs. Borthwick was the first to put her head through the window. The negro, waiting outside, struck her down with one blow, crushing her skull. He then dragged her body out and waited for the next." (*Atlanta Constitution*, August 16, 1914, p. 1)

Other accounts are more consistent and record the events differently. Carlton's first victim was Mamah Borthwick. Carlton plunged the hatchet into the center of her head while she still sat in her chair in the courtyard porch. The head of the hatchet went through her skull and into her brain with such force that it believed that she died instantly. He then attacked her son, John, who was also killed as he sat in his chair. His charred bones were all that were found. It is believed that Carlton doused both corpses with gasoline before igniting them too. (Secrest, pp. 218-220)

Mamah's daughter, Martha, tried to escape, but Carlton caught up to her and struck at least three blows behind her right ear, one above the next, with the hatchet. One penetrated her skill and another wound left the imprint of the hatchet head under her right eye. She was found in the inner courtyard, her clothes burned off, with burns on her arms and legs. When the men finally broke the door down, Carlton attacked them with the hatchet.

Herbert Fritz lived to recall that there were two doors, one leading to the kitchen and the other to the courtyard. After serving them, Carlton left the room and Fritz noticed a fluid flowing under the screen door that led to the courtyard. He and his co-workers thought it was soapsuds until they smelled the gasoline, which was followed by a streak of flame that shot under Fritz's chair and set the room ablaze. They all jumped up and Fritz, realizing his clothes were afire, plunged through a window to a rocky slope. His arm was broken by the fall and the flames were consuming his clothes and burning his body. He rolled down the hill to extinguish his flaming clothes then jumped to his feet to start back up the hill to the house. He saw Carlton running around the house with the hatchet.

Emil Brodelle had also escaped though the window, but Carlton buried the hatchet in his brain at the hairline. Brodelle staggered and fell to his knees. William Weston was on his way through the same window when Carlton knocked him to the ground with two blows with the back of the hatchet. William was not killed and was the only one, along with Fritz, to survive.

Before attacking Brodelle and Weston, Carlton had wounded David Lindblom in the back of the head. Though the wound had not penetrated Lindblom's skull, he had severe burns on his back, arms, legs, head, and neck. Thomas Brunker was struck with a lethal blow that penetrated his brain as he broke through the door into the courtyard. He, too, had severe burns. William Weston's thirteen-year-old son, Ernest, was the final victim. He was beaten in the skull with the hatchet and sustained severe burns.

In less than two minutes Carlton had killed or fatally wounded seven people:

- Martha "Mamah" Borthwick-Cheney,
- John Cheney (age 10), Mamah's son,
- Martha Cheney (age 12), Mamah's daughter,
- David Lindblom (age 38), the gardener and handyman,
- Emil Brodelle (age 26), draftsman, of Milwaukee,
- Thomas Brunker (age 68), foreman,
- Ernest Weston (age 13), William's son,

William (Billy) Weston, a carpenter, and Herbert Fritz, a draftsman, escaped death and were able to give their account of these events.

Help Arrives for the Victims

While Taliesin burned, William Weston got to his feet and found fatally wounded David Lindblom, bleeding and burned. He led Lindblom away, running a half-mile to the nearest house to telephone for help. After summoning assistance, Weston heroically returned to the house to loose a fire hose kept in a niche in the garden wall. He staggered to the fire with the hose.

Frank Sliter was the closest neighbor and came with Jack Farries, Albert Beckley, and Fred Hanke to help and to find Carlton. They found Brodelle on his hands and knees about to collapse. They found young Ernest Weston covered with blood but still standing. He was able to walk a few feet before fainting. Farries carried him to a shade tree. Next they found young Martha Cheney, her clothing nearly completely burned away.

Help came from the Hillside Home School, the Spring Green Fire Department, and a bucket brigade of workers from Tower Hill. By 3:00 p.m., however, Taliesin was completely destroyed. While Wright's uncle, Unitarian minister Jenkin Lloyd Jones, directed the firefighting efforts, Wright's brother-in-law, Andrew Porter, was the first to find Mamah Borthwick, her body still ablaze and her hair nearly burned off completely. The bodies were taken to a neighbor's cottage nearby.

Martha's young friend, Edna, was on her way to Taliesin when she saw the smoke and heard the shouts of men and screams of children. Slipping from her horse with trembling hands she began to cry and prayed over and over, "Hail Mary, full of grace! The Lord is with thee." When she arrived at Taliesin she saw the carnage of the victims' bodies. One was covered with towels, her hair and eyelashes gone but still conscious. The lips on that face mouthed Edna's name but Edna could only stare and think, "That is not Martha!" But she recognized the ring on her playmate's swollen hand and knew the truth that was too horrible to acknowledge. Twelve-year-old Martha Cheney lived for a few hours longer. (Secrest, p. 220)

Ernest Weston and David Lindblom would also linger awhile before dying of their burns. Mamah and John Cheney, Emil Brodelle, and Thomas Brunker were already dead from their wounds. Only Billy Weston and Herbert Fritz survived their wounds and the horrible carnage.

Wright Receives the Heartbreaking and Morbid News

In Chicago with his son John, Wright was taking a break from the Midway Gardens project for lunch. John, a sandwich in one hand and a paintbrush in the other, was painting a mural for a tavern wall. John Wright recounted the notification of the tragedy in his book *My Father Who Is On Earth*:

> Dad was sitting at a table in the far end of the room, eating his lunch. From this point he watched me. The door opened, the stenographer from the Gardens' office walked in. "Mr. Wright, your wanted on the telephone," she said. I was studying my work when he returned and did not turn to look at him.
> (Wright, p. 81)

Charlotte Wallard wrote in her 1972 book *Frank Lloyd Wright: An American Architect*, "Someone said, 'This is Frank Roth calling from Madison. Be prepared for a shock...'" (Wallard, pp. 69-70)

John Wright's account continued:

> Suddenly all was quiet in the room, a strange unnatural silence, his breathing alone was audible, then a groan. I turned to him, startled. He clung to the table for support, his face ashen. I climbed down hurriedly and ran to his side.
> (Wright, p. 81)

Literary accounts of what happened following the murder vary to some degree, particularly in regards to Carlton's apprehension. Wallard wrote, "Numbed by what he heard, Wright turned to his son and mumbled, 'I go to Spring Green at once.' Meanwhile, the sheriff found the madman crouching in the firepot of the steamboiler. He had taken poison. Refusing to say a word, he died a few hours later." (Wallard, pp. 69-70)

John Wright recalled:

"What's happened, Dad?" It was difficult for him to speak. Finally he whispered in a hollow voice, "John – a taxi."

"What for, Dad, what's happened to you? What's the trouble?" I insisted

"Taliesin is on fire – Mamah, the children, the students, what if they're hurt? Why did I leave them today…" His voice broke, his lips were parted and pale. I called a cab and helped him into it. We drove to the station and boarded the first train we could get for Spring Green. It was a slow local.

(Wright, p. 80)

The Manhunt, Capture, and Incarceration

Hundreds arrived to try to extinguish the fire and to search for the mass murderer, Julian Carlton. The Atlanta Constitution and the Sunday Review of Decatur, Illinois, reported that "Sheriff Bauer organized a search for Carlton as soon as he learned of the murder." (*Atlanta Constitution*, August 16, 1914) (Sunday Review of Decatur, Illinois, August 16, 1914) This is the only mention that historic records make mention of "Sheriff Bauer" in connection with this case. All other accounts refer to Sheriff John T. Williams as the head lawman in this investigation. A posse of sheriff's deputies, farmers, and neighbors was organized and bloodhounds were obtained for tracking. It was believed that Carlton had had escaped in a canoe and was making his way down the Wisconsin River. (*Atlanta Constitution*, August 16, 1914, p. 1) This was not the only inaccuracy in names recorded by journalists. *The Washington Post* referred to the suspect as "Robert Carlton" in one of its articles. (*The Washington Post*, October 4, 1914) But, while the historic accuracy of news accounts is not always precise, the essentials of this tale are pretty clear.

Infamous Murders and Mysteries

1890 - Sauk County Jail

Iowa County Sheriff John T. Williams, Sauk County Under-Sheriff George Peck, and Jenkin Lloyd Jones set up a posse. Carlton's wife was found in a daze walking along the highway after the tragic murders. She was taken into custody, but denied participation in the macabre mass murder. It was believed at that time that Carlton had brooded over being reprimanded by Mamah Borthwick and had gone berserk over this incident. (*Atlanta Constitution*, August 16, 1914)

(Courtesy of Sauk County, Wisconsin; public domain)

Under-Sheriff George Peck from nearby Sauk County assisted Iowa County Sheriff John T. Williams in the manhunt and apprehension of Julian Carlton.

Dr. Robert J. Girod, Sr.

Carlton was found and apprehended at about 5:30 p.m. He was found hiding in the basement of the burning house, where he had secreted himself in the unlit furnace which protected him from the flames. It was supposed that he intended to affect his escape once the searches had relinquished the manhunt. He had swallowed muriatic acid and was semiconscious when found. Some accounts say he died then and there, but he did not. The crowd was ready to string him up for lynching, but Sheriff Williams and his posse, though pursued by three car loads of men, stood the would-be lynch mob off at gun point and incarcerated their prisoner in the Iowa County jail at Dodgeville, eighteen miles away.

The Iowa County Courthouse in Dodgeville is Wisconsin's oldest active courthouse. The cornerstone was laid on June 11, 1859. A marker detailing the historic structure is located on-site.
(Courtesy of Iowa County, Wisconsin; public domain)

Carlton's mouth and throat were badly burned by the acid, but his condition was not fatal. Though he was sick, the killer made trouble for the sheriff, throwing drinking glasses and tin plates at him. In one scuffle the murderer grabbed the sheriff's leg and the assistance was required to throw the prisoner back into his cell. There were preliminary hearings at which evidence was given. Seven charges of murder, two of assault and one of setting a building on fire were read to Carlton. The Circuit Court ordered a plea of "not guilty" to be entered for the prisoner and he was remanded to the Iowa County Jail without bail. (*Grand Rapids Tribune*, September 9, 1914, p. 1) Carlton actually made two court appearances, but he never stood trial. Despite medical attention, Carlton starved himself for seven weeks and after loosing nearly sixty pounds succeeded in starving himself to death.

Julian Carlton was scheduled to appear before Judge Clementson on September 20, 1914. Sheriff Williams and five deputies took him to a crowded courtroom. (*Grand Rapids Tribune*, September 9, 1914, p.1) But he would never answer for his charges. He allegedly remarked to a deputy sheriff, at the time of his arrest and when he feared that he would die of the poison, "I'll tell you why I did it before I die." Later when physicians told him he was in no danger of death, he declined to explain except to say, "I did it in self defense." (*The Washington Post*, August 17, 1914) Julian Carlton died on October 7, 1914 (*The Indianapolis Star*, October 8, 1914, p.1), at the Iowa County jail in Dodgeville, Wisconsin.

A Time for Grieving: Mourning at Taliesin

Even Wright's son, John, gave differing details of the tumultuous events. The tragedy occurred on September 15, 1914, but Wright reported in his book, "The first time I went to Taliesin was during the tragedy. Dad needed me then. It was in August of the year 1914, not long after the opening night of the Midway Gardens." (Wright, p. 80)

Mr. Edwin Cheney, Borthwick's husband, was at the train station and took the same train with the Frank and John Wright. John secured a compartment and shoved the two men, Wright and Cheney, into it to save them from the pressing reporters who were already closing in on them. John wrote, "Mr. Cheney was the father of the two little girls who were visiting their mother, his former wife." (Another confusing detail, as the children were one girl, Martha, and one boy, John). (Wright, p. 80)

Wright's aunts, Nell and Jane, waited for them to arrive at the Madison train station. A morbidly curious crowd also waited ghoulishly for hours for the train and the entourage to arrive. Frank Lloyd Wright's face displayed his anguish as he sat in the dimly lit compartment when he learned of the macabre details of the murders from the reporters and the shouts of newsboys along the way calling out the headlines, "Taliesin Burning to the Ground, Seven Slain." Arriving at Spring Green, the night wind filled the countryside with smoke while the shadows of men taking exaggerated proportions in the darkness ran here and there with flashlights and lanterns. The darkness of the night saved Wright from some of the macabre sightseers.

When news of the tragedy flashed over the wires to the *Wisconsin State Journal*, its owner, Richard Lloyd Jones, Wright's cousin and Jenkin Lloyd Jones' son, immediately left for Taliesin and met the Wright's there. John recalled that his father was growing weaker by the moment and was about to collapse. Cousin Richard grabbed Frank by the coat collar, pounded him on the back, shook him vigorously, and said, "Stand up Frank! It couldn't be worse; get hold of yourself." His cousin's thunderous words and rugged strength seemed to flow to Wright. Jones walked with Frank and John to the station car, which sped them to the home of a neighbor where the charred and axed remains of the victims had been taken. (Wright, p. 83)

Final Good-byes

Frank Lloyd Wright cut down flowers from Mamah's garden and filled the homemade casket with them. John helped him place the plain strong box in the little spring board wagon which was also filled with flowers. A little sorrel team pulled the wagon along the road to the family chapel where no one waited.

John Wright recalled the emotionally charged meeting and parting of the two men as a congenial encounter. "From the moment he clasped Dad's hand there was a closeness between them, a grief-stricken, mute understanding. From there the only words I remember hearing uttered between them were when Mr. Cheney took his departure at noon the next day. The remains of his two little girls were in a box he held in one hand." John recalled the conversation as an emotional but peaceful exchange. "Goodbye, Frank, I'm going now," Cheney said. "Goodbye, Ed," Wright said, clasping Cheney's hand. The two men stood looking into each other's eyes. "Goodbye, Frank," Cheney repeated. John records that there was no trouble or strife in their voices. (Wright, pp. 81-82)

There was a hailstorm that weekend that substantially damaged the crops in the surrounding areas. Boils broke out on Wright's back and neck and as one victim after another died, he stoically attended each funeral, one after another. Some believed that Wright entertained the thought of joining Mamah's fate. But on Tuesday, August 18, the heavy rains of the weekend forced the dam of an artificial lake below Taliesin to break. Wright was standing too close to the edge when it happened and was swept into rushing water. In a moment of truth he discovered some desire to live and fought his way to the bank. Yet, Wright later wrote, "All I had left to show for the struggle for freedom of the five years past that had swept most of my former life away, had now been swept away." He was being punished, he thought, by the same hand he had always feared, the wrathful God of Isaiah. "Fate has smashed these wonderful walls. This broken city, has crumbled the works of giants…" (Secrest, p. 222)

John wrote of his father, "Something in him died with her, a something lovable and gentle that I knew and loved in my father." (Wright, p. 86) "He has never marked the spot of her burial, why need he? Taliesin stands as a monument to her love and beauty. I believe that in it she still lives and loves and breathes inspiration to him." (Wright, p. 80)

Frank Lloyd Wright promised to rebuild Taliesin in memory of Mamah and he kept that promise in 1928. Later his wife granted him a divorce and he remarried. His strong-willed wife had his body exhumed from near Mamah's burial site in 1985 and moved to near her own designated gravesite at Taliesin West in Arizona.

CHAPTER NINE

THE "MURDER" AND GHOST OF AGATHA CHRISTIE: THE DUCHESS OF DEATH

It's a wicked world, and when a clever man turns his brain to crime it is the worst of all.

~ Sherlock Holmes ~

Sir Arthur Conan Doyle

The Perfect Crime

It was the perfect crime. The Colonel's wife was missing, which would mean that he was free to marry his mistress. Her car was found, obviously pushed, not driven, into the water. Her fur coat had been left behind on a chilly night, along with her identification and other personal items. The victim was nowhere to be found and her husband had a motive – the mistress. In fact, he had no alibi, as he admitted to the police that he was at a party with the mistress when he heard from his wife that she intended to make a scene at the party over him leaving her. He went home to stop her, only to discover, he said, that she was not there. Now she was missing and presumed dead. It was the perfect crime, but who was the actual perpetrator and who was the actual victim.

The Colonel was married to "The Duchess." But he also had a mistress. When he announced to his wife that he intended to divorce, some say she decided to kill him. Divorce was such a scandal in 1926 that the thought of it was unbearable to "The Duchess." Then there were the financial problems associated with divorce and, more importantly, the Colonel's wife still loved him. She may have loved him to death so, desperate and realizing that there would be no reconciliation, his wife planned the perfect crime.

Yes, the Colonel's wife, not the Colonel, planned the perfect crime. She would fake her own death and implicate her husband. He would then be sent to the gallows and would be denied his illicit affair. His death, if successful, would constitute a murder by design and the plan itself a conspiracy to commit murder. The conspiracy would not involve the executors, but a close, lifelong friend. At least this is how the story goes by some reports, which are diverse and many. But let us back up a bit and look at the author of this who-done-it or the mystery that it would become, because the conspirator-wife was an author and is known today as the "Duchess of Death."

Agatha Christie: The Duchess of Death

Agatha Christie, also known as the "Duchess of Death," was the most renowned mystery writer of her time, perhaps of all time. She is known today as a prolific writer of mystery novels and short stories, the creator of Hercule Poirot, the Belgian detective, and Miss Jane Marple. She wrote more than seventy detective novels under the surname of her first husband, Colonel Archibald Christie. She published a series of romances, a children's book, and her style for contemporary mystery writing came to be among the most popular "who-done-its" in Eastern Europe, Great Britain and the United States.

Agatha May Clarissa Miller was born on September 15, 1890, at Ashfield, the family home of Frederick Alvah Miller and Clara "Clarissa" Miller, in Torquay, England. She was one of three siblings in a well-off, upper-middle-class, late Victorian family. Her father was an American who had business connections in both America and England, and her mother was the niece of Frederick's stepmother.

Dr. Robert J. Girod, Sr.

In 1879, shortly after the birth of their first child, Madge, the family decided to move to New England from Torquay. While in America in 1880, Clara gave birth to their second child, Monty. Soon after, the family returned to England again, but Frederick was forced by business to return to America. He suggested that the family continue on to Torquay and rent a house. Upon his return, however, Frederick found that Clara had actually purchased a house - Ashfield. Eventually the Millers decided to remain at the home and become permanent residents in England.

The household Agatha grew up in seemed to have a significant influence upon her writing style and characters. Though she was raised to be a young lady by her stable parents and eccentric grandparents, her mother had little to do with her upbringing. Agatha grew up as an only child, since Madge and Monty were much older than she was and were away at school most of the time. Her early education was at home where she was schooled by a governesses and tutors until later on in life. Because of her severe shyness, her parents worried that she might be developmentally challenged. This concern was soon allayed and Agatha demonstrated the curiosity and love of learning that characterized her later years. Many of her novels poke fun at the common English mannerisms of her time. When she was not occupied by assignments, she played what might be called a series of mind games with a series of imaginary friends. These too had significant influence upon her writing.

Infamous Murders and Mysteries

A plaque for the Agatha Christie mile at Torre Abbey in Torquay.
(Used by permission of Violetriga. Internet: http://en.wikipedia.org/wiki/
Image:Agatha_Christie_plaque_-Torre_Abbey.jpg)

Agatha's father passed away when she was eleven, in 1901. Agatha's mother had to rent out Ashfield from time to time to make ends meet, meaning that she and Agatha would travel under very austere circumstances during the times when Ashfield was occupied. In 1906, she was sent to Paris to attend a finishing school and have social opportunities similar to what her elder siblings enjoyed. While there, she earned a reputation as a gifted singer and showed a talent for music. Throughout her life she retained a love of music and an ability to play the piano. Her travels also took her to Cairo, where many of her novels take place. She developed a contemptuous amusement with the upper class society and their eccentricity, often including mockery of social quirks into several of her novels and short stories.

When she was about eighteen, a few of her poems were published in *The Poetry Review*, and encouraged her to publish short stories and a novel. At first she was rejected by a publishing agent, who the encouraged her to try again. She was relucatnt to do so until her sister made a remark, during a discussion of Sir Arthur Conan Doyle, about her inability to write a mystery-detective story. Agatha resolved to prove her sister wrong and in 1916, she did when she wrote *A Mysterious Affair at Styles*.

Agatha and Archie

Agatha was an attractive and intelligent young woman and soon became the recipient of a number of marriage proposals. She declined them all until 1912, when she accepted the offer of a major in the Gunners (Artillery). But the following year she met Captain Archibald Christie, a dashing officer in the Flying Royal Corps. He swept her off her feet at a party. He was a guest at Ashfield a few days later and made a grand entrance on a motorcycle. Shortly thereafter she accepted his proposal of marriage and wrote a letter to her first fiancé to break off their wedding plans. On Christmas Eve, 1914, Agatha and Archibald were married and two days later Archie was sent off to fight in The Great War (World War I).

While Archie was away, Agatha volunteered in a local hospital as a nurse and was eventually moved to the hospital pharmacy and dispensary. There, she became familiar with many of the poisons that would be featured in the plots of her mysterys. It was here that she gained firsthand knowledge leading to the idea for at least one possible plot for a murder. By 1916, she had decided to try her hand at writing and had been working on a mystery novel. Partly to alleviate the boredom of being a lonely war wife and because she seemed to have a natural ability to plot the details of a novel, Agatha continued her writing which produced *The Mysterious Affair at Styles*.

When Archie returned at the end of the war, he and Agatha settled in London, where Archie took a position in a bank. Agatha unsuccessfully submitted her work to several publishers. After she had given birth to her daughter and only child, Rosalind Christie in 1919, her first novel was published in 1920. John Lane offered her a contract for the next five novels, in addition to the one that he had already accepted. Due to the terms of her contract, she made virtually no money from the book and she was initially uncertain whether a writing career was feasible. But earning at least some money from her writing persuaded her pursue a career writing detective mysteries and thrillers.

Agatha Christie continued writing and in 1922 her second novel, *The Secret Adversary*, was published. Archie encouraged her in her writing and she soon signed with the literary agents Hughes Massie, Ltd. Soon her unprofitable contract with John Lane expired and she signed a contract with another publisher, William Collins Sons and Co., Ltd. Her first book with them was *The Murder of Roger Ackroyd* (1926). Her relationship with Collins endured to the end of her life.

Agatha dedicated her third novel, *Murder on the Links* (1923), "To my husband," and noted in her autobiography that she was happy during this period. But trouble seemed to develop between the couple as early as 1924. Some reports assert that Archie's obsession with golf was, at least in part, to blame. Others speculated that Agatha's growing independence and financial success may also have contributed to the couple's trouble. While trouble often comes from both directions, Archie eventually became interested in another, less socially rebellious, woman. By 1926, the couple had grown apart to the point that Agatha took a vacation to Corsica without Archie.

When Agatha came home she found that her mother was seriously ill with bronchitis. Clara Miller died a few days later. Archie was in Spain and Agatha endured her tragedy alone. When Archie returned to England and learned of the death of his mother-in-law, he left again. Even after he came back, he still stayed away from Agatha, in London or at the family home, Styles House, in Berkshire. Agatha was still recovering from the death of her mother when Archie announced that he wanted a divorce. He had fallen for another woman, Nancy Neele. But because of their daughter, Rosalind, Archie moved back to Styles House in an attempt toward reconciliation. Agatha described this as a period of sorrow, misery, and heartbreak. When the reconciliation was unsuccessful, Archie announced that he was leaving for good to be with Nancy. It was during this personal crisis that Agatha Christie came into national acclaim with the publishing of *The Murder of Roger Ackroyd*. The bizarre affair that followed remains a mystery and controversy to this day.

The "Murder"

A series of events led to Agatha Christie's disappearance in 1926. Agatha, still mourning her mother, disappeared on 5 December 1926. Two days earlier, on the morning of Friday, 3 December, the Christies had an argument. Colonel Christie left the house with a packed bag to spend the weekend with Madge and Sam James at Hurstmore, near Godalming in Surrey. Colonel Christie's mistress, Nancy Neele, who lived in Croxley Green, was to be there, and the party was held to announce their engagement. (Costello, p. 190)

Agatha spent the afternoon having tea with Archie's mother, Mrs. William Hemsley in Dorking. (Costello, p. 190) Returning home to Styles House, Agatha discovered Archie was gone. Leaving their daughter, Rosalind, asleep in the house, Mrs. Christie packed a bag and drove away. She posted a letter to the Deputy Chief Constable of Surrey, in which she said she feared for her life and asked for his help. (Osborne, p. 51)

Charlotte Fisher, a servant in the employ of the Christies, telephoned Archie, who is said to have left his dinner party in a hurry. It is supposed that he may have made an attempt to head off Agatha from blundering into the James' house and making a scene. (Costello, p. 191)

Her car was found the following morning over an embankment at Newlands Corner, Berkshire, by George Best, a fifteen-year old "gypsy lad." (Osborne, p. 51) The hood was up and the lights were on. Inside the car were a fur coat and a suitcase, as well as Agatha's expired driver's license. The police subsequently issued a missing person report, a news flash that gripped the imagination of the country, especially as *Roger Ackroyd* was still one of the best-selling books of the year.

Agatha's biographer, Charles Osborne, wrote, "*The Murder of Roger Ackroyd* was published in the spring of 1926. Seven months later, on Friday, 3 December, Mrs. Christie disappeared in mysterious circumstances worthy of one of her crime novels." (Osborne, p. 51)

The Daily Mail offered a reward of one hundred pounds for Agatha's discovery and police everywhere were on the lookout for her. Over 15,000 friends, fans and family members searched for her and even offered a reward through *The Daily News* for information on her whereabouts. The Deputy Chief Constable of Surrey said, in the best tradition of the detective novel, "I have handled many important cases during my career, but this is the most baffling mystery ever set me for solution." Police from four counties, Surrey, Essex, Berkshire, and Kent, were brought in. As in an Agatha Christie murder mystery, a number of clues were found, only to be discarded. The police guarded Colonel Christie's house, monitored his phone calls, and followed him to his office. Christie told a city colleague, "They think I've murdered my wife." (Osborne, p. 52)

The Daily Mail published an article by the famous thriller writer, Edgar Wallace, opining that he did not suspect foul play, but had considered it. He characterized the mystery as, "A typical case of 'mental reprisal' on somebody who has hurt her. To put it vulgarly her first intention seems to have been to 'spite' an unknown person who would be distressed by her disappearance." (Osborne, p. 53)

Another fellow writer and friend, Sir Arthur Conan Doyle, author of the Sherlock Holmes mysteries, joined in the investigation. He felt that the Chief Constable of Surrey should ask his advice. Indeed, Conan Doyle seems to have had the assistance of both the police and Colonel Christie, however, it was not the deductive powers of Sherlock Holmes that was called upon to aid in this inquiry. Conan Doyle obtained from the police one of Mrs. Christie's gloves. He took it at once to his friend Horace Leaf, a well-known medium and psychometrist. Conan Doyle gave Leaf no other information at all. This was on Sunday, 12 December, when Mrs. Christie had been missing for eight days. (Costello, p. 191-192)

Horace Leaf at once got the name "Agatha." "There is trouble connected with this article," he said. "The person who owns it is half-dazed and half-purposeful. She is not dead as many think. She is alive. You will hear of her, I think, next Wednesday." That same evening Conan Doyle sent a report of this session to Colonel Christie. (Costello, p. 191-192) Agatha Christie cannot have been happy to discover Conan Doyle's involvement in this incident as she owed him so much for his influence upon her writing.

On the twelfth day, she was finally located. The "mystery" was solved when Bob Tappin (another account reports the name as Bob Leeming), a musician at the Hydro Hotel (now the Old Swan) in Harrogate, recognized Christie as a guest and claimed the reward. In those days the Hydropathic Hotel was an elegant spa resort in Yorkshire. Reportedly the banjo player in the band at the Harrogate informed the police of his suspicion that the Mrs. Neele was in fact, Mrs. Christie. The police stationed a detective in the hotel for two days to keep on eye on Mrs. Neele.

Infamous Murders and Mysteries

The Harrogate Hydropathic Hotel (formerly the Swan Hotel).
(Public domain photo)

Agatha Christie was in fact registered in the Harrogate Hydropathic Hotel under the name of Teresa Neele. The police and Archie Christie rushed to the hotel. By now you have deduced that there was no murder or, at least, Agatha Christie was not the victim of a murder. At most there may have been a conspiracy to commit murder - Archie's, through the faked murder of Agatha. Richie Calder, the journalist who first approached Agatha when she was found, said, "If she had intended suicide and if her body had been found in the Silent Pool, say, I have no doubt from what I know of the police attitude, that Colonel Christie would have been held on circumstantial evidence." Was this her revenge, to have Archie arrested, and then to rescue him from a murder trial, perhaps at the last moment? (Costello, p. 194-195) Or was her intent to send Archie to the gallows to guarantee that he would never leave with his mistress?

After meeting in private with Agatha, Archie made a public statement that his wife "has suffered the most complete loss of memory and does not know who she is." This position was reiterated in public statements by the author, though she never addressed the matter in her autobiography. Those few family members who knew of her whereabouts claimed she was stricken with amnesia, however, this was never confirmed.

The disappearance of Agatha Christie remains one of the most intriguing episodes in the eventful life of the author. There was nationwide interest when the writer vanished after apparently crashing her car near a Surrey chalk pit. Once she was discovered, the speculation as to why she went missing continued for much longer.

Christie's activities during her several days of being "missing" resulted in a great deal of rumor, gossip, speculation, and theory. This caused a tremendous controversy and much of the press considered Agatha Christie's sudden breakdown a publicity stunt. Others thought her inner turmoil was sincere. Still others theorize that the disappearance was a calculated effort by Agatha to humiliate her husband, Archie, or that this was an attempt to implicate Archie in her feigned murder in order to send him to the gallows and prevent him from running away with Nancy Neele. These theories have been rejected by Mathew Prichard, the dedicated defender of his grandmother's memory.

Yet, biographer Charles Osborne wrote that the week before her disappearance, Agatha Christie had lost a diamond ring at Harrods. She wrote to the Knights bridge department store from Harrogate, describing the ring and asking that, if it were found, it be sent to Mrs. Teresa Neele at the Hydro Hotel. Harrods did, in fact, return Mrs. Christie's ring to "Mrs. Neele." In 1980 a very elderly journalist claimed that he remembered that in 1926, on the morning after Mrs. Christie disappeared, her publisher Sir Godfrey Collins had told him not to talk to anyone about Mrs. Christie, as she was in Harrogate resting. (Osborne, p. 56)

There are those who insist that Agatha was far from losing her memory and that she knew exactly what she was doing on December 3, 1926. Some assert that she may even have hoped that Archie would be suspected of having murdered her. Such a dogmatic position on how the author staged her disappearance not only asserts culpability, but with her friend and "sister-in-law" Nan Watts as an alleged accomplice, a conspiracy.

The Conspiracy

Realizing her marriage was over, Agatha and her friend Nan Watts staged the disappearance in manner that would cause the finger of suspicion to point toward her estranged husband, Archie. The plan was to leave him with a motive and no alibi when the police questioned him. Reports have been published by authors and the media that members of the Watts family have confirmed this story and that the family was never allowed to speak to Agatha about this affair. None of the family ever spoke of it to her because they knew she loved Archie very much and it would upset her.

Agatha and Nan Watts had been friends since they were young girls, having been introduced by their mothers who were also childhood friends. Agatha and Nan remained friends for many years and, when Agatha's older sister, Madge Miller, married Nan's brother, James Watts, they became family. When Agatha was in the middle personal tragedy emotional crisis over her mother's death and Archie's request for a divorce, it was her close friend, Nan, whom she turned to for support.

On the morning of 3 December 1926, after Agatha and Archie had their tumultuous fight, some author and reporters say, Agatha and Nan got together that same afternoon to devise their plan. At about 2145 hours (9:45 p.m.), Agatha got into her Morris Cowley car at her Berkshire home, "Styles," and drove off into the night. About five miles outside Guildford in Surrey, at a spot known as Newlands Corner, her car went off the road. The car was discovered the next morning and the police were called. On the back seat of the car were Agatha's fur coat, her driver's license, and a case of clothes.

After abandoning the car and leaving the "clues" on the back seat as "evidence," she had caught a train to Waterloo. Later she arrived at Nan's house at 78 Chelsea Park Gardens in London. The friends spent the next morning, allegedly, shopping for clothes at the Army and Navy Stores and Nan apparently withdrew some cash from her Harrods bank account. Agatha allegedly posted a letter to Archie's brother saying she was going to a spa in Yorkshire and then caught the 1340 (1:40 p.m.) northbound train.

A massive search of woods in the area was initiated and divers began dragging a nearby pond. Archie and thousands of volunteers joined in the search, but to no avail. When her body was not found, the search area was widened but Agatha was already on her way to Harrogate. In Harrogate, she checked into the Hydro Hotel (the Old Swan Hotel) under the name of Teresa Neele, an alias intentionally chosen because it was the last name of her husband's mistress, Nancy.

The plan went awry because the two conspirator-friends had underestimated the amount of publicity that the case would attract. Agatha is reputed to have disliked press coverage and was reportedly shocked by the publicity that the incident received, though some people have suggested that she did it for publicity. She reportedly spent ten days of her sabbatical writing, knitting, doing crosswords, reading and dancing at the hotel, and visiting the local library. It was her love of dancing that eventually revealed the truth about who she was. A bandsman named Bob Leeming (another account reports the name as Bob Tappin) became suspicious about her identity and, on 13 December, the police were notified. The fictional account of this incident was presented in the film *Agatha* (directed in 1978 by Michael Apted), starring Dustin Hoffman and Vanessa Redgrave.

OK, so we do not have a murder here. It may still have been a conspiracy to commit murder, as some have theorized. Conjecture aside, what about the "Ghost of Agatha Christie"? Well, let's finish the tale of her life first; then we will look for her ghost.

"The Story of My Murder Is Greatly Exaggerated" or Life After Death

During a period of recovery, Agatha lived at Styles with Archie, but their marriage was at an end and in 1927she reluctantly granted him a divorce, which was finalized in 1928. Agatha returned to her normal state in society after a brief period of recuperation and she continued to write even more books than ever. Agatha and Nan remained friends and confidantes into old age.

It has been speculated that she may have felt she needed to vent her emotion and frustration through her writing. In the years after her separation, she wrote many of her best selling novels (*The Big Four*, *The Mystery of the Blue Train*, etc.). Her plots became more complex mysteries, rather than the predictably consistent plots charactered by her earlier writing.

In 1928, Agatha Christie also went to the Middle East and visited the archaeological dig at Ur (a providential town near Baghdad). She became friendly with the dig director, Leonard Woolley, and his wife, Katharine. On her second visit, she met Max Mallowan, the twenty-six-year-old archaeological assistant to Woolley. The two were married on 11 September 1930 in Scotland. Their marriage lasted for forty-six years, until Agatha's death. At the time of their marriage, Agatha was thirty-nine and Max was twenty-six. Agatha retained the pen-name Agatha Christie, but in private life she used her married name of Mallowan. In a nonfiction account of life on an archaeological dig, *Come Tell Me How You Live*, she was published under the name Agatha Christie Mallowan.

She published more novels, a couple of stage plays, and lived happily until the start of World War II when Mallowan entered the Air Force. Christie's daughter married a young Major, Hubert Prichard, and they eventually had a son before Prichard was killed in the war in 1944. In her 50's, the personal tragedies that punctuated Agatha Christie's life, no doubt, had a profound influence on her writing, giving them what some observers have referred to as "solemn and morbid undertones." Her later work sold even better than many of her earlier works, possibly due to the increasing popularity of mysteries. Some literary analysts have noted that the influence of her travels and experiences are reflected in her story settings and may be the most intriguing aspect of her writing style, connecting the author and the audience as only Agatha Christie did.

Agatha made her final public appearances at the 1974 gala premiere of the film *Murder on the Orient Express*, screened at the ABC cinema on Shaftesbury Avenue, London, with Queen Elizabeth in attendance, and at the banquet held at Claridge's afterward.

Dr. Robert J. Girod, Sr.

Agatha Christie (*Agatha May Clarissa Miller Christie Mallowan*) died on January 12, 1976, at her home at Wallingford, Berkshire. Max Mallowan survived his beloved Agatha by two years, dying on August 19, 1978. At her request, Christie was buried in a private ceremony at Saint Mary's churchyard, Cholsey, Berkshire. Her simple tombstone was inscribed with two lines from Edmund Spenser's *The Faerie Queene*:

> ***Sleepe after toyle, port after stormie seas,***
> ***Ease after warre, death after life, does greatly please.***

This would be suitable place to end this story of the story-writer, but there is more. There is the "ghost story" part of this "mystery" (for those of you who like stories about "things that go bump in the night").

The Final Mystery of Agatha Christie: A Ghost Story

One of Agatha Christie's best-known stories, *Orient Express*, was written at Istanbul's Pera Palas Hotel, a favorite "haunt" of the rich and famous (pun intended). She stayed in the hotel many times between 1926 and 1932.

Room 411 at the Pera Palas Hotel in Istanbul, Turkey, the room where Agatha Christie wrote Murder on the Orient Express.
(Photo by Steve Hopson, November, 2004; used by permission. Internet: http://en.wikipedia.org/wiki/Image:AgathaChristie.jpg)

Warner Brothers film studios reportedly contacted a famous Hollywood medium and clairvoyant, Tamara Rand, to try to contact Agatha's spirit through a séance.

Rand reported a vision of Agatha Christie walking along a paved street and read the sign *Mesrutiyet Caddesi*. She said that, after she went into a trance, she began to write in a language that she did not know. She allegedly scribbled in Agatha's own handwriting during her trance. The words she wrote were the name of a street in Istanbul and the name of a hotel on that street. Rand asserted that in the trance she saw the hotel and Agatha Christie. Agatha was going into a building called Pera Palas and going up to room 411. Once she closed the door to room 411, she hid a large key beneath the floorboards.

Thus, it was claimed that contact was made with "Agatha Christie's spirit" and that she revealed that the key to the box containing her missing diary was in room 411 at the Pera Palas Hotel in Istanbul, Turkey. The Turkish press and foreign journalists from everywhere went to Pera Palas, room 411, on March 7, 1979. A telephone connection was established with Los Angeles and, under the supervision of Tamara Rand, the floor of the room was disassembled on live American television via satellite. At the point where the wall joined the floor by the door, a rusty, eight centimeter-long key was found.

In January 1986, a second key numbered 411 was found in the Pera Palas Hotel. This time the key was found in room 511. Speculators and the hopeful suggest that the mystery continues on with a new dimension. Thus, Agatha Christie, the Duchess of Death, continues to thrill fans with mysteries even after her death.

CHAPTER TEN

SHERLOCK HOLMES AND HOUDINI: GHOST BUSTERS

It is one of those instances where the reasoner can produce an effect which seems remarkable to his neighbor, because the latter has missed the one little point which is the basis of the deduction.

~ Sherlock Holmes ~

Sir Arthur Conan Doyle

The Doctor and the Detective

Sir Arthur Conan Doyle, creator and author of the Sherlock Holmes mysteries, was a medical doctor. He had a lifelong interest in crime and detection and was more than an author of detective novels. He was a distinguished criminologist and consulting detective in his own right. Sir Arthur was more known as an author, then as a criminologist and consulting detective, but was perhaps most devoted to his interest as a spiritualist.

It was spiritualism that later brought Harry Houdini and Sir Arthur Conan Doyle together. At the time they met, Doyle's life and writing were absorbed in advancing the spiritualist movement, which he regarded as a new

Revelation. Doyle was the literary artist-intellectual Houdini fantasized of becoming. Although trained as a physician and eye specialist, Doyle was a man of letters, the versatile author of stories, novels, plays, poems, histories, articles, and polemical writing. He was high-minded, generous, and often spoke out on social questions. (Silverman, p. 250)

Doyle was fond of being called upon by the Criminal Investigations Division of Scotland Yard's London Metropolitan Police. On Wednesday, 19 April 1905, Conan Doyle was one of a small group from the Crimes Club who met in the East End of London to follow up the case of "Jack the Ripper." Conan Doyle had long been familiar with the mysterious series of murders of White chapel that had claimed the lives of at least five women in the autumn of 1888. That same year, Doyle's Sherlock Holmes mystery, *A Study in Scarlet,* was published as a book. (Costello, p. 57)

The mutilated trunk of a female was been found under a railway bridge in Pinchiu Street on 10 September 1889. The head and legs were never found, and the woman was never identified. Even at the time the police did not connect this crime with Jack the Ripper and, though it received sensational coverage in the papers, it is even now uncertain as to whether it was one of the infamous serial murders. What role would spiritualism play in solving the mystery of Jack the Ripper? Although nothing as sordid as the Whitechapel murders ever appeared in his novels, Conan Doyle, like every other criminologist, was fascinated by Jack the Ripper and the mystery of his identify.

On 2 December 1892 Conan Doyle visited the notorious Black Museum at New Scotland Yard. This gruesome display, housed in a cold, ill-lit room in the basement of the building on the Theme's Embankment, contained relics of crime and murder going back several decades. He reviewed the facts of Friday, 9 November, when Mary Jane Kelly, an Irish girl of about twenty-five, was butchered in her room in Miller's Court off Dorset Street. Behind the safety of a locked door, Mary Kelly was murdered and butchered, her nose, breasts, and intestines cut out and placed on the table beside the bed. This was the last Ripper murder in the series of five, before the killer vanished as mysteriously as he had arrived. (Costello, p. 58-60 and 63)

Dr. Frederick Gordon Brown, the City of London police surgeon (as opposed to the London Metropolitan Police) shared with Doyle that he had told the Coroner that some anatomical knowledge was evidenced by the killer's work, but whether this was from medical training or skill in cutting up animals was not clear. The entrails had been removed and deliberately placed on the right shoulder. This has given some writers to speculate that this was an example of Masonic ritual murder. In the summer of 1894 Doyle outlined to an American journalist how Sherlock Holmes would have investigated the series of murders, but "there is good reason to believe that by then the police knew the culprit was either dead or well out of the way in a lunatic asylum." (Costello, p. 60-61)

Houdini: Criminologist and Escapologist

Harry Houdini was also interested in crime and criminology. Houdini gave a private showing of his skills at Scotland Yard and often bragged about this demonstration at the famed CID. The detectives had no fear of his escaping, he said, so they used easy locks. But the press did not cover the event and it earned him no publicity. (Silverman, p. 47) He developed his magician's skills to become the greatest escapologist ever. Houdini had many and diverse interests.

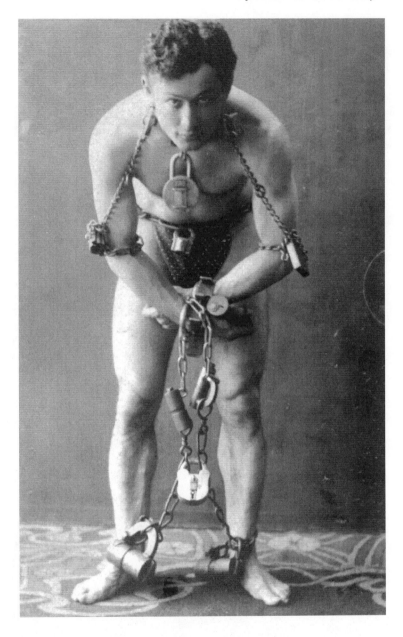

Harry Houdini: Illusionist and Escapologist.
(Public domain photo; Internet: http://en.wikipedia.org/wiki/
Image:HarryHoudini1899.jpg)

Sir Arthur Conan Doyle, physician and author of *Sherlock Holmes*.
(Public domain photo. Internet: http://upload.wikimedia.org/wikipedia/
commons/b/bb/Conan_doyle.jpg)

Harry Houdini was fascinated by the art of illusion and, in pursuit of knowledge, attended several séances, though he was not a spiritualist himself. In fact, Houdini denounced all mediums as cons and tricksters. He learned most of their techniques in order to expose their bunk. Spirit messages upon blank slates were in reality substituted slates, luminous cheesecloth was made to appear as ghosts or ectoplasm, and spirit hands were nothing more than paraffin wax models. Along with spiritualist mediums, Houdini exposed fortune-tellers, palmists, astrologers, and the like as hucksters. But, like Arthur Conan Doyle, Harry Houdini was close to his mother and longed to contact her spirit if possible. (Booth, p. 326-327)

Although Houdini directed four linked motion picture organizations, his interest in film production declined as his involvement in Spiritualism grew. His last production, **Haldane of the Secret Service**, released in 1923, was a failure. He starred in this motion picture as a U.S. Secret Service agent, Heath Haldane. In the film Haldane tracked a gang of international counterfeiters and dope smugglers, headed by a mysterious Dr. Yu. Some say that Houdini tried to out-Holmes Sir Arthur. His newspaper-size publicity book touted Haldane as a "Super-detective" (Silverman, p. 289)

Houdini became "The Handcuff King." He cultivated the friendship of lawmen and stayed abreast of their affairs. "It has been my good fortune," he wrote, "to meet personally and converse with the chiefs of police and the most famous detectives in all the great cities of the world." He even performed for a former NYPD police commissioner, President Theodore Roosevelt. By the end of his career he had a New York City Police Department pass, authorizing him to cross "all police lines." (Silverman, pp. 42 and 189)

Houdini the Spy?

The name Harry Houdini is synonymous with the art of escape and his death-defying escapes and illusions made him famous. It is well known that Houdini was fascinated by crime detection and often associated with the police. But recent reports suggest that Houdini worked as a spy for Scotland Yard, monitoring Russian anarchists, and assisted the U.S. Secret Service in investigating counterfeiters. These same reports suggest that the paranormal sleuth and illusionist may have been murdered.

The theory suggests that Houdini used his career as cover to travel throughout the United States and around the world to collect information for law enforcement authorities. Researchers have posed this hypothesis after reviewing a journal belonging to British spy master William Melville (1850-1918), who mentioned Houdini several times in his writing. Melville joined the Metropolitan Police in 1872 but was sacked for insubordination. Later he was reinstated and promoted to the Criminal Investigation Department (CID). Melville met magician Harry Houdini in June, 1900, when Houdini came to Scotland Yard to demonstrate his abilities as an escapologist. When Houdini released himself easily from the police handcuffs, Melville befriended him and reputedly learned lock picking. Melville became the head of Scotland Yard's Special Branch but resigned as superintendent on 1 November 1903, to become the first chief of the British Secret Service with the code name "M," which is still used today by chiefs of SIS (MI-6).

While at Scotland, Melville helped launch Houdini's European career by allowing the performer to demonstrate his escape skills. Melville arranged a demonstration for Houdini, as an audition for a London theatre owner, where the illusionist slipped free from a pair of Scotland Yard handcuffs. The theory suggests that Melville helped Houdini in exchange for his work as a spy. Later Houdini was similarly aided in Chicago by a police lieutenant who participated in a publicity stunt with him.

The Irish Crown Jewels and Political Murder

Doyle's mother had great interest in the history of her family in Ireland and her second cousin, Sir Arthur Vicars, Ulster King of Arms and the Chief Herald of Ireland, helped her as a leading historian and genealogist of Irish families. In 1907, his office in Dublin Castle was raided and the Irish Crown Jewels were stolen. As Ulster King of Arms he held office directly under the King and was not a government employee. The jewels were the Regalia of the Royal Order of Saint Patrick, founded in 1783, and were worn at knighting ceremonies in Dublin Castle or when a monarch visited Ireland.

The jewels were the Star and Badge of the Order and had been presented to them in 1830 by William IV. Because Sir Arthur Vicars was the custodian, Vicars was relieved when Sir Arthur Conan Doyle wrote his cousin offering advice and assistance. The mystery was replete with sinister political and sexual undertones. There were rumors that Vicars was associated with ring of homosexuals in high levels of government in both London and Ireland. This was quite a scandal in 1907 and the affair was dangerous to the interests of many influential people up to King Edward himself. (Costello, p. 94-96)

The jewels were kept in a safe in the library of the Bedford Tower, where the Office of Arms was located, rather than in the strong room, as required. They were last seen when Vicars showed then to a visitor on 11 June 1907. On 6 July, one of the collars was returned by the Grafton Street jewelers after being altered. Vicars asked the office messenger, William Stivey, to put the collar in the safe. Having second thoughts at having given Stivey the key from his chain, Vicars followed him downstairs. Stivey appeared in the library doorway with an anxious look on his face and said that the safe was already unlocked. There was evidence that the thief had taken his time in stealing the regalia, as well as some of Vicar's own family jewelry.

The theft had political, as well as criminal, ramifications. King Edward was to arrive in Dublin in a few days. The Irish Crown Jewels included an eight-point Star of Brazilian diamonds with a Shamrock (the symbol of Ireland) in the center on a ruby cross (the symbol of England) with a blue enamel background. It was adorned with the motto *"Quis Seperabit?"* (Who will separate?) It represented unity between Britain and Ireland. The king was livid at the thought that the theft may have been a direct insult by Irish Nationalists or Republicans or even an act by Irish monarchists who wished to restore an Irish King. (Costello, p. 96)

Dublin police headquarters, across the Castle Yard from Bedford Tower, had undertaken the investigation. Vicars, who was now in royal disfavor, was nervous when he realized that even he was under suspicion. Chief Inspector John Kane, of Scotland Yard, was contacted for assistance but returned to London when his report naming a suspect was rebuffed. Vicar's and Conan Doyle's suspicions were on Francis Shackleton, the brother of Antarctic explorer Sir Ernest Shackleton. The suspect was a businessman of questionable practice, who was later jailed for fraud, and had a reputation of sexual deviance. Vicars had, however, appointed Shackleton as one of his assistants, despite his reputation. (Costello, p. 95-97)

In 1920, when Ireland was again at issue, the affair was resurrected. Conan Doyle considered the case solved and Shackleton, having served time in prison for his fraud, he was certain was the perpetrator. Shackleton, out of the public view for some time, died anonymously in 1939. Vicars and Doyle also suspected Captain Richard Gorges, a hero of Spion Kop in the South African War. He shared Shackleton's reputation and in 1916, while in prison for manslaughter, implied to a fellow prisoner that he was involved in jewel theft and could help recover them. No one followed-up on this and Gorges took his secret to his grave in the 1950s. (Costello, p. 98)

On 14 April 1921 Sir Arthur Vicars was murdered. Around his neck was hung a label, "Spy. Informers beware. I.R.A. never forgets." The I.R.A. issued a statement that it was not responsible for the murder. While Conan Doyle was unable to save his cousin from the controversy, their suspicions are thought by many to be the correct solution to the crime. Though Shackleton and Gorges were never formally exposed, the Irish Crown Jewel theft was the basis of the plot for Conan Doyle's 1908 mystery **The Bruce-Partington Plans**. (Costello, pp. 97-99 and 100)

"My two sweethearts." Harry Houdini with his wife Beatrice and mother Cecilia Steiner Weiss.
(Public domain photo. Internet: http://en.wikipedia.org/wiki/Image:Weiss_with_mother_and_wife.jpg)

Crime in America

While crime in America was different from what Conan Doyle knew in Britain and Europe, the experiences in his "second homeland" stimulated his imagination and provided new plots for his novels. Doyle met William J. Burns in 1913. Then known as "America's greatest detective," Burns was a long-time admirer of Sherlock Holmes and his fictional "practical methods." Doyle was fascinated by Burns' stories and those of other American private detectives like Allan Pinkerton and the men of Pinkerton's National Detective Agency. Burns' father had been a tailor and a Police Commissioner in Columbus, Ohio. The younger Burns (also a tailor in his 20's) gained a reputation as an amateur sleuth. In 1885, he had cleared up a notorious election fraud for the State of Ohio. In the 1890's Burns joined the U.S. Secret Service, which had been founded by Allan Pinkerton during the Civil War. In 1909 Burns and his son, Raymond, established the William J. Burns National Detective Agency. (Costello, p. 124 and 131-132)

In 1921 Burns was appointed as director of the U.S. Justice Department's Bureau of Investigation (later the Federal Bureau of Investigations) by President Harding's Attorney General. In 1924, he resigned as a result of the "Tea Pot Dome" corruption scandal. A series of other setbacks and scandals diminished Burns reputation following this and Doyle never made mention of him after 1924. (Costello, p. 135)

Conan Doyle maintained an avid interest in crime in America throughout his life. One of the last American cases that Doyle took an interest in before his death was the 1929 Sacco-Vanzetti case. A subject of controversy even today among jurists, forensic scientists, detectives and criminologists of diverse varieties, Doyle was at the end of a trip through Africa when the Boston area press was full of this story. The two Italian-born anarchists were later executed following their conviction of Bridgewater, Massachusetts, payroll robbery and the murder of cashier Frederick A. Parameter and guard Alessandro Berardelli. (Costello, p. 214)

A Common Interest

The friendship between Sir Arthur Conan Doyle and Harry Houdini all began in early 1920, when Harry Houdini, who was touring in Britain, sent Sir Arthur one of his books, ***The Unmasking of Robert-Houdin***. In it he referred to the Davenport Brothers, two American medium-magicians who became very famous in various parts of the world during the middle of the 19th century.

Harry Houdini with Sir Arthur Conan Doyle, June, 1922.
(Photo courtesy of the Portsmouth Public Library, Conan Doyle Collection, Arts and Cultural Development Service).

Dr. Robert J. Girod, Sr.

Back of photo, reading: *"Doyle with Houdini. The Handcuff King. (Last installment)."*
(Photo courtesy of the Portsmouth Public Library, Conan Doyle Collection, Arts and Cultural Development Service).

Infamous Murders and Mysteries

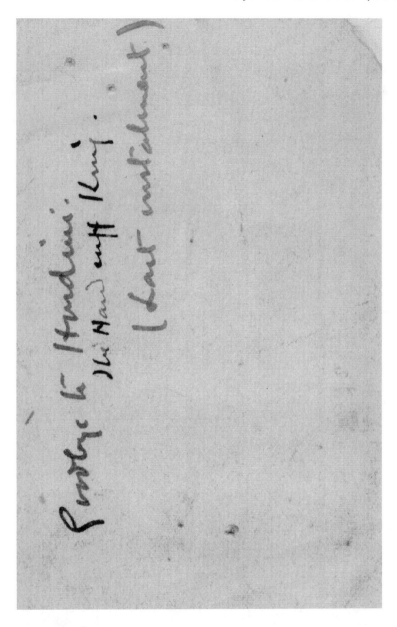

They were known for a specialty presentation which they called the "spirit cabinet." This was a wooden cabinet in which one of them sat securely tied. Once the cabinet doors were closed "rappings" would be heard, a bell and a tambourine would play, and hands would appear at the openings of the doors. Examination during or at the end of the séance revealed that the mediums were still securely tied, leaving many to wonder if they were genuine mediums or clever magicians who somehow managed to free themselves and produce impressive manifestations.

Houdini had had a chance to speak with Ira Davenport in 1910. Ira was the only surviving brother and Houdini felt privileged to learn directly from him the clever secret of their act. The Davenports were forerunners of the escape act that later made Houdini famous and Ira admitted to him that they had always used illusions, but, for publicity reasons, they allowed their audiences to decide for themselves whether it was magic or clever illusions.

In thanking Houdini for the book, Sir Arthur wrote that he did not put much faith in this kind of revelation. He said, "As to Spiritualist 'Confessions,' they are all nonsense. Every famous medium is said to have 'confessed,' and it is an old trick of the opposition." He seemed to believe in one of the oldest ruses used by fake mediums and psychics to convince onlookers of the reality of their powers, that failure is proof of genuine paranormal powers. He wrote, "I can only learn, so far as 'exposures' goes, that there were occasions when they could not undo the knots, but as there are intermittent periods in all real mediumship, that is not against them. It is the man who could always guarantee spirit action whom I should suspect most."

In numerous subsequent letters, Sir Arthur repeatedly referred to the Davenports, writing, "I've been reading the Davenport book you gave me. How people could imagine those men were conjurers is beyond me." After Houdini sent him a picture of himself with Ira, Doyle wrote:

> "...you said that Ira Davenport did his phenomena by normal means. But if he did (which I really don't believe) then he is manifestly not only a liar but a blasphemer, as he went round with Mr. Ferguson, a clergyman, and mixed it all up with religion. And yet you are photographed as a friend with one whom under those circumstances, one would not touch with a muck-rake. Now, how can one reconcile that? It interests me as a problem."

Houdini was anxious to cultivate a friendship with Doyle and replied somewhat ambiguously, "I can make the positive assertion that the Davenport Brothers never were exposed," meaning that no one had ever exposed their tricks. Doyle, however, preferred to interpret this as a confirmation of his beliefs, that they were never exposed because there was nothing to expose. He replied, "Unless I hear to the contrary, I will take it that I may use your authoritative statement as the occasion serves."

In another letter Doyle was more blunt, writing, "I had meant to ask you, in my last, and I will do so now, whether you, with your unique experience, consider that the Davenport phenomena were clever physical tricks, or whether their claim to occult power was a true one." Houdini, again non-committal, merely responded, "Regarding the Davenport Brothers, I am afraid that I cannot say that all their work was accomplished by the spirits." Doyle found the reply satisfying and so their friendship started.

Sherlock Holmes Meets Houdini

Conan Doyle was impressed by Houdini's escape performances and his exceptional muscle control. After a performance he was taken backstage to meet Houdini and the two spent several hours together. Conan Doyle an ardent spiritualist believed Houdini's abilities were at least in part spiritualistic powers. When Houdini did not deny it, Conan Doyle urged him to admit it. Houdini, then, admitted that rather than being a spiritualist he was an illusionist and even offered to demonstrate some of his tricks. Sir Arthur declined the invitation and refused to be dissuaded from his beliefs. (Booth, p. 326-327)

It was about this time that Houdini's interest in the spirit world developed, yet he presented himself to Doyle as a long-time student of spiritualism, saying, "I have gone out of my way for years to unearth mediums, so that I could really find a truthful representative - and regret to say that, so far, I have never witnessed a séance which had the ring of sincerity." In another letter he wrote,

Dr. Robert J. Girod, Sr.

"During my tour in Australia, I met a man who was supposed to have laid low Mrs. Piper; I was in Berlin, Germany, at the trial of Miss Rothe, the flower medium; I know of the methods of the Bangs Sisters, the famous Chicago mediums; I was in court when Anna O'Delia Diss De Bar, who was mixed up with the lawyer Luther Marsh, was sentenced..."

The Houdinis and the Doyles. Back of photo reads "*Denver Colo., ...1923.*"
(Photo courtesy of the Portsmouth Public Library, Conan Doyle Collection, Arts and Cultural Development Service.)

He also proposed himself to Doyle as a disciple, writing, "You will note that I am still a skeptic, but a seeker after the Truth. I am willing to believe, if I can find a Medium who, as you suggest, will not resort to 'manipulation' when the Power does not 'arrive.'" On April 14, 1920, Sir Arthur and Jean were called upon by Houdini at Windlesham, Doyle's country house in Crowborough, Sussex.

After Houdini put on a magic show for the children, the Conan Doyle's conveyed their spiritualistic experiences and the friends talked late into the night. Houdini did not believe in such things, but held his remarks out of respect for his friends. Yet, he was amazed that a man with Sir Arthur's powers of deduction and logic could believe them himself. Houdini wrote in his diary:

"Visited Sir A. Conan Doyle at Crowborough. Met Lady Doyle and the three children. Had lunch with them. They believe implicitly in Spiritualism. Sir Arthur told me he had spoken six times to his son. No possible chance for trickery. Lady Doyle also believes

> and has had test that are beyond belief. Told them all to me."

(Booth, p. 327)

Despite their differences they remained good friends and sent each other articles on spiritualism when they corresponded. (Houdini's own library of books on spiritualism and illusion are preserved in the library of Congress).

Drawn more and more into Spiritualism by his eagerness to know Doyle, Houdini asked him to recommend some mediums who he might have a séance with. He wrote, "I am very, very anxious to have a séance with any medium with whom you could gain me an audience. I promise to go there with my mind absolutely clear, and willing to believe. I will put no obstruction of any nature whatsoever in the medium's way, and will assist in all ways in my power to obtain results." Doyle consented and arranged a number of sittings for him in London and elsewhere. For all of Houdini's tact, Doyle understood that his polite silences represented serious doubt, and warned him at the outset that he must treat the séance receptively, "It wants to be approached not in the spirit of a detective approaching a suspect, but in that of a humble, religious soul, yearning for help and comfort." (Silverman, p. 255)

Houdini's attempt to conceal from Doyle his distrust of spiritualists was wasted. Like Houdini, Doyle was immune to persuasion but he offered little resistance to self-delusion. He considered spirit communication an established fact. His mission was to raise a new moral awareness of spiritualism. (Silverman, p. 258)

In June of 1922 Harry Houdini and his wife visited Sir Arthur and Jean at the Ambassador Hotel in Atlantic City. After Harry put on a show for them Jean suggested a show of her own, offering to conduct a séance in their hotel room. She suggested that they attempt to contact Houdini's beloved, departed mother. Being impressed by his friends' sincerity and wanting to believe that he could contact his mother, he agreed and later said that he put his entire being into the séance. (Booth, p. 327)

Jean Conan Doyle claimed to see Houdini's mother in a vision, carrying a crucifix. While this was unlikely, as his mother was a devout Jewess, Houdini said nothing as the séance continued. Jean then said she had received an automatic writing message to her son which, of course, strongly supported spiritualism. Again, Houdini doubted the message. First, the date was June 17, his mother's birthday, yet she made no mention of it. Second, the message was in English but Houdini's mother spoke Yiddish and wrote in German. Ever vigilant, Houdini knew that it was a common belief that the dead communicated in their own language. He was not impressed but Conan Doyle dismissed the shortcomings by suggesting that spirits often became more educated in the after-life. (Booth, p. 327-328)

Sir Arthur was eager to convert Houdini to spiritualism. This would add powerful credibility and recognition to the movement if the renowned magician affirmed their beliefs. Houdini felt he had been conned but did not want to discredit his friends by revealing the farce the séance turned out to be. Determined that the fraud of spiritualism should not be unnoticed, he said nothing and saw the Conan Doyle's off when they sailed for England on June 24. Four months later however, he published an article with the **New York Sun** which denounced spiritualism. He then wrote to Conan Doyle explaining why he felt that séance was a sham. Their friendship suffered from this revelation. (Booth, p. 327-328)

Séance with Eva C.

The most famous séances which Houdini participated in were those with the French medium known as "Eva C." These séances were held in London, at the Society for Psychical Research (SPR). Houdini was invited to participate in several of them and Eva C., also known as Eva Carrière (although her real name was Marthe Béraud) specialized in the production of "ectoplasm" manifestly emanating from her mouth and other orifices of her body.

The SPR invited Eva to England to study her case and verify these reputed phenomena. Several of the séances which Houdini attended were unproductive and Houdini reported this to Sir Arthur in a letter dated June

19th, 1920, writing, "Bagally and Dingwall [two investigators of the SPR] inform me that she has really mystified them with her manifestations, and I am rather keen to be present, and am going again Monday night." That Monday night was a bit more eventful. Houdini wrote in another letter:

> My Dear Sir Arthur, Well, we had success at the séance last night, as far as productions were concerned, but I am not prepared to say that they were supernormal. I assure you I did not control the medium, so the suggestions were not mine. They made Mlle. Eva drink a cup of coffee and eat some cake (I presume to fill her up with some food stuff), and after she had been sewn into the tights, and a net over her face, she "manifested," 1st. Some froth-like substance, inside of net. It was about 5 inches long; she said it was "elevating," but none of us four watchers saw it "elevate." Committee, Messrs. Feilding, Baggally, Dingwall and myself. 2nd. A white plaster-looking affair over her right eye. 3rd. Something that looked like a small face, say 4 inches in circumference. Was terra-cotta colored, and Dingwall, who held her hands, had the best look at the "object." 4th. Some substance, froth-like, "exuding from her nose." Baggally and Feilding say it protruded from her nose, but Dingwall and I are positive that it was inside of net and was not extending from her nose; I had the best view from two different places. I deliberately took advantage to see just what it was. It was a surprise effect indeed! 5th. Medium asked permission to remove something in her mouth; showed her hands empty, and took out what appeared to be a rubberish substance, which she disengaged and showed us plainly; we held the electric torch; all saw it plainly, when "presto!" it vanished. The séance started at 7.30 and lasted till past midnight. We went over the notes, Mr. Feilding did, and no doubt you will get a full report. I found it highly interesting.

After receiving this letter, Sir Arthur wrote to Houdini, "That is very interesting. It is certainly on the lowest and most mechanical plane of the spiritual world, or borderline world, but at least it is beyond our present knowledge." Houdini did not immediately reveal to Conan Doyle his complete thoughts on the séance. In private he noted, "I was not in any way convinced by the demonstrations." A few years later, in his book *A Magician Among the Spirits*, he explained that he had detected the various illusions and tricks employed by mediums. Houdini's opinions on "mediums" are well documented in his own letters and books. He wrote of one fraudulent medium, "I know positively that the move she made is almost identical with the manner in which I manipulate my experiment" (referring to the "Hindu needle trick"). He believed that Eva and her assistant, Mme. Bisson, were nothing more than talented hucksters. He wrote, "I have no hesitation in saying that I think the two simply took advantage of the credulity and good nature of the various men with whom they had to deal."

Doyle's Persistent Beliefs

It was about this time that Doyle became fascinated by the story of the fairy photographs. He wrote to Houdini:

> I have something far more precious: two photos, one of a goblin, the other of four fairies in a Yorkshire wood. "A fake!" you will say. No, sir, I think not. However, all inquiry will be made. These I am not allowed to send. The fairies are about eight inches high. In one there is a single goblin dancing. In the other four beautiful, luminous creatures. Yes, it is a revelation.

Houdini made no comment in reply to Doyle's letters on this subject. Some suggest this was because he could not discuss it seriously while others suggest, more likely, that he did not want to risk offending his friend.

Meanwhile, Sir Arthur was becoming increasingly convinced that Houdini himself actually had supernatural powers. He wrote Houdini:

> My dear chap, why go around the world seeking a demonstration of the occult when you are giving one all the time? Mrs. Guppy (a well-known medium) could dematerialize, and so could many folk in Holy Writ, and I do honestly believe that you can also, in which case I again ask you why do you want demonstrations of the occult? My reason tells me that you have this wonderful power, for there is no alternative, tho' I have no doubt that, up to a point, your strength and skill avail you... I am amused by your investigating with the S.P.R. Do they never think of investigating you?

When Sir Arthur went to the United States for a series of lectures on Spiritualism in April of 1922, they created a sensation and lecture halls where Doyle was appearing were always filled to capacity. His opening lecture at Carnegie Hall, in New York, had to be repeated seven times to meet demand. Houdini attended one of the lectures but did not mention it to Doyle. Instead, the two men met about a month later, on May 10, when Sir Arthur and his wife went to New York to have lunch at Houdini's house. Houdini showed Doyle his huge collection of books on magic and related arts. Sir Arthur was duly impressed but mentioned the lack of "good books" on Spiritualism. Houdini noted later that day:

> There is no doubt that both Sir Arthur and Lady Doyle believe absolutely in Spiritualism, and sincerely so. They related a number of incidents which they accepted without proof. They stopped for lunch and we enjoyed the visit very much. Lady Doyle passed a comment that this was the most home-like home that she had ever seen. After luncheon we called a car and took them to the Ambassador Hotel.

The Fatal Séance

Sir Arthur had a hectic lecture tour schedule, but he wrote to Houdini, "Until Thursday is over I shall be in turmoil. Then, when I can breathe, I hope to see you - your normal self, not in a tank or hanging by one toe from a skyscraper." Houdini was anxious to see his friend too. In June of that year (1922), Houdini invited Doyle to attend the Society of American Magicians' annual banquet in New York. Houdini enthusiastically wrote to Doyle, "You will meet some notable people and, incidentally, this is quite an affair to our organization, as some of the city officials and big business men will be there... I know that you will be interested in witnessing the magicians' performance from a looker-on viewpoint." Sir Arthur replied, "I fear that the bogus spiritual phenomena must prevent me from attending the banquet... I look upon this subject as sacred."

Houdini assured his friend, "...as a gentleman that there will be nothing performed or said which will offend anyone." Sir Arthur finally consented to attend, writing with a caveat, "Of course we will come. All thanks. But I feel towards faked phenomena as your father would have felt towards a faked Pentecost." It was at this annual banquet of the Society of American Magicians that Sir Arthur showed some of the film that would later be incorporated into the motion picture adapted from his book *The Lost World*.

Later that June, Doyle and his family vacationed in Atlantic City and invited the Houdinis to spend some time with them. "The children would teach you to swim!" Sir Arthur wrote to Houdini, "and the change would do you good." Houdini was pleased with this idea and wrote back to Doyle, "Mrs. Houdini joins me in thanking you for the invitation to come to Atlantic City, and if you will be there next Saturday or Sunday, Mrs. Houdini and I would like to spend the week-end with you... Most important of all, if the kiddies want to teach me to swim I will be there, and in return will show them how to do one or two things that will make it very interesting."

The week-end of June 17-18, 1922, the Houdinis and Doyles stayed at the Ambassador Hotel. Both Houdini and Doyle biographers document this meeting in great detail. The friends spent their Saturday playing with the children in the hotel swimming pool. On Sunday Bess and Harry Houdini were sunning themselves on the beach when Doyle met them. In an often cited turn of events, Sir Arthur suggested that Lady Doyle offer Houdini a private sitting, at which she would attempt to receive a message from Houdini's beloved mother. Houdini was both surprised and intriqued at his friends' offer. Lady Doyle suggested that through her mediumship she would use automatic writing to make such contact. The Doyle's asked Mrs. Houdini if she would mind waiting outside, explaining, "You understand, Mrs. Houdini, that this will be a test to see whether we can make any Spirit come through for Houdini, and conditions may prove better if no other force is present."

Houdini recalled the sitting in his writings:

> I walked with Sir Arthur to the Doyle's suite. Sir Arthur drew down the shades so as to exclude the bright light. We three, Lady Doyle, Sir Arthur and I, sat around the table on which were a number of pencils and a writing pad, placing our hands on the surface of the table. Sir Arthur started the séance with a devout prayer. I had made up my mind that I would be as religious as it was within my power to be and not at any time did I scoff at the ceremony. I excluded all earthly thoughts and gave my whole soul to the séance. I was willing to believe, even wanted to believe. It was weird to me and with a beating heart I waited, hoping that I might feel once more the presence of my beloved Mother... Presently Lady Doyle was "seized by a Spirit." Her hands shook and beat the table, her voice trembled and she called to the Spirits to give her a message. Sir Arthur tried to quiet her, asked her to restrain herself, but her hand thumped on the table, her whole body shook and at last, making a cross at the head of the page, started writing. And as she finished each page, Sir Arthur tore the sheet off and handed it to me. I sat serene through it all, hoping and wishing that I might feel my mother's presence. The first sheet

began: "Oh, my darling, thank God, thank God, at last I'm through. I've tried, oh so often - now I am happy. Why, of course, I want to talk to my boy - my own beloved boy - Friends, thank you, with all my heart for this."

This is one of the most speculated upon encounters between Doyle and Houdini, as the friends views on the affair were at opposite ends of the spectrum. After the séance, Houdini asked about trying automatic writing at his own home. He took a pencil and wrote the name "Powell." Doyle expressed surprise, exclaiming that a friend of his by the name of Powell, the editor of the Financial Times of London, had died just a week before. Doyle insisted that this was evidence that Houdini was a medium, declaring, "Truly Saul is among the Prophets!" Houdini and Doyle had opposing impression of what had happened. According to Doyle, Houdini left "deeply moved."

Houdini's view was much different and he was disturbed by various details which he could not reconcile. He wrote, "Although my sainted mother had been in America for almost fifty years, she could not speak, read nor write English," yet Lady Doyle's message was in perfect English. Her message also began with the sign of a cross, which was unlikely for the wife of a rabbi to have communicated. Houdini had been thinking all the time about familiar things that he had discussed with his mother. He expected some reference to them in the message, but there was none, nor to the fact that the day before the séance, June 17, was his mother's birthday.

Both Houdini and Doyle biographers and many historians opine that this was the beginning of the end of the two sleuths' friendship. Houdini did not confide his reservations to the Doyles at that time, but he did deny Doyle's view of him as a medium. Houdini explained the "Powell" incident to Doyle by revealing that he was referring to a magician friend of his, Frederick Eugene Powell, with whom he was having a great deal of correspondence. "No, the Powell explanation, won't do," was Sir Arthur's insistent reply.

Another often mentioned meeting between the friends occurred just before the Doyles returned to England. Sir Arthur received an invitation from

Houdini saying, "Mrs. Houdini and I are going to celebrate our twenty-eight marriage anniversary June 22nd. Would you care to join us in a little box party?" The Doyles accepted the invitation and the couples went to see the show *Pinwheel* at the Carroll Theater. During the performance Raymond Hitchcock, the star of the show, called the attention of the audience to famous guests. He then asked Houdini to perform an illusion for them. Encouraged by Sir Arthur and the entire audience yelling his name, Houdini went to the stage and performed the "Hindu needle trick," in which he appeared to swallow several needles and some thread and then brought the needles up threaded.

The next day this received a great deal of coverage. One reviewer reported:

> Seldom has there been heard such applause as that with which Houdini was greeted at the conclusion of the mystery. He finally made his way to his seat, but, with the audience speculating on the mystery, the *Pinwheel* performance was curtailed and the show swung into its closing number. Such an incident is unique, for (there is) no mention, in the memory of the theatrical historian, of the feat of an artist not only stopping but curtailing a show in which he was not programmed to have a part.

When Doyle finally left America he had a telegram from Houdini in his pocket, which read, "Bon Voyage. May the Decree of Fate send you back here soon for another pleasant visit." But this was not to be so.

End of a Friendship

It is undisputed by historians and biographers that the decline of Houdini and Doyle's friendship started when Houdini published an article in the New York Sun, in October 1922, in which Houdini declared that he had "never seen or heard anything that could convince me that there is a possibility of communication with the loved ones who have gone beyond." Sir Arthur was obviously hurt by Houdini's implication that Lady Doyle's séance had been a fiasco. He wrote, "I felt rather sore about it. You have all the right in the world to hold your own opinion, but when you say that you have had no evidence of survival, you say what I cannot reconcile with what I saw with my own eyes." He added, "I don't propose to discuss this subject any more with you, for I consider that you have had your proofs and that the responsibility of accepting or rejecting is with you."

Houdini responded, "You write that you are very 'sore.' I trust that is not with me, because you, having been truthful and manly all your life, naturally must admire the same traits in other human beings." He then explained his doubts concerning the séance and trusted Doyle would "not harbor any ill feeling." He wrote, "I know you treat this as a religion, but personally I cannot do so for, up to the present time, and with all my experiences, I have never seen or heard anything that could really convert me."

The Doyle's returned to the United States in April, 1923. In the meantime, **Scientific American** magazine posted a reward for anyone who could authenticate a psychic phenomenon. A committee of doctors, a professor of psychology, and Harry Houdini was formed to oversee this challenge. Sir Arthur was invited to name a genuine medium to prove the spiritualists' assertions. He declined, declaring that he had no confidence in the committee. A number of mediums appeared before the committee but one after another was discredited. One, named Nino Pecorara, had impressed Conan Doyle with his ability to produce psychic manifestations while bound. After being bound by Houdini, Pecorara was unable to produce anything. (Booth, p. 328-329)

Houdini lectured widely against the dangers and cruelty that spiritualism perpetrated by giving false hope. He and Conan Doyle continued to correspond until 1924 when Houdini published a book entitled ***A Magician among the Spirits***. Houdini wrote that he valued Conan Doyle's friendship and his brilliant mind. But he dismissed his religious beliefs and suggested that he was a "deluded man of integrity" who produced an excuse for any medium's shortfalls. This ended their friendship, yet when Houdini died in

1926, Sir Arthur Conan Doyle grieved the loss of his former friend. (Booth, p. 329-330)

Their private quarrel soon became a public battle. Early in 1923, Houdini had become a member of the *Scientific American* committee to investigate mediums, a fact that had left Conan Doyle puzzled: "...you can't sit on an impartial Committee... It becomes biased at once." Later he expressed his opinion publicly: "The Commission is, in my opinion, a farce, and has already killed itself. Can people not understand that 'psychic' means 'of the spirit,' and that it concerns not only the invisible spirit or the spirit of the medium, but equally those of every one of the Investigators?"

Doyle continued his lecture tour and met with Houdini in Denver. They had long discussions about Spiritualism and some recent psychic investigations. Doyle had witnessed a demonstration by the Zancig, a couple of vaudeville mind-readers, and was convinced they were real telepaths. Houdini, however, knew them personally and that they were acknowledged magicians and members of the Society of American Magicians. This was unconvincing to the insistent Dr. Doyle. "Sir Arthur said that he was capable of detecting trickery," wrote Houdini in his notes, "and we had a discussion in which I said that I did not think he could."

While staying in Denver, the local newspaper interviewed Doyle. The reporter told him that Houdini was offering five thousand dollars for any medium's feat he could not duplicate and Doyle was quoted as saying that he would give the same amount of money if Houdini could "show me my mother." Doyle later apologized to Houdini, saying that he had been misquoted. Then it was Houdini's turn to be misquoted by a Los Angeles newspaper. After reading the interview, in which Houdini asserted his views on Spiritualism, Doyle wrote to him:

> I have had to handle you a little roughly in the Oakland Tribune, because they send me a long screed under quotation marks, so it is surely accurate. It is so full of errors that I don't know where to begin... I hate sparring with a friend in public, but what can I do

when you say things which are not correct, and which I have to contradict or else they go by default?

In a another frustrated letter Doyle wrote to Houdini, "I am very sorry this breach has come, as we have felt very friendly towards Mrs. Houdini and yourself, but 'friendly is as friendly does,' and this is not friendly, but on the contrary it is outrageous to make such statements with no atom of truth in them." The riff becoming greater and Doyle wrote again, "Our relations are certainly curious and are likely to become more so, for so long as you attack what I know from experience to be true, I have no alternative but to attack you in return. How long a private friendship can survive such an ordeal I do not know, but at least I did not create the situation."

Doyle wrote the last letter to pass between the two former friends in February of 1924. In reply to some request by Houdini for some kind of information, Sir Arthur wrote, "You probably want these extracts in order to twist them in some way against me or my cause." Some time later, Houdini sent a short note inquiring whether Doyle wanted to receive a copy of his new book, *A Magician Among the Spirits*, but he received no answer. Their friendship was at an end, but their disagreements continued.

The Final Conflict

In the summer of 1924 an attractive, powerful medium named "Margery" (Mina Crandon) was the big, new sensation in the world of psychic research. She had entered the *Scientific American* competition and was thought to be a possible winner of the prize until Houdini sat with her. He immediately detected and exposed her methods. Sir Arthur, who had met Margery and had endorsed her powers, resented this and wrote a newspaper article explaining his version of the story of the investigation, based upon Dr. Crandon's (Margery's husband) correspondence on the subject.

Harry and Bess, circa 1922.
(Public domain photo. Internet: http://en.wikipedia.org/wiki/Image:3c12428r.jpg)

The article, intended to discredit Houdini, bitterly declared, "It should be the end of him as a Psychic Researcher, if he could ever have been called one." The fued became more hateful with each step. When the article was published, Houdini announced that he would "contemplate legal action" against Sir Arthur for slander, responding, "There is not a word of truth in his charges against me. Sir Arthur has been sadly misinformed. Anyhow, I fail to see how he, being 3,500 miles away, qualifies as a judge." He attributed Doyle's attack to his being "a bit senile... and therefore easily bamboozled" and to a desire for revenge because Houdini had "often expressed the belief that Lady Doyle was not a valid medium."

Doyle replied to Houdini's statements by diagnosing an "abnormal frame of mind" that he called "Houdinitis," one symptom of which was the belief "that manual dexterity bears some relation to brain capacity." What had started as an edifying friendship, nourished by mutual respect and admiration, ended in bitter insults, deep resentment and threats of legal actions.

When Houdini died, on 31 October 1926, however, Doyle's ill feelings seemed to melt away as he assimilated the reality of the loss of his former friend. Doyle expressed fondness for Houdini and shock at his death, saying, "I greatly admired him, and cannot understand how the end came for one so youthful. We were great friends... We agreed upon everything excepting spiritualism." In a letter to Beatrice Houdini, Doyle wrote, "Any man who wins the love and respect of a good woman must himself be a fine and honest man." Doyle went on to describe Houdini as "a loving husband, a good friend, a man full of sweet impulses."

Houdini "The Medium"

Sir Arthur Conan Doyle wrote "The Riddle of Houdini," an essay by published in the July 1927 issue of the *Strand Magazine* and, later, in Doyle's last book *The Edge of the Unknown* (1930). He wrote of his late friend, "Who was the greatest medium-baiter of modern times? Undoubtedly Houdini. Who was the greatest medium of modern times? There are some who would be inclined to give the same answer." The essay began by describing Houdini's merits, saying, "Let me say, in the first instance, that in a long life which has touched every side of humanity, Houdini is far and away the most curious and intriguing character whom I have ever encountered." Doyle continued,

"I have met better men, and I have certainly met very many worse ones, but I have never met a man who had such strange contrasts in his nature, and whose actions and motives it was more difficult to foresee or to reconcile."

Doyle expressed an admiration for what he described as Houdini's "essential masculine quality of courage..." He said, "Nobody has ever done, and nobody in all human probability will ever do, such reckless feats of daring." He applauded Houdini's "cheery urbanity" in every day life, again saying, "One could not wish a better companion so long as one was with him, though he might do and say the most unexpected things when one was absent." Doyle also noted, however, that "a prevailing feature of his character was a vanity which was so obvious and childish that it became more amusing than offensive... This enormous vanity was combined with a passion for publicity which knew no bounds, and which must at all costs be gratified."

The primary thesis of the essay, however, was Doyle's theory that Houdini was himself a real medium. Doyle insisted that no tricks or illusions could explain Houdini's amazing feats, such as his escapes from jails. "It take some credulity, I think, to say that this was, in the ordinary sense of the word, a trick," Doyle wrote. "I contend," he continued, "that Houdini's performance was on an utterly different plane, and that it is an outrage against common sense to think otherwise."

According to Doyle's essay and thesis, Houdini possessed strong psychic powers that enabled him to dematerialize from his confinement and then rematerialize outside of it. The fact that Houdini had always told him that he had no psychic powers and that he perfomed ilusions, did not dissuade Doyle's beliefs, despite the fact that Bess affirmed this to him after her husband's death. These denials merely encouraged Doyle to believe that his theory was correct. He opined, "Is it not perfectly evident that if he did not deny them his occupation would have been gone for ever? What would his brother-magicians have to say to a man who admitted that half his tricks were done by what they would regard as illicit powers? It would be 'exit Houdini.'" In one of his last letters, to B. M. L. Ernst, Houdini's lawyer, Sir Arthur wrote, "I write this in bed, as I have broken down badly, and have developed Angina Pectoris. So there is just a chance that I may talk it all over with

Houdini himself before long." Sir Arthur Conan Doyle died on 7 July 1930, four years after the death of Houdini. (Costello, p. 218)

Accidental Death or Murder Conspiracy?

New research suggests the theory that Houdini's zealous investigation and exposure of the Spiritualist movement may also have led to his death. This theory suggests a conspiracy by followers of the Spiritual movement. Members of the movement included "Sherlock Holmes" author and close Houdini friend Sir Arthur Conan Doyle. While there has been little or no no implication that Dr. Doyle or even a majority of the movement's members, participated in a conspiracy against Houdini, some members openly resented Houdini's belief that they were frauds. When he debunked those who claimed that they could contact the dead, many in the movement were hostile toward him and his revelations.

Others are now theorizing that recent evidence that suggests that Houdini was a law enforcement agent and/or a spy may have made him the target of an assassination plot. While Houdini is widely known to have associated with many police officials, presumably to further his knowledge of and publicity for his escape escapades, recent evidence suggests that he may have also aided (officially or unofficially) the United States Secret Service, Scotland Yard (the Criminal Investigation Division of the London Metropolitan Police), and/or The British Secret Intelligence Service (SIS or MI-6).

Proponents of the murder theory point to two incidents in October, 1926, in which Houdini was punched in the stomach. One occurred in his dressing room when a college student, allegedly testing his reputation for being able to withstand such a punch, did so when Houdini was unprepared. The other allegedly occurred later when a stranger in a hotel lobby also punched him. Houdini died days later at Grace Hospital in Detroit. Conspiracy theorists suggest that members of the Spiritualist movement, enemy spies, or syndicated criminals may have arranged the attacks to neutralize his efforts..

Dr. Robert J. Girod, Sr.

The Death of Elrich Weiss

Elrich Weiss, one of four sons of Rabbi Mayer Weiss, was a well-known magician. In October 1926, while rehearsing and upside down water torture trick, the cables hoisting him upside down into the water torture cell twisted and cracked the clamped footstock. The magicians left ankle was fractured. Only eight months before he had broken the bone in the same foot. The physician who attended to him backstage told him that if the stock had not broken it would have amputated his foot. (Booth, p. 406-7)

Already exhausted from long hours, the illusionists kept an engagement the next day to speak to students at Montreal's McGill University. Invited by the

Psychology department and publicized in the university newspaper, the event drew an enthusiastic crowd. Among them was student Samuel Smilovitz. He had expected to see an awe-inspiring figure of the magician with such a great reputation. Instead he saw a sickly-looking man with tired eyes and a drawn face limp to the raised platform. (Booth, p. 406-7)

Having just arrived from New York where the magician with his attorneys discussed impending law suits by several exposed mediums, his voiced cracked when he said, "If I were to die tomorrow, the Spiritualists would declare an International holiday!" To illustrate a point that one can control fear he stuck a needle through his cheek. Whether he felt the pain from that or his broken ankle he later noted, "I spoke for an hour, my leg broken." It was his last entry in his diary. (Booth, p. 406-7)

Three days later an assault was perpetrated on Weiss. The incident is somehow sketchy, but two witnesses, Samuel Smilovitz and the magician's niece, Julia Sawyer, gave their accounts. At about 2315 (11:15 p.m.) Smilovitz and another student, Jacques Price, came to the theater and the magician's dressing room. Weiss reclined on a small couch along the wall. He apologized for reclining, explaining that he had had an accident. (Booth, p. 406-7)

Weiss appeared sallow and in need of rest. His face drawn, his eyes were tense with dark circles, and the muscles of his temples and mouth twitched. He read some mail as Smilovitz sketched him. They talked until a knock came at the door and a secretary admitted another visitor. Some accounts say he was J. Gordon Whitehead, a first-year student at McGill. Others observe that the only Freshmen by the name of Whitehead that year was Wallace (Wallie) Whitehead. He was muscular and came with an armload of books. He came to return a book that Weiss had loaned him and Weiss invited him to take a seat. Smilovitz found that Whiteheads excessive chatter distracted Weiss from his pose, but none the less found the conversation interesting. (Booth, p. 408)

Weiss commented that he had read a number of detective stories and had unraveled many mysteries himself. Whitehead asked the magician his opinion of the miracles mentioned in the Bible, but was surprised when he declined to answer "matters of this nature." Whitehead then asked about the magician's physical strength, asking if it was true "that you can resist the hardest blows struck to the abdomen." (Booth, p. 408)

The magician ignored the question and diverted attention instead to his arm and back muscles. Whitehead persisted but Weiss again mentioned his arms and back. Whitehead then asked the magician, "Would you mind if I delivered a few blows to your abdomen? "Weiss accepted the challenge, still reclining on the couch with his right side nearest Whitehead. Smilovitz reported that as the magician began to rise from the pillows Whitehead began punching him in the stomach. The blows were "terribly forcible, deliberate, well-directed," the witness's affidavit read. Jacques Price, still with them protested, "Hey there you must be crazy. What are you doing? "Whitehead hit Weiss two or three more times. Weiss made a gesture and mumbled, "That will do." (Booth, p. 409)

The three students stayed until about 0115 (1:15 a.m.), Smilovitz finishing the sketch. Weiss commented "You made me look a little tired in this picture. The truth is, I don't feel so well." He signed and dated his portrait. That afternoon his niece, Julia, found her uncle in pain. She gave a different account of the events. Weiss, she reported, said that he had told the students that because of his physical conditioning punches did not affect him. He consented to prove it and intended to stand to brace himself. Before he could do so and while he was still reading his mail one student began punching him. (Booth, pp. 409-410)

Before Weiss was able to finish his performance he took to his couch during a break and broke into a cold sweat. Unable to dress himself, he experienced severe stomach pains aboard the train to Detroit. A physician was summoned ahead to meet them at the Detroit station upon their morning arrival. At Grace Hospital in Detroit, Weiss had a temperature of 102 and displayed symptoms of appendicitis. Determined to perform, however, he checked into the Statler Hotel where he shook with chills as his temperature reached 104. He collapsed during his act; wad revived, finished his show, and collapsed again. (Booth, p. 410)

At 0300 (3:00 a.m.) Dr. Charles S. Kennedy, chief of surgery at Grace Hospital, examined Weiss at the Statler. After hearing of the punching episode, Dr. Kennedy believed Weiss either had a ruptured intestine or a clot in the large blood vessel feeding it. Weiss talked to his physician in New York by phone and was urged to go to Grace. Surgery commenced at 1500 (3:00 p.m.) That afternoon, October 25, 1926, his ruptured appendix was removed, but peritonitis infected the membrane lining of the stomach and the surrounding organs. As the toxins spread, Kennedy and three other physicians released a statement that the famous magician was near death. (Booth, p. 410)

On Sunday, October 31, (Halloween), 1926, Elrich Weiss told his brother, "I can't fight anymore." He died at 1326 (1:26 p.m.) When the bronze coffin the magician had ordered for his "buried alive stunt" was left behind when the set of his show was sent back to New York, it was used for his corpse. The death of the renowned magician, who had often cheated death, was very controversial and remains so more that eighty years later. The *Graphic* called it an "unpunishable crime" and demanded an investigation. (Booth, p. 412-413)

"Sir Arthur Conan Doyle expressed fondness and shock: 'I greatly admired him, and cannot understand how the end came for one so youthful,' he said. 'We were great friends…..We agreed upon everything except spiritualism." (Booth, p. 414)

This story is not really about Sherlock Holmes, but his creator and the author of his adventures, Sir Arthur Conan Doyle. To many the fictional sleuth "Sherlock Holmes" is more renowned than the doctor who brought the character to life. Sir Arthur Conan Doyle first met Elhrich Weiss in 1920. Weiss started in show business as a trapeze artist of the age of eight. The Hungarian Jew was, by the age of forty-eight, a world renowned magician and escapologist, was also better known by his alias or stage name, Harry Houdini. In 1922 Sir Arthur Conan Doyle and his wife Jean made a trip to North America. During many of their visits to several U.S. cities they attended the performance of psychics and mentalists. During their trip they made several visits to Harry Houdini. (Booth, p. 326-327)

Arthur Conan Doyle was not only the creator of the mystery novel detective, Sherlock Holmes, but was much more. Doyle was raised by his mother when his father, a disappointed artist, was consumed by drinking and fishing. Doyle was well-read as a child and by age fourteen had learned French in order to read Jules Verne in the author's language. A brilliant man, Doyle become a medical doctor and served as a physician during the Boer War. (Silverman, p.326)

Dr. Conan Doyle was a sportsman, an adventurer, world traveler, and inventor. He gave up his medical career for a lucrative literary career but was also a crusader against injustice and other social problems. Sir Arthur, as he was often referred to, led several successful efforts to exonerate wrongly convicted prisoners. Another passion he held was the propagation of the doctrines of spiritualism. (Silverman, p.326)

Shortly before his death, Harry Houdini arranged a secret ten-word code with his wife. If there was life after death and if there exists the ability to communicate "from the other side," he would communicate with her within ten years. Despite numerous claims by numerous mediums, contact was never made and the code has never been broken. (Booth, p. 330)

Grave of Harry Houdini (Ehrich Weiss) at Machpelah Cemetery (Jewish) in Queens, New York. The emblem below the bust is of The Society of American Magicians; the bust is no longer on the memorial due to vandals. The headstones are covered with small stones, which is a Jewish custom that indicates morners have passed by. His parents and siblings are buried at this family grave, but wife, Bess, is buried at a Catholic Cemetery.

Sir Arthur Conan Doyle's grave; Minstead Churchyard at Hampshire, England.
(Public domain photo. Internet: http://en.wikipedia.org/wiki/Image:Doyle_
Arthur_Conan_grave.jpg)

CHAPTER ELEVEN

MURDER, HEMINGWAY, AND THE FLORIDA KEYS

... there is no hunting like the hunting of man and those who have hunted armed men long enough and liked it, never really care for anything else thereafter. You will meet them doing various things with resolve, but their interest rarely holds because after the other thing ordinary life is as flat as the taste of wine when the taste buds have been burned off your tongue.
"On the Blue Water," *Esquire*, April 1936

The Florida Keys

The Florida Keys are an archipelago of about 1,700 islands which begin at the southeastern tip of the Florida peninsula (about 15 miles south of Miami) and extend south-southwest and then westward to Key West. Key West is the far western of the inhabited islands and on to the uninhabited Dry Tortugas. These island-keys are along the Florida Straits, dividing the Atlantic Ocean on the east from the Gulf of Mexico on the west. The southern tip, known as the "Southern Most Point," of Key West is just 98 miles from Cuba. The Florida Keys are geographically in the subtropics, but are classified as having a tropical climate. The total land area of the Keys is approximately 137 square

Infamous Murders and Mysteries

miles, with more than 95 percent of the land area in Monroe County. A small portion extends northeast into Miami-Dade County. The City of Key West is the county seat of Monroe County, which includes a section on the mainland which is almost entirely in Everglades National Park and the Keys islands from Key Largo to the Dry Tortugas.

More than twenty-seven years before Hemingway moved to the Keys, murder took the life of one of its lawmen. Deputy Sheriff Frank Adams, Monroe County Sheriff's Office, was shot and killed in the line of duty October 7, 1901. While it was not commonplace for black men to be police officers at the turn of the century (1900s), Deputy Adams was indeed a black deputy sheriff. (No photo is available, although his family survives in the Miami area). He was attempting to arrest a man who was interfering with the discharge of his duty. Two drunken men started fighting near Jackson Square in Key West, the county seat. They separated and one of the men began to use profane language as he walked up Thomas Street. Deputy Adams, who was sitting near the corner of Southard and Thomas Streets, arrested the man and was taking him to jail, when the man resisted. Deputy Adams called out for assistance and two men named Fleming and Gabriel took hold of the man to assist the deputy.

Sheriff Francis Knight, Sheriff Richard T. Hicks, 1901-1905   1893-1901 and 1905-1909 (Monroe County during Adams' time)
(Used with permission; Sheriff Richard Roth, Monroe County Sheriff's Office, Florida).

Another man pushed some bystanders aside and said that he would not allow them to arrest his brother. Deputy Adams released the first man he had arrested and grabbed the man who interfered. They began to struggle and the suspect gained control of Deputy Adams' service weapon. After a short scuffle a pistol shot rang out. The bystanders, with the exception of a mate on the steamer *Laurel*, ran away. Fleming and Gabriel, the two men holding the arrested man, let him go and also fled. Adams had been shot in the arm and he fell to the ground, with the man who shot him falling on top of him. The suspect then shot Deputy Adams two more times, with one bullet hitting him in the left chest, penetrating his heart, and another wounding him in the face. After shooting Adams, the assailant got up and ran down Southard Street toward what was then the Government Reservation.

A large crowd soon gathered around the body of Deputy Adams and the mate from the *Laurel*, who was the only one to stay at the scene. The mate told the crowd how the murder had happened. The 42 year-old Deputy Adams was taken to his home where he was pronounced dead. The following day the shooter, Robert J. Frank, was caught and identified by the mate from the *Laurel* as the perpetrator who shot and killed Adams. He was arrested and charged with murdering the deputy. At the preliminary hearing Robert Frank admitted to the shooting and said that he was sorry for it. He said that had anyone attempted to arrest him, he would have shot them as well. When searched he had some empty cartridges and a loaded pistol, with extra ammunition in his pocket.

Frank Adams was born to William and Miranda Adams July 12, 1859, one of six children. He and his wife, Clementine also had six children - Lillian (died in 1957), Lenora (died as a toddler), Willard (died in 1918), James (died in the 1940s), Gladys (died in the 1930s) and Bernard (died in the 1980s). Gladys married William McGee and had one child, Wilhelmina. Gladys died when Wilhelmina was very young and the child was raised by Lillian. None of Frank's other children had children, making Wilhelmina the sole descendent of Deputy Adams. Wilhelmina married and had two girls, Lillian and Angela. Lillian, who lives in Atlanta, Georgia, has one son, William, and one grandchild, Alexa (Frank's great, great grandchild). Both William and Alexa live in Miami, Florida. Angela has one son (Frank's great grandchild), who served in Iraq before returning to Hunter Army Airfield in Savannah, Georgia.

The character of Deputy Clyde Sawyer (played by John Rodney) may have closely resembled any one of the Florida Keys lawmen who lost their lives before and during the Hemingway period (1901-1961). It was the murder of a Monroe County Sheriff's deputy that was a part of the plot in director John Huston's **Key Largo** (1948), starring Humphrey Bogart, Lauren Bacall, Edward G. Robinson, and Claire Trevor. The gathering force of a hurricane like the one that really did devastate the Florida Keys in the 1930s is a backdrop to the perspiring passions of murderers, molls and Bogart and Bacall. Bogart journeys to visit his buddy's father and widow, finding them in the backwater Key Largo Hotel, occupied by invading gangsters. Hardened criminal Johnny Rocco isn't afraid of any man, but God's fury is another matter.

To create the proper atmosphere, Huston and Richard Brooks worked out the details of the script in the only hotel in Key Largo at the time, which was deserted in the off season. The criminal boss, Johnny Rocco, was modeled after real-life gangster Lucky Luciano, who had just been deported to Cuba, with his mistress, Gaye Orlova, who resembled the character Gaye Dawn, played by Claire Trevor. The film's ending was changed to incorporate one added from Hemingway's *To Have and Have Not*, since Howard Hawks' film of that name had previously dispensed with Hemingway's ending.

Ernest Hemingway (1899-1961)

Ernest Miller Hemingway was born in Oak Park, Illinois, on July 21, 1899, the second of six children. He was one of the most famous of American novelists, short-story writers and essayists. Many of his works are now considered classics of American literature. His mother Grace Hall had a career in the opera before marrying Dr. Clarence Edmonds Hemingway. Hemingway's physician-father personally attended to the birth of Ernest and blew a horn on his front porch to announce the birth of his son to the neighbors. The Hemingways lived in a six-bedroom Victorian house built by Grace's widowed father, Ernest Hall. Ernest's grandfather Ernest, who was an English immigrant and Civil War veteran, lived with the Hemingway family.

Hemingway's mother was a homemaker who had aspired to an opera career before marrying Dr. Hemingway and she earned money giving voice and music lessons. She was known as a domineering woman who was described as narrowly religious. She had wanted twins, but when this did not happen, she dressed Ernest and his sister Marcelline (eighteen months older) in similar clothes and with similar hairstyles.

Rather than adopting an interest in music, as his mother had hoped, Ernest acquired his father's interests in hunting, fishing and the outdoors as he roamed the woods and lakes of northern Michigan. Hemingway liked other sports, as well, like boxing and football. Academically, he excelled in his English classes. The family owned a house called Windemere, on Michigan's Walloon Lake, and the family often spent summers vacationing there. These early experiences with nature resulted in Hemingway's lifelong passion for outdoor adventure and remote, isolated parts of the world.

When Hemingway graduated from high school in 1917, he did not pursue a college education, but began his writing career as a cub reporter. He worked for six months as a reporter for *The Kansas City Star*. He tried, against his father's wishes, to join the United States Army to see action in World War I. He reputedly failed the medical examination due to poor vision, but there is no record of this. He then joined the American Field Service Ambulance Corps and left for Italy. En route to the Italian front, he stopped in Paris, which was under constant bombardment from German artillery. When he arrived on the Italian front, he witnessed first-hand the brutalities of the war. On his first day of duty, an ammunition factory near Milan exploded. Hemingway had to pick up the human remains, which were mostly of women who had worked at the factory. This experince with death made a disturbing and profound impression on the young Hemingway. On 8 July 1918 he was severely wounded in a leg by an Austrian trench mortar shell while he was delivering supplies to soldiers. He was decorated twice by the Italian government, receiving the *medaglia d'argento* or Silver Medal of Military Valor.

Hemingway recovered from his wound in an American Red Cross hospital in Milan, where he drank heavily and read newspapers to pass the time. There he met Sister Agnes von Kurowsky of Washington, D.C., who was one of eighteen nurses who attended to groups of four patients each. Hemingway fell in love with Sister Agnes, who was more than six years older than him. But after he returned to the United States, Sister Agnes fell in love with and married another man. This relationship inspired Hemingway's early novel, A Farewell to Arms (1929). This tragic love story, filmed for the first time in 1932, starred Gary Cooper, Helen Hayes, and Adolphe Menjou. A 1957 remake, starred Rock Hudson and Jennifer Jones. Its lack of success reputedly led David O. Selznick to stop producing films.

Hemingway returned from his experiences with war and love to a less emotional and dramatic life, for a time. He worked for a short time as a journalist in Chicago and married his first wife, Hadley Richardson, in 1921. That September they moved to a small fourth floor apartment at 1239 North Dearborn in a poor, run down section of Chicago. The building still stands with a plaque on the front of it calling it the Hemingway Apartment. It was not long after this, however, that the Hemingways moved to Paris where Ernest wrote articles for the *Toronto Star*. In Europe Hemingway associated with successful writers, such as Gertrude Stein and F. Scott Fitzgerald. He was part of the 1920s expatriate community in Paris, known as "The Lost Generation," a name coined and popularized by Ms. Stein.

In 1922 Hemingway went to Greece and Turkey to report on the war between those countries. In 1923 made two trips to Spain, on the second to see bullfights at Pamplona's annual festival. On October 10 of that year his first son, John Hadley Nicanor Hemingway, was born. Then his first books, *Three Stories and Ten Poems* (1923) and *In Our Time* (1924), were published in Paris. His writings began to reflect his sense of adventure and mystery. *The Torrents of Spring* and his first serious novel, *The Sun Also Rises*, were published in 1926.

In the fall of 1926, Ernest's grandfather, Anson Hemingway, died. Ernest's father, Clarence, wrote to his son, saying, "My dear father died this morning at Seven o'clock… The day before he had written several letters and paid up all his bills… He was eighty-two and one month and eleven days, his birthday was August 26th 1844." Ernest replied, "Dear Dad, I am dreadfully sorry to learn of grandfather's death. It makes me very sad not to have seen him again before he died, but it is good he died so happily and peacefully." (Mellow, 371) In 1927 Ernest and Hadley separated and that same year he published Men Without Women, a collection of short stories, containing "The Killers," one of Hemingway's most popular works. After the publication, Hemingway returned to the United States, to live in Key West, Florida.

Hemingway in Key West

Following the separation, Hemingway divorced Hadley Richardson in 1927 and in May he married Pauline Pfeiffer. Pauline was a fashion editor and devout Roman Catholic from Piggott, Arkansas, and Hemingway converted to Catholicism himself. On June 28, 1928, Hemingway's second son, Patrick, was born in Kansas City. John Dos Passos, a friend of Hemingway's, suggested that the outdoors-lover move to Key West, Florida. In November, 1928, Hemingway rented a house there. He occasionally traveled to Spain to gather material for his next works, Death in the Afternoon and Winner Take Nothing. There he also wrote *A Farewell to Arms*, which was published in 1929. It was not until 1931 that Pauline's Uncle Gus gave them the old stone house as a wedding present.

By the time he moved to the Keys, Hemingway may have heard the story of the murder of Deputy Sheriff Frank Adams in 1901. If he hadn't heard the tale by the time he arrived, he was sure to hear it soon thereafter, as he frequented the gin-mills and pubs of the island-city. The story probably lingered and was still told in the bars of Key West. He just as likely, may have also heard the murder story of Key West Police Officer Clarence Till, who was shot down in cold blood in March of 1904, just three years after the murder of Deputy Adams. These were the type of tales of men in conflict that may have interested the author. Here, in the Keys, Hemingway fished in the Dry Tortugas waters with his longtime friend Waldo Peirce and went to the famous Sloppy Joe's bar. Here he may have heard the stories of Adams and Till.

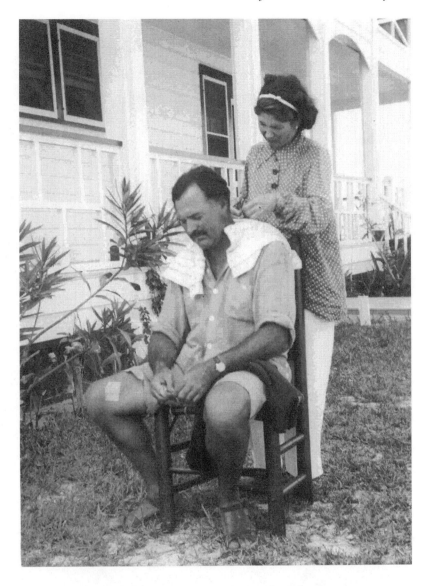

Ernest Hemingway and second wife, Pauline, in Key West, Florida.
(Used by permission of the Ernest Hemingway Collection, The John F. Kennedy Presidential Library and Museum, Boston).

Officer Till was called to a disturbance at a coffee shop near the corner of Division Street (now Truman Avenue) and White Street where a drunken crowd had smashed a store window. When Officer Till tried to arrest one of the perpetrators, Herbert "Dutchy" Melbourne, the crowd beat him and took his pistol. Till escaped and got another gun from Mayor Benjamin Trevor, who apparently lived nearby. The officer returned to the scene where the gang, apparently expecting his return, had prepared an ambush. Melbourne shot him with his own pistol then fired several times into the body. Till died without regaining consciousness. Melbourne was arrested at his mother's house early the next morning.

Sheriff Cleveland Niles, 1925-1933, and Monroe County Sheriff's motorcycle (1929); the law when Hemingway lived in Key West.
(Used with permission; Sheriff Richard Roth, Monroe County Sheriff's Office, Florida).

The following year, another Monroe county peace officer was murdered. Guy M. Bradley, age 35, was a game warden hired by the Audubon Society and deputized by the Monroe County Sheriff's Office. He was shot and killed July 8, 1905, while attempting to arrest a man for poaching Egrets in the Everglades. Walter Smith, a well-known plume hunter, sailed out to Oyster Keys Rookery. Smith was already angry with Officer Bradley for arresting his son, Tom, on two previous occasions. Smith had threatened that if Guy Bradley ever attempted to arrest him or any of his family again, he would kill him. Within view of Guy Bradley's cottage home, Tom Smith and a friend went ashore and started killing Egrets. Bradley approached Smith in his skiff and announced that he was arresting Tom and his friend, "under a charge of violating the law by shooting plume-birds." Smith replied, "Well, if you want him you have got to come aboard of this boat and take him" at the same time picking up his rifle. Bradley said, "Put down that rifle and I will come aboard." According to Smith's statement, Bradley immediately fired at him with his pistol, the bullet striking the mast of the boat. Smith fired his rifle back at Bradley, killing him.

Deputy Guy M. Bradley, 1870-1905 (killed 1905)
(Used with permission; Sheriff Richard Roth, Monroe County Sheriff's Office, Florida).

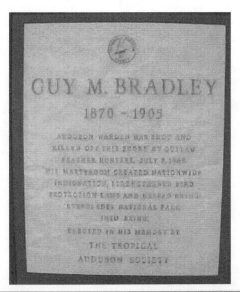

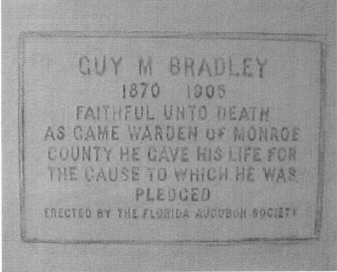

Memorial stones dedicated to Bradley by the Tropical Audubon Society and the Florida Audubon Society.
(Used with permission; Sheriff Richard Roth, Monroe County Sheriff's Office, Florida).

Louis Bradley found his brother's body the next day still adrift in the small skiff. Bradley was buried on a shell ridge at Cape Sable overlooking Florida Bay. Walter Smith turned himself into the authorities in Key West, where he spent five months in jail unable to raise the $5,000 bond. A case was made that he had deliberately plotted to murder Bradley. Bradley's pistol showed no evidence of having been fired. But the only witnesses were friends of Smith who were below deck at the time, and claimed to have heard two shots close together. The grand jury failed to indict Smith, and he was released. A few weeks after Bradley's murder, a sort of frontier justice was extracted by the two young brothers of Sophronia Bradley, Guy's widow, who burned down Smith's house. A monument was erected by the Florida Audubon Society. The grave was later washed away in a storm.

Personal Tragedy

Just a month after Hemingway moved to Key West, tragedy would strike his own family. In December, 1928, his father, Clarence Hemingway, was troubled by his health due to diabetes and his financial losses due to the instabilities of the Florida real-estate market. Dr. Hemingway (Clarence) had become over-protective of his younger son, Leicester, who was home sick with a cold at their Oak Park residence. When the physician came home at lunchtime he asked his wife, Grace, how their young son was. She said that he was feeling better but was sleeping. Dr. Hemingway went down to the basement and burned some personal papers in the furnace. Then he walked slowly upstairs to his bedroom and closed the door. He took out his father's Civil War Smith & Wesson revolver and sat for a moment on the bed. In a cold, tragic moment he put the gun to his right temple and fired a single shot. Young Leicester hurried to the bedroom, pushing the door open to find the shocking scene of his father slumped on the bed. (Mellow, pp. 367-368)

The medical examiner's report was cold, clinical, and graphic:
> The bullet pierced the brain looping under the skin, after shattering the bone of the skull in the left temple 5 cm above and 7 cm posterior to the external auditory meatus. There were powder burns at the point of entrance of the bullet. Blood was oozing from the bullet wound. (Mellow, p. 368)

Sheriff Karl Thompson, 1933-1941, and a Monroe County Sheriff's patrol car (1931).
(Used with permission; Sheriff Richard Roth, Monroe County Sheriff's Office, Florida).

The Coroner's inquest convened the next day and determined that Dr. Clarence Hemingway's death was a suicide. (Mellow, p. 368) This hurt Hemingway deeply and he immediately traveled to Oak Park to arrange the funeral. A controversy resulted when he vocalized the Catholic idea that suicides go to Hell. At about the same time, Harry Crosby, founder of the Black Sun Press and friend of Hemingway from his days in Paris, also committed suicide. The deaths left deep emotional scars on Hemingway. The Coroner later returned the pistol that his father killed himself to his mother. She sent it to him in the same package that she also sent with cookies for his sister, Sunny, a cake for Pauline, and a book for his son, Bumby. A note was enclosed that read, "Les wants you to leave it to him, when you are through with it – but you have first choice." (Mellow, p. 375)

Ernest Hemingway's grief may have been somewhat assuaged by the birth of his third son, Gregory, a few short years later in 1931. The 1930s also ushered in new literary works as Hemingway wrote *Death in the Afternoon* in 1932, *The Green Hill of Africa* in 1935, and *To Have and Have Not* in 1937. Among his most famous stories is *The Snows of Kilimanjaro*. In 1937 Hemingway observed the Spanish Civil war firsthand and, as many writers, he supported the cause of the Loyalist. In Madrid he met Martha Gellhorn, a writer and war correspondent. In the spring of 1939 Francisco Franco won the Spanish Civil War and Hemingway lost an adopted homeland to Franco's fascist nationalists. In 1940 he also lost his Key West home in a divorce. A few weeks after the divorce, Hemingway married his third wife, Martha Gellhorn, and published his novel, For Whom the Bell Tolls.

Hemingway's home and its feline residents made a brief appearance in the James Bond film License to Kill in 1989. Hemingway was given his first polydactyl-cat (those having extra toes characterized by a genetic trait) by a ship's captain. Sailors have been known to value the six-toed cats due to their proficiency in climbing and hunting, which was helpful in controlling shipboard pests. Some seamen even considered them to be good luck. Hemingway's former home in Key West is now a popular museum and remains the home of more than sixty descendents of his cats, most of whom are polydactyl.

Infamous Murders and Mysteries

Victor Licata: The Ax Murders of 1933

Hemingway had lived in the Keys for about five years when a number of gruesome and macabre murders that occurred in nearby Tampa, Florida, made the news. On October 17, 1933, Victor Licata, a seventeen-year-old boy in Tampa smoked two marijuana cigarettes handed to him one afternoon in a poolroom. That night when he arrived home, he imagined that his family had been conspiring to dismember him. To avert this, he crushed the skulls of and hacked to death his father, mother, sister and two brothers with an ax while they slept in their beds.

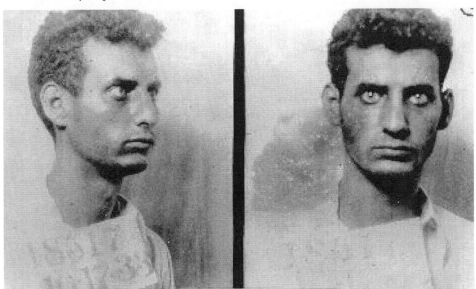

Tampa Police Department booking photo (1933)

When officers arrived at the home they found Licata staggering about in what they described as a human slaughterhouse. The officers knew him to be a sane, quiet young man. But now he seemed almost maniacal and in a daze.

"I've had a terrible dream," he said. "People tried to hack off my arms!" he exclaimed to the police. "Who were they?" an officer asked. "I don't know. Maybe one was my uncle. They slashed me with knives and I saw blood dripping from an ax," Licata answered. He said that he had no recollection of having committed the multiple murders. He said that he had been in the habit of smoking something which his friends called "muggles," a name at the time for marijuana. The story made national headlines and stunned residents of south Florida, even in the usually peaceful Keys.

Ernest and Pauline Hemingway in Key West.
(Used by permission of the Ernest Hemingway Collection, The John F. Kennedy Presidential Library and Museum, Boston).

World War II and the Fourth Wife

Hemingway developed a passion for deep-sea fishing in the waters off Key West, the Bahamas, and Cuba. Following his divorce from Pauline in 1939, he and Martha Gellhorn moved to Cuba. In 1940 Hemingway and Gellhorn were married and bought *Finca Vigia*, a house outside Havana, Cuba. He also armed his fishing boat, the *Pilar*, and he and his crew monitored Nazi submarine activities in that area during World War II.

Who can say what events may have inspired tales of intrigue in Hemingway's writing. He may or may not have shared the stories of the murders of Adams, Till, and Bradley. Just two days before the United States entered the war and just after Hemingway left the Keys, another Florida law man would be murdered just north of the Keys. On Friday, December 5, 1941, Trooper Luther Paul Daniels was shot and killed while questioning the driver of a stolen car in Miami. The suspect was taken into custody by two U.S. Immigration Agents four miles from the crime scene two days later. The gun used to murder Trooper Daniels had been used in another murder in Ohio several months earlier. Trooper Daniels, age 32, had served with the Florida Highway Patrol for six months. Hemingway may have read this account in passing in a morning newspaper or may have been struck by the reality of "… *those who have hunted armed men long enough*…" This homicidal tragedy would be lost in the news just two days later as attention was riveted on the Japanese attack on Pearl Harbor, thrusting the United States into World War II.

The first years of his marriage with Gellhorn were happy, but Ernest soon realized that Martha was not a housewife, but an ambitious journalist. Gellhorn called Hemingway her "unwilling companion." Just before the D-Day Invasion of Normandy in 1944, Hemingway managed to get to London, where he settled at the Dorchester Hotel. He had taken Martha's position as *Collier's* leading correspondent. She arrived two weeks later and took a separate room at the hotel. Hemingway observed the D-Day landing from below the Normandy cliffs; Gellhorn went ashore with the troops. Back in Paris after many years, Hemingway spent a great deal of his time at the Ritz Hotel. During this time he also met Mary Welsh, a correspondent for *Time* magazine and future Hemingway spouse, in a London restaurant.

Hemingway's divorce from Martha Gellhorn in 1945 was a bitter fight as tumultuous as the war they were covering. Gellhorn said that she had been living with a "mythomaniac." She said such people are characterized, not by being conscious liars, but by believing their own lies. They fabricate to magnify everything about themselves and their lives and believe in their own fabrications. Recovering quickly, as he had in the past, Hemingway returned to Cuba in 1946 and married his fourth wife, Mary Welsh.

Hemingway was overweight and his blood pressure was high. His excessive drinking had started years before when he was a young reporter and he had come to tolerate large amounts of alcohol. It did not seem to affect the quality of his writing at first, but by the late 1940s he had started to hear voices in his head. He taught his son Patrick to drink, when he was only 12-years old, as he did his other sons. Patrick later developed problems with alcohol and Gregory, who became a transvestite, abused drugs. In October, 1951, Pauline, Ernest's second ex-wife (during his Key West days) and Patrick and Gregory's mother, died at the age of 56.

The Old Man and the Sea, published first in *Life* magazine the following year in 1952, renewed Hemingway's fame. The story was of an old Cuban fisherman named Santiago, who finally catches a giant marlin after weeks of not catching anything. As he returned to the harbor, the sharks eat the fish, which is lashed to his boat. The model for Santiago was a Cuban fisherman, Gregorio Fuentes, who died in January, 2002, at the age of 104. Fuentes had served as the captain of Hemingway's boat *Pilar* in the late 1930s. Hemingway also made a fishing trip to Peru, in part to shoot footage for a film version of the *Old Man and the Sea*.

On July 3, 1955, Hemingway's friend, A.E. Hotchner, flew to Miami and caught an afternoon plane to Key West. A taxi took him to 414 Olivia Street, as Ernest had directed. When Ernest lived there in the 1930's, the neighborhood had only a few residents and nice houses. Ernest had the large main house and a smaller, more modern house beside the pool. Hotchner observed that the years had not been kind to the neighborhood, which was now crowded and seedy. Ernest had not lived there since 1940 when he and Pauline were divorced and the property became hers in the settlement. She continued to live there with the children until her recent death and the property passed to the children. They did not want to live there and were not around to look after it, so it fell to Ernest to try to keep it rented for them and provide for its upkeep. (Hotchner, p. 155)

Murder of the Judge

When A.E. Hotchner flew into Key West in July of 1955, a murder story was barely two weeks old in south Florida. Hemingway and Hotchner may have been so busy that they missed reading the story in the newspapers or they may have found the story intriguing enough to discuss over drinks at the local watering hole. In any event, a judge was missing and presumed murdered.

Curtis Eugene Chillingworth was a Florida attorney and state judge who disappeared from his Manapalan, Florida, home. He and his wife, Marjorie Chillingworth, are believed to have become the victims of a murder plot. Chillingworth and his wife were last seen at a dinner in West Palm Beach, Florida, on the evening June 14, 1955. They left the dinner at about 2200 (10:00 p.m.) for their Manapalan home. They went to bed expecting a carpenter to arrive the next morning of June 15 to build a playground for their grandchildren.

The carpenter arrived on time at 0800 (8:00 a.m.), but he noticed that the door had been left open and that the Chllingworth home appeared to be empty. Later that same day, Judge Chillingworth failed to appear at a previously scheduled 1000 (10:00 a.m.) hearing at the courthouse in West Palm Beach. When the police were notified they began their investigation upon arrival at the Chillingworth's home. There they found a shattered porch light, drops of blood on the walkway to the beach, and two used spools of adhesive tape (one in the sand and one in the living room). The $40 found in Mrs. Chillingworth's pocketbook seemed to rule out robbery and the keys were still in the ignition of Chillingworth's Plymouth. No further clues were found and the case went cold.

Two years later, in 1957, Curtis and Marjorie Chillingworth were legally declared dead. While no bodies were ever recovered, one theory of what happened to the Chillingworths centered on Judge Chillingworth's known previous association with a Florida municipal court judge named Joseph Peel. Peel, allegedly, was protecting bolita (gambling) operators and moonshiners. In 1953, Peel represented both sides in a divorce, which was unethical by the legal standards of conduct at that time. His superior at that time, Judge Curtis Eugene Chillingworth, reprimanded him, warning that this was his last warning for ethics violations. Peel was allegedly so angry that there was some speculation that he arranged for the Chillingworths to be killed.

By June, 1955, Peel was worried that his ethical detours were about to be exposed by Judge Chillingworth, threatening to end Peel's career as an attorney. Peel reputedly hired "Lucky" Holzapfel (a carpenter's apprentice and known criminal) to murder the Chillingworths. On the night of June 14, Holzapfel and an accomplice named Bobby Lincoln are believed to have gone to Manalapan. They landed on the warm, breezy beach behind the Chillingworth's house around 0100 (1:00 a.m.). Bobby Lincoln crouched in the bushes that gave a Floridian landscape to the home. Lucky knocked on the door and awaited a response. The judge answered the door in his pajamas. Lucky pulled a pistol from under his shirt and forced the Judge back inside where his wife waited. Holzaphel and Lincoln restrained the judge and his wife with tape and led them toward the beach beneath the partially obscured south Florida moonlight. There they forced their captives into the boat, the victims objections muffled by strips of the same tape that bound them. After the boat drifted for about an hour, the couple was thrown overboard with lead weights strapped to their legs. Their last desperate efforts to breath filled their lungs with sea water.

This is the theory that has been postulated the most in this still unsolved mystery. However, it is believed that the truth is that Peel did not hire Holzapfel or Lincoln to murder Chillingworth. They are, however, believed to have committed these murders in the hope that their illegal activities with Peel would be allowed to continue. On December 12, Lucky Holzapfel pleaded guilty to both murders and was sent to Death Row. Judge Joseph Peel was not in the clear, however. On March 30, 1961, he was found guilty of accessory to murder and he received two life sentences. The accomplice to the murder, Bobby Lincoln, finished his federal prison term in Michigan in 1962. Lucky died in prison in 1996.

Just a few months after the judge and his wife were murdered, another Florida Keys peace officer was murdered. Lieutenant Robert J. Staab, age 32, of the Bal Harbour Police Department, had been in law enforcement for five years. He was a U.S. Marine Corps veteran of World War II. On Thursday, October 31, 1957, he was on a plainclothes detail at a large convention. He and his partner observed a suspicious man going from door to door in the hotel and attempted to question him. The suspect and Staab's partner began to scuffle. As Lieutenant Staab came around a corner to help his partner in the struggle, the suspect shot and killed him. The perpetrator fled the scene but was arrested a short time later when he was stopped by police in Hollywood, Florida. The suspect was apprehended and executed for the murder in 1961. Lieutenant Staab was survived by his wife and three sons.

For Whom the Bell Tolls

He led a turbulent social life, was married four times, and allegedly had various romantic relationships during his lifetime. Hemingway received the Pulitzer Prize (1953) for The Old Man and the Sea and the Nobel Prize in Literature in 1954. But his fortunes were about to change to tragedy.

Hemingway spent much of his time in Cuba until Fidel Castro's 1959 revolution. He supported Castro but when the living became too difficult, he moved to the United States. He also lost Finca Vigía, his estate outside Havana, Cuba, which he had owned for more than twenty years. He was forced into virtual exile in Ketchum, Idaho, when the conflict in Cuba began to escalate. Hemingway allegedly came under surveillance by the U.S. federal government due to his activities and his living in Cuba.

During this period of Hemingway's life he was alleged to suffer from a variety of health problems: hemorrhoids, grippe, kidney trouble from a fishing trip in Spain, a torn groin muscle, a gash on his forehead, a finger gashed to the bone in an accident with a punching ball, lacerations (to arms, legs, and face) from a ride on a runaway horse through a deep Wyoming forest, a broken arm from a car accident, a cut eyeball, and an anthrax infection. Oh, and he also complained of a toothache. He was receiving treatment in Ketchum, Idaho, for high blood pressure and liver problems, as well as electroconvulsive therapy (ECT) for depression and his continued paranoia.

In 1960 Hemingway was hospitalized at the Mayo Clinic in Rochester, Minnesota, for treatment of his depression. He was released in early 1961. But in April, Mary interrupted a suicide attempt and, after two more attempts, Hemingway was taken back to the Mayo. During this time he was given electric shock therapy (ECT) for two months. On June 26, 1961, he was again released from the hospital. Mary and a friend, George Brown, drove him back to their Ketchum, Idaho, home.

Ernest had been cheerful during the three-day drive from Rochester, Minnesota, to Ketchum, Idaho. On his first night home he had a pleasant dinner and even joined Mary in singing one of their favorite songs, "*Tutti Mi Chiamano Bionda.*" (Hotchner, p. 303)

> *And then it just occurred to him that he was going to die. It came with a rush, not as a rush of water nor of wind; but of a sudden evil-smelling emptiness, and the odd thing was that the hyena slipped lightly along the edge of it.* ("The Snows of Kilimanjaro")

Early on the morning of July 2, 1961, according to Mary, a shot from a shotgun exploded in the house. She ran downstairs. Ernest had been cleaning one of his guns, she said, and it had accidentally discharged, killing him. His friend, A.E. Hotchner wrote, "I could not fault Mary for covering up. She was not prepared to accept what had happened and that's what came out when she had to explain." (Hotchner, p. 303) Hemingway had committed suicide by a shotgun blast to the head with his favorite shotgun at his home in Ketchum, Idaho. Hemingway himself blamed the ECT treatments for "putting him out of business" by destroying his memory.

Hemingway's daughter-in-law, Valerie, wrote, "She did not have to imagine the gruesome self-inflicted shot that sent her husband into blood-splattered oblivion. She had been a witness, she and George Brown." She said, "... Mary vehemently denied that suicide was the cause, claiming her husband's death resulted from a gun-cleaning accident. She was not so much trying to hide the facts from the world as from herself." She characterized Mary as being in a state of denial, saying, "The cruel, unbearable truth would only add to her tragic loss." Valerie had met the Hemingways just two years before and met their son, Gregory, at the funeral and later married him. (Hemingway, pp. 4-7)

Hemingway was still writing new works up to the time of his death in 1961. All of these unfinished works, which were Hemingway's sole creation, have been published posthumously. These include Islands in the Stream, The Dangerous Summer, and The Garden of Eden. The Associated Press reported, in February 2005, on the progress of what was purported to be the final work to be posthumously published that was written by Hemingway. Entitled Under Kilimanjaro, the novel is a fictional account of Hemingway's final African safari in 1953–1954. Also published after Hemingway's death were several collections of his work as a journalist. These collections contain his columns and articles for *Esquire Magazine*, *The North American Newspaper Alliance*, and the *Toronto Star*. They include *Byline: Ernest Hemingway* (edited by William White) and *Hemingway: The Wild Years*.

A.E. Hotchner recalled Hemingway being asked by a German journalist, "Herr Hemingway, can you sum up your feelings about death?" The author simply replied, "Yes. Just another whore." (Hotchner, p. 303) Ernest Hemingway is interred in the town cemetery in Ketchum, at the north end of town. A memorial, erected in 1966, is just off of Trail Creek Road, one mile northeast of the Sun Valley Lodge.

The Family Curse

Some believe that certain members of Hemingway's paternal line had a genetic condition or hereditary disease known as *hemochromatosis*, in which an excess of iron concentration in the blood causes damage to the pancreas and depression or instability in the cerebrum. The hereditary form of the disease is most common among those of Northern European ancestry, in particular those of British descent. Hemingway's physician-father is known to have developed the disease, also known as bronze diabetes. Ernest was known as a heavy drinker and some think he suffered from bipolar disorder (commonly referred to as manic depression disorder, characterized by extreme mood swings from mania to depression).

Ernest Hemingway followed his father, Clarence Hemingway, in taking his own life, his father in 1928 and himself in 1961. Two of his siblings, Ursula and Leicester, would also follow this tragic course. Ursula Hemingway Jepson, Ernest's younger sister, having survived three cancer operations, committed suicide with a drug overdose in 1966 at age 64. His younger brother, Leicester Clarence Hemingway shot himself to death in 1982 at age 67 after a series of health problems. He was the fourth to take his life and the third to use a firearm.

John Hadley Nicanor "Jack" Hemingway (aka Bumby), Ernest's oldest son, was born on October 10, 1923. Just as Ernest's mother had given him the gun that his father had killed himself with, Mary gave Jack the gun that Ernest used to take his life. The Idaho conservationist died in New York in December, 2000, of heart failure at the age of 77. Jack had three daughters - Joan (Muffet) Hemingway (1950), Margaux Hemingway (1955), and Mariel Hemingway (1961). The two younger daughters became famous actresses in their own rights. Margaux Hemingway would also take her own life – the fifth member of the immediate family.

Margaux Louise Hemingway, the granddaughter of Ernest Hemingway, was born on February 16, 1954, in 1955 in Portland, Oregon. She moved to New York City in 1974 to begin her modeling career. She was was a model, singer, and film actress who appeared in several movies. She was only 41 years old when she died by suicide near the anniversary of her grandfather's suicide 35 years earlier. She was found on July 1, 1996, having overdosed on prescription drugs. She was interred in the same Ketchum Cemetery at Ketchum, Idaho, as her grandfather. Her sister, Mariel Hemingway was interviewed by CNN News reporter Connie Chung on January 17, 2003. When asked about the "Hemingway Curse," she responded: "I just think that it's an easy way for the media to go – it's just such a hook, the Hemingway curse and suicide and this, that, and the other thing. That's not my life."

"There was no sign of forced entry and no obvious foul play," reported a Santa Monica Police spokesman. "No guns or illegal substances were found in the apartment." Margaux Hemingway was last seen on Saturday by a neighbor and her body was found the following Monday by a friend. She had been trying to get her career back on track throughout the 1990s. Her efforts included a nude spread in *Playboy* magazine. She suffered from alcohol problems, as her grandfather had, and with bulimia. She was married and divorced twice and often compared her life to that of her hard-drinking grandfather, Ernest "Papa" Hemingway. But unlike the famous writer, his granddaughter sought treatment for alcoholism.

Santa Monica police investigators said they found no illegal drugs or suicide note in the apartment but they had not ruled out the possibility that Hemingway killed herself. Three vials of Klonopin, a barbiturate, were found in her apartment. Two vials were empty and one vial still contained five tablets. The Los Angeles Coroner's Office ruled the death of Margaux Hemingway a suicide by taking an overdose of a sedative following a final determination made after toxicological tests completed. Hemingway did not have a prescription for the drug.

Ernest's middle son, Patrick, was born on June 28, 1928. At this writing, Patrick Hemingway, age 80, is the only surviving son of Ernest Hemingway. His only daughter, Mina Rothenberg, is a bookstore owner in Naples, Florida.

Gregory Hemingway, Hems youngest son, (known as Gigi and later calling himself Gloria), was born on November 12, 1931. Gregory (Gloria) had eight children: Patrick, Edward, Sean, Brendan, Vanessa, Maria, John and Lorian Hemingway. Like his father, Gregory would be married four times. He met his third wife, Valerie, at his father's funeral. She wrote, "Over the years since I met him, Greg Hemingway kept in touch with me by phone and letter, and we saw each other whenever he was in Manhattan…. And he invited me to his graduation from medical school on June 7, 1964, at the University of Miami." (Hemingway, pp. 226-227)

When Greg started his fellowship in orthopedics at Boston City Hospital, he visited Valerie in New York on his days off, sometimes staying over night. He told her that he was divorcing his second wife, Alice, and wanted to know if she would go out with him. (Hemingway, pp. 226-227) After they were married, Greg's behavior became a concern. Valerie wrote, "I came across more articles of clothing tucked in unexpected corners, and sometimes my own clothes vanished. I asked Greg if he could explain…" When he finally confided in her, he begged her to keep it a secret. "…whenever he was under stress, he put on a pair of nylon stocking…," she wrote, "It gave him comfort and strength…" (Hemingway, pp. 235-236)

Valerie conjectured that it all may have started at or before birth. His father had two sons and wanted a daughter. As Greg grew up, he felt the tension between his parents and his mother blamed him. After Greg's second birthday, Ernest took Pauline to Africa. Greg was left in Key West with the nurse, Ada, who terrorized him. When he was bad, she threatened to leave him, as his parents had done. "She would put on her hat and coat," Valerie wrote, "and walk out slamming the door and not return until his screams and imploring reached an unbearable pitch." He assured her, "I am not a transvestite. I do not want to dress up as a woman." (Hemingway, pp. 235-237)

Valerie told his psychiatrist, Dr. Robert Arnot, that Greg had become obsessed with his ex-wife, Alice, and fantasized her death, even plotting how he would kill her if only he could get away with it. "Finally, we talked about the history of suicide in the Hemingway family," she said. Dr. Arnot said that Greg was a transvestite (someone with a compulsion to wear clothes of the opposite sex), but that he would not commit suicide. (Hemingway, p. 242)

He was killing Greg (himself) in another way. In 1995 he had a sex change operation and called himself "Gloria." (Hemingway, p. 293)

Valerie wrote, "My son Edward telephoned me from New York on October 1, 2001. He told me his dad had died in a woman's prison that morning." Gregory Hemingway died on October 1, 2001, at age 69 in Florida's Miami-Dade Women's Detention Center. He was reportedly picked up in a disoriented state while walking home from a party early one morning. He was booked for "indecent exposure" when he was found naked, carrying a dress and high-heeled shoes. Five days later he was found in his cell dead of "heart disease" by an officer who came to get him for a court appearance. (Hemingway, p. 294) Homicide detectives reported that the death was due to natural causes. The autopsy report listed hypertension and cardiovascular disease, according to Miami-Dade police spokesman.

Dr. Robert J. Girod, Sr.

Hemingway posing for a dust jacket photo by Lloyd Arnold for *For Whom the Bell Tolls*, at the Sun Valley Lodge, Idaho, late 1939. It was common to not renew the promotional materials (the dust jacket and occasionally the preface and forward) when creating a new edition of the book. This dust jacket was only used on the 1940 edition.
(Public domain photo: httpen.wikipedia.orgwikiImageErnestHemingway.jpg)

Postscript

The life of Ernest Miller Hemingway was often characterized by adventure and often by tragedy. Beginning with his father, then himself, two siblings and a granddaughter, what some have called a curse has followed his family. While he wrote about, read, and lived near many tragically macabre incidents, many within his own household were just as bizarre and tragic. He and many of his offspring have experienced numerous marriages and divorce or other personal tragedy. Following the death of their father, Gregory, in 2001, Ernest Hemingway's eight grandchildren by his youngest son brought a suit to keep control of the $7.5m estate, left by Gregory, from his fourth wife, Ida, who he had divorce and remarried.

Meanwhile, Hemingway and his work remain cherished and admired by fans around the world. His work continues to inspire other authors and scholars of literature. Many of his offspring continue to contribute greatly to our culture, unaffected by the so-called curse of the Hemingways. And the curious will continue to speculate and wonder.

PART IV –

THEY'VE KILLED THE MARSHAL: 1907

One drawback of an active mind is that one can always conceive alternate explanations which would make our scent a false one.
~ Sherlock Holmes ~
Sir Arthur Conan Doyle

CHAPTER TWELVE

THE MURDER OF MARSHAL COLUMBUS L. CROY

Nothing clears up a case so much as stating it to another person.
~ Sherlock Holmes ~

Sir Arthur Conan Doyle

The Marshal Has Been Shot!

The story of a town marshal being gunned down by outlaws is not a new story to Americana, but it was 1907 in rural Indiana. The town was Woodburn and, although the town (now city) is located just outside of Fort Wayne (Indiana's second largest city), this sort of violence stirred the entire town. The day following the murder of Town Marshal Columbus L. Croy the Fort Wayne Journal-Gazette included this headline:

NO CLUE TO MURDERS

Slaying of Marshal Croy Stirs Up Town of Woodburn

Citizens and Commissioners Offer Reward – Bloodhounds Were Put on Trail Last Night

(Fort Wayne Journal-Gazette, June 8, 1907, p. 1)

    The Allen County Commissioners offered a $250 reward, making the sum $500, and the citizen committee raised the sum total to $1,000. The newspapers reported the next day:
    The slaying of Town Marshal Columbus Croy at Woodburn at an early hour yesterday morning has stirred the citizens of the village to a high pitch of excitement and indignation and in order that absolutely nothing be left undone to apprehend the burglar-murderers of the official, the citizens of the town, headed by Mr. Frank Butt, last night started the work of raising a reward for the apprehension of the outlaws.
    (Fort Wayne Journal-Gazette, June 8, 1907, p. 1)

William L. Wearley ran a butcher shop next door to the Faulkner saloon. He and his wife lived at the same location, with their residence at the rear and above the butcher shop. At about 1:00 a.m. on June 7, 1907, Mrs. Wearley was awakened by a noise. Apparently she was often hearing "noises" and her husband told her that she was crazy and to go back to sleep. Mrs. Wearley listened and heard the noise again and again awakened her husband. When William got up they saw a light in the saloon. William sent his wife upstairs to keep her "out of the way of harm," as he telephoned Marshal Columbus L. Croy. (Fort Wayne Journal-Gazette, June 8, 1907, p. 3)

Infamous Murders and Mysteries

Marshal Columbus L. Croy
(Photos courtesy of Loretta McCann and the Woodburn Historical Society)

Marshal Croy was called from his bed at home by a telephone report of three burglars in saloon of Joseph Faulkner, which was only about 500 feet from the marshal's home. Mrs. Amelia Croy said she heard the telephone ring at about 1:00 a.m. and called her husband. The caller, William L. Wearley, reported that burglars had entered the saloon, were rifling through the cash drawer, and were preparing to blow the safe. The marshal slipped on his clothes, not taking the time to tie his shoes.

As the marshal approached with revolver in hand, he rounded the corner in view of the saloon and heard a voice command, "Halt!" The newspaper account read, "The words came from an outlaw on guard at one of the windows of the saloon, but the officer, a man unknown to fear, gripped his revolver tighter, preparing to fire, and advanced upon the burglars." (Fort Wayne Journal-Gazette, June 8, 1907, p. 1)

Mr. Wearley stood back in his sitting room, looking out through the shop and waiting to go out to Marshal Croy as he passed. Wearley saw the marshal pass, then saw the reflection in the windows across the street of flashes from two shots. Mrs. Wearley watched out of a window and saw two flashes and heard two reports that seemed to come from a window at the side of the saloon – the window that one of the burglars had entered. One shot rang out, imbedding itself in a nearby building, followed by the second shot which mortally wounded Marshal Croy. Witnesses say the marshal advanced ahead a short distance, up to twenty feet, before falling. (Fort Wayne Journal-Gazette, June 8, 1907, p. 3)

Mr. Wearley called Mr. Faulkner, the saloonkeeper, and he and his wife came to the Wearley's. As they came into the Wearley's side entrance, someone said that someone was lying by the side of the pavement just west of the Shirley City Entertainer office. They all went out to find Marshal Croy's body laying there.

When assistance arrived Marshal Croy was already dead. Dr. A. P. Betts was summoned within a few moments, but found Croy dead. Mrs. Amelia Croy said that not three minutes after Marshal Croy left the house she heard *three* shots and did not see her husband again until they brought him home dead. "Oh, if I hadn't heard that 'phone he would not have been shot down like this," the widow said. (Fort Wayne Journal-Gazette, June 8, 1907, p. 3)

Coroner J.E. Stults later determined that Croy's death must have been instantaneous. The fatal bullet entered one and a half inches below and two inches to the left of the right nipple. The bullet penetrated Croy's heart from right to left and exited the left side, leaving a one-half by three-eighths inch wound. While the bullet passed completely through the body, it was not found until later. Yet, because of the wound dimensions, Coroner Stults concluded that the wound was from a large caliber firearm.

Within twenty minutes the entire population of the town was aroused following the murder, which occurred between 1:00 and 2:00 a.m. But news did not reach Fort Wayne, the county seat, until 4:00 a.m., at which time Sheriff Jesse Grice was notified by telephone. Sheriff Grice, Deputy Sheriff Jules Huguenard, and Coroner Stults boarded a Wabash railroad train at 5:00 a.m. en route to the murder scene at Woodburn.

Sheriff Jesse Grice, Allen County, Indiana
(Used by permission from the Allen County – Fort Wayne Historical Society: The History Center)

Upon their arrival the officers roped off each area where the burglars were believed to have been. Hoping to preserve any clues and scents, the cordoned areas were barred to everyone, but the area had already been well attended by the time the county officials arrived. The officers concentrated on interviewing all possible witnesses to the incident.

Coroner Stults did not think enough rain had fallen since the crime had occurred to obliterate the scent of the outlaws and that the crime scene had been effectively preserved. He hoped dogs would be useful in tracking the murderers. The sheriff and his deputy stayed on the scene all night until the arrival of bloodhounds from Dayton, Ohio, at about 10:00 p.m. At 10:40 p.m. Sheriff Grice and Deputy Huguenard initiated a posse led by the trailing dogs.

By 2:30 a.m. on June 8, 1907, the bloodhounds were on a trail from the murder scene at Faulkner's saloon in Woodburn. Tracking despite the time delay and rains that had fallen since the crimes, the dogs followed a trail out the front door of the saloon and went north on Main Street. The trail did not stop at the Wabash railroad, but continued to the Bull Rapids public road. The trail then followed the highway north for six miles and turned west toward Maysville. The dogs continued northwest one and one-half miles beyond Maysville. (Fort Wayne Journal-Gazette, June 8, 1907, p. 1)

Two Wabash railroad trains were standing by in Woodburn at the time of the crimes – one eastbound and one westbound. There was speculation that the three desperadoes took the eastbound train in order to cross the state line into Ohio. By 3:00 a.m. reports came from Antwerp, Ohio, that three men in a buggy drawn by two brown horses had stopped at the edge of the town and were involved in an argument over which road they should take. Other accounts reported that for several days before the murder a stranger dressed in a black suit and having a hair lip had been hanging around Woodburn.

The Times in Perspective

Had Marshal Columbus L. Croy not been killed the early morning of June 7, 1907, he might have read the Fort Wayne Journal-Gazette, one of the newspapers from the county seat. He may have read of the "Ugly Army Scandal at West Point."

The Highland Falls, New York, headliner read, in part, "After reading a communication from the war department, Lieutenant Colonel Charles G. Ayres tonight declared that he would support his wife in the action she has instructed her attorney to institute against Superintendent Hugh Scott, and other officers of the West Point military academy." (Fort Wayne Journal-Gazette, June 8, 1907, p. 1)

He may have read of two other crime stories. On June 7, 1907, President Theodore Roosevelt ordered an investigation of the relations between the railroads and the post office department. Thirty-two postal inspectors (postal law enforcement officers) were assigned to conduct a conspiracy investigation in not-so-far away Cincinnati, Ohio. While these "shrewdest in the service of Uncle Sam" investigated the alleged conspiracy, other postal inspectors were at trial at the state capital in Indianapolis.

Main Street, Woodburn, Indiana, 1907
(Photos courtesy of Loretta McCann and the Woodburn Historical Society)

Fred C. Boltz, of Fort Wayne, was charged and convicted of knowingly receiving and selling $1,600 worth of stolen postage stamps. Judge A.B. Anderson of the Federal District Court sentenced Boltz to three years at hard labor at Fort Leavenworth prison and fined him the, then, sizable sum of $100 for each of three counts. In addition to testimony by a private detective, Boltz stood against the testimony of a fellow criminal. The judge said, "I believe the *yeggman*, Moore, told the truth, seemingly the jurors believed him – they ought to believe him." (Remember this term "*yeggman*").

Main Street 1908
(Photos courtesy of Loretta McCann and the Woodburn Historical Society)

What do these headlines have to do with the Croy murder investigation? Not a great deal, but the heinous crime of stolen stamps and the term "yeggman" provide a bit of historic reference here. You will soon discover that the Croy murderers included the theft of stamps in the felonious spree and this became a clue later. They were also referred to by the same antiquated (to us today) term "yeggmen." I had to look this up myself, despite being a career lawman and a sometimes historian. Webster defines "*yegg*" as a slang term for a safecracker; therefore a "yeggman" is a safe burglar.

The Investigation Continues

Marshal Columbus L. Croy, age forty-five, had the reputation for not knowing fear and being a "superb specimen of physical manhood." He had been the Woodburn marshal for six years and is said to have "filled the position in a highly creditable manner." A number of petty thefts had occurred in the town at the time and he had been working to discover the identity of the thieves. It is believed that when he went to the Faulkner saloon, he expected to find the men he was looking for.

Croy came to Allen County from near Portland, Indiana, and had been the manager of the L. M. Rogers farm near New Haven for a number of years. He later moved to Gar Creek and then to Woodburn. He was a member of the Fort Wayne aerie Number 248, Fraternal Order of Eagles and was survived by his wife, two daughters, and a sister, Mrs. Lanning, of the Bloomingdale section of Fort Wayne.

It is believed that the burglars intended to blow the safe at Faulkner's saloon, as well as the safe at the town bank. A sledgehammer and some chisels were among the evidence found near the saloon. They had been stolen nearby from the William F. Keller machine shop. As mentioned previously, the theft of postage stamps would become an issue in this case. In addition to the recovered tools, Mr. Benjamin Thomas found some postage stamps at the rear of his saloon which he believed had been stolen and dropped after the murderers burglarized his saloon. It was deduced from this that burglar-murderers were members of a gang of post office robbers which had been operating in the area for some time. (Fort Wayne Journal-Gazette, June 8, 1907, p. 3)

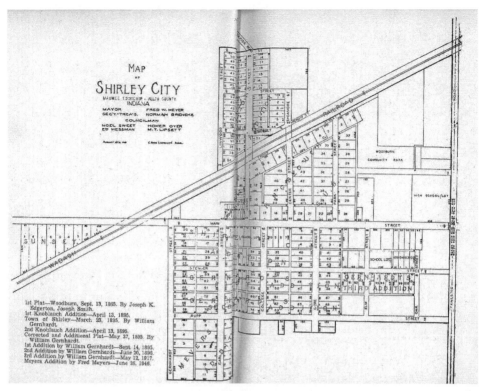

Woodburn (Shirley City) mid-1900s

(Photos courtesy of Loretta McCann and the Woodburn Historical Society)

Coroner Stults collected no evidence at the scene, but held a Coroner's inquest at his office at the county seat in Fort Wayne. He summoned all witnesses in the case to give testimony. Meanwhile the county officers determined that the killers had committed the burglary and taken the officer's life for naught. The Fort Wayne Journal-Gazette reported, "The cash drawer at the Faulkner saloon contained only a few cents and the safe had nothing in whatever save a few papers that would have been absolutely worthless to the yeggmen." (Fort Wayne Journal-Gazette, June 8, 1907, p. 3) Remember the term "yeggmen?" A "*yegg*" is defined as a slang term for a safecracker; therefore a "yeggman" is a safe burglar.

Collecting the Usual Suspects

Services for the slain peace officer were scheduled for 9:00 a.m. on June 8, 1907, at his residence in Woodburn. His remains were then transferred by a westbound Wabash train at 10:10 a.m. to the city of New Haven for interment at the Odd Fellows cemetery. The funeral expenses were paid for by the Fraternal Order of Eagles lodge. The Saturday morning edition of the Fort Wayne Journal-Gazette on June 8, 1907, had a brief notice regarding Marshal Croy's funeral and memorial:

ATTENTION, EAGLES!

All Eagles are requested to be at the Wabash depot at 7:15 o'clock Sunday morning to attend the funeral of Brother Columbus Croy, at Woodburn, Indiana

J.W. EGGEMAN,
President
CHARLES RULO,
Secretary

John W. Eggeman, attorney and president of the Eagles lodge, Mr. John Pfeiffer, lodge chaplain, and the Rev. Johnson of Woodburn conducted the services. Services were attended by most of the town of Woodburn, as well as Sheriff Grice, Deputy Sheriff Martin Detzer, and (Fort Wayne) Police Captain A.M. Reichelderfer.

The next day reports said that due to the hour, everyone was in bed in Maysville and no one there noted or observed the fugitives. While the initial investigation suggested, based upon witness statements, that there were three perpetrators, it was now believed that there were only two. The tracks indicated two sets of prints that were clearly discernible in the mud. At several points the trail departed from the road and into muddy fields, which led the posse to believe they were made by fugitives, with no legitimate purpose, who left the roadways to avoid meeting passersby.

Dr. Robert J. Girod, Sr.

Woodburn 1908
(Photos courtesy of Loretta McCann and the Woodburn Historical Society)

The trail led from Faulkner's saloon over mired roads and through muddy fields and barns. The trail led through the barn of Mr. Fred Fuelling four and a half miles north of Woodburn then back to the road. It was concluded that the perpetrators had walked northward eleven miles to the Wabash depot at Grabill where they may have taken a Wabash train to Chicago, Detroit, or Toledo. The track ended at the Grabill depot, the dog indicating that the trail concluded there. The pursuit, headed by Sheriff Jesse Grice, along with Deputy Jules Huguenard, Coroner J.E. Stults and sixty members of a posse, ended there at 3:00 a.m. Sheriff Grice was convinced that that dog had tracked successfully and that the perpetrators had boarded a train there at Grabill. (The services of the bloodhound cost $65 and were paid for with money raised for that purpose).

Later that day a Detective Lieburger from adjoining Whitley County was in Woodburn. While returning through New Haven he "picked up a strange negro" and took him to the county seat in Fort Wayne. Since this "suspect" did not even match the description of who the sheriff was looking for, "The negro was turned loose, however, when he reached Fort Wayne, as no suspicion was directed against him." Sheriff Grice continued to look for the "hair-lipped man who was seen hanging about Woodburn for several days prior to the shooting and disappeared on the night of the tragedy." (The Fort Wayne Journal-Gazette on June 8, 1907, p. 14)

Meanwhile, a man was arrested in Toledo, Ohio, who had a revolver from which two shots had been fired. He was a Hungarian and Toledo police suspected him as one of Croy's slayers, though they had little more than the revolver to go on.

The Coroner's Inquest and Physical Evidence

Coroner J.E. Stults began taking testimony on June 8, 1907, at his office in the Allen County Court House in Fort Wayne. He examined Mr. and Mrs. William Wearley, who reported the crime from the home at the butcher shop, and Mrs. Wearley's sister, Miss Jennie Heltzel. In addition to these three "eye-witnesses," the coroner interviewed Mr. Joseph Faulkner, owner of the burglarized saloon. (The newspaper used the term "which the burglars were trying to rob," but an unoccupied building cannot be robbed; it can only be burgled). Dr. A.P. Betts, the physician who pronounced Croy dead at the scene, was the next to be examined. He was followed by Mr. Henry Scheppelmann, a retired farmer and president of the Woodburn Tile and Brick Company and Mr. A.J. Bennett, a blacksmith in Woodburn, who were among the first on the scene. (The Fort Wayne Journal-Gazette on June 8, 1907, p. 1)

Scheppelmann was a prominent resident of Woodburn and was one of those citizens heading the fund-raising for the costs of the bloodhound and for funds for Croy's widow and children. Croy did not have life insurance and left his family almost no money. Bennett was apparently something of an assistant to Marshal Croy. Mr. Elmer Voirol, a stenographer for Allen County Prosecuting Attorney Dan B. Ninde, recorded the notes of testimony.

The bullet which passed through Marshal Croy, killing him, was recovered and found to be a .44-calibre, confirming the coroner's theory that it was a large caliber round. After the fatal bullet entered one and a half inches below and two inches to the left of the marshal's right nipple, the bullet penetrated Croy's heart from right to left and exited the left side. Leaving a one-half by three-eighths inch wound, the bullet passed through and exited the marshal (Fort Wayne Journal-Gazette, June 8, 1907, p. 3) and imbedded in a small icehouse across the street, where it was later dug out and recovered. (The Fort Wayne Journal-Gazette on June 8, 1907, p. 14)

The fatal shot was the second shot fired by the burglar-murderer. The first shot fired hit the corner of the Wearley meat market and residence, where it was deflected by a brick in the foundation and imbedded in a plank in the house. It was also recovered later in the investigation.

Examination of Marshal Croy's revolver indicated that he too had fired one shot, but the bullet was not located. Croy carried a .38-caliber pistol. His sometimes assistant and town blacksmith A.J. Bennett told the coroner that Croy's revolver "worked very hard," but examination by the coroner indicated that it was working properly. (The Fort Wayne Journal-Gazette on June 8, 1907, p. 14)

Angle of the Fatal Shot

In her testimony at the Coroner's inquest, Mrs. Wearley stated that she believed the man who killed Croy fired from a side window of the Faulkner saloon. A high board fence stood in front of the window, making it unlikely that the shot could have been fired from that position. The Wearley's shop and residence was just south of the Faulkner saloon. Adjoining their building to the south was the Shirley Entertainer office. Between their house and the saloon was an open lot with a board fence obstructing the view for part of the distance. When the marshal arrived, he turned the corner around the Entertainer office and north of Union Street, on which the Faulkner saloon and Wearley meat market were located.

When Marshal Croy reached the corner of the meat market he was ordered to halt by one of the burglars. Mrs. Wearley testified that she saw a man inside the saloon come to the side window. She then saw a flash and heard a report and thought it came from the man at the window. The county authorities believed she must have been mistaken in her belief. They believed that a second man stood watch at the street end of the high board fence and that he fired at Croy. Because he would have stood only a short distance from the window, Mrs. Wearley could have easily mistaken the point from which the shots came.

Dr. Robert J. Girod, Sr.

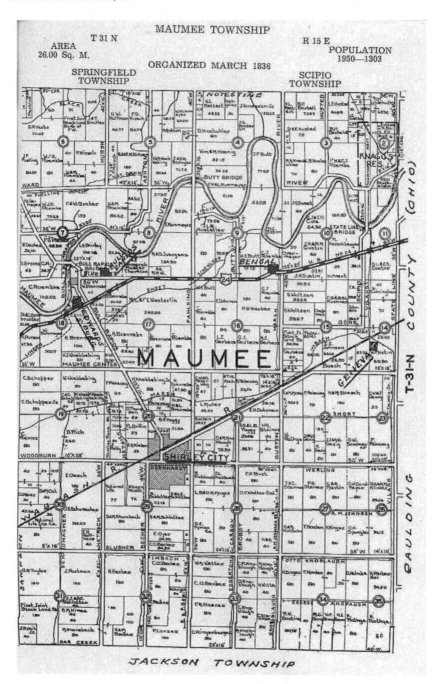

Maumee Township, Allen County, Indiana
(Photos courtesy of Loretta McCann and the Woodburn Historical Society)

Infamous Murders and Mysteries

Woodburn 1910
(Photos courtesy of Loretta McCann and the Woodburn Historical Society)

Had the shots came from the window, the county officials theorized, the bullets would have passed through the fence. If they were fired from the end of the fence, as they theorized, a shot fired toward the corner of the meat market could have struck the icehouse across the street. Croy was at the corner of the meat market when he was shot and it is thought that he leaned around the building to fire when the fatal shot hit him. Investigators speculated that had he been left-handed he may have fired without exposing as much of his body and not been hit by his assailant's round.

Dr. Robert J. Girod, Sr.

Hair-Lipped Man in Custody

The morning headline read:

SUSPECT IS ARRESTED

Hair-Lipped Man in Custody; Tells Good Story

Denies Any Knowledge of Woodburn Murder – Funeral of Marshal Croy Largely Attended – No Further Trace of Murderers

(The Fort Wayne Journal-Gazette on June 10, 1907, p. 1)

The "hair-lipped man" seen in Woodburn before the murder was located in Fort Wayne on June 9, 1907. Robert Krueger, age twenty-five, of 3401 South Barr Street, was locked up at the county jail "for investigation." Krueger was taken into custody at about 1:00 p.m. by Deputy Sheriffs Jules Huguenard and James Hattery and taken to (Fort Wayne) police headquarters to be interviewed. He was then transferred to the hospital wing of the county jail to separate him from the other prisoners.

Sheriff H. A. Betts of Paulding County, Ohio, tipped Allen County, Indiana, authorities about Krueger. Sheriff Betts knew Kreuger had resided in Cecil, Ohio, and that he had been through Woodburn within the past few days. Certain that Krueger was the wanted man, Sheriff Betts came to Fort Wayne and notified the Sheriff's office that the man was in the city.

When Deputies Huguenard and Hattery went to Kreuger's father's house at 3401 South Barr Street they found Kreuger sitting on the porch. Though he protested his innocence, he went with the officers without trouble. He was unmarried and the second eldest of five children of John Kreuger, a house mover for Contractor William Witte. The family had lived in Clay Center, Ohio, then in Cecil, Ohio, for about ten years. They had moved to Fort Wayne just two months before Robert's detention.

Kreuger said that on the Tuesday prior to the murder he left Fort Wayne at about 1:00 p.m. to return to Cecil, Ohio, to retrieve his clothes. He said he walked to New Haven, took shelter at a depot for about fifteen minutes during a rainstorm, and then walked to Woodburn. Once in Woodburn, Kreuger said he went to Wearley's meat market and bought some bologna for lunch. He then started looking for Marshal Croy to help him find a place to sleep for the night. He said he had only one dollar at the time.

Unable to locate the marshal, Kreuger said he crawled into a boxcar and stayed the night. At about 5:00 a.m. (Wednesday morning) he walked to Antwerp, Ohio, and said he paid his fare for a train to Cecil, Ohio. Once there he said he had lunch and went to Samuel Lehman's for his clothes. (It is interesting to note that he could pay a train fare and buy lunch with only one dollar). He said he stayed the night in Cecil with a friend and left at about 9:00 a.m. Thursday morning and walked back to Antwerp. Arriving there at about 12:00 noon, he again purchased a lunch, and then walked to Woodburn, arriving between 4:00 and 5:00 p.m.

Kreuger said he then waited for the westbound Wabash local freight, which arrived at about 7:00 p.m. He said he boarded the train and paid his fare by helping the train crew load and unload freight at the stations. He said he arrived in Fort Wayne at between 9:00 and 10:00 p.m.

Officers worked to check Kreuger's alibi. It was determined that he did talk with Marshal Croy on Thursday about being unable to find him on Tuesday. Kreuger also admitted to officers that he had been arrested once in Toledo for drunkenness. Three days later, on Wednesday, June 12, 1907, Robert Krueger, having proven his alibi, was released from jail.

The Nosy Critic

Krueger, having proven his alibi (after three days in custody) was released. The reward offered by the citizens of Woodburn was increased on June 12 to $1,200, in addition to the $250 reward offered by the Allen County Commissioners. Meanwhile, new suspects began to emerge.

A scene looking west on Main Street showing the Meyer Block. The businesses which are visible are l. to r. The Minder Harness Shop, The Woodburn Banking Company, The J. A. Eby Store, The Neuenschwander Hardware Company, A Furniture Store (which also advertised musical instruments), The Old Band Stand, and the Schoolhouse.

Main Street and the John A. Eby Store
(Photos courtesy of Loretta McCann and the Woodburn Historical Society)

Fort Wayne Police received a report from an east side resident who lived on Walton Avenue near the Wabash railroad tracks that a hobo had been sleeping in a boxcar near his home all day the Sunday following the murder. Though dozens of hobos were known to sleep in the boxcars, the suspicious man ran when the resident approached him to talk. Railroad detectives later tried to locate and capture the tramp, but were not successful.

A new suspect was emerging and arousing the suspicions of residents. George Moore, of Fort Wayne, was reportedly "running down to Woodburn at frequent intervals since the murder of Croy, and, it is alleged, talking too much and criticizing too freely citizens of the little town..." (The Fort Wayne Journal-Gazette on June 13, 1907, p. 1).

While Robert Krueger was being released from the Allen County Jail in Fort Wayne, citizens read in the news of another macabre, though unrelated, finding. The headline next to the Croy murder story read:

"TWO SKELETONS TURNED TO DUST"

The story began, "A grewsome sight was that which met the eyes of the excavators making the first floor improvements in the west room of the Fort Wayne Printing company on East Main street last week when at a depth of about four feet their shovels sank suddenly through the board covers of two rude caskets, long since decayed by the dampness under the building, and each containing a human skeleton." (Spelling errors not edited). (The Fort Wayne Journal-Gazette on June 12, 1907, p. 6)

The excavators had discovered the remains from a century-old burial ground from the old military fort. The story also reports that Indian tribes had also buried their dead north of the city (at the time) near the confluence of the Saint Joseph's and Saint Mary's rivers (which is now within the city limits). (The Fort Wayne Journal-Gazette on June 12, 1907, p. 6)

The next day, June 13, 1907, the reward was again increased to $1,400 and the county commissioners increased their offer to $500. Meanwhile, the citizens of Woodburn had taken George Moore "in charge and notified Sheriff Grice." The headline read:

Man Who Talked to Much At Woodburn Is Arrested And Will Be Investigated

(The Fort Wayne Journal-Gazette on June 13, 1907, p. 1)

The sheriff telephoned back (to Woodburn) that "if there was anything suspicious about the actions of Moore to arrest him and hold him for investigation." Moore, who lived at 914 Cottage Avenue in Fort Wayne, was married with a family and was recently unemployed from the electric works. (The Fort Wayne Journal-Gazette on June 13, 1907, p. 1)

Moore showed up in Woodburn when the bloodhounds from Dayton, Ohio, arrived to track the trail of the murderers. The newspaper reported that, "he criticised a number of things which were done and the citizens of the town got tired of it." (Spelling errors not edited). While the report said that there was no suspicion of connection between Moore and the murder, "it is desired to know why he has taken such an interest in the case." (The Fort Wayne Journal-Gazette on June 13, 1907, p. 1)

Headlines the following day (June 14) reported that eight leading men of the community of Woodburn had been appointed to help find Croy's slayers. The meeting was attended by "every male inhabitant of Woodburn and many of the leading farmers of the surrounding country" at the town hall to establish a committee of public safety. (The Fort Wayne Journal-Gazette on June 14, 1907, p. 1)

Unrelated crime headlines that day included a story about a state constitutional challenge to the new statute licensing the sale of intoxicating liquors and a story of a deputy game warden who shot up the town of Mexico, Indiana. Meanwhile, the Woodburn safety committee organized to take charge of the reward fund and assist in securing information leading to the apprehension of the killers. The reward, increasing daily, now was raised again to $1,655 "in negotiable paper" deposited in the Woodburn bank and the $500 offered by the county. They also established a fund to hire bloodhounds to track criminals in the event of future "predications of any kind, large or petty." (The Fort Wayne Journal-Gazette on June 14, 1907, p. 1)

The town board also met to take applications for a new town marshal. The board took no action on this, just one week after the murder, as there was not a single applicant.

Meanwhile, George Moore had been taken into custody the night before, on June 13. Town Marshal Barney Schoenfeldt arrested him in New Haven when he was thought to have been under the influence of liquor and "his talk directed the suspicion of the officer to him." He was released the next day, June 14, when it was determined that he too had no knowledge of the murder. Detectives from a number of surrounding cities were keeping their eyes out for clues to assist in the murder investigation.

The Manhunt Continues

On June 17 Coroner Stults returned a finding that Croy came to his death as a result of the gunshot wound to his chest while in the performance of his official duty in protecting property and preventing crime. The shot, the coroner ruled, was fired by an unknown person with murderous intent.

On June 18 the total reward had reached $2,175 and the protective board (committee of public safety) had printed thousands of posters advertising the reward. The citizen felt that it was in their interest to deter thieves and murderers by apprehending the killers of their marshal. The newspapers account read, "Located far from any large town, Woodburn has no protection, whatever, save in one lone marshal, who stands no show whatever in a battle with outlaws such as those whom the brave Croy went after on the occasion in which he met his death."

Bull Rapids Road (Union Street) 1907
(Photos courtesy of Loretta McCann and the Woodburn Historical Society)

The posters from the committee read:

> **Arrest the murderer. $2, 175 reward for the murderers of Columbus L. Croy.** $2,175 reward will be paid for the arrest and conviction of the slayer or slayers of Columbus L. Croy, late marshal of the town of Shirley City (Woodburn), Ind. Of the above amount the commissioners of Allen County, Ind., will pay the sum of $500. The balance, $1,675, has been raised by subscription and is secured by negotiable paper in the hands of the Woodburn Banking Co., of Woodburn, Ind. **"CITIZENS COMMITTEE, Woodburn, Ind."**

(The Fort Wayne Journal-Gazette on June 18, 1907, p. 6)

Bull Rapids Road (Union Street)
(Photos courtesy of Loretta McCann and the Woodburn Historical Society)

On June 19 Herman Miller, a blacksmith and former deputy sheriff and town marshal in Woodburn, found forty cigars hidden in his firebox. Another man, named Saylors, found a fake mustache in an alley behind Miller's shop, not far from Faulkner's saloon. Sheriff Grice and Deputy Hughes (first name not recorded) went to Woodburn to collect the items, but did not attach any significance to them as evidence. They believed the cigars were the fruits of a crime pulled off by local crooks and the mustache another local crook, as the murderers of Croy did not have time to secret the items before their flight. There was some speculation that the "clues" had been dropped to throw off the investigators. Croy was investigating a number of petty thefts before his murder and some citizens speculated that his killers were neither hoboes nor professional burglars, but local crooks.

Local crime continued on a smaller scale. Fort Wayne Police Detective George Soliday arrested fourteen-year-old Johnnie Kessinger, of 120 West Jefferson Street in Fort Wayne after Kessinger confessed to a burglary of the A. Furthmiller grocery at Lewis and Harmer streets. Patrolman Bevelheimer (first name not recorded) arrested his accomplice, James McDeppert of Fletcher Avenue. McDeppert used a penknife to gain entry and the juveniles stole $3.03, some firecrackers and chewing gum.

Allen County Sheriff's Deputy Ritcha (first name not recorded) was also busy making an arrest of Johnnie Coughlin, AKA "Johnnie Appleseed" (after the local folklore hero), for drunkenness.

Sheriff Grice continued his investigation and his efforts to add a pair of bloodhounds to his office after the successful but delayed track of the Croy murderers by dogs from Dayton, Ohio.

One of the blacksmith shops in Woodburn
(Unknown if this is Herman Miller's or A.J. Bennett's shop)
(Photos courtesy of Loretta McCann and the Woodburn Historical Society)

The Grand Jury Meets

The Allen County Prosecutor, Dan B. Ninde, and his assistant and brother, Harry W. Ninde left the state on July 31, 1907, to escape the controversy raging between saloon keepers and the temperance movement of the Good Citizens' League. The work of the prosecutor's office was in the hands of local attorney Harry Hogan and the prosecutor's stenographer, Elmer Voirol, who had been appointed as deputy prosecuting attorneys while the bother took a hideout at a Leland, Michigan, resort.

On September 26, 1907, less than two months later, the Grand Jury held a late night session lasting until 10:30 p.m. and resuming the following morning raising hopes that an indictment was imminent. (The Fort Wayne Journal-Gazette on September 26, 1907, p. 9) When this did not materialize, the citizens of Woodburn felt the prosecutor had not handled the case properly. (The Fort Wayne Journal-Gazette on November 5, 1907, p. 7)

After the Grand Jury met, Marshal Croy's widow and two children left to live at a home provided by Mrs. Croy's brother in Lusk, Wyoming. Because the family was destitute following the marshal's death, the citizens of the town collected a fund to get them to their new home. Saloonkeeper Joseph Faulkner and John Conners organized the subscription.

The citizens of Woodburn believed the previous inquiry was not a thorough examination of the facts known and that the facts of the investigation had been treated in a cavalier manner by the former prosecutor. Dissatisfied with the grand jury's results, a new prosecutor took office and a new grand jury was seated. They looked to Prosecutor Albert E. Thomas to remedy the shortcomings of Prosecutor Ninde's September grand jury.

CHAPTER THIRTEEN

MARSHAL CROY MURDER: THE PROSECUTION AND TRIAL

I have no desire to make mysteries, but it is impossible at the moment of action to enter into long and complex explanations.

~ Sherlock Holmes ~

Sir Arthur Conan Doyle

Former Marshal Arraigned: Four Suspects Brought to Trial

With a new prosecutor in office and the investigation progressing, new leads were developed. Four suspects were subsequently arrested. They were Fred LaDuke, who would become the state's key witness, John Baker, and the alleged shooter, John Stout. The fourth suspect was former deputy sheriff and town marshal Herman Miller, the blacksmith who reported finding the stolen cigars in his firebox. All four suspects were from Woodburn and knew Marshal Croy.

FORT WAYNE NEWS

SATURDAY EVENING, APRIL 11, 1908   TWELVE PA

THE WOODBURN MURDER SUSPECTS WILL NOT BE TRIED AT PRESENT TERM

| FRED A. LA DUKE. | JOHN STOUT. | JOHN BAKER. | HERMAN MILLER. |

Late this afternoon the News secured positive information to the effect that Fred A. LaDuke, Herman Miller, John Stout and John Baker, charged with the murder of Columbus Croy last year in Woodburn, will not be tried at the present term of the circuit court.

(Photos courtesy of Loretta McCann and the Woodburn Historical Society)

 The Fort Wayne Daily News reported on Saturday, April 18, 1908, that John Baker was one of four men arrested in the murder. He had retained the services of Attorneys W. and E. Leonard but was waiting for money from his relatives to pay them to go ahead with his defense. He asserted that he could establish an alibi that would clear him. The case was to be heard by Judge Edward O'Rourke in circuit court, where Baker would have to enter as a poor person in order for the county to appropriate funds for his defense. The state had already appropriated $1,000 for James M. Robinson to assist Prosecutor Thomas in the prosecution of the murder cases. (Fort Wayne Daily News, April 18, 1908, p. 10)

Dr. Robert J. Girod, Sr.

The only available photo of Herman Miller
(Photos courtesy of Loretta McCann and the Woodburn Historical Society)

Infamous Murders and Mysteries

ALBERT E. THOMAS
State's Attorney Who Conducted the Case Against Herman Miller.

Prosecutor Albert E. Thomas
(Photos courtesy of Loretta McCann and the Woodburn Historical Society)

John Stout, the alleged shooter, was also without funds and Attorney P. B. Colerick was appointed to defend him. The former marshal, Herman Miller, had retained the services of the Aiken & Underwood law firm. (Fort Wayne Daily News, April 18, 1908, p. 10) Judge R. K. Erwin of Erwin & Underwood (the firms name was reported differently in the same newspaper two days later) denounced the confession of co-defendant Fred LaDuke and said he would demand that the state go to trial in the case of *State vs. Miller* immediately upon his return from Missouri later in the week on April 20, 1908. (Fort Wayne Daily News, April 20, 1908, p. 2)

On April 22, 1908, Prosecutor Albert E. Thomas announced that he, assisted by James M. Robinson, was ready to go to trial. Herman Miller would be the first arraigned and to go to trial. (The Fort Wayne Journal-Gazette on April 23, 1908, p. 1) At 11:30 a.m. on April 23, 1908, Judge O'Rourke arranged to hear the case of *State vs. Miller*. Miller was brought from the county jail by Sheriff Grice and his deputies at 1:30 p.m. on April 23 and arraigned in circuit court on the grand jury indictment for the murder of Woodburn Marshal Columbus Croy. Trial was set for May 28, 1908. The firm of Erwin & Underwood appeared for Miller's defense. (Fort Wayne Daily News, April 23, 1908, p. 2)

Miller did not seem to mind or be bothered in the least as he firmly walked into the courtroom to enter his plea of "not guilty" to the capital charge. His attorney, Judge Erwin, asked for a speedy trial for his client. All four suspects were to be tried separately. Both Miller and Baker were depending upon their alibis as their defense.

The Marshals Widow Testifies About Disputes

Amelia Croy, the widow of Marshal Croy, was brought back from Wyoming to testify. Clad in black, the forty-year-old widow told of her marriage to the marshal in 1888 and their two children, who were now aged fifteen and ten. The defense sought to deter her incrimination of Herman Miller by showing a letter she had written to Miller's defense attorney, Judge Erwin, in which she expressed the opinion that Teddy Moulter, the baker, was her husband's killer. On cross-examination the state objected to the letter being admitted as evidence, but Judge O'Rourke held his ruling until later in the trial. (Fort Wayne Journal-Gazette, June 10, 1908, p. 1)

Infamous Murders and Mysteries

JAMES M. ROBINSON
Assistant to Prosecuting Attorney Thomas in the Woodburn Murder Case.

Special Assistant Prosecuting Attorney James M. Robinson
(Photos courtesy of Loretta McCann and the Woodburn Historical Society)

Mrs. Croy laid the foundation for part of the murder motive. She said that after they moved to Woodburn her husband worked at clearing land, then as a watchman and lamp tender. She recounted an occasion when her husband and, then town marshal, Herman Miller had arrested some turkey thieves. Then one morning about four years ago (from that date in 1908) she heard loud talking in the garden and went out to find her husband standing near the barn with Herman Miller, who had a revolver in his hand. She said she heard Miller say, "I'll shoot you" and call her husband a liar. Mr. Croy responded, "Shoot and be damned." With the children near her Mrs. Croy asked what the matter was, but Miller ignored her and took Mr. Croy by the arm and the two men went uptown. (Fort Wayne Journal-Gazette, June 10, 1908, p. 3)

Later, when her husband was the town marshal, she heard about the burglary at the Eby barbershop. For a number of nights after that Marshal Croy stayed out until after midnight and began locking the doors at night and keeping his revolver in bed, neither of which he had done before. She said that the marshal feared that someone would attempt to kill him.

Then, on the night of June 6, 1907, Marshal Croy came home earlier than usual at about 11:00 p.m. and retired for the night, saying that he intended to go fishing with Mr. Faulkner the next morning. At about 1:15 a.m. the phone rang. She heard her husband tell the caller, "I'll be over." Mrs. Croy helped him get his clothes and their nine-year-old daughter awakened. The phone rang again, but the Marshal left without lacing his shoes.

A few minutes after the marshal left Mrs. Croy heard two shots. She went to the window and listened. The Croy home was almost directly across from the Miller house. She and their little girl sat at the south window and saw no one pass on the street. The Miller back yard was in the deep shadow cast by the Faulkner saloon building. She went to the north window for a moment to look out. About forty-five minutes later Mrs. Croy was told of her husband's death by Dr. Betts and his body was brought to the home a few minutes later. Herman Miller never came to view the marshal's remains. (Fort Wayne Journal-Gazette, June 10, 1908, p. 3)

On cross-examination the defense asked Mrs. Croy if her husband was afraid that Ted Moulter would try to kill him and that was the reason he locked his doors and slept with his gun. "Did you not send me a letter from Lusk, Wyoming, saying you thought it was Moulter who killed your husband," asked Judge Erwin. "You must not have read the letter right," Mrs. Croy replied. Judge Erwin submitted a letter, which Mrs. Croy identified as her handwriting and the state objected to its admission. The objection was sustained.

When asked further about the quarrel between Croy and Miller, the witness, Mrs. Croy, said that it was about the rumor Mr. Croy had told Mr. Wearley that Miller had stolen gasoline from the town pumps (five years earlier). It was then brought out that Mrs. Miller was at the Croy home between 7:00 and 8:00 a.m. the morning after the murder. Mrs. Moulter also came.

Erwin: "Did you let her see your husband?"

Mrs. Croy: "No, sir."

Erwin: "Why not?"

Mrs. Croy: "The doctor had forbidden it."

Erwin: "Is that the reason you gave in your letter to me why you wouldn't let Mrs. Moulter see the body?"

Objection by the prosecution was made and sustained. Judge Erwin contended that because the state brought Mrs. Croy as a witness to testify that Miller did not come to see the body, it was fair and proper for the defense to show that Moulter also did not come to view the body. Judge O'Rourke held that this was proper at cross-examination.

Erwin: "Didn't you write to me that Moulter was the only one that didn't come to see your husband?"

Mrs. Croy: "I don't remember writing that."

Erwin handed Mrs. Croy the letter that she had identified as her handwriting and she admitted that she had written that Moulter did not come to view her husband as others did. Erwin handed the letter to Prosecutor Robinson for examination when it was introduced for cross-examination. At redirect examination Robinson asked Mrs. Croy, "Did your husband associate with Mr. Miller during the last three or four months of his life?"

Mrs. Croy: "No, sir."

Robinson: "Why not?"

Mrs. Croy: "I know what my husband told . . ."

Judge Erwin objected.

Robinson: "Then I object to all the evidence of the cross-examination."

Erwin: "I withdraw the objection."

The remaining testimony by Mrs. Croy involved ancillary issues about whether Mr. Croy had asked Mr. Miller to kill a cat for him that was killing Mrs. Croy's chickens, whether Mr. Croy had asked Mr. Miller to fix an ax and a hand plow for him, and whether she recalled Croy and Miller having a conversation in the Croy back yard about the Eby barbershop burglary. Mrs. Croy's testimony ended by confirming that Ted Moulter had been to the Croy house once to borrow something and that neither Fred LaDuke, John Baker, nor John Stout had ever been to their house.

Allen County Court House, circa 1907
(Used by permission of the Allen County – Fort Wayne Historical Society: The History Center)

Co-Defendant Fred A. J. LaDuke Takes the Stand

On June 10, 1908, Fred A. J. LaDuke took the witness stand against his co-defendant, Herman Miller. LaDuke, described as a "swarthy, low set man," was born in Carp Lake, Michigan, and had also lived in Cadillac and Traverse City, Michigan. His mother died when he was about ten years old and his father died about four or five years later. LaDuke lived with his brother, Henry, in Traverse City and, later, Empire, Michigan, before moving to Leo, Indiana, in Allen county.

Once in Leo, he met Ted Moulter, the baker, through relatives. LaDuke held various jobs, including helping Moulter at the bakeshop occasionally. That is where LaDuke first met Herman Miller, when the latter came to the bakeshop to buy some bread. They often met on the street and began to frequent Ben Thomas' saloon and drank together. LaDuke also became acquainted with Marshal Croy.

LaDuke said that Miller had been the one to break into the Eby barbershop before the Croy murder occurred. He said that Miller had the cigars in his possession the whole time, which he later reported to Sheriff Grice as having found in his fire box at his blacksmith shop. (Fort Wayne Journal Gazette, June 10, 1908, p. 1)

LaDuke seemed to have his story committed to memory. More than once, when the prosecution asked questions during examination, he responded, "I haven't come to that yet." At another point he repeated a portion of his story as if to regain the sequence of events. (Fort Wayne Journal Gazette, June 10, 1908, p. 1)

Robinson: "Do you know anything about the robbery of Eby's barber shop?" (referring to the burglary in which the cigars were taken that were recovered at Miller's blacksmith shop).

LaDuke: "Yes, sir."

Robinson: "Who did it?"

LaDuke: "Herman Miller."

Robinson: "Who was with him?"

LaDuke: "I and John Stout."

Robinson: "Who is Herman Miller; this man at the table?"

LaDuke: "Yes, sir."

For the first time since the trial started Herman Miller seemed perturbed and nervous. He lost his confident air as he wiped perspiration from his head with his handkerchief. LaDuke said that he and Stout met Miller on a street corner after coming from the Redderson saloon (some accounts refer to the "Retison saloon") and Miller brought up the idea of breaking into the barbershop for the purpose getting some cigars.

LaDuke continued his testimony:

> Miller said, "Let's get some cigars." "Where?" I said. Miller said, "In the barber shop." I said, "Not tonight." Stout also said, "Not tonight. I guess there is someone watching." "Tomorrow night we'll go," I said. The next night we again met and Miller said, "Are you going to do what we said?" Stout was ready and I said I didn't care about going in. I stood on the left side of the door of the barbershop and Stout on the right side. Miller pushed the door in very easy. In a couple of minutes he came out with six or eight boxes of cigars. One box was open and he gave us some of them and went away saying not to tell anyone. Before he went to the barbershop Miller said Croy wouldn't know anything about it if me and John wouldn't tell.
>
> (Fort Wayne Journal Gazette, June 10, 1908, p. 3)

LaDuke said that he was at Miller's blacksmith shop when the cigars were in the stove and they joked about how funny it was that someone would put cigars in the stove. LaDuke said that he, Baker, and Stout committed three other robberies (again meaning burglaries, not holdups), but that Miller was not with them on the other three jobs.

The night before Croy was shot LaDuke was tending bar for Ben Thomas, having left Moulter's place. On June 6 Croy came into the saloon at about 9:00 p.m. Stout and Baker were there but left for about forty-five minutes after Croy left. Baker brought in a chicken and he and Stout dressed it outside behind the saloon. LaDuke cooked it, put out the lights in the front and the three men ate it in the poolroom, along with a deaf mute named Billy Kerns. They finished at about 11:30 p.m. and Kerns left. Baker was the next to leave. LaDuke put out the lights and locked the door. He and Stout stayed and drank until about 12:00 or 12:30 a.m.

LaDuke and Stout went out the front door and LaDuke locked up, intending to go home to bed. Stout said, "Let's go down by Moulter's." They stood at the corner a few moments and were rejoined by John Baker. They walked up to Dr. Bett's corner and talked for about ten minutes, then headed toward Faulkner's. They went north toward Miller's home and stood at the fence corner for a few moments, then Baker said, "Let's go get a drink." LaDuke asked, "Where?" Baker replied, "At Joe's."

Prosecutor Robinson asked, "Did you see Herman Miller?" "Yes, he climbed over the fence," LaDuke answered. The questions continued:

Robinson: "Did you walk up together, or how?"

LaDuke: "We went single file. Baker went first, Stout next, then Miller, and I was last."

Robinson: "What happened then?"

LaDuke continued his testimony:

> Baker said, "Come on, let's get a drink." Stout said, "Yes, come on; we're ready." Miller was in his yard and climbed over the fence. He wore a cap and a coat. I couldn't see if his coat was light or dark. It was dark back there. We all went up the alley and through a back gate into the Faulkner yard, past the icehouse. Baker stooped down and picked up something. He went to the back door and knocked, and then listened. Then he said, "By God, I can't get in here; let's go around to the window."
>
> (Fort Wayne Journal Gazette, June 10, 1908, p. 3)

Baker pried at the back door with some instrument, LaDuke recounted. He was shown a rasp and said it looked like the instrument Baker used. Then Baker went around to the window that faced Wearley's building and the other men followed him. Baker and Miller were whispering and LaDuke heard glass breaking just as Baker struck with his left hand. (The rasp and Baker's left-handedness would become issues that would be raised later). There was a light in the street out front. Baker pried the window up and told LaDuke and Miller to watch the back yard and for Stout to watch the front.

LaDuke continued his testimony, recounting the actual murder:

> Then we went to watching and Baker went in. Next thing I saw was a light over the meat market. Stout went close to the sidewalk and then came back again. Next thing I heard a noise coming down the alley along the printing office. The noise was somebody walking in the alley. I didn't say anything and didn't hear Miller say anything. Next thing I heard John Stout say, "Stand back there, I say!" and fired. (Fort Wayne Journal Gazette, June 10, 1908, p. 3)

The prosecutor asked how he knew Stout fired and LaDuke said, "I seen him. I seen him hold out his hand and I seen the flash." He said Miller was about ten feet from Stout when Stout fired and Stout moved after firing the first shot and was near the end of the fence when he fired a second time. LaDuke said he did not see who Stout was firing at and did not wait to see any more, but "skipped for home" through the alley gate.

The following day LaDuke was again called to the stand. He said that after the shot was fired Miller ran to the window and called to John Baker, "Hustle out of there." He remembered Baker was wearing a black slouch hat. LaDuke did not wait to find out if anyone had been shot and did not know until the next morning when Reddison, the saloonkeeper, told him. He said that after he left Faulkner's saloon he went back to his room and was in bed within ten minutes. He said that it took him more than an hour to get to sleep and he did not see his roommate, Stout, until he awoke the next morning and found Stout in bed with him.

LaDuke stayed in Woodburn for three more weeks, and then went to Paulding, Ohio, and for awhile before going for one night to Toledo. From there he went to his former home of Cadillac, Michigan. Prosecutor Thomas and Sheriff Grice met with LaDuke in Kalamazoo, Michigan, along with Dr. Donald C. Gorrell, the dentist-detective of Payne, Ohio, and Will Landis.

There LaDuke related his story and gave his confession. He was free at the time and was not arrested until he was returned to Fort Wayne, Indiana. He said that he was not threatened or offered immunity and gave his confession because his conscience was troubling him. He said, "It was bothering my mind so I could hardly stand it."

Prosecutor Thomas tried to introduce LaDuke's written statement into evidence, but Judge Erwin objected and the court ruled the confession out. At cross-examination, Erwin asked, "Don't you know that Miller was not in Woodburn, nor within twenty miles of Woodburn that night?" LaDuke emphatically replied, "No, sir, I don't know that. He was there that night." LaDuke said he had eight to ten drinks of whiskey the night of the murder and when they started out, he did not know where they were going. He said he was not so drunk as to not know what was going on, but that he simply was not in on plot, but went with the crowd.

Cross-examination continued. "Now when Stout fired that shot up there did he say halt, halt?" Erwin asked. "No, sir; I didn't hear him say that," LaDuke answered. "Well," Erwin asked, "who was standing between you and Stout when he fired?" "Nobody," LaDuke said.

Erwin: "Where did he get that gun?"

LaDuke: "I don't know."

Erwin: "Didn't Stout have the gun down there at Thomas' saloon and show it to you all?"

LaDuke: "No, sir."

Erwin: "Where did you get your gun?"

LaDuke: "I didn't have any gun."

(Fort Wayne Journal Gazette, June 11, 1908, p. 5)

LaDuke repeated his story of the shooting and described running through the alley south of the printing office. Though he would have passed within a few feet of Croy's body, he said he did not see him as he ran past. He said that he never spoke to Miller, Stout, or Baker about the murder afterwards and never discussed making their escape from town. He said that he had talked with Prosecutor Thomas several times since his arrest and knew that he was jointly charged with the murder.

Cross-examination continued:

Erwin: "Say, LaDuke, isn't it a fact that you and Gorrell fixed this thing all up to get the reward out of it?"

LaDuke: "No, sir."

Erwin: "Didn't you fix this all up in Cadillac and then come down to Kalamazoo?"

LaDuke: "No, sir."

Erwin: "Are you willing to come into this court and plead guilty to the murder of Columbus Croy?"

LaDuke: "I'm willing to confess to being along."

Erwin: "You know they can hang you for that, don't you?"

LaDuke: "I don't know about that."

Erwin: "Why do you want to do this when you know what can be done with you?"

LaDuke: "Well, I wanted to get it off my mind."

(Fort Wayne Journal Gazette, June 11, 1908, p. 5)

LaDuke was asked whether he had told William Wearley and J. A. Baker, the new marshal of Woodburn, that he was in the Thomas saloon when the shots were fired and that he had dodged behind the ice box. LaDuke said that he did not tell them that.

The Testimony of Dr. A. J. Betts

Dr. Betts testimony had begun on the previous Friday and was continued on Tuesday for a four-hour course of questioning. Dr. Betts not only pronounced the marshal dead at the scene, but was a member of the town board for three years and when the defendant, Miller, was appointed as marshal prior to Croy.

> Claim No 69
>
> Shirley City Allen Co. Indiana
> May 11th 1903
>
> For Services as Marshall of the
> Town of Shirley City for Six Months
> due me (Thirty dollars) $30.00
>   Herman A Miller
>   Marshall
>
> Shirley City }
> Allen County } S.S.
> Indiana }
>
> I Herman A Miller solemnly
> swear that this is due me and unpaid
>   x Herman A Miller
>
> Sworn before me this the 11th day
> of May 1903
>   Henry S. Yehrly
>   Town Clerk,

Claim form submitted by Herman Miller while he was the Woodburn Marshal (signed as "Marshall," which was a common misspelling).
(Photos courtesy of Loretta McCann and the Woodburn Historical Society)

Miller was appointed as marshal in 1901 at a salary of $150 a year. In December, 1903, Miller threatened to resign unless the salary was raised. On May 11, 1905, the salary was increased to $500 but Miller complained that he should be paid $75 a month because thieves were trying to break into business houses and his life was in peril. Columbus Croy was employed at that time to attend to the streetlights at night and as a night watchman at a salary of $10 per month. Miller's resignation was accepted in November,

1905, and Columbus L. Croy was appointed as marshal at a salary of $75 per month.

Dr. Betts testified that one night while Miller was the marshal Miller woke him up and told him that thieves were trying to steal his horse. A moment later Miller ran away calling "Halt!" and firing his revolver. Dr. Betts found Fred Rohrer at the back door and going out to the barn found the horse asleep and nothing disturbed.

There were so many arrests while Miller was the marshal that it was necessary to construct a calaboose. The fighting and near rioting that had been frequent in Woodburn for years prior stopped. The fights began again after Miller resigned and a number of burglaries occurred after Croy became the marshal.

Dr. Betts testified that he was in Defiance, Ohio, all day the day the cigars were discovered in the Miller blacksmith shop stove. Defense attorney Judge Erwin tried to get the doctor to admit that he was in Woodburn that day and had talked with Mr. Chapman and Detective John B. Ryan about the murder. Dr. Betts continued to insist that he was in Ohio.

The defense then raised the issue that Dr. Betts had contacted the Leonard brothers' law firm about prosecuting Miller (for something not specified, but presumably about the murder of Croy). In regards to the murder charge Erwin asked, "You have been trying for a year to fasten this thing on Miller, haven't you?" "No," replied Dr. Betts, "I want Miller to have a chance. I am after the man that killed Croy."

Judge Erwin then asked Dr. Betts about his examination of the body and tried to raise the issue that Croy could have accidentally shot himself. Dr. Betts countered that it was not possible because there were no powder burns on Croy's coat and the path the bullet took clearly showed that Croy was stooping in manner making self-infliction impossible.

On redirect Dr. Betts said that at one time he had a good opinion of Miller as an officer and helped him to get appointed as a deputy sheriff. But later, after Miller had served as town marshal, Betts opinion of Miller changed. There were several complaints about Miller. Shooting was often heard late at night and the following days Miller would brag about chasing criminals out of town. The criminals always seemed to get away with no sign of any criminal activity.

While Croy was night watchman the lock was broken off of the town gas tank and Croy reported this to Dr. Betts as a member of the town board. (This is the incident that precipitated the argument that Mrs. Croy testified about).

More Witnesses Called

Deputy County Auditor Clayton A. Lindemuth was the next witness called. He too had been a member of the town board when Miller was the marshal. He said Miller often complained of his low salary for the services he rendered and that his life was frequently in danger. He said Miller had once discovered men trying to steal Dr. Betts horse and fired shots at them, coming close to capturing them. He said Miller often told of chasing criminals at other times as well. Lindemuth said that Miller once told him that Croy was a coward and had accused him of taking gasoline from the town pump. Lindeman testified that he thought Miller had been an efficient officer when he served as town marshal.

East Main Street, Woodburn, Indiana
(Probably around 1910)

(Photos courtesy of Loretta McCann and the Woodburn Historical Society)

Postmaster Henry Chapman, whose activities in the quest for the murderers won him the enmity of the Miller, was called on Wednesday. Miller allegedly had threatened to kill Chapman. Chapman also testified that he observed footprints in the mud behind the Faulkner saloon leading toward Miller's home. Chapman said he was positive that the tracks were made by rubber boots with corrugated soles which were worn down. He said the tracks led from the gate at the rear of the saloon to Miller's lot on the opposite side of the alley and that Miller sometimes wore rubber boots. Chapman did admit that many people in the neighborhood wear rubber boots as well.

Chapman also said he saw the bullet mark on the Wearley building and saw John Baker looking at it, but did not see him dig it out. He said another bullet was found across the street when some men drew lines to determine where the shot was fired. Later at trial a letter written to Miller was introduced. It contained vicious language and allegations, which the defense said, were from Chapman, in an attempt to discredit the witness.

Both the defense and the prosecution called a number of witnesses, including several young people who attended a dance at a home in the country. Several of them reported hearing the shots and some testified about the presence or absence of passing traffic at that hour. The state called nearly eighty witnesses in all.

The Woodburn Post Office
(Possibly the same Post Office manned by Postmaster Chapman in 1907)
(Photos courtesy of Loretta McCann and the Woodburn Historical Society)

Dr. Edward Moser testified that he was returning from calling on Mr. Colby's baby, after being called by Mr. Rohrer. Dr. Moser said he heard someone running on the boardwalk in the direction of Miller's house but did not see anything when he looked in that direction. He stopped to listen to the footsteps and a minute or so later heard two shots. He then met Dr. Betts, who told him of the murder.

George Overmeyer, night watchman for the Woodburn Lumber Company, testified that he was in the office when he heard a shot and stepped to the door, then over to the railroad. He stayed there for about ten minutes until the trains left then made his rounds and returned to the office. He did not see anyone. After making his rounds, he went to the Thomas saloon, met the Baker boys coming home from a dance, and learned of Croy's murder by phone.

Documents submitted to the Town Board of Shirley City (Woodburn) by Columbus Croy in 1905 before he was appointed as marshal.
(Photos courtesy of Loretta McCann and the Woodburn Historical Society)

Fred Sprunger refused to swear but gave his affirmation when called to testify. He said that he was friendly with Miller when he was the marshal and they sometimes spoke to each other in German. Miller once told him that Croy wasn't smart enough to be the marshal, that he didn't make the rounds late enough, and there wasn't as much trouble when he (Miller) was the marshal.

When Sprunger asked Miller who he thought broke into the barbershop, Miller said that it was better not to give an opinion of such things but that he could spot the guilty men. He also said he didn't think Croy would last long and that if he (Miller) ever got into any trouble he had friends in Fort Wayne who would stand beside him.

"How did he happen to say that?" Prosecutor Thomas asked. "One evening when I was kind of afraid he said it. We were fishing," Sprunger said. "Were you violating the law," Thomas asked. "Well, yes," Sprunger replied. Judge Erwin asked at cross-examination whether Miller mentioned Prosecutor Thomas as one of his friends. Sprunger said that he did not.

Austin Augsburger was questioned about seeing Miller before and after the barber shop burglary and about whether or not he knew Miller was divorced and remarried just after the burglary. Jennie Faulkner, wife of saloonkeeper Joseph Faulkner, was questioned about receiving a phone call about the burglars being in their saloon. Not much of consequence was brought out in their testimonies.

Former deputy sheriff Jules Huguenard was examined by Deputy Prosecutor Hilgeman and testified that he examined the crime scene at Faulkner's saloon in Woodburn following the murder. He said that he had observed footprints, which appeared to have been made by old rubber boots.

Eleven-year-old Sylvanus Heltzell was called by the state to testify that he had seen a shotgun, two revolvers, a billy club, and a belt at the Miller house when they were moving out. The prosecution showed the boy the two revolvers taken from Miller's house.

Burglary Tools Evidence to the Murder

Although the saloon and lot, which was the scene of the murder, were supposedly carefully guarded from the time Croy's body was discovered and no one was allowed in the yard, Herman Miller allegedly knew what tools the burglars used and their methods of forced entry. Henry Yaggy, one of

Woodburn's most reputable residents, was a poultry dealer and a stockholder in the bank. He testified that on the morning following the murder he was in front of his building, across the street from the Faulkner saloon. He said the crime scene at the saloon was guarded from intrusion. Herman Miller called him to the side of the building and in a secret and covert manner asked him his opinion as to who committed the murder. He gave his own opinion and told Yaggy that the burglars had used a sledgehammer and rasp to gain entry. No one had said anything about discovering the tools used to that point. After the bloodhounds had been sent out on the trail and the guards removed from the scene, a sledgehammer with a shortened handle was found in the yard and a rasp was found on the floor inside the saloon.

The Chase of Burglars Defense

On the afternoon of June 12, 1908, the defense attempted to strengthen their position by proving that Herman Miller's claims to have chased burglars, while he was the marshal, were true. The state tried to establish that Miller's bravado claims were nothing more than subterfuge in an attempt to gain an increase in his salary by a display of bravery and vigilance. The defense tried to substantiate that he did see and chase burglars.

Fred Rohrer, the former night watchman at the lumberyard, said Miller called him one night to help him catch some burglars at "Doc" Betts house. "He told me to take off my shoes and put on some light shoes. I went with him. It was about three-quarters of a mile to Bett's house. He told me I better take my revolver," Rohrer said. "Miller went to a window and called Dr. Betts' and told him burglars were after his horse. The doctor came downstairs. We walked along the alley and Miller said, 'There they go,' but I didn't see anybody," Rohrer continued. The witness said Miller darted away on a run, firing several shots. When Miller came back he said he saw one of the burglars lying down and one getting up, then both running. He didn't say anything about the burglars getting away.

The defense considered Rohrer's testimony of value that it "proved" that there were "marauders" about in Woodburn and that this somehow made Herman Miller more credible and less guilty. Rohrer also testified about having Dr. Moser at his place the night of the murder.

Herman Miller (court sketch)
(Photos courtesy of Loretta McCann and the Woodburn Historical Society)

Miller's Bullets

George Miller (it is unknown if he was in any way related to Herman Miller) was a former bartender at the Faulkner saloon. He testified that on one occasion Herman Miller, while he was the marshal, came into the saloon to make a purchase and laid three cartridges on the counter with his money. Bartender Miller asked Marshal Miller for the cartridges and Herman gave them to him. George put them in the cash drawer where he left them when he quit working for Faulkner. This was four or five years before the murder and George testified that he did not know what caliber they were. But after the murder he called them to Faulkner's attention.

Frank Faulkner, bartender and brother of Joseph, the saloon owner, testified that there were three or four cartridges in the drawer. After the murder the cartridges "were taken away," but a day or two later Shirley Faulkner brought "a large caliber cartridge" into the saloon and gave it to Joseph. Judge Erwin objected to the admission of this "evidence," as it was submitted after nearly three of "everyone in town" having trampled the scene. His objection was overruled. (Fort Wayne Journal Gazette, June 12, 1908, p. 5)

Postmaster Henry Chapman was recalled and testified that he had weighed the .41 caliber bullet produced by the Faulkners and compared it to a .44 recovered at the scene. He said that he did not compare it to the bullet found in and recovered from the wall. The cartridges were then sealed in an envelope and sent to the sheriff.

Next called was Elmer Halfly who was in Woodburn at about 7:00 a.m. on June 7. He met with Herman Miller between 8:00 and 9:00 a.m. "He asked me what I thought," Halfly said, "And afterwards asked me if I didn't think yeggmen had come to town to rob the bank. I said I thought yeggmen wouldn't go to rob a saloon and Miller said he thought they were after the bank but went to the saloon to get a little courage."

Then George Stenger, justice of the peace of Maumee Township and blacksmith, testified that he heard Miller say the day after the murder that the marauders wanted to get some booze to give them courage to rob the bank.

Town Father Called as Witness

Robert B. Shirley, candidate for representative and former member of the state legislature, was called as a witness. The town of Shirley City (Woodburn) had been named after him. This distinguished witness testified that he and Herman Miller were long-time friends. He said that he was in Miller's blacksmith shop the day the cigars were found. He went in with Henry Chapman. Miller was working on some horses and, when he looked up, asked angrily, "Were you in my shop yesterday?" Shirley said he was angry and thought he was asking him, but was relieved that he was speaking to Chapman.

Shirley said that Miller told them that he had placed a toothpick in the door when he went to church. Miller said that someone was in the place while he was at church. Someone had placed cigars in the stove and Miller was angry that someone was trying to make it appear that he had stolen them. Someone suggested using the dogs to track, but Miller said it was too late for that. Chapman said, "Whoever put the cigars in there knows who killed Croy." Shirley said that he shared that opinion.

Mr. Shirley also testified that he had met Miller in Assessor Eggeman's office in the courthouse in Fort Wayne. He asked the assessor for the newspaper because he heard that there was something in it about the Croy murder. Miller said that he had heard that "they" were accusing Bradley Staley of the murder. Staley was a local in Woodburn who had once been arrested for robbery. When Mr. Eggeman came back with the newspaper Miller called Mr. Shirley to the side and again said that he understood that they were looking for Staley. Mr. Shirley said that he had not heard that. At cross-examination Mr. Shirley was asked if Miller had said that he had reported Staley to the sheriff. Shirley said, "I think not." (Fort Wayne Journal Gazette, June 12, 1908, p. 5)

The Trial and Testimony Continues

Judge Erwin introduced a letter that Postmaster Henry Chapman had written to Detective John B. Ryan expressing his belief that whoever stole the cigars (from the Eby barbershop) knew who killed Marshal Croy. Another letter was produced that was addressed to Mrs. Miller (Herman's wife) that was replete with profanity. Chapman was asked if the two letters were not written in the same hand-writing., but the witness pointed out several differences in the formation of the letters.

Referring to the second letter Erwin asked Chapman if he knew that Mrs. Miller had received the vicious note. Chapman said that he had heard about it. "Did you ask Detective Lenz to get it from her?" Erwin asked. "No, sir, I did not," Chapman replied. (Fort Wayne Journal Gazette, June 12, 1908, p. 5)

Jake McNuller, Ed Sprunger (witness), and Harley Wearley (William Wearley's son) in front of the Woodburn Post Office
(Photos courtesy of Loretta McCann and the Woodburn Historical Society)

Sheriff Grice Gives Important Testimony for the State

The headlines on Saturday, June 13, 1908, read:
"Miller's Guns Had Disappeared When Officers Searched House,"

"Sheriff Grice Gives Important Testimony for the State in the Woodburn Murder Case," and

"Evidence of Prisoner's Anxiety to Avert Suspicion from Himself – Threatened His Accusers Since Beginning of the Trial."

(Fort Wayne Journal Gazette, June 13, 1908, p. 1)

Jesse Grice, the Sheriff of Allen County, Indiana, was called at 3:30 p.m. as the last witness before the State was to rest their case. Sheriff Grice testified that he was informed of Marshal Croy's murder the morning of June 7, 1907, and that he left Fort Wayne with his deputies at 6:00 a.m. and arrived in Woodburn at 7:00 a.m. (The news account on June 8 reported that the sheriff boarded a train at 5:00 a.m.). Before leaving Fort Wayne, Sheriff Grice telephoned instructions to Woodburn officers and his deputies to make a thorough search. The sheriff said that it was misty and it started to rain hard at about 8:00 or 9:00 a.m.

When Sheriff Grice and his deputies arrived, the scene at the Faulkner saloon was already under guard and he ordered that the entire lot be roped off. No one was allowed in the yard between the saloon and the Wearley meat market. John Baker, one of the co-defendants now in jail, was on guard at the corner of the meat market. Sheriff Grice, Deputy Jules Huguenard, and Postmaster Chapman were all on guard until 10:00 or 11:00 p.m. Sheriff Grice said that he saw small pieces of a spattered bullet taken from the Wearley building. The prosecutor showed him broken pieces of lead, which he identified as the same fragments.

Testimony to this point had tended to indicate that Miller had always kept firearms in his house. The sheriff's testimony explained that an extensive search of Miller's house produced no firearms whatsoever and the State hoped to show that this was due to Miller's overzealous attempt to remove any connection between himself and the murder of Croy. Even Mrs. Miller was noted for having said that Croy might have saved himself if he had called her husband, as Mr. Miller had a revolver and a shotgun in the house.

A key part of the prosecution's case of circumstantial evidence was that after Miller was arrested two revolvers were found in his house. Yet when

Sheriff Grice and his deputies searched Miller's home eleven days after the murder he was unable to find firearms of any kind.

Sheriff Grice testified that on June 14 Herman Miller came to the sheriff's office with a bundle. It was a piece of a buggy pole wrapped in a stone-colored paper. Miller asked the sheriff if he could leave it in the office. When Sheriff Grice and Deputy Hughes went to Miller's blacksmith shop on June 17, the cigars, which Miller had allegedly found in his stove, were wrapped in paper similar to that which Miller had brought to the sheriff's office on the previous Friday. The sheriff would not positively say that the paper found in the stove was the same as the paper that Miller had wrapped the buggy pole in at his office.

The prosecutor then asked the sheriff to identify in court the box of cigars, which he had recovered from Miller's shop. Sheriff Grice identified the box as the same one he collected and turned over to Mr. Detzer, his office deputy.

Miller told the sheriff that he had seen suspicious characters the evening before finding the cigars in his stove and that they had been placed there to put suspicion on him. He told the sheriff that before going to church on Sunday he had placed a toothpick in the door latch and when he returned it was on the floor.

On June 18 Sheriff Grice, Deputy Hughes and Mr. Ninde made a thorough search of Miller's house in Miller's presence, but found no firearms at all. Later Miller came to the sheriff and said that he had heard that Croy was killed with a .44 caliber bullet and that he never heard of a .44 caliber gun in Woodburn except one that had been stolen from him ten years earlier by Bradley Staley. He said Staley had gone to Michigan. After hearing Miller's story, the sheriff said that he would look into it.

Miller seemed to be working hard to place suspicion on Staley, who had also mentioned to Mr. Shirley (described in previous testimony). Sheriff Grice said:

> At still another time Miller came in and asked if I had heard of Staley. I told him that I had not, but I knew the woman who raised Staley and I would ask

her if she knew where he was. Miller never talked of anything else in connection with murder except Staley. Miller never gave me any other information. I knew Staley twenty-three or twenty-four years ago. He lived at Bull Rapids. The last I heard of him he took a trip to the penitentiary. Miller called two or three times to ask about Staley. Miller never mentioned any Woodburn people being implicated in the murder. Miller said he the .44 caliber gun he used to own was of German make, an army gun with an eight cornered barrel and had two marks on it made by blows from a sword. He said the gun was used in battle and was thrown up to ward off a sword cut.

(Fort Wayne Journal Gazette, June 13, 1908, p. 6)

Sheriff Grice related that he had received information about Fred LaDuke and that he and Prosecutor Thomas left for Kalamazoo, Michigan, on January 26, 1907. They met with LaDuke the next day, then returned with him to Fort Wayne, where LaDuke had been in jail since.

The sheriff's testimony also highlighted Miller's vindictive spirit. Since the trial began Miller had told the sheriff that he would get even with the men who had "put the cuffs on him," referring to the shackles that Miller wore to and from the jail. He said that on June 3, 1908, he took Miller back from the courthouse to the jail. On the way Miller said, "Sheriff, I'm pretty well satisfied that the evidence showed up some of the witnesses and when we get through we'll show up more of them. Then I'll get even with some of the _____ _____ _____ that made me wear these cuffs." The defense objected that this testimony had nothing to do with the crime and showed no intention on the part of the defendant to intimidate witnesses, but was solely intended to prejudice the jury against the defendant. The court ruled that the testimony was competent. (Fort Wayne Journal Gazette, June 13, 1908, pp. 1 and 6)

At cross-examination the defense raised the question of the bloodhounds. The prosecution objected but was overruled. The sheriff said, "It was raining.

The man in charge of the dog took it inside. The dog trailed past the bar, out the back door, and right straight north. I followed eight or ten miles."

Erwin: "To Grabill?"

Sheriff Grice: "Yes, sir."

Erwin: "Did he stop anywhere on the way?"

The state objected but was, again, overruled. The sheriff said the dog stopped once at a house.

Erwin: "Whose house?"

Sheriff Grice: "It was said to be Bennett's He went up over the steps, then across the yard and the field, and out into the road again, went through Maysville and on to Grabill. He went to the south part of the depot platform and stopped."

(Fort Wayne Journal Gazette, June 13, 1908, p. 6)

The posse then returned to Woodburn. Baker had been there on guard all day and stood by when the dog was put on the scent. The dog did not approach Baker or Miller, but went straight north from the saloon. Sheriff Grice said that the man in charge of the dog appeared to be under the influence of liquor and that it had been raining since early morning. He said that it rained for eighteen hours before the dog was put on the trail and pointed out that the roads were cut up and the holes were full of water. He also noted that there was a crowd of nearly three hundred in Woodburn and that there were tracks everywhere.

CHAPTER FOURTEEN

THE CROY MURDER: DEFENSE AND THE VERDICT

What one man can invent another can discover.

~ Sherlock Holmes ~

Sir Arthur Conan Doyle

The Defense Calls Witnesses

The defense called Deputy Sheriff Martin Detzer who identified the broken cigar box as the one Sheriff Grice gave him as evidence on June 18, 1907. He had fixed the lid and testified that the stamps were also broken. The defense said that they did not wish to imply that the evidence had been intentionally tampered with, but objected to having the box presented to the jury on the grounds that it had never been shown to have been in the possession of the defendant. The objection was overruled. Detzer was questioned about the cancellation marks on the stamps and he said that they were not distinguishable.

The defense then called Henry Yaggy and tried to determine why he had declined to answer certain questions asked by the prosecution at his previous testimony. Judge Erwin asked him if he had told Miller that he was suspicious of Jack Bennett because he was on the street all day following the murder and went to work late, which was not his custom. Yaggy reluctantly admitted that he did say that. The defense persisted in its strategy to place suspicion on others.

Next, Cooney Bayer, a cigar manufacturer, was called and identified the cigar box found in Miller's stove. He stated that while it bore the union label and was dated September 14, the year could not be made out.

John Trautman, Jr., a dealer in sporting goods and reputed expert in firearms, was called and identified a cartridge shown to him as a .41 caliber short, which, he said, was an unusual revolver cartridge. Peter Conrad, a hardware salesman, was called to testify that in his thirty years of experience he had never seen a cartridge of that caliber. Henry L. Wearley, a jeweler in Garrett and former town clerk of Woodburn, testified that the stolen gasoline incident occurred during his term of office and that he started the story as a joke on Miller. (But previous testimony by Dr. Betts indicated that Croy had discovered the theft while he was the night watchman). Wearley did mention that he thought that there was a rivalry between Miller and Croy.

Other Witnesses Report Observations

Sylvester Perkins, a local farmer, testified that he was on the train with Miller, Chapman, and J. Frank Butt going to Fort Wayne when Miller accused him of trying to get evidence against him in the Croy murder. When Perkins denied the accusation, Miller allegedly threatened him.

J. Frank Butt, proprietor of the Oxbow Farm, north of Woodburn, said that he and Miller had been good friends up to the time of the murder. He said that he saw John Baker digging a bullet out of the Wearley building the morning after the murder. He referred to him as "Left Handed John" to distinguish him from the John Baker who had become the new marshal at Woodburn. He also said that Herman Miller had told him that Ted Moulter needed to be watched and that the Moulter crowd was a bad crowd.

Shirley Faulkner, a twelve-year-old boy, testified that he had found a cartridge in the yard of his father's saloon on the Saturday following the murder. He gave it to his uncle Frank who was tending the bar.

William Driver, a farmer living a half mile from Woodburn, said that Miller had told him that robbers had intended to rob the bank. He, too, said that he saw John Baker (Left Handed John) digging the bullet out of Wearley's building. He said that Miller had also threatened him. He admitted to the defense that Miller had arrested him twice for drunkenness, but that he was acquitted both times. When the defense accused Driver of not liking Miller, Driver said with emphasis that he did not, but said that this did not affect his testimony in any way.

County Clerk Joseph N. Mason was called and testified from the county records that Herman A. Miller and Louisa M. Miller had procured a marriage license on February 20, 1907. The return certifying that they were married by the Rev. J. W. Miller was signed with the same date.

The Defense Raises a Suspect and the State Suggests an Affair

Continuing its strategy of suggesting other suspects and casting suspicion on others, the defense called William Keller, owner of the machine shop. Keller testified that he was a former member of the town board and was a member when Columbus Croy applied for the position of town marshal. He testified that Jack Bennett was also an applicant.

The state objected to this line of questioning and while the prosecutor, Mr. Robinson, was citing authorities in support of his objection to bringing Bennett's interest in Croy's job, Judge Erwin stood and said, "If it please the court we expect to bring in evidence to show not only that he had a motive, but that he did it."

Judge O'Rourke said that such a line of questioning would result in two trials going on simultaneously and thought that only direct evidence should be brought. The newspaper account read, "The pile of leather bound law books on the attorneys' table was rifled, and judge and lawyers were immersed in the large volumes, and conflicting opinions and rulings were presented by the opposing sides." After arguments, citations, and examination of decisions consumed much of the afternoon, the defense intended to meet the State's contention involving Miller's motive with evidence showing that others had equal motives. (Fort Wayne Journal Gazette, June 14, 1908, pp. 1 and 9)

Judge O'Rourke conceded, "You may show overt acts, but not threats." Judge Erwin cited Supreme Court decisions that threats were admissible in cases in cases with similar circumstances. Judge O'Rourke took the issue under advisement for the weekend. (Fort Wayne Journal Gazette, June 14, 1908, p. 1)

The next surprise in the trial was when Mrs. Wesley Saylor was called by the defense. John Baker boarded with Mrs. Saylor for five years and she testified that at the time of the murder she lived next door to the Redderson saloon. (This was also referred to as the Retison and Rettison saloon, as spelling errors were not uncommon in newspapers at that time). She said that on the night of June 6 she was taking care of her daughter's baby while her daughter and son-in-law were at a dance. Her husband and their two younger children were in the house and she said that John Baker came in at about 11:45 p.m., going to bed without leaving again. If the defense could establish that LaDuke's testimony about Baker was not true, it could prove that none of his testimony was reliable and that Miller was not guilty.

The State, on cross-examination, attempted to impeach Mrs. Saylor's testimony by showing that she had an intimate relation with Baker. She admitted that Baker was a longtime boarder at her house and that they were very familiar with each other, but denied any impropriety in their relations. She denied any intimacy with Baker, but Prosecutor Robinson asked, "Didn't Wes leave you because of that?" "No, sir," she replied. (Fort Wayne Journal Gazette, June 14, 1908, p. 9)

Mrs. Baker testified that she heard the shots the night of June 6 or morning of June 7. "Didn't you tell Wearley that you never heard any shots?" the prosecutor asked. "No, sir," she again responded. She said that her daughter and her husband went to a dance that night at about 8:30 p.m. She went upstairs shortly after that and into Baker's room. Mr. Baker was in bed at about 9:00 p.m., but she said she did not see him come in. When Mrs.

Baker's grandchild cried, she took it into Baker's room. (Fort Wayne Journal Gazette, June 14, 1908, p. 9)

When Baker came in, Mrs. Saylor said, he went straight to bed and she heard him snoring. She said that she did not see Baker come in, but saw him when he went upstairs. He was in his shirtsleeves, bareheaded, and barefooted. She said she went into his room about five times and was just coming out of her room again with the infant when she heard the shots fired. "When you saw Baker in bed don't you know he had his clothes on?" Mr. Robinson asked. "No, sir; he was covered with a quilt," Mrs. Saylor answered.

Mrs. Baker admitted that she had engaged an attorney for Baker, but said that she did so because she knew he was innocent. "Isn't it a fact that you told no one about the shots except your little girl because you knew Baker was out and wanted to shield him?" Robinson asked. "No, sir; Mr. Baker was in the house," Mrs. Saylor said. A lengthy dialogue of questioning followed. Then Mr. Robinson asked, "You walked into Baker's room five times that night. Why didn't you go into your husband's room?" "Well," Mrs. Saylor replied, "Baker's room was larger and there was a chair where I could sit down." She admitted that she felt free to enter Baker's bedroom at all times, even after her husband had left for Michigan. She also admitted that she had intended to move to a farm that Baker had purchased and that Baker said she would not have to pay any rent. "He lived with you five years?" Robinson asked. "He boarded with us five years," Saylor quickly replied, emphasizing the word "boarded." She said that she had frequently gone to parties with Baker, but that her daughter or someone else was always along and that she never went with him alone. (Fort Wayne Journal Gazette, June 14, 1908, p. 9)

Mrs. Saylor said that she looked at a watch after Baker came in and it was at 11:45 p.m. The prosecutor asked when she looked at the watch again and she said that she didn't remember. He asked if Baker didn't quietly turn the watch backward or forward, and, again, she said that she did not know.

When all witnesses had testified, the prosecution and the defense gave their closing arguments. At the conclusion of the arguments, the verdict was given.

Dr. Robert J. Girod, Sr.

Police Chief Martin J. Ankenbruck
(Photos courtesy of Fort Wayne Police Department Training Academy)

The Trial of John Stout

On September 13, 1908, the press credited Sheriff Jesse Grice, Prosecutor Albert E. Thomas, and Fort Wayne Police Chief Martin J. Ankenbruck with their cooperative investigations, which lead to the arrest of the murderers of

Marshal Columbus L. Croy. On September 22, 1908, John Stout presented an affidavit to the Circuit Court that he was without means to hire attorneys for his defense. Judge O'Rourke appointed Judge R.K. Erwin and former State's Attorney P. B. Colerick to defend Stout, who was charged with complicity in the assassination of Marshal Croy. The case was set for November 16, 1908, at 9:00 a.m.

Deputy Prosecutor Harry F. Hilgeman
(Photos courtesy of Loretta McCann and the Woodburn Historical Society)

Prosecutor Thomas would again be assisted by Attorney James M. Robinson, as well as Deputy Prosecutor Harry F. Hilgeman. The prosecution would concentrate on Stout's shooting ability, as he was fingered as the shooter. The defense would concentrate on his alibi.

Meanwhile, Fort Wayne police were called to the scene of a new, but unrelated case of suspected foul play. Mrs. Julia (Harmon) Stahl, the widow of Boston American league baseball player "Chick" Stahl, was found dead in her doorway. Mrs. Stahl had come to Fort Wayne with her husband following their marriage in November, 1906. They lived in Fort Wayne until training camp started on March 1, 1907. Her husband had committed suicide on March 28, 1907, by drinking carbolic acid at West Baden, Indiana. Mrs. Stahl was found dead on November 15, 1908.

While baseball fans followed the Stahl deaths in the news, an Allen County jury of twelve was selected from a special venire of one hundred men. Each side made peremptory challenges and Deputy Sheriff Hall and Bailiff Plumadore would bring a new prospective juror. Seventy-eight were dismissed from the jury pool before both the defense and the prosecution were satisfied with the jury selection. One prospect was excused for having served on a jury in the Superior Court during the previous year and two took advantage of the excuse of being over the age of sixty. All of the selected jurors were farmers. Six were approximately forty-five years of age and six were over the age of sixty.

Few of the men examined as prospective jurors had not read something or talked about the crime. Most had some opinion about the case as well and several seemed intent upon enlightening the court as to their opinion, but succeeded in sharing their beliefs in open court. The jurors would be kept together during the course of the trial, which was expected to take about two weeks. The jurors were dismissed at about 6:00 p.m. on November 17, the first day, and Deputy Bailiff Daily arranged for their beds in the courthouse.

While curious crowds were typical at murder trials, the first day was lightly attended, as most people probably speculated that jury selection would take up most of that day. The newspaper reported, "There was a noticeable lack of the fair sex in the audience." The interest in the Stout may have been less keen since most of the evidence and testimony would be the same as in the Miller case. (Fort Wayne Journal Gazette, November 17, 1908, p. 9)

Stout had been indicted by the Grand Jury on three counts of murder in the first degree. The distinction between the three depended upon whether the shooting was for the purpose of killing Croy, whether it was merely for the purpose of robbing the Faulkner saloon, or whether it occurred incidentally in the course of the robbery. Each count, however, carried a potential death penalty.

Once the trial commenced, Mrs. William Wearley, the butcher's wife, was called and testified that she lived opposite the Faulkner saloon and that she saw and heard most of the circumstances at the scene of the murder. She said, "I was awakened about 1:00 o'clock by a noise over toward the Faulkner saloon and I went over to the window to look. I saw a man leaning out of the saloon window and standing on the floor, I supposed. He was large and wore a soft hat." (Fort Wayne Journal Gazette, June 18, 1908, p. 1)

Mrs. Wearley continued, saying, "Inside of the saloon we saw a light, as though a man was scratching a match, and I heard a rattling of beer bottles. Then, I heard a voice holler, 'Halt! There.' And a shot was fired. Then the voice hollered again, 'Stand back, there,' and there was another shot. "Did you ever hear that voice before?" asked Prosecutor Thomas. Mrs. Wearley said that she had and, pointing toward the defendant, said that it was the voice of John Stout. (Fort Wayne Journal Gazette, June 18, 1908, p. 1)

Stout seemed calm during Mrs. Wearley's testimony. She went on to relate that several weeks later she was walking along the street when she passed John Stout sitting on a fence. Stout said something in a loud voice and it startled her. When the prosecutor asked her why she was startled, she said, "Because it sounded so much like the voice I heard on the night of the murder." (Fort Wayne Journal Gazette, June 18, 1908, p. 1)

The defense then questioned Mrs. Wearley about her inconsistent testimony before the two grand juries, particularly that she had not heard the voice the night of the murder. She said that she was afraid to tell everything because the killers were still at large. "You admit that you falsified to me?" Judge Erwin asked. Mrs. Wearley admitted that she had.

Mr. William Wearley reiterated the testimony of his wife and testified that Stout was in the habit of using the expression, "I say," which Stout was said to have shouted at the time of the shooting. Yet, Wearley also admitted that he was not certain that it was Stout's voice that he heard the night of the murder. Wearley also reported anonymous letters that Dr. Betts, Mr. Chapman and other witnesses had received threatening dire punishment if they gave damaging evidence in their testimony. He, too, gave his fear of these threats as the reason he also withheld information from the Grand Jury until he "got in a proper place."

The prosecution reiterated many of the details brought out in the Miller trial, including six conflicting stories that Stout allegedly told about the incident. More than fifty witnesses were called, including co-defendant Fred LaDuke. County Surveyor David Spindler identified and testified about a chart of the scene of the murder made from his measurements. Particular attention was given to testimony about the location of the body and the position of the recovered bullet.

Looking East on Main Street
(Compare to other Main Street photos)
(Photos courtesy of Loretta McCann and the Woodburn Historical Society)

Still hoping to transfer suspicion on someone else and raise doubt in the jury's mind, the defense called Jack Bennett and maneuvered to discredit him. Bennett was a blacksmith and a deputy marshal under Croy. When questioned about his confinement in the Ohio state penitentiary at Columbus, Ohio, Bennett bristled and said, "I worked there until I quit." "Do you know how many years or months it was?" Judge Erwin asked. "Yes, I know, but I won't tell," Bennett snapped back. "Then you refuse to answer the question?" Erwin responded. Just then Judge O'Rourke announced a noon recess. (Fort Wayne Journal Gazette, June 18, 1908, p. 5)

For the State Bennett provided only minor testimony and contributed to establishing the corpus delicti. When court resumed at 1:45 p.m. for the afternoon session the defense established that Bennett had been incarcerated at the Ohio penitentiary for three years and some months for a conviction of highway robbery. The witness countered with a long and eloquent explanation of the merits of his case and vindication of himself. The State finally suggested that he had defended himself sufficiently after he declared his innocence several times.

Judge Erwin then attempted to point out several discrepancies between Bennett's current testimony and his testimonies at the coroner's inquest and at Miller's trial. Bennett attempted to explain the discrepancies by asserting that they were the result of his hearing deficiency. The defense then pursued a minute examination of Bennett's movements on the day after the murder and attempted to show the inaccuracy of his memory.

The exchange between Judge Erwin and Bennett continued in heated fashion:

Bennett: "If you don't know nothing you can't tell it, can you?"

Erwin: "How does it come you can't tell me what you did that morning?"

Bennett: "If you can tell me what I did in my shop after seeing me do it I will tell you too!"

Erwin: "Have you been drinking intoxicants today?"

Bennett: "No more than you have. I ..."

While the crowd thought this exchange was a great joke and had to be quieted by Deputy Bailiff John Daly, the court intervened in the heated exchange.

Stout's Personal Statement

Stout's daughter, Ethel, and her aunt (Stout's sister) came to only a single day of the trial and only for a half-hour. They were the only members of Stout's family to attend the trial. Ethel lived with an aunt just outside of Fort Wayne. No greeting passed between them and Stout was oblivious to their presence. Ethel made no attempt to attract anyone's attention, but sat quietly with her head down, looking at the floor. Described as a beautiful girl of sixteen, observers noted that her face was sad and somber. Meanwhile, Stout watched the proceedings with interest but not a trace of concern on his face. He readily exchanged pleasantries and laughed, but his attorneys only consulted him a couple of times during recesses.

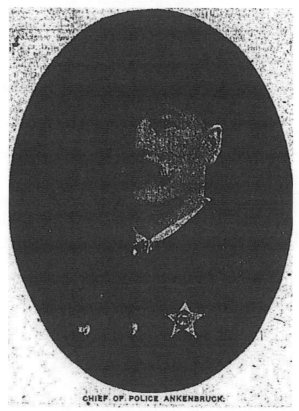

Fort Wayne Police Chief Martin J. Ankenbruck
(Photos courtesy of Loretta McCann and the Woodburn Historical Society)

Infamous Murders and Mysteries

The defense fought to prevent Stout's statement, made on the evening of his arrest, from being admitted into evidence. Judge Erwin was permitted to examine Fort Wayne Police Chief Martin J. Ankenbruck, who testified to identify Stout's statement before it was admitted. Erwin attempted to show that the statement was made under duress or unusual and prejudicial circumstances. He declared that law officers elicited the statement at a very late hour after the defendant had put in a hard day's work. He also attempted to demonstrate that the statements given by LaDuke and Baker had been made after inducements were presented by the State.

Court Reporter John C. Capron read the stenographic notes of John Stout's statement to the Grand Jury in September, 1907. Judge Erwin objected to the materiality of the statement, but his objection was overruled. In the statement were minor discrepancies, which the prosecution attempted to exploit. Stout also denied, in his statement, seeing "Red" Baker (possibly referring to John Baker's brother, rather than John himself) and Herman Miller on the night of the murder.

Fred LaDuke Testifies Against John Stout

Fred LaDuke again took the stand against the second of his co-defendants. His testimony was described as calm and naïve candor. One news account said that observers felt convinced that LaDuke was either a consummate liar or an absolute truth-teller. One spectator was heard to remark, "I don't believe that fellow has brains enough to tell a good lie." LaDuke reiterated the story he had related at the Miller trial about the "chicken dinner," about going to the Faulkner saloon and about the shooting and running home afterwards. LaDuke said that about three weeks after the shooting, he left his job in Woodburn and went to Paulding, Ohio, to work for Ben Rhiopel, an amateur detective. (Fort Wayne Journal Gazette, June 21, 1908, p. 1)

LaDuke was as a small, swarthy man with a jet-black mustache and hair. He was described as looking more like an Italian or Hungarian than a Frenchman. He spoke with a high, mildly expostulating voice. The news account said, "His face, although blank and ignorant, is not nearly so repulsive as might be supposed." He calmly gave his direct, simple testimony and damaging admissions of guilt while keeping his eyes on his interrogator.

While Judge Erwin played freely on LaDuke's ignorance and lack of advantages, the witness freely admitted his ignorance and observers felt that his candor reinforced the credibility of his testimony. The defense followed a line of questioning about LaDuke's ignorance:

>Erwin:"What month does Christmas come in?"
>
>LaDuke:"I don't know."
>
>Erwin:"What month comes after November?"
>
>LaDuke:"I don't know."
>
>Erwin:"How many weeks are there in a month?"
>
>LaDuke:"Four."
>
>Erwin:"How did you find that out?"
>
>LaDuke:"Oh, I always knew that."
>
>(Fort Wayne Journal Gazette, June 21, 1908, p. 6)

Failing to lead the witness into contradictions, the defense then tried to impeach LaDuke's credibility by suggesting that he was drunk the night of the murder.

>Erwin:"Why did you break in after hours when you could get all you wanted during hours?"
>
>LaDuke:"Well, because I was drunk," (adding that his employer's orders were not to go into the saloon after hours and he was afraid to use his key to enter).
>
>Erwin:"How often did you get drunk at Woodburn? Every day?"
>
>LaDuke:"Pretty nearly."
>
>Erwin:"Were you drunk the day of the murder?"
>
>LaDuke:"Not very."
>
>Erwin:"Were you drunk that night?"
>
>LaDuke:"Pretty full."
>
>(Fort Wayne Journal Gazette, June 21, 1908, p. 6)

LaDuke reiterated the testimony he had given at Miller's trial, staying consistent in his tale. He said that he talked with Miller, Stout, and Baker after the murder, but that they did not discuss the murder at all. Judge Erwin asked LaDuke if he had been promised anything in exchange for his testimony and he said that he had not. Erwin then asked if he had burglarized the Grand Hotel in Bay City, Michigan, and jumped in the lake to escape. LaDuke denied any involvement in that incident. Upon reexamination LaDuke said that the only school he had ever attended was one summer at school. He was excused from the stand at 2:15 p.m.

Testimony by Other State's Witnesses

The November 21 session of the trial brought testimony of minutiae by supporting witnesses. John Conners, who lived near Woodburn, was in town the night of the murder and saw a man he believed to be Herman Miller near the Keller machine shop where the burglar tools were stolen.

John Eby, the Main Street barber, told of a conversation with John Stout in which Stout said that he knew Fred LaDuke had nothing to do with the murder because they had spent the entire night together. Daniel Rothgeb, a farmer living near Woodburn, testified that Stout was in the habit of using the expression, "I say." Mrs. Miller reported a conversation in which John Stout said that he was afraid, "they would stick some innocent man for the murder." Frank Wilson saw Stout and Baker talking together the morning of the murder. (Fort Wayne Journal Gazette, June 21, 1908, p. 6)

Rudolph Redderson, a Woodburn saloonkeeper, testified of waking Stout and LaDuke, who roomed above his house, by pounding on the ceiling with a pool cue the morning after the murder. This was what LaDuke reported, but Stout asserted that Redderson came upstairs to wake them up and told them at that time of the murder.

William Classon testified about a conversation with Stout on the night after the murder. Someone said that the tracking dog was coming and Classon observed that Stout immediately turned and went into the house. The prosecution hoped to demonstrate that Stout feared that the bloodhound would alert searchers to him.

Mrs. Ephraim Lotz, a boarding house keeper, said that Stout told her, "I don't think they will get them, because it is too long after the murder." At another time she observed Stout and Baker acting out the murder on the street and heard them speculating upon the probable positions of Croy and the murderer at the time of the shooting. She said, however, that many townspeople also speculated about this. She said that on another occasion she heard Stout say, "I don't think they came with the intention of killing. They were run in on and rather than being caught they shot." Her daughter, Mrs. Noah Cotterel also gave confirming testimony of these events. (Fort Wayne Journal Gazette, June 21, 1908, p. 6)

When the witnesses and evidence for both the State and the defense had been presented, the prosecution and defense each gave their closing arguments. At the conclusion of the arguments, the verdict was given.

The Trial of John Baker

The trial of John Baker started in mid-February, 1909, and continued for three weeks. The trial had been moved from Allen County to Judge Cook's court in Huntington County, just west of Fort Wayne. On March 9, Baker testified on his own behalf. Baker, as had his co-defendants, was described as being cool, without apparent concern or nervousness, and at times even disinterested in the examination of other witnesses. Defense attorneys asserted that Baker was confident in his innocence and had no doubt of his acquittal. Baker's father, John, and brother, "Red," were in the courtroom with him.

Baker's story was the same as that told at the two trials of his co-defendants. He admitted to stealing the chicken at Faulkner's saloon for the famous "chicken dinner" with Stout, LaDuke, and "Dummy" Kerns. He told of going home to the Saylors' boarding house and going to bed. He reported that the next day when he was told of the Croy murder, former Sheriff Jesse Grice asked him to guard the Wearley corner of the crime scene.

During cross-examination by former Congressman J. M. Robinson, a letter allegedly dictated to Fort Wayne Police Detective Lenz by John Baker was read to the jury. Baker identified the signature as his, but said that it was not the same letter that Detective Lenz had read to him. Baker said that part of the letter was wrong and contested some of the minor details contained therein.

> Robinson: "Did you, while talking to Faulkner on the morning after the murder, say to him as you saw Miller coming up the alley, 'There comes the s___ of a b_____ that killed Croy'?"
>
> Baker: "No, sir. I never expressed any theory as to who did the killing."
>
> Robinson: "Did you not make arrangements with Stout for him to get Mr. Miller to help you rob the Faulkner saloon?"
>
> Baker: "No, sir."

(Fort Wayne Journal Gazette, March 9, 1909)

When questioned about asking Dave Spindler if they hung men in Indiana for murder, Baker denied asking the question. He also denied telling Ralph Gunther, "I don't think it is right to have a law that would take a man's life." Baker said, "I don't remember saying it, but I suppose that if we were talking about it I might have made such a statement as I don't believe in capital punishment." (Fort Wayne Journal Gazette, March 9, 1909)

Baker testified that Dr. Betts met him on the street soon after the murder and offered him $1,000 to swear that he saw Herman Miller on the street the night before the murder. "You know that Dr. Betts did not want to hire you," said Mr. Robinson. "I know that he did," answered Baker. "Wasn't it true that Dr. Betts, as a member of the citizens' committee, just wanted to find out who did the murder?" Robinson responded. "No, sir. He was anxious to have me swear that I saw Miller on the street the night of the murder," Baker replied back. (Fort Wayne Journal Gazette, March 9, 1909, p.2)

Co-defendant Herman Miller also testified for the defense at the Baker trial. John Stout's testimony about his whereabouts on the night of the murder was refuted by testimony by Bert Furney, a farmer from near Maysville, who saw Stout on the morning following the murder. He said that in the morning Stout told him that he was in bed the night before, but in the afternoon while discussing the murder and robbery said that it was a good thing that the guilty men did not try to get into the Redderson saloon as he and LaDuke slept there all night and they would have filled them full of shot.

Allen County Court Reporter John Capron to give testimony from the transcripts of the Stout trial the previous November. The prosecution called rebuttal witnesses concerning the character of Baker, including Perry Smith and Effie Heltzel. Dr. Mosier testified to refute the character of the defenses' key witnesses – Mr. and Mrs. Miller and Mrs. Saylor. A motion by the defense was made to strike this testimony, as Dr. Mosier would not say who had asserted that the defense witnesses were dishonest or ruffians. The objection was sustained, but was then followed by more than a half dozen of Woodburn's leading citizens in confirmation of Dr. Mosier's testimony and in rebuttal of the defense witnesses. The prosecution called another sixty witnesses.

Martin Detzer, who was chief deputy sheriff at the time of the murder, said that Mrs. Miller visited his office on the morning after the murder and told him that she had wrapped up Herman's revolver in a piece of paper and thrown it in the attic. When Mrs. Miller took the stand again, she denied this.

More from Fred LaDuke

The day ended on March 9, 1909, with much speculation about the fate of Fred LaDuke, who had testified against his co-defendants. LaDuke had been incarcerated in the Allen County jail since his return from Michigan with the sheriff and prosecutor. Anxious to establish that LaDuke would be given immunity for his testimony, making him free to collect or share the reward money, it was reported by the defense counsel that LaDuke was now in a position to claim freedom. Judge Erwin asserted that the State, whether by design or not, would be forced to let LaDuke go because he had been carried over three terms of court on the single charge.

More Allegations of Impropriety by the State

Clarence Omo, a driver for the Fort Wayne Supply Company, testified that in January, 1908, he was at the Bogenschuetz saloon. He testified that he had overheard a conversation between John Stout and Herman Miller and that Stout said to Miller, "Forget it, Herman. We fixed him and they can't get us." On cross-examination Judge Erwin noted that Omo had testified in both the Miller and Stout trials that he heard the conversation in June, 1907, but had just testified that he heard it in January, 1908. (Fort Wayne Journal Gazette, March 10, 1909, p. 2)

Erwin asked Deputy Prosecutor Eberhardt to draw up an affidavit charging Omo with perjury. The defense also called Attorneys Ray McAdams and Harley Graftmiller who testified that Omo had been called from a meeting of the Modern Woodmen Lodge to the office of former Congressman J. M. Robinson, who was assisting the State in the prosecution. They both testified that when Omo returned to the lodge room, he said that Robinson and Prosecutor Thomas wanted him to "tell a lot of stuff that was not true" but that he had refused because he was afraid that he would get "balled up" in the cross-examination. (Fort Wayne Journal Gazette, March 10, 1909, p. 2)

Next, former Deputy Sheriff Harvey Hughes was called to the stand to testify about his interview with John Stout. Hughes asked to use his notes to aid in his testimony, but the defense objected, asserting that the notes had been arranged after he heard the testimony given at the Miller trial.

Postmaster Henry Chapman was again called and the defense attempted to impeach him by suggesting impropriety. "Did you tell Detective John Ryan that you were going to furnish evidence against Miller to convict him of the crime even if he wasn't guilty?" Erwin asked. "No, sir," Chapman replied. "Did you tell one of the jurymen, not mentioning names, that you had evidence to prove that Miller was the guilty man?" Erwin questioned. "Yes, sir. He came into the post office after his mail and said that he would hate to sit on a jury. I told him that I thought the boys were guilty and that I couldn't see it any other way," Chapman answered. Erwin asked the postmaster if he knew that the man was to be on the pending jury and he said that he did. (Fort Wayne Journal Gazette, March 10, 1909, p. 2)

Samuel Schneck testified that during a conversation that took place in Miller's blacksmith shop, Herman Miller said that Croy ought to be killed. Isaac Sprunger testified that at 5:00 a.m. on the morning of the murder Miller told him that he (Sprunger) could not go up to the Faulkner saloon as they were keeping people away. He said that chisels, hammers and other tools had been found, even though no one had been allowed in to find them to that point. Sprunger later told Miller that it was too bad that people in Woodburn were connecting him (Miller) to the murder. Miller said, "They will have to prove it."

Milton Augsberger testified that John Stout saw him (Augsberger) the morning of the murder and said, "Hello, Butch. Ain't it a shame that Croy was killed? He and I were going fishing today." Dr. A. J. Betts testified again that Miller had threatened to kill him, Chapman, and F. J. Butt – the citizens' committee. State Representative Robert B. Shirley, the founder of Shirley City (inaccurately reported in some accounts as Shirleyville), which later became known as Woodburn, was summoned from a session of the Indiana State Legislature to corroborate testimony given by former Sheriff Grice that Miller wanted the sheriff to look for Bradley Staley as a suspect in the murder. (Fort Wayne Journal Gazette, March 11, 1909, p. 5)

At the end of the testimony by both the prosecution and the defense, both sides rested their cases and each side was allocated five hours for closing arguments. At the conclusion of the arguments, the verdict was given.

The Verdicts in the Trials of Miller, Stout, and Baker

In June, 1908, the jury in Allen Circuit Court in the case of State v. Herman Miller came to a verdict. The jury found Herman Miller guilty of murder in the first degree, a capital crime, and he was sentenced to life in prison.

In November, 1908, the jury in Allen Circuit Court in the case of State v. John Stout came to a verdict. At Stout's side was his sixteen-year-old daughter, Ethel, who was the only one of his seven children to visit him while the trial was in progress. She came in as Judge O'Rourke was reading instructions to the jury and once the jury had retired she went to her father. Stout seemed pleased to see her and greeted her with a hearty handshake. The father and daughter sat and talked until a knock at the jury door indicated that Stout's fate had been determined.

After only a half-hour of deliberation the jury reached its verdict. At 3:25 p.m. Bailiff Plumadore answered the knock on the jury door. He stepped into the room for a moment then returned to notify the judge and the counsel for the State and the defense and then returned to the jury room. At 3:30 p.m. the jury members filed to the seats in the jury box for the last time in this case. "Gentleman of the jury," Judge O'Rourke said, "have you arrived at a verdict in this case?" Jury Foreman Horace G. McDuffy replied, "We have." (Fort Wayne Journal Gazette, November 28, 1908, p. 6)

Stout kept his eyes on the Judge the entire time, showing no sign of emotion but a hint of flush. His daughter looked at the floor with a downcast expression described as dejection. Neither moved until the judge read the verdict:

> *We, the jury, in the case of the State of Indiana versus John Stout find the defendant guilty of murder in the first degree. We further find that he be imprisoned in the state penitentiary during his life.*
> *(Signed)*
> *Horace G. McDuffy, Foreman*
> (Fort Wayne Journal Gazette, November 28, 1908, p. 6)

"Is this your verdict, gentlemen?" the judge asked. "It is," the jury responded together. "During the reading of the verdict John Stout never moved a muscle or showed any sign of anxiety," observers noted. After hearing the verdict, Stout and his daughter resumed their interrupted conversation, appearing no more concerned than before the verdict had been read. (Fort Wayne Journal Gazette, November 28, 1908, p. 6)

There was no discussion of the death penalty for the shooter of Marshal Columbus L. Croy, though this was a capital offense in Indiana. The defense announced that it would ask for a new trial within the allotted thirty days and present its reasons at that time.

In March, 1909, the jury in Huntington Circuit Court in the case of State v. John Baker came to a verdict. While Herman Miller and John Stout had been convicted of murder in the first degree and sentenced to life in the penitentiary in Michigan City, Indiana, John Baker was found guilty of manslaughter and given an indeterminate sentence. The defense would also ask for a new trial within the thirty days time limit.

Meanwhile, there was a new sheriff in town. Allen County Sheriff Reichelderfer announced that John Baker would remain in the Huntington County jail until transferred to the state pen in Michigan City. Allen County would pay Huntington County forty cents per day to board the prisoner and another $1,101.80 for the trial. One hundred and one witnesses had been called in the Baker trail – eighty for the State and twenty-one for the defense. One of the ironies in this case was that Woodburn's new town marshal was John Baker – another man by the same name from the same small town. Meanwhile "Left-handed John" prepared for prison and an appeal for a retrial.

Post-Conviction Prologue and the Appeal

Ten months after John Stout's conviction and six months after the conviction of John Baker, the third trial in the murder case, Stout's daughter was back in court. On September 22, 1909, sixteen year old Ethel Stout brought a complaint in Fort Wayne City Court against Edward Lynch.

Ethel alleged that she was asleep in her bedroom at the Hugh Welsh boarding house at Clinton and Superior streets in Fort Wayne. She was awakened by a burning match that fell on her arm. When she awoke, she saw Edward Lynch bending over her bed. Ethel asserted that she got up from bed and tried to get Lynch to leave but he pushed her back, holding a knife to her face, and threatened her.

Edward Lynch said that while he was in jail, Ethel Stout wrote to him and wanted to run away with him. When he got out of jail, he went to South Bend, Indiana, then returned to Fort Wayne and went to see Ethel. Ethel's "steady" boyfriend later found him on the street, knocked him down and dragged him to the police station. The city court judge did not buy Lynch's story and fined him $5 in court costs and sentenced him to thirty days in jail for assault and battery.

Jack Bennett, one of the many individuals who Judge Erwin tried to transfer suspicion to in the Croy murder case, was also back in court – divorce court. On the same day Ethel Stout appeared in city court with her complaint against Edward Lynch, Jack Bennett, a witness in the Croy murder case, was in Allen Superior Court in a divorce action against his wife, Minnie Bennett.

The Bennett's were married in February, 1903, and Jack said they got along until her folks got her started and she "got to jawin' around" and would not cook his meals. He asserted that he had only had five warm meals in two weeks and that he had cooked three of them himself. The judge gave Bennett his freedom and granted the divorce.

On February 16, 1910, the Woodburn Banking Company was given permission to turn over funds to the clerk of the Allen Circuit Court which was money held for the reward for the capture of the murderers of Marshal Columbus L. Croy. Dr. Don E. Gorrell (the dentist-detective from Ohio) had instituted legal action to claim the reward.

Sheriff Jesse Grice had left office and was succeeded by Sheriff A. M. Reichelderfer. Chief Ben Elliott had succeeded Fort Wayne Police Chief Martin J. Ankenbruck. Marshal Columbus Croy had been succeeded, ironically, by Marshal John Baker, a different man from Woodburn by the same name as one of the murderers ("Left-handed" John Baker).

On August 23, 1910, defense attorney Judge Erwin brought an appeal to the conviction of Herman Miller in DeKalb Circuit Court in Auburn, Indiana. The appeal was based upon the contention the key witness and co-defendant, Fred LaDuke, was a delinquent and degenerate and, therefore, not entitled to belief. The defense also filed a motion that the State specify which one of the three counts in the indictment that they would try Miller on. The motion was overruled. The re-trial started on August 26 and on September 7 the defense began trying to impeach Fred LaDuke's credibility as a witness.

Dr. Robert J. Girod, Sr.

East Main Street, Woodburn, 1912
(Photos courtesy of Loretta McCann and the Woodburn Historical Society)

The defense cross-examined LaDuke for two and one half-hours in an attempt to establish that his testimony was an attempt to collect the reward after being released with immunity. The defense asked LaDuke if he had told Secretary Amos Butler of the Indiana Board of Corrections and Charities that he expected to be out of jail soon. He was also asked if he didn't tell Deputy Sheriff Walter Immel, at the time he was being taken to Huntington to testify against John Stout, that he wished the whole thing was over so he could be as free as a little girl they saw playing in a yard on their way to court. The prosecution rebutted by showing that, while LaDuke had expressed a wish to be out of jail, he had not been promised anything during his nearly three years in jail. Curiosity in the case had diminished and crowds in the courtroom were minimal.

Life and history was moving on. In a compromise reached between the prosecution and the defense, John Stout pleaded guilty to burglary and received a new sentence of ten to twenty years in prison. In December of

1912 the Indiana Board of Pardons paroled John Stout, just six years after the murder of Marshal Croy. Herman Miller was sentenced in the same plea agreement to two to four years in prison and died in October, 1911, at the Indiana State Penitentiary in Michigan City, Indiana. John Baker, the third defendant in the plea bargain served three years in prison for his complicity in the burglary.

In 1914 John Baker was arrested for fighting and again on December 13, 1915, he and his brother, Alex, a convicted thief, were arrested for beating and elderly man from Antwerp, Ohio. Oscar Wilson had had trouble with the Baker brothers several years earlier and when Wilson entered the Maxwell saloon at 617 Calhoun Street in Fort Wayne the two pounced on him and beat him, causing severe head injuries. The Baker's resisted six police officers before being apprehended. They claimed that they were merely blowing the foam off of their schooners of suds when the police viciously assaulted them. Alex and John were each fined $25 for assault and resisting, respectively.

History does not record much of Fred LaDuke or even whether he was tried for his part in the burglary and murder, despite his testimony. The Croy family had moved to Wyoming, but there are citizens in the Woodburn area that still bear the Croy family name.

Croy's mother, Fanny Croy, grieved over her son's death and never recovered from the shock. She died in February, 1908. Croy's father, A.J. Croy, and only five of the thirteen Croy children survived her death. Her last words were, "Oh, how I would like to see Mr. Ankenbruck and Sheriff Grice and the officers who helped get those men who did that awful deed. Tell them if I can't see them, how I thank them most sincerely with all my heart and I know the Lord will reward them for it some day. Now I am ready to go." (Fort Wayne Journal Gazette, February 26, 1908, p. 3)

Amelia E. Croy died thirty-five years after her husband. She returned to Woodburn at some point to live with her daughter, Ellen. She was buried next to her husband in the IOOF Cemetery in New Haven when she died on April 3, 1942.

Ellen Croy Smith, Columbus' and Amelia's daughter, died in 1990 and is buried nearby in the IOOF Cemetery in New Haven. She and her husband left Marshal Croy six grandchildren and four great grandchildren. Marshal Columbus L. Croy is still remembered and memorialized as the first name on the list of police officers killed in the line of duty in Allen County, Indiana.

Amelia E. Croy (January 3, 1862, - April 3, 1942);
Columbus L. Croy (August 26, 1862, - June 7, 1907.
IOOF Cemetery, New Haven, Indiana.
(Photos courtesy of Loretta McCann and the Woodburn Historical Society)

REFERENCES

I suppose I am the only one in the world. I'm a consulting detective, if you can understand what that is.

~ Sherlock Holmes ~

Sir Arthur Conan Doyle

Chapter 1
Autopsy Number A-49-60, Mackinac County Coroner's Office, July 29, 1960.

Barfknecht, Gary. **Unexplained Michigan Mysteries**, 1993. 0-923756-05-1

The Detroit News, "Woman's Trip to Tragedy Is Retraced on Mackinac," page 1A, July 30, 1960.

The Detroit News, "Jacket Is Clue in Slaying; Mackinac Search Spurred," page 1B, July 30, 1960.

The Detroit News, "Island clings to murder secret," August 22, 1969.

Mackinac Island Town Crier, The Saint Ignace News, Saint Ignace, Michigan, July 17, 1960.

Dr. Robert J. Girod, Sr.

Mackinac Island Town Crier, The Saint Ignace News, Saint Ignace, Michigan, July 31, 1960.

Michigan Department of Health, Division of Laboratories memo, August 9, 1960.

Michigan State Police Complaint Report 83-862-60, July 24, 1960, p. 1.

Michigan State Police Complaint Report 83-862-60, July 27, 1960, pp. 12-16.

Michigan State Police Complaint Report 83-862-60, July 28, 1960, pp. 17-18.

Michigan State Police Complaint Report 83-862-60, July 28, 1960, pp. 21-22.

Michigan State Police Complaint Report 83-862-60, August 2, 1960. Michigan State Police Complaint Report 83-862-60, Report on Property, August 10, 1960.

Michigan State Police Complaint Report 83-862-60, July 28, 1960, pp. 23-25.

Michigan State Police Complaint Report 83-862-60, July 28, 1960, pp. 31-32.

Michigan State Police Complaint Report 83-862-60, September 11, 1964, p. 157

Michigan State Police Complaint Report 83-862-60, August 18, 1960, pp. 236-239.

Michigan State Police Complaint Report 83-862-60, October 18, 1962, pp. 297-298.

Michigan State Police Complaint Report 83-862-60, August 18, 1960, pp. 760-761.

Michigan State Police Complaint Report 83-862-60, March 3, 1961, pp. 814-815.

Pond v. People, 8 Mich. 150 (1860)

Stonehouse, Frederick. ***Great Lakes Crime: Murder, Mayhem, Booze & Broads***. Avery Color Studios, Inc., Gwinn, MI: 2004.

Chapter 2

Daily Republican Times, "Check Leads for Slayer, Await Pathologist Report; Round up Sex Criminals," L.S. Clemens, March 17, 1960, pp. 1 and 10.

Daily Republican Times, "Study Comb found near Murder," March 28, 1960.

Petition for Executive Clemency, LaSalle County Case Number 60-11-753, April 2005.

Inbau, Fred E., John E. Reid, Joseph P. Buckley, and Brian C. Jayne. ***Criminal Interrogation and Confessions*** (Fourth Edition), Aspen Publishers, Inc., Gaithersburg, Maryland: 2001.

Stout, Steve. ***The Starved Rock Murders***, Utica House Publishing Company, Utica, Illinois: 1982.

The Times, "Families of victims, Weger relatives attend," Dan Churney, April 14, 2005: Ottawa, Illinois.

The Times, "Murder case figure found dead," Dan Churney, May 4, 2005: Ottawa, Illinois.

The Times, "Hettel: Cancer, not guilt possible reason murder case figure killed himself," Dan Churney, May 6, 2005: Ottawa, Illinois.

The Times, "Spiros death ruled a suicide," Dan Churney, June 18, 2005: Ottawa, Illinois.

The Times, "Starved Rock murderer Chester Weger went before a parole board this morning at Menard Correctional Center," Chester Dan Churney, August 18, 2005: Ottawa, Illinois.

Small Newspaper Group, "Weger," Stephanie Sievers, September 27, 2005: Springfield Bureau, Springfield, Illinois.

The Times, "Scene of the Crime: Documentary film crew camps out at site of 1960 slayings," Dan Churney, April 4, 2006: Ottawa, Illinois.

The Times, "Detective to write about Starved Rock Slayings," Dan Churney, June 10, 2006: Ottawa, Illinois.

Chapter 3
Internet: http://www.ohiodeathrow.com/

Internet: http://www.drc.state.oh.us/Public/capital.htm

Internet: http://www.drc.state.oh.us/web/inst/ohioref.htm

Mansfield News Journal, John Futty, December 9, 1990.

Martin, John Bartlow. **The Edge of the Chair** (Joan Kahn, Editor). Harper & Row Publishers, New York, New York: 1967.

Internet: http://www.zerotime.com/storefront/ghosthunter/sample3.htm

Internet: http://www.forgottenoh.com/OSR/osr.html

Chapter 4
Internet: http://www.courttv.com/news/hiddentraces/heist/stupid_crimes.html

Internet: http://www.rediff.com/news/2003/oct/06spec1.htm

Internet: http://en.wikipedia.org/wiki/Charles_Sobhraj

Internet: http://news.bbc.co.uk/1/hi/england/2029166.stm

Internet: http://www.thisislocallondon.co.uk/ specialreports/ ameliemurder/display.var. 576848.0.0php

Harvard Magazine, *Map* Miscreant, September-October 2006 (Volume 109, Number 1), Cambridge, Massachusetts, p. 72

Patch, Susanne Steinem. **Blue Mystery: The Story of the Hope Diamond**, Washington D.C.: Smithsonian Institution Press, 1976.

Internet: http://www.courttv.com/news/hiddentraces/heist/stupid_crimes.html, March 24, 2005.

Internet: http://news.bbc.co.uk/1/hi/england/2029166.stm, March 24, 2005.

Internet: http://www.thisislocallondon.co.uk/specialreports/ameliemurder/display.var.576848.0.0php, March 24, 2005.

Chapter 5

Deacon, Richard. *The* Cambridge Apostles*: a History of Cambridge University's Elite Intellectual Secret Society*. 1986.

Dorril, Stephen. ***MI6: Inside the Covert World of Her Majesty's Secret Intelligence Service***. Free Press (Simon & Schuster, Inc.), New York, NY: 2000.

Fleming, Ian. ***From Russia, With Love***. The Macmillan Company (Glidrose Productions, Ltd.), New York, NY: 1957.

Modin, Yuri. ***My Five Cambridge Friends: Burgess, Maclean, Philby, Blunt, and Cairncross***. Farrar, Straus& Giroux: 1994.

Owen, David. ***Hidden Secrets: A Complete History of Espionage and the Technology Used to Support It***. Firefly Books, Ltd., Buffalo, NY: 2002.

Perry, Roland. ***The Fifth Man***. Pan Books, London: 1994.

Wright, Peter. ***Spy Catcher: The Candid Autobiography of a Senior Intelligence Officer***. Viking Penguin, Inc., New York, NY: 1987.

Chapter 6
National Archives records.

Chapter 7
National Archives records.

Chapter 8
Secrest, Meryle. *Frank Lloyd Wright: A Biography*. Alfred A Knopf, New York, New York: 1992.

Wallard, Charlotte. *Frank Lloyd Wright: An American Architect.* The McMillan Company, New York, New York: 1972.

Wright, John Lloyd. *My Father Who Is On Earth.* G.P. Putnam's Sons, New York, New York: 1946.

The Indianapolis Star, October 8, 1914.

The Atlanta Constitution, August 16, 1914.

The Grand Rapids Tribune, September 9, 1914.

The Sunday Review, Decatur, Illinois, August 16, 1914.

The Washington Post, August 17, 1914.

The Washington Post, October 4, 1914.

Martha "Mamah" Borthwick Cheney, Steven Hurder, http://www.oprf.com/flw/bio/cheney.html, December 20, 2004.

Frank Lloyd Wright, http://www.ds.arch.tue.nl/education/students/MultiMedia/FallingWater/flw.htm, December 20, 2004.

Taliesin, http://www.planetclaire.org/fllw/twi.html, December 20, 2004.

Map of the Estate at Taliesin, http://www.planetclaire.org/fllw/twi.html, December 20, 2004.

Julian Carlton, Caribbean Voice, **http://www.caribvoice.org/Features/carlton.html**, December 20, 2004.

Taliesin (Frank Lloyd Wright Foundation), Frank Lloyd Wright Foundation, http://www.pbs.org/flw/buildings/taliesin/taliesin.html, December 20, 2004.

Sauk County Jail, Sauk County Sheriff's Office, ***http://www.saukcounty.com/sheriffhistory.htm***, December 21, 2004.

Iowa County Courthouse, Iowa County Government, http://www.iowacounty.org/, December 21, 2004.

Mamah, Frank Lloyd Wright Foundation, http://www.pbs.org/flw/buildings/taliesin/taliesin_wright02.html, December 20, 2004.

Chapter 9
Osborne, Charles. ***The Life and Crimes of Agatha Christie.*** St. Martin's Press, New York, HY: 1999.

Chapter 10
Costello, Peter. ***The Real World of Sherlock Holmes: The True Crimes Investigated by Arthur Conan Doyle.*** Carroll & Graf Publishers, Inc., New York, NY: 1991.

Booth, Martin. ***The Doctor and the Detective: A Biography of Sir Arthur Conan Doyle.*** Thomas Dunne Books, NY, NY: 1997.

Costello, Peter. ***The Real World of Sherlock Holmes: The True Crimes Investigated by Arthur Conan Doyle.*** Carroll & Graf Publishers, Inc., New York, NY: 1991.

Silverman, Kenneth. ***Houdini!!! The Career of Elrich Weiss.*** Harper Collins Publishers, New York, NY: 1996.

Chapter 11
Mellow, James R. ***Hemingway: A Life Without Consequences.*** Houghton Mifflin Co., New York, New York: 1992.

Hemingway, Valerie. ***Running with the Bulls: My Years with the Hemingways.*** Random House Publishing group (Ballantine Books), New York, NY: 2004.

Hotchner, A.E. *Papa Hemingway: A Personal Memoir by A.E. Hotchner.* Random House, New York, New York: 1966.

Chapter 12
Fort Wayne Journal-Gazette, June 8, 1907

Fort Wayne Journal-Gazette, June 10, 1907

Fort Wayne Journal-Gazette, June 12, 1907

Fort Wayne Journal-Gazette, June 13, 1907

Fort Wayne Journal-Gazette, June 14, 1907

Fort Wayne Journal-Gazette, June 18, 1907

Fort Wayne Journal-Gazette, November 5, 1907

Chapter 13
Fort Wayne Daily News, April 18, 1908

Fort Wayne Daily News, April 20, 1908

Fort Wayne Daily News, April 23, 1908

Fort Wayne Journal-Gazette, June 10, 1908

Fort Wayne Journal-Gazette, June 11, 1908

Fort Wayne Journal-Gazette, June 12, 1908

Fort Wayne Journal-Gazette, June 13, 1908

Chapter 14
Fort Wayne Journal-Gazette, June 14, 1908

Fort Wayne Journal Gazette, November 17, 1908

Fort Wayne Journal Gazette, June 18, 1908

Fort Wayne Journal Gazette, June 21, 1908

Fort Wayne Journal Gazette, March 9, 1909

Fort Wayne Journal Gazette, March 10, 1909

Fort Wayne Journal Gazette, March 11, 1909

Fort Wayne Journal Gazette, November 28, 1908

Fort Wayne Journal Gazette, February 26, 1908

ABOUT THE AUTHOR

DR. ROBERT J. GIROD, SR.

Dr. Robert Girod earned a double Ph.D. in Criminology and Public Administration from the Union Institute and University in Cincinnati, Ohio, and a Post-Doctoral Executive Development Certificate in Leadership for the 21st Century from Harvard University, John F. Kennedy School of Government. He is currently pursuing a J.D. (Doctor of Jurisprudence) at Thomas M. Cooley Law School in Lansing, MI. He also earned a Master of Science in Criminal Justice Administration from Central Missouri State University, a Bachelor of Arts in Sociology from Huntington College, and a Bachelor of General Studies in Social and Behavioral Science and an Associate of Science in Criminal Justice from Indiana University. Dr. Girod also received a technical diploma in Forensic Science from the Institute of Applied Science.

Girod is a graduate of the Indiana Law Enforcement Academy, the Fort Wayne Police Academy, the National Police Institute Command & Staff School, and more than sixty advanced police and instructor schools. He is also a graduate of more than a dozen military training programs, including the U.S. Naval War College, the U.S. Marine Corps Command & Staff College, and the U.S. Air Force Squadron Officer's School.

Dr. Robert J. Girod, Sr.

Girod has served the Fort Wayne Police Department since 1989, with duties as a supervisor of the Robbery-Homicide Section and the Federal Bank Robbery Task Force, the Juvenile Section, and all four Detective Bureau Quadrants, and the Auto Theft Section. He was a patrol supervisor on B- and C-Shifts, a detective in nearly every section of the Detective Bureau, and a patrol officer on B- and C-Shifts. He has served on the Police Reserves Board, the Police Pension Board, and has lectured as an instructor at the Fort Wayne Police Academy.

Girod has also served as special deputy for the United States Marshal's Service and as a police officer with the Indianapolis Police Department and the Indiana University Police Department. He was a special agent with the Ohio Bureau of Criminal Investigations (BCI) and an investigator with the Indiana Department of Insurance and the Wells County Prosecutor's Office, beginning his career in 1979. Prior to this he was a private detective and security officer with Zeis Security Systems.

Major Girod Served for four years in the Indiana Guard Reserve and for eighteen years in the U.S. Army Reserve, attaining the rank of captain. He held command and staff positions in the military police, basic training (infantry), and Special Forces, but most of his duty was with the U.S. Army Criminal Investigations Command (USACIDC).

Professor Girod has taught more than thirty subjects in Management, Criminal Justice, Public Administration, Political Science, History, and Sociology at seven universities. He has been an associate faculty member at Indiana University in Fort Wayne and an adjunct professor at Concordia University of Wisconsin and at Taylor University, both in Fort Wayne. He has also taught graduate courses at Indiana Wesleyan University, graduate Internet courses at Boston University, and through the doctoral level via Internet at Northcentral University in Prescott, Arizona.

Dr. Girod and his wife, Mimi, prior to her death, both served on their church board at First Church of the Nazarene and were active in political and civic service. In addition to his military awards, Girod was awarded the Meritorious Service Medal and the Commendation Medal by the Fort Wayne Police Department and a Letter of Commendation by the Director of the Federal

Bureau of Investigation. He was listed in the *Who's Who in Law Enforcement* in 1991 and the *International Who's Who in Public Service* in 2000.

Dr. Girod is a member of numerous professional and civic associations and organizations, including the Fraternal Order of Police, the American Legion, and the Fort Wayne-Allen County Historical Society (The History Center). He has authored numerous articles for various professional periodicals, such as *FBI Law Enforcement Bulletin*, *Security Management*, *The Police Marksman*, and *Musubi* and is the author of a book, **Profiling the Criminal Mind: Behavioral Science and Criminal Investigative Analysis**. His two new books are **Infamous Murders and Mysteries** and **Character Management**.

Made in the USA
San Bernardino, CA
12 December 2013